There Were Also Many Women There

Katharine E. Harmon

There Were Also Many Women There

Lay Women in the Liturgical Movement in the United States, 1926–59

Foreword by
Nathan D. Mitchell

A PUEBLO BOOK

Liturgical Press   Collegeville, Minnesota

www.litpress.org

A Pueblo Book published by Liturgical Press

Cover design by Ann Blattner. Photo: istockphotos.com. Illustration: *He Has Risen: He is Not Here* by Ade Bethune, used with permission from St. Catherine's University, Special Collections, St. Paul, Minnesota.

1   2   3   4   5   6   7   8   9

Library of Congress Control Number: 2012952897

ISBN: 978-0-8146-6271-7

To my teachers, in gratitude
for all they envisioned

Contents

Abbreviations

ACUA	The American Catholic History Research Center and University Archives
CAA	Catholic Arts Association
CLIT	Liturgical Arts Society Records
CMRH	Reynold Hillenbrand Papers
CPOL	Nina Polcyn Moore Collection
CSWD	Sheed and Ward Family Papers
EGSP	Ellen Gates Starr Papers
LAS	Liturgical Arts Society
NCCB	National Conference of Catholic Bishops
NCCM	National Council of Catholic Men
NCCW	National Council of Catholic Women
NCRLC	National Catholic Rural Life Conference
NCWC	National Catholic Welfare Conference
PGEN	General Collection Printed Materials
SJAA	Saint John's Abbey Archives
UNDA	University of Notre Dame Archives
USCC	United States Catholic Conference

Foreword

I am delighted to write these few words for a book that I greatly admire, as it focuses on a topic, the liturgical movement in the United States (1926–59), that I myself have been very passionate about and that has fueled my work over the past forty years or so. It is a hard task indeed to add anything to Katie's scholarly acumen and in-depth analysis of this momentous watershed moment within the Church, which, I am sure, will attract the attention of many readers. There is, however, one aspect that I would like to focus on here: its timeliness. Katie's book could not have appeared at a better moment as its publication coincides with the celebration of the fiftieth anniversary of the opening of the Second Vatican Council, which, I strongly believe, can never be celebrated enough, especially now, when its spirit is frequently under attack or risks nefarious distortions. Reform-minded Cardinal Carlo Maria Martini's recent remarks, published posthumously, about the current Church as stuck "two hundred years behind the times" is dead right. As I have stated elsewhere, it seems to me that in these last years the Vatican has lost its sense of priority. While under persistent attack for its sluggish dealing with the sexual abuse scandals that have emerged in recent years, it has nevertheless found plenty of time to teach us American Catholics "good liturgical English" (when not promoting the Latin of the professed one and only "authentic" Missal of 1962); to force the government to eliminate the entire contraception mandate, thus denying (and silencing) the fact that many (98 percent) Catholic women have their own legitimate ideas when it comes to using methods of contraception other than natural family planning; and, more disquietingly, to persist in having the last and only word on all issues pertaining to sexuality and reproduction without feeling the necessity to address lay women and men who, in both these matters and for obvious reasons, might have a word or two to say to the Church's venerable hierarchy of celibate men. Yet, as far as I know, it hasn't slapped an interdict on the American church for failing to feed the hungry or wash the feet of the most vulnerable citizens of our chaotic world. We are therefore profoundly grateful to a group of hardworking nuns, currently on buses across the country, who, instead of becoming propaganda voices for the current Vatican agenda, remind us all, including Peter's successor in Rome, that, as laywoman Daria Donnelly wrote from her deathbed at forty-five, struck with a terminal illness, "[t]he only thing that matters is showing love and compassion in the time that is given us."[1] Further, with their unwavering commitment to the poor, these women powerfully teach us that the liturgy is reduced to an ostentatious, self-congratulatory display of pomp and wealth when it does not trigger in us the ethical response to feed the hungry, dress the naked, visit the prisoners, console the sick, and educate the young ones. As Christians, these will always remain our foremost priorities.

This fascinating book reminds us that "there were also many women there" (Matt 27:55-56) whose priorities were exactly the same: providing for Jesus and his disciples "out of their resources" (Luke 8:3). More to the point, "there were also many women there" who were an integral and active part of the liturgical movement in the United States and, as Katie writes, were "led by a lay apostolate inspired to affect the renewal of society by taking the celebration of the liturgy to heart, participating in the Eucharist to truly be the Body of Christ in the world" (p. xvi). These many women had truly become Christ-like and had very little to do with the fictive Mrs. Murphy, the "primary theologian," as somewhat patronizingly defined by Aidan Kavanagh. The lay women presented in the following pages, such as liturgical theologian Aemiliana Löhr, OSB, Ellen Gates Starr, Justine B. Ward, the members of the National Council of Catholic Women, Maisie Ward of Sheed & Ward, Dorothy Day of the Catholic Worker Movement, Catherine de Hueck Doherty of Friendship House, Ade Bethune, Therese Mueller, Mary Perkins Ryan, Florence Berger, and their companions were not only first-rate theologians but also supreme disciples of Christ through whom "Jesus himself sent out . . . from east to west, the sacred and imperishable proclamation of eternal salvation" (Mark 16:8d).

I have known Katie first as a talented doctoral student at the University of Notre Dame, and now as a brilliant liturgical scholar. In her book, she brings together many of the previously silenced and marginalized voices that need to be known and remembered *now* for the future generation of Catholics in this country and beyond. We are profoundly grateful to her for this much-needed book and for being today among the "many women there."

Nathan D. Mitchell

[1] Cited in *Give Us This Day* (Collegeville, MN: Liturgical Press, September 2012): 214.

Preface

> "There were [also] many women there, looking on from a distance, who had followed Jesus from Galilee, ministering to him. Among them were Mary Magdalene and Mary the mother of James and Joseph, and the mother of the sons of Zebedee." (Matt 27:55-57)

The goal of this volume is to provide a new resource for further analyses of the classical liturgical movement in the United States, 1926 to 1959, ones which might include the many lay women who were integral, and not marginal, to its narrative.[1] The Roman Catholic liturgical movement in the first half of the twentieth century is aptly named by liturgical scholar Keith Pecklers, SJ, as the "unread vision," the hopes and dreams of which have yet to be fully realized.[2] Historical scholarship rightly describes the liturgical movement as the necessary context out of which to interpret the key issues addressed by the Second Vatican Council: the Church's role in the modern world, the reform of the liturgy, and the perception of ecclesiology, among other elements.[3] Yet, while the "liturgical" outcomes of the Council were most tangibly felt in the revised texts and translations of the liturgies, the fullness of the liturgical movement's aims did not rest solely in the revision of texts. The liturgical movement as realized in the United States describes a comprehensive vision for a renewed social order, one led by a lay

[1] Hereafter, the "classical liturgical movement," describing the mid-twentieth century, will be referred to as the "liturgical movement."

[2] Keith F. Pecklers, *The Unread Vision: The Liturgical Movement in the United States of America: 1926–1955* (Collegeville, MN: Liturgical Press, 1998).

[3] See, for example, Herbert Vorgrimler, ed., *Commentary on the Documents of Vatican II* (New York: Herder and Herder, 1969); Karl Rahner, "Towards a Fundamental Theological Interpretation of Vatican II," *Theological Studies* 40, no. 4 (1979): 716–27; Massimo Faggioli, *Vatican II: The Battle for Meaning* (New York: Paulist Press, 2012); and Richard R. Gaillardetz and Catherine E. Clifford, *Keys to the Council: Unlocking the Teaching of Vatican II* (Collegeville, MN: Liturgical Press, 2012).

apostolate inspired to affect the renewal of society by taking the celebration of the liturgy to heart, participating in the Eucharist to truly be the Body of Christ in the world.[4]

Sighting the work of women in the vision of the broader liturgical movement asks the contemporary reader to revisit old sources in a new way. From the liturgical movement's American debut in November 1926, neither the content of its central journal, *Orate Fratres* (later *Worship*), nor its audience was devoid of the presence of lay women. In Advent 1933, a woman who identified herself simply as "Miss B. M." wrote a somewhat disgruntled letter to the editor (Virgil Michel, OSB) regarding her home parish:

> The word "liturgical" is not known here. Our parish church is wonderfully decorated with streamers of pink, yellow, orange, and greenish blue and red, supplemented by yards of soiled Nottingham lace, dirty paper flowers and endless vigil lights. The altar looks more like a soda fountain than an altar. Any comment brings the reply that it would hurt the feelings of the dear Brother sacristan if it were changed. The feelings of the thousands of Catholics and Protestants that come here every year are not considered.
>
> In this atmosphere *Orate Fratres* is a great consolation. I have had it since the very first number.[5]

While the anonymous Miss B. M. is particularly appalled by the gaucherie of her parish altar, there are two other important notes about her letter to Michel: first, she is a "miss" and, second, this "miss" has been receiving *Orate Fratres* since its inaugural number.

In short, revisiting some of the usual suspects for the liturgical movement, including journals like *Orate Fratres* and proceedings from the National Liturgical Weeks, renders a more robust picture of the liturgical movement on the American scene, one that reveals not only the presence of faithful and committed priests and religious but also

---

[4] Godfrey Diekmann, "Is There a Distinct American Contribution to the Liturgical Renewal?," *Worship* 45, no. 10 (1971): 578–87; H. A. Reinhold, "More or Less Liturgical," *Orate Fratres* 13, no. 4: 152–55; H. A. Reinhold, *The Dynamics of Liturgy* (New York: The Macmillan Company, 1961); and Mary Perkins Ryan, ed., "Introduction," *The Sacramental Way* (New York: Sheed and Ward, 1948), vii–xii.

[5] Miss B. M. "A Neglected Parish Church," "The Apostolate," *Orate Fratres* 7, no. 12 (1933): 571.

lay women. These usual sources must be paired with the unsuspected: not only lead articles, but letters to the editor; not only printed and published liturgical histories, but letters to Godfrey Diekmann, to H. A. Reinhold, and to Virgil Michel; not only revised rituals for Holy Week, but recipes for the paschal lamb. As the narrative of the gospel reminds us in the very heart of the Paschal Season, "There were also many women there."[6] Women have always been witness to Christ, even if their words were unrecorded.

In present histories, the absence of women in the liturgical-historical narrative should no longer be assumed. It is, in fact, the responsibility of the liturgical historian to be attentive to the presence of women and to integrate that presence within the historical narrative, rather than treat "women's stuff" always as a sidebar or a paragraph of that narrative.[7] A critical-historical retrieval of laywomen's voices in the liturgical movement does not make much of nothing but makes much of voices that too long have been silent in a period of modern liturgical history in great need of further study. Doing so provides a practical and concrete account of ways in which women were formed by the primary practice of liturgy, how women actively engaged in liturgical life, and how women taught others to realize the liturgy of the

[6] Matt 27:55-56, read on Passion Sunday, Year A.

[7] Several liturgical scholars have worked to identify and retrieve women's experiences in various areas and eras in liturgical studies, most extensively in considering rituals for women (e.g., Joanne M. Pierce, "'Green Women' and Blood Pollution: Some Medieval Rituals for the Churching of Women after Childbirth," *Studia Liturgica* 2, no. 2 [1999]: 191–215); women's eucharistic devotions (e.g., Caroline Walker Bynum, *Holy Feast and Holy Fast: the Religious Significance of Food to Medieval Women* [Berkeley: University of California Press, 1987]; and Miri Rubin, *Corpus Christi: The Eucharist in Late Medieval Culture* [New York: Cambridge University Press, 1991]); and the significance of gender in interpreting liturgical history and sacramental practice (e.g., Teresa Berger, *Women's Ways of Worship: Gender Analysis and Liturgical History* [Collegeville, MN: Liturgical Press, 1999]; Berger, *Gender Differences and the Making of Liturgical History: Lifting a Veil on Liturgy's Past* [New Haven, CT: Yale University Press, 2011]; and Susan A. Ross, *Extravagant Affections: A Feminist Sacramental Theology* [New York: Continuum Publishing Company, 1998]). With respect to feminist studies and liturgical and sacramental theology, a useful review of twentieth-century literature can be found in David Power, "Sacramental Theology: A Review of Literature; Feminist Theology," *Theological Studies* 55, no. 4 (1994): 693–702.

Church in authentic and vitalizing ways. Such an endeavor invites a new vision for the liturgical movement in the United States: there were also many women there, women ministered to the Mystical Body of Christ, and women too should be remembered by those of us who look on from a distance.

The uniqueness of the liturgical movement, which sought to fully integrate the lay apostolate within the life of the Church, and the changing sociocultural status of women in the United States during this same period provide a particularly striking landscape within which to discover and reinterpret the presence of these women. To accomplish this, this volume is divided into five overlapping, historical chapters. The first chapter examines women's involvement in the European liturgical movement (c.1870–1926), noting both continuities and contrasts between women of the European liturgical movement and their American counterparts. In particular, liturgical theologian Aemiliana Löhr, OSB, and the Dutch Grail movement provide insight into the issue of gender at play in the foundation of the modern liturgical movement. Aside from this first chapter, the volume focuses only on the work of lay, non-religious women, that is, single women, wives/divorcées, and mothers. This is not for lack of zeal on the part of American women religious[8] but for the sake of a concise and manageable history, and for the sake of seeking those lay women who have even less organizational power and access to institutional preservation of their work and memories.

Following the stage setting in the European scene, the second chapter recounts the liturgical movement's beginning in the United States (c. 1926–38), with the inaugural issue of *Orate Fratres* and the context of Progressivism, examining the liturgical movement through the work of Ellen Gates Starr, Justine B. Ward, and national Catholic women's organizations, such as the National Council of Catholic Women. The

---

[8] Among their contributions to and participation in the liturgical movement at large, religious sisters served as editorial board members of *Orate Fratres* (Mother Mary Ellerker, OSB, of Duluth, Minnesota), championed and created tools for liturgical catechesis (Estelle Hackett, OP, and Jane Marie Murray, OP, of Grand Rapids, Michigan, and Mary Roberta Mellinger, OSB), and attended the National Liturgical Weeks, as one liturgical pioneer would describe, in "gobs." See Godfrey Diekmann to Florence Berger, June 21, 1957. The Godfrey Diekmann Papers Box 1013, Folder 6, Saint John's Abbey Archives [hereafter cited as SJAA].

third chapter more specifically focuses on how lay initiative, particularly Catholic Action, the Catholic intellectual revival, and social activism, affected the liturgical movement during the interwar period (c. 1930–40). This decade between the world wars saw the establishment of dynamic, radical, and influential lay-controlled, lay-led organizations that compelled members to live out the Mystical Body in the world. The principal women examined include Maisie Ward of Sheed & Ward (a company that began in England but found a ready audience on American soil), Dorothy Day of the Catholic Worker Movement, and Catherine de Hueck Doherty of Friendship House.

Pressing further into the frontier opened by liturgical movement advocates in education, liturgical participation, and social activism in the 1930s, the fourth chapter elaborates on more specific strains inspired by Catholic Action (c. 1933–45) by following how labor, lifestyles, and the arts intertwined with the liturgical movement. These avenues are explored especially through the work of liturgical artist and social activist Ade Bethune and the American Grail Movement, a program designed specifically to invite young women to embrace their Catholic faith through study, work, and prayer. Finally, the fifth chapter focuses on the period following the Second World War until the end of the liturgical movement (c. 1945–59), turning to the development of the liturgical life in the home and how women strategized methods to act as domestic leaders of the liturgy for their families, husbands, and children. Therese Mueller, Mary Perkins Ryan, and Florence Berger are central to this turn toward the liturgical life in the family. While each era of the movement concentrates on several key voices, dozens of examples from other women—women in the pews, women writers, women in schools and study clubs—invite the reader to see the extent to which lay women moved the American liturgical movement from theory into practice.

Here, I am grateful for the opportunity to identify and thank those who made the research and writing of this book possible: first, the University of Notre Dame's Institute for Scholarship in the Liberal Arts, which provided a research travel grant; and to my friends at the Cushwa Center for American Catholicism at the University of Notre Dame, who provided me with a research grant and their hospitality: Timothy Matovina, past director; Kathleen Sprows Cummings, current director; and Paula Brach, senior administrative assistant. Research for this work was indispensably aided by many kind, resourceful, and committed archivists: David Klingeman, OSB, of Saint John's Abbey

Archives in Collegeville, Minnesota; Deborah Kloiber, overseer of the Ade Bethune Collection at St. Catherine University in St. Paul, Minnesota; Lynn Wingert, archivist at the Diocese of Des Moines, Iowa; Mary Kraft, CSJ, of the Sisters of St. Joseph of Carondelet, St. Paul Province, in St. Paul, Minnesota; Maria Mazzenger, Timothy Meagher, John Shepherd, Jane Stoeffler, and the archive staff of the American Catholic History Research Center at The Catholic University of America in Washington, DC; Justine Sundaram and the staff of the John J. Burns Library at Boston College in Chestnut Hill, Massachusetts; Beth Poley of the Ohioana Library Association in Columbus, Ohio; and, finally, Kevin Cawley, Sharon Sumpter, and the staff of the University of Notre Dame Archives, in Notre Dame, Indiana.

A word of deep thanks to those who oversaw the earliest version of this work as a doctoral dissertation: first, my teacher, Nathan Mitchell, professor of liturgical studies, University of Notre Dame, who first suggested I turn through the pages of *Orate Fratres*, who directed this project as a doctoral dissertation, and who graciously agreed to write the foreword; thanks also to Teresa Berger, professor of liturgical studies, Yale Divinity School; Mary Catherine Hilkert, OP, professor of theology, University of Notre Dame; and Maxwell E. Johnson, professor of liturgical studies, University of Notre Dame, who read this work through its various stages and offered their suggestions and guidance. I am also grateful to my colleagues and friends from the liturgical studies program at Notre Dame for conversations and for reading portions of this work, especially Sheila McCarthy, Anne McGowan, Melanie C. Ross, and Noel Terranova.

I am thankful for the conversations, interviews, and insights of many people with whom I discussed this project, including Paul Bradshaw, professor of liturgical studies, University of Notre Dame; Ann Berger Frutkin, daughter of Alfred and Florence Berger, Indianapolis, Indiana; Martha Marie Grogan, personal assistant to Ade Bethune in the 1990s, Newport, Rhode Island; Kathleen Harmon, SNDdeN, music director, Institute for Liturgical Ministry, Dayton, Ohio; Mary Ann Hinsdale, IHM, professor of theology, Boston College; Mary Berger Kelly, daughter of Alfred and Florence Berger and artist, Hilton Head, South Carolina; Mary E. McGann, RSCJ, professor of liturgy, Graduate Theological Union, Berkeley, California; Gertrud Mueller Nelson, liturgical artist, author, and daughter of Therese and Franz Mueller, San Diego, California; Catherine Osborne, graduate student at Fordham University, New York City, New York; Keith Pecklers, SJ, professor of liturgical history, Pontifical Liturgical Institute, Sant'Anselmo, Rome; Gerard Pottebaum, publisher and writer, Love-land, Ohio; Mary Sparks, parishioner and forty-year liturgical commis-sion member at St. Joseph's Parish, South Bend, Indiana; and William Storey, retired professor of liturgical studies, University of Notre Dame, author, and bookseller. Finally, thanks to Hans Christoffersen, the editorial director of Liturgical Press, for his interest and advocacy for publishing this work and to all at Liturgical Press. I am deeply in-debted to those who shared their personal reminiscences and love of the liturgical movement and for the suggestions and discussions that led me to greater knowledge of the liturgical movement as a whole.

Finally, my thanks to my own Harmon family: Millie, John, Andy, Emma, and Billy, for their encouragement and continual support; and to my husband, Matthew J. Sherman, with whom I look for-ward to many more conversations about faith, history, and American Catholics.

Katharine E. Harmon
August 27, 2012
Feast of St. Monica

The Need for a Liturgical Movement: Beginnings in Europe, Preparations for America (c. 1870–1926)

INTRODUCTION

The Bloody Face of Modernity and the Mystical Body of Christ

In her collection of essays, *Not Under Forty*, Willa Cather reflects, "The world broke in two in 1922 or thereabouts."[1] Cather's observation about her own writing—that she found it impossible to write in the same romantic, mythic scope as she had previous to some turning point she felt after the close of World War I—is no unique conclusion about the profound shift for moderns in the first quarter of the twentieth century. Literary narratives continued to echo Cather's sentiments about this bend in time, such as Barbara Tuchman's analysis of the first weeks of World War I in *The Guns of August*. Tuchman describes the starkness with which a new reality emerged after the horrors of this most technological war:

> When at last it was over, the war had many diverse results and one dominant one transcending all others: disillusion. "All the great words were cancelled out for that generation," wrote D. H. Lawrence in simple summary for his contemporaries. . . . There was no looking back . . . . The nations were caught in a trap, a trap made during the first thirty days out of battles that failed to be decisive, a trap from which there was, and has been, no exit.[2]

This "disillusionment" or "trap" in which the world was caught brought to a new and provocative head the threat of modernism or

[1] Willa Cather, "Prefatory Note," *Not Under Forty* (New York: Alfred Knopf, 1936), v.

[2] Barbara Tuchman, *The Guns of August* (New York: Dell Publishing Co., 1962), 16.

secularism as expressed by mid-nineteenth-century theologians, historians, artists, and other commentators. The myth of a culturally advanced, enlightened, and economically powerful Western world was crushed in light of the menacing cruelty that boiled and burst through the surface of these same cultured, civilized, *Christianized* nations. The long and bloodied narrative of the First World War sundered each of the nineteenth-century myths that Christianity had supported: unimpeded progress, the unassailable assumption that the best of science and technology should be used despite effect, the superiority of "rational minds" controlling the "more ignorant races," and the unbridled pursuit of individual "happiness" through the garnering of wealth and power.[3]

While technology and the autonomy of the individual were viewed as potentially deplorable, these "modern" characteristics also provided the very mechanisms or conditions for increased independence, literacy, and textuality that enabled Christians to find the Church's complacency toward (through sanction or silence) modern evils indefensible.[4] By the time the world "broke in two," the Christian Churches were faced with increasingly intense questioning about their support of the illusions that seemingly had led to the incredible destruction experienced in Europe. At the same time, both Protestant and Catholic churches of the Western hemisphere experienced more organized and educated congregational bodies who became active in secular social reforms. From the horrific African slave trade to the destruction of Native American Indians in body and culture to the Church's seeming disinterest with regard to vast social ills resulting from increased urbanization, rising populations, and deplorable working conditions, the Christian Churches by the nineteenth century brought scores of

[3] Douglas John Hall, "'The Great War' and the Theologians," in *The Twentieth Century: A Theological Overview*, ed. Gregory Baum (Maryknoll, NY: Orbis Books, 1999), 7; see also William M. Halsey, *The Survival of American Innocence in an Era of Disillusionment, 1920–1940* (Notre Dame, IN: University of Notre Dame Press, 1980); Margaret Mary Reher, "The Path to Pluralism, 1920–1985," in *Catholic Intellectual Life in America: A Historical Study of Persons and Movements*, The Bicentennial History of the Catholic Church in America Series, ed. Christopher J. Kauffman (New York: Macmillan Publishing Company, 1989), 114–41.

[4] See Michel Foucault, "Technologies of the Self," in *Technologies of the Self: A Seminar with Michel Foucault*, ed. Luther H. Martin, et al. (Amherst: University of Massachusetts Press, 1988), 16–49.

reformers and social activists preaching a new Gospel grounded in the belief that the rule of love should rule society. Experiences of the twentieth century served to intensify the sense of disillusionment and the need to reclaim the lost Christian spirit in a dangerously secularized, callous, and demoralized society.

The Need for a Liturgical Movement

The liturgical movement responded to both social and spiritual fronts, embracing the possibility of the reformation of the world through the reformation of the Christian spirit. As the 1949 pamphlet *What Is the Liturgical Movement?* would reflect, the "liturgical movement" gave "the one name for that many-sided work going on throughout the Church today whose purpose is to bring the lives and actions of Christians into closer, more vital contact with the sacramental Life and Action of Christ in the Church."[5] This many-sided work encouraged a more vital sacramental life through a revisioned experience of worship—an "active participation of the laity," liturgical education and active comprehension of liturgical prayer, a newfound interest in liturgical historical scholarship, and the creation of soundly crafted, symbolically informed liturgical arts. Such integration of mind, spirit, and craftship would open up the serious social nature of the liturgy flowing from liturgical worship, freeing liturgy from its stigma as a science stuffed in a rubrical box as well as from its limiting identification as an individual experience. The promoters of the liturgical life quickly found affirmation in their desires for reform, for they could claim that taking liturgy seriously meant taking Pius X's (1835–1914) instruction seriously, that the liturgy was "the primary and indispensable source" of the true Christian spirit.[6] Reformers would later draw on Pius X's words to affirm their instinct that the liturgy should cease being an *individual act* and be restored to its proper place as nourishment of the Mystical Body of Christ. All the Church—lay, cleric, and religious—were part of this Mystical Body, and all were sacramentally called, through the Eucharist, to act as leaven in this thick and airless society. Active, intelligent, responsible participation in the Mystical Body would allow the grace of Christ given in the Church to permeate the density of modern life and to uplift it to form a new

---

[5] Liturgical Conference, Inc., *What Is the Liturgical Movement?* (Boston: The Liturgical Conference, 1948), 7.
[6] Pius X, *Tra le Sollecitudini* (On Sacred Music, 1903).

3

world, one that yielded nourishment, good work, human development, and peace.

The American Liturgical Movement as a Social Response

By the liturgical movement's entrance onto the American scene,
marked by its official American debut with the inaugural issue of *Orate
Fratres* in Advent 1926, American liturgical reformers saw themselves
as responding both within the immediate reality of their twentieth-
century experience and within the broader scope of history. Reformers
shared a common drive to draw both themselves and others closer to
Christ through liturgical worship, a drive identified as being shared
with reformers and activists throughout the atemporal Mystical Body
of Christ:

> As saints' biographies show, holy men and women have always found
> the source of their life and strength in the Mass, the Sacraments, the
> Feasts and seasons, the Sacramentals, the full life of the Church; the ap-
> ostolic aim of their prayers and labors has always been to draw others
> closer to this same source. [The] "Movement" within the Church today
> [exists], not to promote any special form of Catholic life or action, but
> to further the essential work of the Church herself, the communication
> of the life and Action of Christ to His members, and through them to
> the world; the re-heading of all things in Christ to offer them, by Him,
> with Him and in Him, to God.[7]

Considering the liturgical movement's development as, among other
things, a social response unfolds the subsequent pursuits of particular
women activists within the liturgical movement from its earliest
years (1920s) until the twilight before the dawn of the Second Vatican
Council in the closing years of the 1950s. As will be apparent, an exploration of the liturgical movement as it was taken up by American
Roman Catholic lay women in its American beginning requires both a
temporal and a sociocultural contextualization of the movement and
the women themselves: the liturgical movement reforms did not begin
in America, the liturgical movement in Europe did not begin without
women, and the American women's reforms did not begin in the
liturgical movement. Again, the disillusionment and deconstruction
of the myths of unimpeded progress, power of the individual, and

---

[7] *What Is the Liturgical Movement?*, 7. The pamphlet poses this point in the
form of a question.

4

capitalism—a disenchantment already gurgling in the heated reforms and cultural tensions of the nineteenth century in both Europe and the United States—dissolved in the aftermath of the First World War. An identification of what the reformers meant when they spoke of the plagues of "modernism," "secularism," "rampant individualism," "technologization," or, interestingly enough, "masculinization" upon the world is critical for comprehending the ethos of the liturgical movement. Response to social need is the very reason that so many women were involved as proponents of liturgical reform, particularly in the early years of the liturgical movement in the United States.

An exploration of the formative ingredients for the American liturgical movement begins, however, in Western Europe with the establishment of modern liturgical scholarship in the earliest refounded Benedictine monasteries of Beuron (Germany) and Solesmes (France). The agency of Benedictine monks was undoubtedly a key force in founding these and other "liturgical centers," as they came to be called, but the presence and contribution of European women as students and scholars at these and other liturgical centers was also part of this narrative. Women were exposed to the study of liturgy by liturgical centers such as the Benedictine Abbey of the Holy Cross at Herstelle in Germany, home to liturgical scholar Aemiliana Löhr, OSB (1892–1972), and the liturgical center of the Benedictine Abbey at Wépion in Belgium, which was founded in the early 1920s in order to introduce the "'modern woman' to the richness of the liturgical life."[8] Furthermore, investigating the circumstances and interests of the women religious and lay women involved with the liturgical movement as it began in Europe, while defining the heritage of American women's involvement, also alerts us to some distinctive contrasts. First, unlike the programs of study established in monastic centers for learning during the late nineteenth and early twentieth centuries, American women had scarce venues for formal exposure to liturgical studies but might have had advanced degrees or training in sociology, education, or the arts.[9] Second, an important theme of these European women's understanding of the liturgy was that the liturgy was in some way *gendered*.

---

[8] Teresa Berger, "The Classical Liturgical Movement in Germany and Austria: Moved by Women?," *Worship* 66, no. 3 (1992): 234.

[9] For a discussion of American women's professional roles, see Nancy F. Cott, "Professionalism and Feminism," in *The Grounding of Modern Feminism* (New Haven, CT: Yale University Press, 1987), 215–39.

Liturgy, the life of the Church, had a distinctive feminine value and, thus, females had a special responsibility in sustaining the life of the Church and the liturgy. The role of the Christian woman was repeatedly treated by European women (and men) in a way which would not be parroted by their American women counterparts who self-identified as being part of the burgeoning American liturgical movement.[10]

WOMEN AND LITURGY IN THE EUROPEAN LITURGICAL MOVEMENT

Traditional Narrative, Historical Absence

Though a European doorway might be the right avenue through which to begin a study of American women in the liturgical movement, a recycling of previous liturgical histories which construct the most commonly known landscape is not an appropriate tack, either for a history for the involvement of American women or for any aspect of the liturgical movement. As Teresa Berger suggests, one might begin looking at women's activity and presence in the liturgical movement by observing women's *absence* in the traditional image of the narrative.[11] Reading the foreword by Odo Casel, OSB (1886–1948), for one of the important early journals of the liturgical movement, *Jahrbuch für Liturgiewissenschaft*, provides a succinct example:

> The liturgy is not an intellectual construct of a world of speculations far away from earthly concerns; it is the worship of the Church, born out of historical facts, out of the life and suffering of Christ, and developed through the mind and prayer of the Church *and its great men*, in whose soul the Spirit of God dug and found gold.[12]

---

[10] The role of the Christian woman, as described by Americans, is taken up more by those writing with regard to Catholic identity but not necessarily by those interested in liturgical reform; this is prevalent in popular Catholic serials such as *The Messenger of the Sacred Heart*, *The Christian Century*, or *Catholic World*.

[11] Teresa Berger, *Women's Ways of Worship: Gender Analysis and Liturgical History* (Collegeville, MN: Liturgical Press, 1994), 71.

[12] Odo Casel, "Zur Einführung," *Jahrbuch für Liturgiewissenschaft* 1 (1921): 21, quoted in Berger, *Women's Ways of Worship*, 72. See also Berger, *Liturgie und Frauenseele: Die Liturgische Bewegung aus der Sicht der Frauenforschung*, Praktische Theologie heute, Band 10 (Stuttgart: Verlag W. Kohlhammer, 1993), 9; emphasis author's. Here and in all excerpted material, the noninclusive language of the original will be retained.

Berger notes that Casel, in his native German, refers to *"Männer,"* that is, male human beings.[13] And, both within its early days and within later evaluations of the 1950s in the days preceding the Council, there seems to be an erasure of the activity of women and of women's concerns in the liturgical movement.[14] These brief histories often share similar characteristics, considering staple personalities such as Prosper Guéranger at Solesmes (either in praise or critique) as founding father of the liturgical movement and pointing to Pius X's 1903 *motu proprio*, Instruction on Sacred Music (*Tra le Sollecitudini*), as providing papal legitimization of the movement.

The movement's self-reflection about and "canonization" of its members in the days leading up to the Second Vatican Council, however, reveal no prominent women, a fact which, as Berger notes, is not necessarily surprising. An awareness of the societal context of early twentieth-century European women, at least, compounded by the political embroilment of two world wars that surrounded these liturgical centers in the first half of the twentieth century, would suggest women would not have had a particularly active part in society, let alone leadership or influence over liturgical matters.[15] Yet, even in the earliest issues of *Jahrbuch für Liturgiewissenschaft*, one sees that the liturgical movement, at least in German-speaking countries, was fed by the leadership and lifeblood not of men alone but also of women and was repeatedly and explicitly concerned with women's issues.[16] Thus,

[13] Berger, "Moved by Women?," 232.

[14] Though authors detail the liturgical movement, few, if any, women are mentioned. For example, see Bernard Botte, *From Silence to Participation: An Insider's View of Liturgical Renewal*, trans. John Sullivan (Washington, DC: Pastoral Press, 1988); Ernst B. Koenker, *The Liturgical Renaissance in the Roman Catholic Church* (Chicago: University of Chicago Press, 1954); Paul Marx, *Virgil Michel and the Liturgical Movement* (Collegeville, MN: Liturgical Press, 1957); Olivier Rousseau, *The Progress of the Liturgy: An Historical Sketch from the Beginning of the Nineteenth Century to the Pontificate of Pius X*, trans. Benedictines of Westminster Priory (Westminster, MD: Newman Press, 1951); Massey Hamilton Shepherd, *The Reform of Liturgical Worship: Perspectives and Prospects* (New York: Oxford University Press, 1961).

[15] Berger, "Moved by Women?," 233.

[16] Ibid., 232. Berger describes how, within the first several issues of *Jahrbuch für Liturgiewissenschaft*, one reads references to women's issues (called "Frauenfragen" in German) as "an important problem" (*Jahrbuch für Liturgiewissenschaft* 3 [1923]: 127); a "beautiful subject" (*Jahrbuch für Liturgiewissenschaft* 12 [1932]:

although women's presence is not immediately apparent in the evidence surrounding the founding fathers of the liturgical movement, briefly overviewing the origins of the liturgical movement, as described by those within the liturgical movement itself, and considering its theological inspiration reveal the presence of women. Second, such an overview provides the foundations for core issues of realizing the liturgical life which would remain in play throughout the liturgical movement, in the hands of both men and women.

Prosper Guéranger and Liturgical Romanticism in France

In an address given to the Liturgical Conference held in Madison, Wisconsin, in 1958, Massey Hamilton Shepherd (1913–90) characterized the liturgical movement as having three steps: first, its origin in the revival of Benedictine monasticism with Prosper Guéranger's (1805–75) refounding of the Abbey of Solesmes, France, in 1832; a second phase with the movement's "sponsorship" by papal authority during the pontificate of Pius X (1903–14); and the final, contemporary phase, which Shepherd described as the character of the movement during the Second World War and into the present (that is, 1958).[17] Shepherd began by noting his contemporaries' tendency to disparage the work of Dom Guéranger, as Guéranger's liturgical interests and reforms were "colored by the romanticism of his age, in its strong reaction to the ultrarationalism and classicism of eighteenth-century culture. Like all romanticists, Guéranger was more at home in the piety of the Middle Ages than in that of the Patristic age—and everyone knows, of course, that the medieval period was one of liturgical deterioration."[18]

Modern scholars could well criticize (or bemoan) Guéranger, not only for his incorrect assumptions about the formation of liturgical

---

298); and a "fundamental question" "of particular importance" (*Jahrbuch für Liturgiewissenschaft* 13 [1933]: 211).

[17] Massey Hamilton Shepherd, "History of the Liturgical Renewal," in *The Liturgical Renewal of the Church: Addresses of the Liturgical Conference in 1958*, ed. Massey Hamilton Shepherd (New York: Oxford University Press, 1960), 24.

[18] Ibid., 24–25. Among others, Joanne M. Pierce presents a contrasting view of the medieval liturgy, describing the benefits of learning from the medieval period, a time of "cultural crisis," and draws from its approach to liturgy as a resource for the present. See Joanne Pierce, "Early Medieval Liturgy: Some Implications for Contemporary Liturgical Practice," *Worship* 65, no. 6 (1991): 509–22.

rite, but for his very active realization of uniformity in liturgical practices by his "zealous campaign" to hasten the suppression of the Gallican rite in France.[19] Yet, a positive aspect of liturgical reform encouraged by Guéranger was his emphasis on the social character of Christian worship. First using the term the "liturgical movement" in 1851, Guéranger hoped to focus on the liturgy as the central act of the pastoral nature of the Church and to demonstrate the preeminence of the official prayer of the Church.[20] Comparing his desires to that of St. Benedict, Guéranger suggested that one could recivilize Europe through the liturgy, which was, in fact, what he imagined his newly reestablished abbey at Solesmes doing. Solesmes was particularly famous for its study and restoration of plain chant, a practical realization of reforming the liturgy and, with hope, the souls who worshiped. Aside from considering the social/communal potential of liturgical performance, Guéranger's largest work, l'Année liturgique, a twenty-eight-volume (unfinished) exegesis of the liturgical year of the Roman Rite, considered the broader social potential of the liturgy: he wanted to exegete the Mass so as to describe what it could yield spiritually, attempting to produce instructions for the people, particularly those

---

[19] Shepherd, 25. Paul Marx's biography of Virgil Michel, written only two years earlier than Shepherd's speech, is not as critical of Guéranger, and merely notes, "no name looms so large as that of Abbot Prosper Guéranger (1805–75). In 1840 he began his monumental work of research and publication. His *Institutions liturgiques* (1840–51) showed the beauties of the Roman rite in contrast of some fifteen local, Gallicanized diocesan liturgies." Marx, *Virgil Michel*, 73. An evaluation of Guéranger's method, which sought uniformity and universality, encouraging the various liturgical practices to fall in line with one sort of über-liturgy, must take into consideration the influence of wider cultural moves of his time, namely, German Romanticism. As Thomas O'Meara describes in his article, "The Origins of the Liturgical Movement and German Romanticism," *Worship* 59, no. 4 (1985): 326–42, "romanticism" defined itself in opposition to the enlightenment which preceded it. Enlightenment-era liturgy was increasingly interpreted as suited to individual formation, seeking to educate the individual by means of rational methods. Romanticism reacted by striving for totality, universality, and organization into a unified system, one which was more focused on spirituality or the worship of God in a public setting and as a communal effort.

[20] Ernst B. Koenker, *The Liturgical Renaissance in the Roman Catholic Church* (Chicago: University of Chicago Press, 1954), 10.

who did not understand Latin, to inspire the emergence of a popular liturgical spirituality.[21]

A desire for a popular, universal, and accessible liturgy also explains Guéranger's suppression of Gallicanism and sharp criticism of Jansenism. He was chiefly concerned with three issues. First, nationalism, in that he viewed the plethora of diocesan liturgies in France as indicative of the vainglorious nationalistic spirit of the country and believed worship should reflect a unity of forms resonating with the Universal Church, not nationalistic particularities. Second, elitism, in that the Gallican texts tended to focus on a sort of "elect" body of believers, somewhat obscuring the emphasis that Christ died for "all"; in short, communal prayers should be of a communal nature. Finally, individualism, in that rampant individualism, private devotion, and individual piety were the result of "Jansenistic" temptations into heresies in the enlightenment-bound seventeenth and eighteenth centuries; this was in direct opposition to the social character of liturgical worship.[22] Early European liturgical reformers vociferously distanced themselves from any suspect of "Jansenism" or the "Enlightenment" until the liturgical movement was safely under the patronage of the Holy See.[23]

---

[21] The abbey at Solesmes began publishing a number of journals to this end, such as *L'auxilière Catholique*. Rather than describe the liturgical movement's origins with the refounding of Solesmes, Ernst Koenker, in his *The Liturgical Renaissance in the Roman Catholic Church*, claimed that it was "commonplace" in Roman Catholic literature to identify the beginning of the monumental *L'Année liturgique* in 1840 as the beginning of the liturgical movement, a trend which is also followed by both Anglican and Lutheran histories of the movement (Koenker, 10). See also Olivier Rousseau, *Histoire du mouvement liturgique: Esquisse historique depuis le début de XIXe siècle jusqu'au pontificat de Pie X* (Paris: Éditions du Cerf, 1945), 1–53.

[22] See R. William Franklin, "The People's Work: Anti-Jansenist Prejudice in the Benedictine Movement for Popular Participation in the Nineteenth Century," *Studia Liturgica* 19, no. 1 (1989): 60–77; Cuthbert Johnson, *Prosper Guéranger (1805–1875): A Liturgical Tradition* (Rome: Pontificio Ateneo S. Anselmo, 1984). Some liturgical scholars saw the Gallican liturgies as scenes of rampant individualism, which defied the unity of the ancient Roman Rite.

[23] As Olivier Rousseau explained in *The Progress of the Liturgy*, "Originating in France, [the liturgical movement] soon spread beyond the French borders and became known through its relationship with other movements which it finally incorporated, giving them its own name. Its profound Catholicity could not be vitiated. From the very beginning, it energetically rejected any counterfeit and refused false alliances; and this all the more, once the Holy See

At the end of the day, while Guéranger may have provided more of an interpretation or reimaging of the process of liturgical evolution, the very methods he supported or instituted for the "restoration of a pure Roman liturgy," in text, ceremony, and chant were, as Massey Shepherd described in 1959, "an essential starting point for any progressive work of reform."[24] But, instead of simply creating a perfect reproduction or a snapshot of liturgical purity, Massey noted that the *intent* of reformed text, ceremony, and chant was to allow the spiritual quality of the liturgy to flourish, inspiring the liturgical worshiper through the performance and practice of the liturgy into union with the Christian community and, thus inspired, to expand this spirit outward for the renewal of a degenerate society.

Despite the intent of Guéranger's development of reform, liturgical histories, such as Ernst Koenker's *The Liturgical Renaissance* (1954), evaluated the European movement as, ultimately, stymied by its inability to effectively transcend the theoretical level and enter the practical. As Koenker described:

> [The European liturgical movement] gave great impetus to the study and use of Gregorian music, but the modern Roman Catholic Liturgical Movement is much more than a concern for the proper rendition of the chant. Moreover, though Guéranger envisaged a return to the official prayer of the Church rather than remain with the meager nourishment of devotional books then popular, his work did not involve bringing the liturgy to the masses as does the work of the modern movement.[25]

The extent to which the European movement can be described as reaching into the popular realm changes radically from reviewer to reviewer. Koenker actually described Guéranger as *not* aiming to incorporate general participation, claiming that Guéranger did not embrace

-----

assumed its patronage. We will see how the cockle tries constantly to mix with this grain, so that it will often be necessary to do some weeding. Very likely it will always be thus" (Rousseau, *The Progress of the Liturgy*, viii). Rousseau described the liturgical movement as that which "will one day be looked upon as something characteristic of present-day Catholicism" and admitted it had yet to achieve a "final synthesis" at the point of his writing in the late 1940s.

[24] Shepherd, 25.

[25] Koenker, 10–11.

the "all-pervading social concern" which is that of the modern era.[26] The differing evaluations of Guéranger are, not surprisingly, negligent in describing another aspect of his interest in liturgical reform and the restoration of the Benedictine community at Solesmes: his interest in refounding the Benedictine order also prompted him to establish a community of Benedictine sisters at Solesmes, the Abbey of St. Cecilia, in collaboration with its first abbess, Mother Cécile Bruyère, OSB (1845–1909).

Benedictine Men and Women, Liturgical Scholarship and Pastoral Initiative in Germany

The revival of Benedictine monasticism for men and women in France influenced its neighbors, including Germany, Belgium, and Austria. Subsequent scholarly work, both by the Belgian Benedictine houses of Maredsous (founded in 1872) and its daughter monastery, Mont César (founded in 1899), advanced liturgical studies both scholarly and practically. As Shepherd described, "The significance of such scholarly work, as these men promoted, lies in the new foundation that their studies laid for liturgical science, by shifting the base of liturgical enthusiasm from medieval to patristic standards."[27]

In Germany, influential liturgical pioneers Odo Casel and Ildefons Herwegen, OSB (1874–1946), met while Casel was a student at the University of Bonn, and, with Herwegen's influence, Casel entered the German monastery at Maria Laach in 1905. Casel wrote hundreds of articles and several books, most significant of which was *Das christliche Kultmysterium*, in which he spoke of the sacraments as mysteries, likening them to the pagan mystery cults. Though one can see why this view might be controversial,[28] he did, as Keith Pecklers notes, prepare

---

[26] Ibid., 11. This same phenomenon occurred within the American movement. Despite its interest in social activism from the beginning, the early stages of the American movement were characterized by an educated populace, the learning of Latin, the Catholic intellectual life, and the cultivation of the fine arts for those with the leisure and resources to do so. The movement took on different valences and more "popular" elements, such as family liturgical practices, in the decade following the Second World War.

[27] Shepherd, 26.

[28] Keith F. Pecklers, *The Unread Vision: The Liturgical Movement in the United States of America; 1926–1955* (Collegeville, MN: Liturgical Press, 1998), 6. As Pecklers summarizes, not only Casel but the entire German liturgical movement was called into question by critics; one of the best circulated was a

the ground for a theologically rich view of the Church as Mystical Body of Christ, which expressed itself "relationally and symbolically" through sacramental participation of the faithful.[29] The view of the Church as the Mystical Body of Christ would be fundamental for the liturgical movement both in Europe and the United States.

While Shepherd mused about the "men" who contributed to this scholarly work, he failed to take notice of the women who were also involved in liturgical scholarship. The German Abbey of the Holy Cross at Herstelle was the home of several prominent Benedictine women students of liturgy, including Aemiliana Löhr, OSB, liturgical theologian, and Agape Kiesgen, OSB (1899–1933), who prepared much of the initial work in compiling the index for the *Jahrbuch für Liturgiewissenschaft*. The sisters of Herstelle were familiar with the freshest theological work, as their prioress, Margareta Blanché, OSB, invited Casel to serve as *pater spiritalis* for the sisters there in 1922, a position he retained until his death in 1948. Some of Casel's most well-developed theological thought, summarized by the term *Mysterientheologie*, found expression in his talks given to the women's community there.[30] Yet, as Teresa Berger observes, the women liturgical scholars or retreatants at Herstelle are rarely mentioned by most liturgical histories and, when they are, are often portrayed in such a way as being dependent on Casel; Aemiliana Löhr, for example, is described as "Casel's master pupil,"[31] though one might wonder at which point a woman with over three hundred publications, including articles, books, and poems, might cease to be considered a "pupil" of another and begin to be considered a scholar in her own right.

Löhr and her fellow Benedictine sisters were students of Casel and (as her liturgical reflection on the liturgical year indicates) were shaped

---

two-part pamphlet written by M. Kassiepe, OMI, "Irrwege und Umwege im Frömmigkeitsleben der Gegenwart," vol. 1 (1939) and vol. 2 (1940).

[29] Pecklers, 6. See also Jeremy Hall, *The Full Stature of Christ: The Ecclesiology of Virgil Michel, OSB* (Collegeville, MN: Liturgical Press, 1976).

[30] Berger, "Moved by Women?," 234. See also Berger, *Liturgie und Frauenseele*, 11–12. Burkhard Neunhueser in his introduction to *Mysterium der Ekklesia Von der Gemeinschaft aller Erlosten in Christus Jesus*, ed. Theophora Schneider (Mainz: Grunewald, 1961), 11–17, here 17, notes that in Odo Casel's writings "much of importance is said about the Christian image of women in our times."

[31] Theodor Schnitzler, review of *Die Heilige Woche*, by Aemiliana Löhr, *Liturgisches Jahrbuch* 7 (1957): 126.

by his teaching. Nevertheless, liturgical roads go both ways. One must ask to what extent persons such as Odo Casel, chaplain to this women's community for twenty-six years, were influenced by the women with whom they regularly spoke. As Berger notes, Casel regularly reflected on women's issues, and the journal he edited, *Jahrbuch für Liturgiewissenschaft*, contained a surprising number of reviews by and about women and their liturgical writings.[32] Women contributed regularly not only to the *Jahrbuch für Liturgiewissenschaft* but also to other liturgically oriented journals, such as *Bibel und Liturgie, Liturgische Zeitschrift*, and *Quickborn*. Subjects ranged from theological reflection on the nature of Christian womanhood and woman's relation to the Church as liturgical subject, to historical analysis of rites and feasts, to discussions of scriptural, patristic, and medieval texts in relation to the liturgy. Even lacking a more thorough analysis of European women's original contributions, it appears reasonable to conclude that religious and non-religious lay women shared in liturgical reflection and scholarly dialogue with their male counterparts.[33]

[32] Berger, *Women's Ways of Worship*, 74. Berger adds that Casel had an American counterpart in Martin Hellriegel, who served as chaplain to the Sisters of the Adoration of the Most Precious Blood at O'Fallon, Missouri, for twenty-two years, also forming much of his liturgical reflection in this context of a woman's community.

[33] To give some sense of the breadth of women's involvement in liturgical scholarship, some examples follow which are readily found in these liturgical journals: Dr. Josepha Fischer, "Das katholische Wertbild der Frau und die deutsche Frauenfrage," in *Die Kirche im deutschen Aufbruch: Gesammelte Aufsätze*, ed. Franz Joseph Wothe (Heider: Bergisch Gladbach, 1934), 112–34; Maria Fuerth, *Caritas und Humanitas: Zur Form und Wandlung des Christlichen Liebesgedankens* (Stuttgart: Frommann, 1933); Dr. Oda Hagemeyer, OSB, "St. Polykarp betet liturgisch,"*Bibel und Liturgie* 9 (1934/1935): 189–95; Dr. Edith Hegemann, "Das Heil des Liebes in den liturgischen Gebeten," *Liturgische Zeitschrift* 4 (1931/1932): 418–22; Edith Hegemann-Springer, "Juristische Formulierungen in den Gebeten der Kirche," *Liturgische Zeitschrift* 5 (1932/1933): 254–60; Agape Kiesgen, OSB, "Die grosse Doxologie der Kirche," *Bibel und Liturgie* 2 (1927/1928): 273–79, 320–26; Makrina Kloeppel, OSB, "Der Hymnus zu den Vigilien am Sonntag im Herbst und Winter," *Bibel und Liturgie* 3 (1928/1929): 33–38; Dr. Maria Louise Lascar, "Abendländische und griechisch-orthodoze Mönchsprofess als Tauferneuerung," *Liturgische Zeitschrift* 2 (1930): 205–13; Dr. Paula Schäfer, "Antwort auf Dr. Hugo Zettels Aufsatz zum Book of Common Prayer," *Liturgisches Leben* 2 (1935): 300–304; Seraphie Schaneng, "Das neue Mädchen," *Quickborn* 6 (1918/1919): 6–10, 22–25; and Irene Schleef, OSB,

Also influential for the German liturgical movement, Romano Guardini, OSB (1885–1968), whose work had also influenced Aemiliana Löhr, presented to a group of women active in the Catholic Women's Movement on "women's nature and mission" in 1921, later published in a popular German Catholic women's journal.[34] Guardini also maintained a friendship with Dr. Gerta Krabbel (1881–1961), president of an important Catholic women's organization in Germany, Katholische Deutsche Frauenbund, and served on the editorial board of a journal for girls and young women, *Der neue Ring*. Meanwhile, Johannes Pinsk (1891–1957) was also interested in the education and professional life of women, publishing multiple essays on women and women's issues. A collection of his unpublished writings on women, titled *Frau im Beruf*, was published in 1957, posthumously.[35]

Abbot Ildefons Herwegen also encouraged others of the abbey to work on theological reflections about and for women and suggested to Athanasius Wintersig, OSB (1900–1942), that he write *Liturgy and*

"Der Hymnus zur Prim (Nach dem monastichen Brevier)," *Bibel und Liturgie* 3 (1928/1929): 336.

The women listed here are both religious (e.g., Agape Kiesgen, OSB, Makrina Kloeppel, OSB, Irene Schleef, OSB, Oda Hagemeyer, OSB) and lay, nonreligious (e.g., Maria Louise Lascar and Edith Hegemann-Springer). With regard to the nonreligious women, Teresa Berger notes that some more "elite" women, such as Dr. Lascar, wrote frequently in liturgical journals and were identified by name, but "ordinary" women who wrote about their "liturgical experiences" in the more popular *Bibel und Liturgie* were not identified. Teresa Berger, personal correspondence with the author, April 15, 2011.

[34] See Romano Guardini, "Wahr-Nehmung der Frau," in *Wie Theologen Frauen sehen—von der Macht der Bilder*, ed. Renate Jost and Ursula Kubera (Freiburg: Herder, 1993): 127–41. Helen McConnell describes how Löhr's work rests in Guardini's approach to "liturgical-ecclesial mystagogy" in "Aemiliana Löhr's Theology of Liturgical Worship," 192–99. Helen H. McConnell, *Aemiliana Löhr's Theology of Liturgical Worship* (PhD diss., Catholic University of America, 2001).

[35] Johannes Pinsk, *Frau im Beruf* (Salzburg: O. Müller, 1959). Some examples of Pinsk's work include: "Das Heil des Leibes in den liturgischen Gebeten," *Liturgische Zeitschrift* 4 (1931/1932): 418–22; "Zu einem Aufsatz uber 'Das Priestertum der Frau,'" *Liturgische Zeitschrift* 3 (1930/1931): 256–79; "Juristische Formulierungen in den Gebeten der Kirche," *Liturgische Zeitschrift* 5 (1932/1933): 254–60; and "Liturgische Gedanken zur Enzyklika 'Quadragesimo Anno,'" *Liturgische Zeitschrift* 3 (1930/1931): 385–92.

Woman's Soul (1925),[36] which appeared in the *Ecclesia Orans* series.[37] Continuing his interest in women's role in the lay apostolate, in 1931 Herwegen presented a paper to Catholic teachers (all of whom were women) titled "Church and Woman." And, ten years later, he wrote the introduction to *The Great Sign* by Maura Böckeler, OSB,[38] a text in which she described woman as symbolizing the Divine, particularly the Holy Spirit.

Pastoral Focus in Belgium

In Belgium, the newly formed Beuron Congregation at Mont César Abbey was perhaps better known for its pastoral focus. Mont César's role in the liturgical movement follows the leadership of Dom Lambert Beauduin, OSB (1873–1960), who remained with the congregation from 1906 to 1925, when he left to found the Belgian Chevetogne Abbey. Beauduin, who had served as a diocesan priest engaged in social work for eight years before coming to Mont César, was convinced that the "work" of saving souls had to be rooted in the liturgy.[39] Shortly after his arrival, in 1909, Beauduin organized the National Congress of Catholic Works [Action] held at Malines, Belgium, a national gather-

[36] Athanasius Wintersig, *Liturgie und Frauenseele*, Ecclesia Orans Series 17 (Freiburg im Breisgau: Herder, 1925). This very popular book was published in 6 eds., 1925–32, which Teresa Berger describes as "the most sustained expression" of the "woman-script" of the liturgical movement. See Berger, *Women's Ways*, 91.

[37] The second edition is reviewed in *Orate Fratres* in 1927, and the reviewer describes that Wintersig's treatise brings out the various callings of woman "in their true Christian light," showing how all activities reflect the qualities of the Church as the Spouse of her divine Bridegroom: "The contents are both profound and inspiring, especially in the light of modern effusions on woman, which parade as the sublimated wisdom of a new enlightenment." "Liturgie und Frauenseele," review, *Orate Fratres* 2, no. 12 (1928): 384.

[38] Maura Böckeler, *Das grosse zeichen*, Apokalypse Series 12, 1 (Salzburg–Leipzig: O. Müller, 1941).

[39] See Paul Marx, *Virgil Michel and the Liturgical Movement*, 27. These interests were taken up by Virgil Michel. In Paul Marx's biography of Michel, Marx includes a letter from Lambert reflecting upon his impressions of Michel while at Rome: "I knew him well at Rome, and when he discovered that I was concerned with the liturgical movement at Louvain, we became quite friendly, and he often came to talk to me in private; but liturgy was not for him just a matter of study; it was above all a powerful means of doing apostolic work, by increasing the faith and devotion of the faithful" (Marx, 28).

ing at which he delivered a speech titled "La vraie prière de l'Eglise," in which he claimed "active participation in the liturgical life of the Church" to be the most fundamental factor in the life of a Christian.[40] Following Pius X's *Tra le Sollecitudini*, Beauduin encouraged the faithful to participate in the ritual, opening eyes and ears to the words of the liturgy and the songs of the Church, thus drawing the laity into participation with the action of Christ and the priestly hierarchy.[41]

Despite Beauduin's more pastoral focus even in 1909, the liturgical movement continued to be misinterpreted by its contemporaries. It was completely misdefined (as the writers in *Orate Fratres* would frequently lament) either as being interested in liturgical dress or candlesticks or as being too far separated from the actual needs and responsibilities of pastoral work.[42] Absent from the narrative, however, was an account of one of Beauduin's most influential pastoral initiatives, that which found expression at the women's Benedictine Abbey at Wépion in Belgium. Founded in the early 1920s, the community was founded in order to provide opportunity for women to experience and

[40] Lambert Beauduin, *Liturgy the Life of the Church*, Popular Liturgical Library Series (Collegeville, MN: Liturgical Press, 1926), 17. This volume is the inaugural issue of the Popular Liturgical Library, established by Virgil Michel, OSB, in 1926. Beauduin, teacher of apologetics, ecclesiology, and liturgy at St. Anselmo in Rome, profoundly influenced Virgil Michel (Marx, 73). For a description of the state of Belgian liturgy prior to Beauduin's influence, see Belgian Benedictine, "Belgium-American-Liturgy," *Placidian* 4 (1927): 103–23.

[41] Beauduin, *Liturgy the Life of the Church*, 14–15. "Let us sing, then; let us lend our ears, open our eyes, unite ourselves completely to the priestly acts according to all the demands of the ritual; let us participate freely in all the functions of parochial life, assimilate all the riches of the liturgical texts, surrender ourselves to the action of our holy Church, in a word, *live the mystery of the hierarchy*, whatever may be our degree of interior prayer, our private method, or our attraction for solitude. It is thus that we shall find the manna of the desert, the family table, the embrace of our Mother Church, nay, Jesus Himself, God" (Beauduin, 15).

[42] Shepherd notes, "If asked for an opinion about some particular liturgical usage [the great scholars in the field of liturgics] are likely to offer an idealistic solution based upon an historical precedent or norm. Liturgical reform often means to them little more than the restoration of some ancient text or custom in its pristine purity. One suspects that for this reason the Liturgical Movement has suffered, until recent years, from the charge of being archaeological and academic. Too many enthusiasts for liturgical reform have sought their inspiration from the liturgiologists" (Shepherd, 28).

be formed by the liturgical life; here, Belgian and German lay women, not only from religious orders, but from the wider lay apostolate, attended liturgical retreats.[43] Also influential for the developing trope of the Christian woman and liturgical renewal, in 1922, Belgian Abbot Auguste Croegaert, OSB, wrote *The Christian Woman and the Liturgical Renewal*.[44] Croegaert's presentation of the task of the Christian woman would influence Virgil Michel, who drew on this source for his paper, "The Liturgical Movement and the Catholic Woman,"[45] and the article "The Christian Woman."[46]

Liturgical Life and the Feminine: The Feminization of the Liturgy

In short, an overview of some of the key figures in the European scene reveals that there were also many women present in the European liturgical movement. The assumption that women were influenced by their teachers and did not, in turn, give their teachers cause for theological reflection is not supportable, even by a quick review of the sources, particularly in Germany and Belgium. Reflections on both women's issues (*Frauenfragen* in German) and women's liturgical writing are clearly present. The social impact of the women's movement in these locales in Europe, the increased interest in the cooperation of the lay apostolate in the work and prayer life of the Church understood as the Mystical Body of Christ, and the beginnings of organized women's movements within the Church as groups of study, retreat, or Catholic identity, all contributed to the presence and activity of women in liturgical praxis and study during the early years of the twentieth century. It is significant that the liturgical movement grew in the same years in which women's roles in society and the Church were being redefined. As Berger surmises, the liturgical movement was one voice in a larger debate attempting to define the nature of woman.[47]

[43] See Teresa Berger, "Moved by Women?," 234.

[44] Auguste Croegaert, *La femme chrétienne et la restauration liturgique* (Bruxelles: Vromant & Co., 1922).

[45] Virgil Michel, "The Liturgical Movement and the Catholic Woman," in Central Catholic Verein of America, *32nd Annual Convention: Catholic Central Verein of America (New York State Branch): And 10th Annual Convention Catholic Women's Union of America (Section New York)* (New York: [n.p.], 1929), 57–62.

[46] Virgil Michel, "The Christian Woman," *Orate Fratres* 13, no. 6 (1939): 248–56.

[47] Berger, "Moved by Women?," 242.

For liturgical pioneers, the connection of the liturgy and the feminine served to rekindle both a feminization of the Church and conversation about women's roles as Christians. The fathers of the liturgical movement typified the ideal of the Christian woman by likening her to the Church, the *ecclesia*, beautiful and timeless; as Guardini identified, the "awakening of the Church in the souls" which was the heart of the liturgical movement also awakened "an intensely feminine image" of the Church.[48] The identification of women's roles as virgin, mother, and bride with the Church, complemented with more conservative readings of the nature of womanhood, paired well with an understanding of women's receptive nature which fostered a longing to nurture her young, just as Mother Church desired to care for her children. The receptive nature of woman was in concert with the writings of women themselves, and Aemiliana Löhr, for example, wrote that, "As the representative of Christ, man is by his very nature essentially priest, lord, and bridegroom; as the image of the *ekklesia*, woman is by her very nature essentially victim, servant, and bride."[49]

These assertions about women's likeness to the Church and liturgy stressed her potential or actual responsibility to use her feminine influence to save the world from masculine, technological, and ruthless degeneration. Women were described as having a certain monopoly or stronghold on being able to understand the liturgy and to convert those around her to the liturgy and, thus, to Christ.[50] Members of the liturgical movement in this early period even explicitly identified women as the key, so to speak, to liturgical renewal, as did, for example, Pius Parsch (1884–1954): "Everybody working at the center of the liturgical movement is able to see that woman is far more receptive

[48] Ibid., 242. Ildefons Herwegen writes, "Woman and Church is to a certain extent an equation . . . for the Church has always remained feminine . . . the Church is the archetype of the Christian Woman" (Herwegen, "Kirche und Frau," *Wom christlichen Sein und Leben Gesammelte Vortrage* [Berlin: Sankt Augustinus Verlag, 1931], 131).

[49] Aemiliana Löhr, review of *Vom Priestertum der Frau*, by Oda Schneider, *Jahrbuch fur Liturgiewissenschaft* 14 (1934): 278. Quoted in Berger, "Moved by Women?," 243.

[50] This seems to be a theological explanation for a cultural phenomenon in which religion had increasingly become associated with the realm of women and children, not the domain of men. Women far outnumbered men in devotional exercises and church attendance, a condition which would be repeated in immigrant populations as they arrived in America.

to liturgical prayer and celebration than man. Woman . . . is the best apostle of the liturgy. . . . Particularly young women . . . are today the primary carriers of the liturgical renewal."[51]

Parsch suggested the manner in which interest in the liturgical movement was realized in parishes where it had been introduced, that women were more active and interested. Additionally, the monasteries that produced liturgical scholarship were not the only locales of liturgical interest, but lay persons (often women), inspired by liturgical or spiritual retreats, sustained a liturgical life of prayer in smaller communities, such as Berger describes:

> These communities were largely made up of women, and also were not infrequently initiated and led by women. The structure of these groups resembled in many ways what today would be called base ecclesial communities, that is, small groups which met to pray, sing, and reflect together on the text of the eucharistic liturgy for the following Sunday. These liturgical base communities certainly provided women with an authentic liturgical apostolate of their own, an apostolate which lay outside of the traditional woman's domain of her home and family. In other words, women who were active in the liturgical movement were not confined to the home, and so they were not confined to a "private" apostolate.[52]

Including the vast social changes for women into the historical account of the liturgical movement begins to open a more complex narrative.

---

[51] Pius Parsch, "Die Mitarbeit der Frau in der liturgischen Bewegung," *Bibel und Liturgie* 7 (1933/1934): 436. Somewhat ironically, Martin Hellriegel, OSB, employed a decidedly choice metaphor when describing Prosper Guéranger's campaign to revitalize the liturgy of France: "In 1840 [Guéranger] began the monumental works which he intended as an antidote to the spiritual torpor of the France of his day. He fought to have the *virile Roman liturgy* substituted for the *somewhat emasculated diocesan liturgies*, and he lived to see his efforts in this line crowned with complete success." Though one might wonder exactly what Hellriegel wished to convey with the adjective "emasculated," he chooses to describe liturgical renewal (according to the methodological assumptions of unification and centralization as employed by Guéranger) as that which would re-masculinize the liturgy. This is a somewhat curious contrast as the liturgy is often described in feminine terms which combat the masculinizing tendencies of society. What does seem clear is "that which is feminine" is identified as inferior. Hellriegel, "A Survey of the Liturgical Movement," in *The Liturgical Movement*, Popular Liturgical Library Series 4, no. 3 (Collegeville, MN: Liturgical Press, 1930), 24.

[52] Berger, "Moved by Women?," 240.

Women's issues were crucially important social questions of the time, and women's role in society, the workforce, and the academy was rapidly changing in the post–World War I era.[53] Yet these *Frauenfragen* are far from the pages of history covering the liturgical movement, and the relative silence with which women and women's issues are greeted by evaluations of the liturgical movement buoys the assumption that women and their women's issues are irrelevant.[54]

Yet, as evidenced above, this silence is not matched by the primary sources of the era, where women not only appear among liturgical dialogue and research but are themselves the subject of liturgical reflection. The same rediscovery of the liturgy as revelatory for the meaning of Church, with the newfound emphasis on the laity's participation alongside the hierarchy, opened up renewal of thought not only on lay participation in the Church and her action within liturgy and in society but also on women's liturgical activity and in the world. Importantly, promoting women's "liturgical activity" did not necessarily mean "ordained activity," though questions about women's ministerial possibilities were part of some European conversations. For example, in Germany, the same early twentieth-century secular questions regarding women's role in society had led to a "lively discussion" of women's priesthood by the 1920s. And by the 1930s, Dr. Josephine Mayer argued for the restoration of the diaconate for women.[55] Yet, questions

[53] Teresa Berger summarizes that, during the Weimar Republic, nearly one-third of the German workforce was women and women's advancement to the university was far more common; when the nationalist-socialist regime, i.e., the Nazis, seized control of the political system, new governmental programs urged women to concentrate on home and family, rejecting "women's emancipation" as an enemy, and quotas were placed upon the number of women who could enter the university (no more than ten percent of any given student population). Berger, "Moved by Women?," 238.

[54] Ibid., 238. Berger concludes, "The scholarly consensus on the liturgical movement, namely, that women and women's issues are of little relevance for the movement, is not developed and established through lengthy arguments, but through silence."

[55] See Josephine Mayer, "Vom Diakonat der Frau," *Hochland* 36, no. 1 (1938/1939): 98–108. See also Teresa Berger, *Liturgie und Frauenseele*, 83–88. Berger describes a variety of discussions regarding women's ministerial roles in *Liturgie und Frauenseele*, 73–93. I am grateful to Teresa Berger for this insight into women's interest in ordained ministry alongside that of the liturgical movement in Europe.

regarding women's ordained activity tended not to enter American conversations until much later, in the era of the Second Vatican Council, and women's ordination was simply not the focus of concern for American writers during the liturgical movement, either for men or for women.[56] Promoting liturgical activity meant, at its simplest, active participation in the rites of the Church's public worship and emphasized that women too were members of the Church and the lay apostolate, and equally had access to and responsibility to be formed by the rites of the Church's liturgy.

The Liturgical Movement Moves outside of Theory
and into the Lay Apostolate

Interpreting the liturgical movement as a means for the faithful, regardless of vocation, to spiritually and intellectually grasp their identity as Christians developed in concert with a number of contemporary movements which advocated for lay Catholic activity. Advocates of liturgical reform resonated with Dom Odo Casel's *Mysterientheologie*, which emphasized that Christ's paschal mystery was present in the liturgical act of worship, not just in its effects.[57] In turn, liturgical reformers sought to involve individual lay persons in the activity of the hierarchical apostolate through their assistance and participation (rather than simple attendance) at Mass. This involvement would serve to revitalize the understanding of the significance of public litur-

---

[56] One such venue would be the "Deaconess Movement," begun in the latter 1960s with a small group of women interested in becoming part of the newly restored permanent diaconate following the Second Vatican Council. See Katharine E. Harmon, "A Historical Perspective for Women and Sacrament: The American Deaconess Movement in the Roman Catholic Church, 1964–1976," *Studia Liturgica* 41, no. 2 (2011): 186–210.

[57] See Kevin W. Irwin, "Contributions of European Authors," in *Liturgical Theology: A Primer*, American Essays in Liturgy, ed. Edward Foley (Collegeville, MN: Liturgical Press, 1990), 20. Casel's work may be criticized for too freely applying Hellenistic mystery religions to Christianity, neglecting the role of the Holy Spirit, or divorcing liturgy from cultural context (see Irénée Henri Dalmais, "La liturgie célébration du mystère du salut," in *L'Église en prière*, vol. 1, *Principes de la liturgie*, ed. A. G. Martimont [Paris: Desclée, 1983], 262–81). However, his presentation of the liturgy as formative for the mystical body was influential for the liturgical reformers' development of the liturgy as a social act.

gical worship as forming the laity in the Mystical Body of Christ.[58] R. P. Chenu, OP, described these two impulses as deeply entwined external and internal developments within modern Catholicism. The first, external element was the Catholic called to participate in the hierarchical apostolate of the Church, described as Catholic Action. A Christianity of the apostolate could not be reserved to priests, good though the work of priests might be, nor could it exist cut off from life, barricading itself against the world. Indeed, a Christian could live no other way than *as a Christian* fully in society:

> Catholic Action is the restoration of this apostolic sense in the Christian soul. It is the yeast thrust once more into the middle of the mass. It is the divine life elevating the whole of human life without rejecting anything, the Incarnation continued in the Mystical Body of Christ. Work, business, firms, trades, offices: everything must be brought into the Christian life. The whole of human civilization is the subject matter of Christianity.[59]

[58] The notion of the *Mysterium* of Christianity is greatly influenced by the liturgical theology of Odo Casel. The reality of redemption, made present in the incarnation, passion, and resurrection of Christ, is made present in the participation of the body of the faithful in the worship of the liturgy. The liturgy forms the faithful to Christ himself, through the sacraments of initiation and continuing in the Eucharist. Through them we are formed to Christ, as members of his Mystical Body. Casel described the liturgical *Mysterium* as follows: "The Mysterium is a holy, cultic action in which the redemptive act is rendered present in the rite; since the cultic community accomplishes this rite, it participates in the saving act and through it attains redemption" (*Das Christliche Kultmysterium* [Regensburg: F. Pustet, 1935], 101).

Ernst Koenker summarized Casel's concept of liturgical action: "In the liturgical rites of sacrifice and sacrament we meet the mystical making-present-again of the *totum opus redemptionis*; not only the Passion of Christ but his whole life, from the Incarnation to his Second Coming, is rendered sacramentally present in the cultic mysteries. It is rather ontological action, a *signum efficax*, a reality which efficaciously heightens man's natural existence through an activity in a higher sphere; as such, of course, it works *ex opera operato*. The symbol really and actually *is* in the supernatural-divine order what in its outward, natural appearance it signifies" (Koenker, 107). See also Leo M. McMahon, "Towards a Theology of the Liturgy: Dom Odo Casel and the 'Mysterientheologie,'" *Studia Liturgica* 3, no. 3 (1964): 129–54.

[59] R. P. Chenu, "Catholic Action and the Mystical Body," in *Restoring All Things: A Guide to Catholic Action*, ed. John Fitzsimons and Paul McGuire (New York: Sheed & Ward, 1938), 13.

This external manifestation of the Church through the activity of the laity is the structure through which the second half, the internal development, the Mystical Body of Christ, might attain its fullness in the social life of the world.[60] If the Word was made flesh, and this was the law for the incarnation of Christ, then it was also the law of incarnation of the divine life throughout the centuries in Christ's Church: the Word is continually made flesh in the community of Christians; it is made of individuals but remains necessarily social.[61]

The emphases on the activity of the laity, the Mystical Body of Christ, and the social nature of the liturgy are particularly important characteristics of the liturgical movement, as they point attention to the lay apostolate. The liturgy's potential for societal reform was an issue broader than the liturgical movement, perhaps, but it highlights an issue taken up by liturgical reformers (i.e., an answer to the evils of the modern world) and also unfolds the connection of liturgy to social activism which was a mainstay of the liturgical movement in its earli-

[60] Ibid.

[61] "Thus the Christian, far from seeing the permanent presence of the community and the common good as an obstacle to his personal perfection, will rejoice in it as a broadening and assuring influence, whence this 'socialness' is the matter and instrument of incarnation. The more the common good is woven into the warp and woof of social life, to that extent will there be eminent matter for grace, and it will be, if one can say it thus, the soil of the Mystical Body—not an agglomeration of individuals but a community of men in the deepest sense of the word.

"So we are quite ready to acclaim the grandeur of the social and communitarian aspirations which have traversed the nineteenth aspirations which exalt the minds of the twentieth; for we see in it a magnificent field of work of Christianity; the flowering of apostolates, specialised according to the different functions of men in society, is in truth the beginning of the cultivation of this field; it is the mystical incorporation of Christ in the community life of man" (R. P. Chenu, "Catholic Action and the Mystical Body," 10). See also G. Lefebvre, "Catholic Action and the Liturgy," in *Restoring All Things: A Guide to Catholic Action*, ed. John Fitzsimons and Paul McGuire (New York: Sheed and Ward, 1938), 16–50; John J. Griffin, "Catholic Action and the Liturgical Life,'" *Orate Fratres* 9, no. 8 (1935): 360; John J. Griffin, "The Spiritual Foundations of Catholic Action," *Orate Fratres* 9, no. 10 (1935): 463–64; for commentary on the connection between Catholic Action and liturgy, see Marx, *Virgil Michel and the Liturgical Movement*, 374; and Pecklers, *The Unread Vision*, 104–13.

est years.[62] An increasing identification of the evils of modern society and the Church's potential or, indeed, responsibility to respond to it occurs within this time. One could point to papal statements such as Pope Leo XIII's (1878–1903) On Capital and Labor (*Rerum novarum*; 1891), described as the first social encyclical, which expressed concern for the harsh life of the working class, or more widely, to the changing atmosphere for inquiry represented by theological reflection produced within the Oxford Movement, an Anglo-Catholic renewal in the Church of England.[63]

Engagement of the laity in the Church and the laity's potential for extending the Church's activity within the world was also witnessed by the founding of a number of lay action groups; some groups were politically oriented, such as the Center Party of Germany, formed largely of Catholics, or nonpolitical parties, such as the *Association Catholique de la Jeunesse Française* (ACJF) in 1886, which sought to apply Catholic principles to social problems of the day.[64] After his election in 1903, Pius X further encouraged lay action, in rather militant language, calling for "select Catholic troops" to fight against anti-Christian lures which were destroying families, schools, and society. But as historian Alden Brown critiques, Pius X encouraged lay action only "when it suited his purposes."[65] Brown suggests that the strictures on lay

[62] Liturgy and social activism is a recurring refrain of Virgil Michel, who was deeply influenced by his European teachers. The development of intentional communities such as the Catholic Worker and Friendship House, which had strong interest in the liturgical movement, resonate with this impulse.

[63] See J. E. B. Munson, "Oxford Movement by the End of the Nineteenth Century: The Anglo-Catholic Clergy," *Church History* 44, no. 3 (1975): 382–95; C. T. McIntire, "The Oxford Movement and the Anglican Newman," *Journal of the Canadian Church Historical Society* 33, no. 2 (1991): 141–48; Geoffrey Rowell, ed., *Tradition Renewed: The Oxford Movement Conference Papers* (Allison Park, PA: Pickwick Press, 1986).

[64] Alden V. Brown, *The Grail Movement and American Catholicism, 1940–1975*, Notre Dame Studies in American Catholicism Series (Notre Dame, IN: University of Notre Dame Press, 1989), 3. See also Etienne Gilson, ed., *The Church Speaks to the Modern World: The Social Teachings of Leo XIII* (Garden City, NY: Image Books, 1954).

[65] Brown, *The Grail Movement*, 3. Pius X's encyclical, On the Doctrines of the Modernists (*Pascendi Dominici Gregis*), 1907, condemns Modernism and instructs bishops to hold suspect "the appearance of that pernicious doctrine which would make the laity a factor in the progress of the Church." Colman

activity that Pius X created actually induced the theological development of the lay apostolate: a deep sense of corporate identity in the
Mystical Body of Christ, flowing from the individual's baptism, would
instill, in turn, a deep commitment to act as the Mystical Body in the
world, responding to the rampant needs of an increasingly secularized
and assailed modern society.[66]

European Mothers of the Liturgical Movement

Looking at two different examples of women's activity in the European liturgical scene, one scholarly and one a popular enactment
of Catholic Action, provides a more robust picture of the extent and
breadth of women's activity in the European liturgical movement, as
well as the sociocultural context of early twentieth-century Catholic
women.[67] First, liturgical theologian Aemiliana Löhr was one of the
more prolific and influential European women writers. While Aemiliana Löhr was a Benedictine sister, she provides an apt example of a
liturgical scholar who was directly influential on the American front;
access to her scholarship was greatly expanded by translations of her
The Liturgical Year into multiple languages, including English, and was
frequently read by American liturgical reformers, men and women.[68]
And an understanding of the American liturgical movement's heritage
cannot ignore the influence of its inspiration by European liturgical

---

James Barry, "The Modern Era: 1789 to the Present," *Readings in Church History*,
vol. 3 (Westminster, MD: Newman Press, 1960), 119–20.

[66] Brown, *The Grail Movement*, 3–4. A number of lay movements developed in
response to this, including the more famous *Jeunesse Syndicaliste* (later the *Jeunesse Ouvrière Chrétienne* [JOC]). Founded by the Belgian abbot, Joseph Cardijn,
the movement encouraged that lay persons, in this case, working men, be
trained to serve as apostles to their peers, a movement which spread outside
the boundaries of its origin. See Michael De la Bedoyere, *The Cardijn Story: A
Study of the Life of Msgr. Joseph Cardijn and the Young Christian Workers' Movement Which He Founded* (London: Longmans and Green, 1958).

[67] For a discussion of Catholic Action, see James O'Toole, "The Church of
Catholic Action," in *The Faithful: A History of Catholics in America* (Cambridge,
MA: Belknap Press, 2008): 145–98.

[68] In a letter from Florence Berger to Godfrey Diekmann discussing recommendations for liturgical readings, Berger notes that she, among other items,
has read Aemiliana Löhr's *The Year of Our Lord*. Florence Berger to Godfrey
Diekmann, 12 September 1957, The Godfrey Diekmann Papers 1013/6, The
Archives of Saint John's Abbey, Collegeville, Minnesota.

centers, especially the Benedictines. The second example examined here is an organized lay movement, eventually known as the Grail Movement. The Grail, which would later immigrate to the United States out of necessity in response to the political unrest in its Dutch homeland, was an organization of lay, non-religious women led by women interested, foremost, in the reformation of society according to a Catholic worldview. They did so via internal formation of their members in prayer and external demonstration in service and grandiose, paraliturgical apostolic endeavors. The Grail, when transplanted to the United States, readily connected with those persons actively involved with the liturgical movement.

AEMILIANA LÖHR, OSB, LITURGICAL THEOLOGIAN

In her introduction to *The Year of Our Lord*, Aemiliana Löhr reflected on the sacramental reality of the Mass:

> Of what does this work consist? Of all that God's Son did to save us; His Incarnation, Death, Resurrection, and his *perfecting* of redeemed mankind through the sending of that vitalizing Spirit who is the divine Life and Love proceeding from both Father and Son. All these are His saving deeds, all these combine to make up His work of world-redemption; and though historically they happened but once, God makes them present again for His faithful, year by year, day after day, beneath the veil of sacred rite and symbol.[69]

In this work, first published in 1934, Löhr described the various courses through which the Lord makes known our salvation, so beyond the powers of human understanding, in a way in which we might "view it slowly" and "draw fruit from each phase separately and in due proportion."[70] The drawing of this fruit occurred not only within the daily celebration of the Holy Mass but throughout the course of the year which traced the course of redemption from Advent to the last Sunday after Pentecost. Using the imagery of a lively tree planted by a stream and exposed to the light, Löhr reflected on the ability of our small souls to "receive and reflect that Light" of Christ with the hope of one day becoming as radiant as the Sun:

[69] Aemiliana Löhr, *The Year of Our Lord: The Mystery of Christ in the Liturgical Year*, trans. A Monk of St. Benedict (New York: P.J. Kenedy & Sons, Publishers, 1937), 4.
[70] Ibid., 5.

For indeed, there is so tremendous an abundance of vitality contained in this heavenly stream of light that we can assimilate it only by slow degrees. Wherefore the Lord has planted the "Tree" of the liturgical year within our midst warmed by the radiance of the divine Sun, it produces month by month its "twelve fruits": the twelve months of the sacred cycle. All the Sun's redemptive power is contained in these "fruits"; and by consuming them we partake of divine Light and Life. And the surrounding foliage, the beauteous leaves whose fragrance and symmetry attract us to pluck these fruits, are the sacred words through which the mysteries are accomplished.[71]

Rather than focusing on the historical development of the liturgical year, Löhr's book centered on contemplating the "Mysterium," as she described, of Christ that a human imagination could never comprehend in the space of a single Mass: "God has expanded and extended His redemptive work in Holy Mass, in the sacraments, in the feasts of *The Year of Our Lord* with its changing liturgy; so that now we have a constant re-presenting [Mysterium] of that work in all its phases."[72] She stated in her preface to *The Year of Our Lord* that her object was "solely an attempt on the basis of the Mass formulae as they appear in today's missal to comprehend and experience the church year as the liturgical celebration of the divine work of salvation—as the 'mystery of Christ.'"[73]

Löhr's introductory contemplation could be described as mystical, as Virgil Michel interpreted *The Year of Our Lord* in his review for *Orate Fratres*: "Yet the mysticism is always the same simple mysticism of this liturgy, permeated by and centered in the Mystery of Christ in His Church, the living action of the Redeemer constantly operative in her liturgical life, sharing this life at all times with every true member of Christ's Body."[74] Indeed, Löhr relied on absorbing images and a poetic, meditative form in her analysis of the liturgical year which exposed her reader to the different liturgical moods of the year. In her comments on the First Sunday after Pentecost, for example, she described how the rhythm of the sacred year "becomes calmer and more subdued," once the great event has happened, yet, in this quiet time, the

[71] Ibid., 6.
[72] Ibid.
[73] Löhr, *The Year of Our Lord*, quoted in McConnell, 220–21. Virgil Michel, review of *Jahr des Herrn*, by Aemiliana Löhr, *Orate Fratres* 9, no. 3 (1935): 140–41.
[74] Michel, review of *Jahr des Herrn*, 141.

Church must grasp her task to become "strong and ardent," to *become Christ*" more and more.[75] This time after Pentecost was devoted to the "unfolding and expansion" of the Church, a time for the Church to strengthen and develop the new Life she had received:

> It is as though after a long arduous climb she had now reached the broad sunny plateau of some high mountain. There, she is able to take grateful rest, and meditate in peace and quiet, for with her glorified Lord she has now entered upon her new and timeless Life in eternity. With Him, her "conversation," her very existence is in heaven. His Passover was hers too; and she is now no more "of this world." So the Sundays after Pentecost bear the stamp of calm glorious repose: they seem to exhale the very atmosphere of heaven.
>
> But the new celestial Life of the Church is contained in earthly vessels. She is still open to the attacks of the world and of evil, and so is unable to take her full repose. She must remain ever-vigilant and ready to repel the enemy. He never sleeps, but always prowls about seeking to invade her newly-won paradise. The New Life is to be proved and tested in battle and dire affliction, and thus take firmer root. So during the Sundays after Pentecost we shall often hear the shouts and cries of battle, and groans of distress, and piteous cries for help.[76]

This new life of the Church in Pentecost, mixed with glorious freedom and repose in Christ but, at the same time, charged with the duty of remaining ever-vigilant for battle, had to be developed for the remainder of the liturgical year. Löhr suggested that the plan "upon which this Life is to be developed" could be summarized in the brief prayer "Speak, Lord, thy servant heareth," which the Church used as the *Magnificat* antiphon at Vespers on that day: the Church sought to understand the Life to which she was called by relying on faith.[77]

More precisely than "mystical," Aemiliana Löhr developed a theology of liturgical worship that, Helen McConnell proposes, is best understood as mystagogy, a mystagogy which prepares the faithful "for a genuine liturgical experience of the paschal mystery through informed, active participation in the liturgical action so that their lives can be transformed into Christlikeness."[78] McConnell connects

---

[75] Löhr, *The Year of Our Lord*, 225.
[76] Ibid., 225–26.
[77] Ibid., 228.
[78] Ibid., i.

Löhr's desire to promote informed liturgical participation to Löhr's own commitment to discover an authentic, living expression of the Christian experience—a quest which led her, finally, to Benedictine monasticism.[79] Löhr was concerned that the liturgical movement, at least in Germany, which she first experienced through her attendance at a series of lectures at Maria Laach,[80] had developed "as a privilege of the Benedictines and well-educated Catholic laity."[81] Particularly, she believed a fundamental problem of liturgical worship, which she had experienced in her own liturgical involvement, first as a Franciscan tertiary and then as a member of the Benedictine community, was a separation of liturgical content and form, an erasure of the relation between priest and community:

> To us the content [of the liturgy] has become everything, the form nothing. The connection between content and form has been lost. We no longer pray the Mass, the offertory prayers of the community; we pray during the Mass whatever happens to please us. But our prayer has become formless and limited to the personal. It has lost its sacrificial and communal character. One does not neglect the form without also seeing the content slowly drift by and become diluted.[82]

Löhr encouraged others to reclaim liturgical catechesis as a primary venue for Christian formation. Evaluating the prayers and gestures of the eucharistic liturgy to be incomprehensible to many, Löhr believed that "only through full understanding, lively and active participation . . . by co-sacrifice and co-dying with Christ in the offering of gifts and

---

[79] Ibid., 12–17.

[80] See McConnell, 15–16, n. 8. McConnell draws this conclusion from Löhr's first article published on the liturgy, "Ostern im Geiste der Liturgie," *Düsseldorfer Tagesblatt* 157/158 (1921); after which, Löhr's focus on liturgical themes becomes increasingly prominent in her writings.

[81] Löhr, "Liturgie und Dritter Orden," *Der Ordensdirektor* 17, no. 4 (1923), 86. Löhr had entered the Benedictines already having established a strong connection with the Franciscans, having become a tertiary shortly after she passed a teaching examination in 1917. See McConnell, 13, 17. Some of the tensions Löhr discussed in her early liturgical writings focus on what she interpreted as a tension between Benedictine and Franciscan understandings of spiritual formation in liturgical worship. See McConnell, 15–20.

[82] Löhr, "Liturgie und Dritter Orden," *Der Ordensdirektor* 17, no. 4, 86–87. Quoted in McConnell, 19.

consecration of the Mass" would the faithful authentically experience the Christ-life.[83]

As McConnell describes, three of the most influential strains of twentieth-century European mystagogical thought directly influenced Löhr's work: Odo Casel's *Mysterientheologie*, Romano Guardini's ecclesial-liturgical mystagogy, and Pierre Teilhard de Chardin's theology as cosmic mystagogy.[84] McConnell analyzes Löhr's use of four "classical" mystagogical devices in her writings on liturgical worship, the most extensive of which are the aforementioned *The Year of Our Lord* (1934) and *The Holy Week* (1957): (1) symbolism, in which the meanings of images within liturgical texts are placed in relation to the paschal mystery and within the context of the liturgical year; (2) typology, in which biblical revelation is connected to liturgical and sacramental events to expound meaning; (3) sacramental analysis, in which liturgical texts serve as tools to interpret sacramental meaning; and (4) a correlation of modernity with the Christian spiritual tradition, allowing the scope of Christian spiritual tradition to comment upon and critique the present.[85] While Löhr did not identify her work as mystagogy or herself as a mystagogue, her works focused on the mystery and transformation which took place within the Christian experience and are imbued with a pastoral concern for liturgical catechesis.

This same desire brought Löhr to study the liturgical year as a source for Christian formation—that the liturgical year provided a source for the Christian to learn of God, Christ, the Holy Spirit, eschatology, ecclesiology, soteriology, anthropology, conversion, discipleship, and the role of Christianity in the modern world.[86] Löhr's work in liturgical scholarship is wide-ranging, and her familiarity with liturgical topics is evidenced by her frequent contributions of book reviews of liturgical publications in *Jahrbuch für Liturgiewissenschaft* (and later in *Archiv für Liturgiewissenschaft*) from the 1920s through the 1950s. Her topics include the Christian hymn tradition, the liturgy and psychology,

---

[83] Löhr, "Liturgie und Dritter Orden," *Der Ordensdirektor* 17, no. 5 (1923): 105. Löhr wrote a series of articles titled "Liturgie und Dritter Orden" in which she argued for liturgical catechesis to be foundational for Franciscan tertiary formation. See McConnell, 22.

[84] McConnell, 163. For a thorough analysis of these three mystagogues, see McConnell, 163–201.

[85] Ibid., 233–34.

[86] Ibid., 23.

the liturgical year, spirituality and philosophy, spiritual poetry, sacraments, patristic theology, women and the priesthood, and women in the liturgical year.[87]

When the English translation of *The Year of Our Lord* appeared in 1937, Godfrey Diekmann, OSB, "unreservedly" recommended her book "to all who are desirous of living with the Church throughout the liturgical year," adding, "Together with Dr. Parsch's *Liturgy of the Mass* . . . it will form a good nucleus of a small liturgical library."[88] Diekmann added an interesting conclusion to his review:

> Particularly striking is the thorough theological background which this nun of Herstelle has given to her treatise. It serves as a timely reminder that the "science of God" is for all the children of God, especially also for His chosen children, the religious, and not exclusively for priests. Dom Odo Casel, chaplain of Herstelle, and one of the greatest liturgical scholars of our day (who also contributes the Introduction to the volume) has done his work well. The solidly theological and spiritual training received by the members of this convent, of which this volume is eloquent witness, is an ideal to be striven for elsewhere.[89]

While Diekmann still places Löhr at the behest of Casel's excellent tutelage, he gently reminds readers that the children of God who give life to the liturgical movement are both men and women.[90]

---

[87] Ibid., 48.

[88] Godfrey Diekmann, "The Year or Our Lord," Review, *Orate Fratres* 11, no. 7 (1937): 336.

[89] Ibid.

[90] For more information on Aemiliana Löhr, see, Corona Bamberg, OSB, "Aemiliana Löhr zum 100. Geburtstag," *Erbe und auftrag* 72 (1996): 428–29; Bamberg, "Monastische Partnerschaft: zum Miteinander von Männer-und Frauenklöstern in der Beuroner Kongregation," in *Ecclesia Lacensis: Beiträge aus Anlass der Wiederbesiedlung der Abtei Maria Laach durch Benediktiner aus Beuron vor 100 Jahren am 25. November 1892 und der Gründung des Klosters durch Pfalzgraf Heinrich II. Von Laach vor 900 Jahren 1993*, ed. Emmanuel von Severus, OSB (Münster: Aschendorff, 1993), 502–17. Aside from hundreds of articles, Löhr's other books include *Ein Lebensbild einer begnadeten Künstlerin: Eucharis Gorissen* (Paderborn: Bonifatius Verlag, 1938); *Des Endes Ende: Zwei Gespräche* (Regensburg: Gregorius Verlag, 1948); *Das Herrenjahr: Das Mysterium Christi im Jahreskreis der Kirche*, 6th rev. and enl. ed. in 1 vol. (Regensburg: Verlag Friedrich Pustet, 1951); and *Abend und Morgen ein Tag: Die Hymnen der Herrentage und Wochentage im Stundengebet* (Regensburg: Verlag Friedrich Pustet, 1955).

An Apostolate for Young Catholic Women

"In spite of the humid climate and unreliable weather of their country there is nothing the Dutch people enjoy more than open-air plays
and pageants," began an American commentator, reporting on a recent
pageant performed by the ladies of the Grail Movement.[91] While these
enjoyable outdoor plays often took place in Dutch open-air theaters
on playing fields of cricket or football, this particular pageant was so
massive that it required the use of the stadium built for Amsterdam's
1928 summer Olympics. This was the only field large enough to conve-
niently house the some *ten thousand* Dutch Catholic girls who took part
in "The Blessing of Pentecost" in 1932.[92] The Grail chose the Holy Spirit
for its topic, for it was the goal of the Grail to "remould the spirits of
young folk" in love of God and the Church; this love should be a "rich,
fiery love," not timid, passive, or halfhearted.[93]

The massiveness of the project was impressive, as the organizers
needed to coordinate ten thousand young women, aged sixteen to
twenty. The text for the play and its directions were sent out to the
young women of dioceses across the Netherlands for preparation prior
to their arrival in Amsterdam for the final rehearsal. Often working
women, they had little opportunity for rehearsal until the final days
before the performance; furthermore, the collaborative nature of the
Grail demanded that no role should be held by an individual, solo
parts being antithetical to the social nature of the project. The intensity

[91] Herbert Antcliffe, "A Dutch Catholic Pageant," *The Ave Maria* 36, no. 1
(1932): 49.

[92] The previous year, in 1931, the Grail's first pageant, "The Triumph of the
Living," had been greeted with such enthusiasm (by the bishop of the diocese
and other ecclesiastical and civil authorities alike) that a pageant of an even
grander scale was planned for 1932, necessitating the use of the Olympic-sized
stadium.

[93] Ibid., 50. Antcliffe includes the poem about the Grail's "watchword," of
"red love":

> Red love is the watchword of The Grail;
> Love that to the cross nor in death shall fail.
> Each one we love, the blind, the erring,
> So to the fullness of Christ all stirring.
> Thus we go out the world to win.
> God, how great and good art Thou!
> All hail, red Love!

of the pageant came from the sheer mass of visual spectacle, with thousands of young women dressed in bright colors. Moments of action in choreographed dance and motion complemented more reflective moments in fixed tableaux,[94] with music ranging from translations of the Gregorian *Veni, Sancte Spiritus* to modern Dutch hymns (e.g., "O happy day, when at last the stream of grace may flow" to a setting of the *Te Deum*).[95] This effort of the Grail was an expression of faith and

[94] Tableaux were a popular form of "parlor entertainment" in the nineteenth century and, in this case of the Grail's Pentecost play in 1932, still common media for drama. Tableaux consisted of costuming and arrangement of a person or group of persons so as to represent a well-known character or scene.

[95] Antcliffe, 51–52. Antcliffe, reflecting on the pageant in his article for the American monthly, *The Ave Maria*, described the scope of the choreography in movement and song: "The largest feature of the design was a huge Grail Star, which, for reasons of seniority, Amsterdam being the place where The Grail was started, and also for convenience, was allotted to the capital city. Here there are seven Grail houses, and to each of the houses was allotted one of the points. These points represented each one of the gifts of the Holy Spirit and each has its own color—red, green, orange, yellow, blue and purple, —which not only makes a very beautiful effect with an instructive value, but helps in the organization by making it easy for each girl to find and remain in her own section. While this star was in course of formation on the broad open space of the Stadium by each point approaching from a separate direction, from 'the seven winds of the world,' 'Veni Creator' was sung to a nearly literal translation and a version of the Gregorian melody taken from a hymn-book of 1621. Almost before the seven points of the Star were in their places they were followed by groups of Guardian Angels in yellow who ranged themselves on two sides of the Star, while the verse 'Send forth Thy Spirit and they shall be re-made, And Thou shalt renew the face of the earth' was sung. Then, while the tableaux remained fixed was sung a modern hymn, 'O happy day, when at least the stream of grace may flow.' These Guardian Angels, working so intimately with the great Star, were drawn from the three houses in the nearby city of Harlem.

"At the close of this tableau took place a feature that would have delighted the heart of the psalmist, for it was no less than a dance to the sacred strains of 'Veni, sancte Spiritus.' This dance, in which three hundred girls drawn from the different points of the Star took part, was an underlining, joining in action with the words of the hymn. At the opening words their arms were spread out in supplication; at 'et emitte coelitus lucis tuae radium,' their faces uplifted to miss no ray of the heavenly beam; at 'da perenne gaudium. Amen,' all knelt with bowed heads in a prayer for the eternal joy of the Holy Spirit, while

a moment of instruction—for the spectators and perhaps even more powerfully for the members of the Grail taking part. Reflecting on the sight of the women's dancing to *Veni, Sancte Spiritus*, Herbert Antcliffe, writing for the popular magazine *Ave Maria*, supposed that their dance and its fine execution "may be commended as a means of teaching the significance of the words of the familiar Latin hymn which supplements and strengthens, and may even do more than can be done by all the verbal teaching possible."[96] Antcliffe concluded that the Grail women's dramatic interpretation of "The Blessing of Pentecost" was a sign, not only to the Dutch people, but also to the world, of the potential for effectively combining enthusiasm for faith and healthy play:

> This is the message of The Grail, and it is a message that is already, in the short history of the organization, bearing fruit, and will continue to bear fruit, not only in little Holland and in its great colonies, and not only for a short time while the girls are of an age to belong to it, but all over the world where they go or are heard of, and for all eternity in their hearts and in the hearts of those whom they directly or indirectly influence by their actions and prayers.[97]

Thus, the Grail Movement, originally called the Women of Nazareth, became one of the most courageous and public realizations of Catholic Action in the years between the world wars. As evidenced by their spectacular (and well-received, according to contemporary reviewers) enactments of feasts in the liturgical calendar, the Grail sought to reach young Catholic women and form them into faithful Christian witnesses with social awareness.

Founding of the Grail and Feminism

The movement was inspired by a Dutch Jesuit and philologist, Jacques van Ginneken (1879–1949), who wished to encourage his fellow Dutch Catholics, long nervous about engaging their faith publically after centuries of oppression following the Reformation, to take initiative and bring the Gospel to the contemporary world. Van Ginneken, in the aftermath of the First World War, sought to understand the suffering of the world as opening a "great blessing" for the Church and

---

the dance closed with a sudden spring of joy, with arms raised high, in the 'Alleluia.'"

[96] Ibid., 51.
[97] Ibid., 52.

society, in that it proffered clear and precise reason for the West to finally respond to the spiritual degeneration and confusion which, he believed, had caused the war. He believed that there was "a spiritual current passing through the modern world which leads to Catholicism"[98] and that this spiritual current could be tapped and fill the world with energy if Catholics were willing to "give themselves to God in the midst of the world" and lead a life radically different from what the world expects, people who bring the Cross of Christ back among humanity."[99] In order to realize this desire, he founded four lay communities, each intended to work with a sector of the Dutch population. The Women of Nazareth (later the Grail Movement) intended to work with girls who had left school and entered the workforce.[100] Founded by van Ginneken on the Feast of All Saints in 1921, the Women of Nazareth consisted of just four members who made simple promises of chastity, obedience, and apostolic poverty rather than canonical vows.[101] Though the Grail bore some similarities to religious

[98] Brown, *The Grail Movement*, 4; See Jacques van Ginneken, *Voordrachten over het Katholicisme voor niet-Katholieken* (Rotterdam: W. L. & J. Brusse, 1927), 201. Quoted in Eleanor Walker, "The Spirit of Father van Ginneken," *Grail Review* 7, no. 2 (1965): 25.

[99] Brown, *The Grail Movement*, 4; See also Rachel Donders, *History of the International Grail 1921–1979* (Grailville, Loveland, Ohio, 1983), 3; and L. J. Rogier and P. Brachin, *Histoire du Catholicisme Hollandais Depuis le XVI Siècle* (Paris, 1974), 201.

[100] The other groups were the Ladies of Bethany, founded in 1919 with the intention to work with de-Christianized young people in big cities, who forsook their lay status to become a religious order; the Knights of St. Willibrord, founded shortly afterward, who were to work among the "well-to-do" elite, or the "drawing room" apostolate; and the Crusaders of St. John, who were to work with boys to help them learn a trade after they left school (Janet Kalven, "Grail Beginnings: The Germinal Ideas and the Pioneers," in *Women Breaking Boundaries: A Grail Journey, 1940–1995* (Albany: State University of New York Press, 1999), 32.

[101] Jacques van Ginneken, "The Grail as a Young Woman's Movement," Lecture 20, 2, quoted in Alden V. Brown, "The Grail Movement to 1962: Laywomen and a New Christendom," *U.S. Catholic Historian* 3, no. 3 (1983): 151. Interestingly, while accounts usually describe van Ginneken as the founder who convinced some students to join him, E. J. Ross of *The Commonweal* reports in November 6, 1936, that "a handful of Dutch women founded a new religious order in 1921" (E. J. Ross, "Successful Youth," *The Commonweal* [November 6, 1936]: 41).

houses and operated under a "rule" based somewhat on what their founder was most familiar with, St. Ignatius of Loyola's *Spiritual Exercises*, the women did not take formal vows and were not cloistered.[102] The ethos of the movement was, as Janet Kalven of the American Grail Movement would later describe, that of spiritually oriented lay persons penetrating the world. This tension between the religious and the secular continually caused outside observers to question the Grail's identity

---

E. J. Ross reveals another issue that plagued the Grail Movement, which was their popular identification as a religious order. Janet Kalven relates that an infamous article in *Time* magazine haunted the Grail members during their early days in the United States; the article described the Grail members as "nuns in *mufti*" and featured a photograph of Dutch members in their in-house "habit." "Mufti" means "not in uniform," or, in the case of the Grail, not in habit. As Kalven relates, "The reporter who coined the phrase, impressed by the red flowered dress Mary Louise (Tully) was wearing, evidently thought we were nuns in disguise. In fact, there are nuns in mufti in the Catholic Church. . . . They maintain secrecy about their religious commitment. That was emphatically not the Grail idea. We were laywomen, striving to demonstrate that holiness was for everyone. . . . The article haunted us for years—every reporter writing on the Grail and doing any research quickly found it in the *Guide to Periodical Literature*" (Kalven, "Grail Beginnings," 47). The public confusion about the Grail's self-understanding as a "quasi-religious nucleus of the lay apostolate" prompted members to abandon any form of habit. Kalven, "Grail Beginnings," 38.

[102] The Movement held some fascinating tensions in its identity as a lay movement. John G. Vance, Canon of Westminster, London, wrote a short history, titled *Ladies of the Grail*, in which he described the flourishing of lay movements in the ever-adaptable Church. Active lay people are crucial, he said, as the "laity are able to move in circles where neither priest nor religious may have easy access, and they may sometimes try to christianise people in ways other than those specially suited to the clergy" (John G. Vance, *The Ladies of the Grail* [London: Catholic Truth Society, 1935], 9). Part of the Grail's early difficulty (and small numbers) seems to have been an uncertainty about their seemingly liminal status between a religious order and a lay women's group; as Vance summarized: "The idea of a vowed life without a religious habit was new to many, and they laughed it to scorn as something new. 'A worldly dress and a religious life? Impossible!' said many. 'They can't be serious; they won't persevere. They are just a group of girls who lack the courage to enter a convent or a religious order and they just want to give their lives a religious cache and make themselves interesting. There is nothing in the whole thing but a half-hearted compromise and it won't last'" (Vance, 14).

as a lay movement, and articles singing in praise of the Grail women sometimes wrongly identified them as a "new religious order" or "new group of nuns."[103]

The fledgling group of a few interested women found inspiration in van Ginneken's energetic proposal for an active Christian life. In concert with many of his contemporaries, van Ginneken claimed that the world was in a crisis in which the old order was breaking down. This "elbow of time" meant not doom, however, but opportunity and, interestingly, an opportunity particularly for *women*. In the fallout of World War I, van Ginneken saw three forces in the world rushing for control: Russia with its communism, America with its capitalism, and Christianity. These vying forces were met, however, with a new social condition—that of feminism. He explained:

> [E]conomic and technical conditions have been the cause of a new matrilineal culture which is now coming into existence, now—to put it in a more correct way—a civilization with a more feminine orientation is about to materialize. The cause of all this is the invention of machinery. Machinery does two things; in the first place, it brings the woman out of the home into the factory where she earns money, a good deal of money, sometimes even more than a man. And, on the other hand, it takes a great deal of the housekeeping out of her hands. . . . Housekeeping has fallen to pieces, and in another generation, it will have gone completely, except for the upbringing of children.[104]

This changing role of women afforded by feminism, van Ginneken believed, would prove to be an essential force in correcting the crises of the world and setting the world in proper balance:

[103] For example, see John G. Rowe, "The Grail; the Modern Movement for Catholic Girls," *The Ave Maria* 39 (1934): 424–27, here at 427: "The Holy Father's call for Catholic Action has been responded to in a remarkable way in Holland. A new order of nuns was founded there in 1921, calling themselves the Congregation of the Ladies of the Grail."

[104] Van Ginneken, Lecture 18, 3–9. Quoted in Kalven, "Grail Beginnings," 33. Kalven indicates in her history of the Grail movement (*Women Breaking Boundaries*) that most of van Ginneken's lectures were delivered in Dutch, taken down on a recording machine, and transcribed, but they were never edited by van Ginneken. The Dutch transcriptions were translated into English and are available at the United States Grail Movement Archives, Grailville, Loveland, Ohio.

If only we could stop considering the man as the only force in public life. . . . Feminism is working in that direction. . . . Oh, if that feminism would succeed . . . if indeed that becomes true, we will have mobilized that half of humanity which up till now did not count, and this half will make its choice of party and will become itself a great party, a great force. . . . Feminism is a terrific rising force and if it will go at the speed which technology proves, it may well happen that we return to our former matriarchal culture . . . then woman will get the greatest chance to let the conversion of the world succeed.[105]

Feminism in this sense was understood as an antidote for the problems caused by a power-driven and, assumably, masculinized modern culture. For example, as social historian Nancy Cott describes this view of feminism, if both men and women were to gain access to education, work, and citizenship, women might be better able to balance society with their "characteristic contribution."[106] Indeed, the Women of Nazareth were not only to convert the world with the newfound social responsibilities and public voice of women but to do so by making use of all their *femininity*—dressing well and practicing "charm":

If [woman] wanted to do good, [the Church] has shut her up in great cloisters behind thick walls; and has thought that every woman who walked along the street in a nice dress was a permanent danger to good morals and to all decent piety. It's of tremendous importance for the Grail movement that you should appear in the streets as well-dressed women. You must be women from all classes and attractive women. If you want to win the world and you are not charming, we can not use you.[107]

Though the Grail's insistence on wearing bright, stylish dresses would be a continual source for questions about their identity (not to mention

[105] Van Ginneken, Lecture 24, 24. Quoted in Kalven, "Grail Beginnings," 33.
[106] Cott, "The Birth of Feminism," in *The Grounding of Modern Feminism* (New Haven, CT: Yale University Press, 1987), 19. Van Ginneken believed that a "matrilineal culture" in the chivalric tradition had been stifled by the "masculine outburst" of events such as the French Revolution; the modern woman's movement, as van Ginneken viewed it, had also adopted a "masculine stance" (Van Ginneken, "The Grail as a Young Woman's Movement: Aims, Methods, and Basic Ideas," available in English in American Grail Archives, quoted in Brown, *The Grail Movement*, 12).
[107] Van Ginneken, Lecture 1, 1. Quoted in Kalven, "Grail Beginnings," 35.

the implicit assumption that Grail women would be in an economic position to afford to be well-dressed), the intent behind the insistence upon feminine women charming the world was an insistence upon lay women, women who would be married and would be mothers, that they might employ their charisms *as women* to convert the world to Christ. As Janet Kalven would later describe, the only way to take "millions of young women and through them create a stream, a veritable torrent, of love and self-sacrifice to change the world"[108] was by being *in the world*—acting as lay women in the midst of contemporary society, using the newest and brightest of modern science and technology.[109]

Thus, the particular power of the Grail was its uplifting of women in their very femininity, emphasizing that women's unique feminine traits were crucial in meeting the rough masculinity which had overtaken society, that the Grail's responsibility might be "to counterbalance in the world all masculine hardness, all the angles of the masculine character, all cruelty, all the results of alcoholism and prostitution and sin and capitalism, which are ultra-masculine, and to Christianize that with a womanly charity. Well, what is that [but] the conversion of the world?"[110]

Catholicism was seen as a remedy for social evils, but Catholic women had a particular potential to serve as a life force for spiritual renewal. A movement such as the Grail might mold young women to a Catholic mind, a stark contrast to the wake of the immoral perils besetting the young women of the modern world. As van Ginneken surmised, there were throngs of young women wasting away with time heavy on their hands. These young women, after the conclusion of their life in devout Catholic homes or convent schools, were beset by new temptations and confusing worldly aims as they, more increas-

[108] Kalven, "Grail Beginnings," 34.

[109] Kalven relates that van Ginneken "had no patience" with the "siege mentality" of modern Catholicism which was antimodern, antiliberal, antidemocratic, and antitechnology: "On the contrary, he urged the Women of Nazareth to utilize all modern means in their work, mentioning particularly automobiles, airplanes, audio, film, cabarets, theaters, stadiums. They should establish their own film studios, design and build their own airplanes, emblazon the Grail symbol in neon lights over the doors of the Grail houses" (Kalven, "Grail Beginnings," 35).

[110] Van Ginneken, "The Grail as a Young Woman's Movement," Lecture 22, 6. See Brown, *The Grail Movement*, 12.

ingly, entered the workforce: "Bewildered by the contrast, and intoxicated with their new liberty, often intensified by a sudden increase of money to spend, they are apt either to lose their heads completely or to succumb within a year or so to the low ideals of the world."[111] Certainly, a paternal (or patronizing) sentiment seems to guide this notion of corralling herds of aimless, vulnerable young women into more useful, wholesome employment. And Kalven, in reflecting on that which the American Movement inherited from the founding Grail women, admits that the early Grail Movement had both hierarchical as well as dualistic tendencies.[112] Yet, the original Grail Movement saw itself as not so much controlling but training young women for their permanent vocation (most often matrimony or a religious life) in the Christian apostolate during the crucial years of adolescence.[113] The immense

[111] E. Boland, "The Grail Movement," Reprinted from the *Month* (London, July 1933), *Catholic Mind* 31 (1933): 293. See also Kalven, "Grail Beginnings," 34. She reflects on van Ginneken's view of the young women which, she notes, is often pragmatic, as he says, "The world has (I shall make a rough guess) some ten million women too many, who have no longer enough to do, and we shall organize these women and we shall convert the world with them." See Kalven, 34, where she quotes from Jacques van Ginneken's "The Grail as a Young Woman's Movement."

[112] See Kalven, "From Feminist Actions to Feminist Consciousness," in *Women Breaking Boundaries*, 217–41. In this chapter, Kalven discusses how the Grail developed as a locus for American feminism and, in fact, has been identified by Rosemary Radford Ruether as one of the major roots of feminism: "One needs to have . . . autonomous spaces, where feminist theology is normative rather than marginal, where the immediate struggle against patriarchy does not define the context of the discussion, where the agenda of feminist theology can be more fully and freely developed. Such autonomous spaces for feminist theology have already begun. The Grailville summer quarter in feminist theology was an important arena in the 1970s" (Rosemary Radford Ruether, "Feminist Theology in the Academy," *Christianity and Crisis* 45 [1985]: 62).

[113] In the Grail Centers, young members kept in touch with the permanent members, while those who trained young girls in convent schools were compelled "like the poor hen that fosters ducklings, to see their charges swim away from them on the waters of life at the most critical time of their development. . . . Educators of girls everywhere have to face the same problem. Everywhere,—to put the matter in its most favorable light—good schools and good Catholic homes are turning out girls in thousands who, as they approach maturity, are plunged at once from a warm atmosphere of quiet piety into the temptations of a new world whose aims and ideals are, most of them, in direct

number of women who eventually joined the Grail, its organization and leadership provided by core women members, and the ingenuity and independence which the members of the Grail asserted through the course of their history indicate that the Grail Movement was an authentic venue for uplifting Catholic women.

Development of the Grail Movement

Though the first five years of the Women of Nazareth yielded them only six members[114] and minimal apostolic activity, the influence of van Ginneken as a lecturer at Nijmegen compelled five of his students to abandon their studies and join the Women of Nazareth, among them Lydwine van Kersbergen.[115] As noted above, the Women of Nazareth sought to aid young working women, first at home in the Netherlands and then on a much larger scale, and they set about working to found a university for women in Indonesia (which had experienced Dutch colonialism) and developing a comprehensive program in which native Javanese culture, rather than imported Western ideals, would drive education. Ready to the task, the women began their own intensive study of local languages and culture. The death of Bishop Callier of Haarlem, however, who had supported the Women of Nazareth's international endeavors, brought a successor, Monsignor J. D. J. Aengenent, who was more concerned with the secularization of the mostly urban diocese of Haarlem; he insisted that the women focus solely on the education and formation of local Catholic girls, working with van Ginneken to run retreats and lead the working-girls' clubs they had established.[116]

---

opposition to all they have been taught to hold sacred" (Boland, "The Grail Movement," 293).

[114] See Brown, *The Grail Movement*, 7. Brown notes that his account of the Grail's early years is based primarily on Gerti Lauscher, "The Grain of Wheat in the Soil," an unpublished manuscript which draws on the few surviving archival materials at Tiltenberg, Vogelensang, Holland, and interviews with long-term Grail members. See also Vance, 11–21.

[115] In 1926, Lydwine van Kersbergen, Mia van der Kallen, Liesbeth Allard, Louisa Veldhuis, and Yvonne Bosch van Drakestein joined; their fellow students referred to their leaving the university to follow Fr. Van Ginneken, in an unfortunate attempt at artistic allusion, as "The Rape of the Sabine Women."

[116] Brown, *The Grail Movement*, 8–9; Brown notes that Bishop Aengenent decreed the Grail should be the only Catholic young women's group in the diocese of Haarlem, "directed according to the aims of the Grail under the

Choosing to act in obedience to authority, the group began to realize itself for the first time, in an intensive opportunity to advance the lay apostolate of women, as commissioned not simply to serve as another social work agency in the Netherlands but to "organize all Catholic adolescent girls, not only to protect them from dangers, but primarily to train them to be fervent Catholic women who are an example in everything."[117] This program harmonized with van Ginneken's own philosophy of Catholicism acting as leaven in the world. Now, instead of attending to the conversion of non-Catholic girls and women through their retreat houses and other social events, the Women of Nazareth would focus on the conversion of *Catholics* to "a full realization of the vast implications of their Faith, and particularly of the *duty* of being, according to their talents, Apostles."[118]

Thus, in 1928, the Women of Nazareth took on a new face as a youth movement, and Lydwine van Kersbergen was chosen as president of, as Kalven described, "a swiftly burgeoning, colorful, assertive movement of young women."[119] Father van Ginneken chose the name "the Grail" as one that would translate easily into most European languages as well as suggest a more exotic or romantic identity, appropriate to youth. The original center, De Voorde, became the first Grail Center, with nine more soon to follow in each major Dutch city. The development of the Grail as an attractive and formative lay group

---

leadership of the Women of Nazareth" (Brown, 9; quoted in "The Grail Begins To Be," *Grail Review* 5, no. 4 [1963]: 8).

[117] Quoted in Rachel Donders, *History of the International Grail 1921–1979: A Short Description* (Loveland, OH: Grailville, 1983), 10.

[118] Boland, "The Grail Movement," 291.

[119] Kalven, "Grail Beginnings," 40. As a youth movement, the Grail possessed attractive qualities of identity to which young women could ascribe: rites of passage, prayers, meetings, uniforms and badges, and distinctive colors assigned to various Grail houses. Such rituals of membership were common for other women's groups as well, including the early European Grail's American contemporaries such as the Daughters of Isabella. A 1935 manual for the Daughters of Isabella, titled "Complete Ceremonial," details rituals of all types to which only members had knowledge: special codes, hand gestures, signs indicating sitting, rising, and prayer, in addition to rubrics of a particularly religious nature, including the carrying of items like votive candles or a crucifix. "Complete Ceremonial," 1935, The Daughters of Isabella, 11/Folder titled "Ritual," The American Catholic History Research Center and University Archives, The Catholic University of America, Washington, DC.

blossomed in these last years of the twenties: the Grail Centers provided its young members with "all the amenities of a club," including sports, evening classes, and recreational and cultural facilities which fostered a positive communal atmosphere for its members.[120] But, different from a secular club, Grail Centers had at their heart a strong Catholic character, and most centers also housed a chapel where the Blessed Sacrament was reserved.

The Grail Movement intended to train the character of its members by developing their mental, physical, and spiritual powers and gifts; though the Grail was "a mass movement of individuals," great care in attentiveness to individual development and cultivation of gifts allowed the women to develop their own charisms, as a prayer of the Grail suggested, "Lord, let me grow into that for which Thou has destined me."[121] The Grail worked not only to mold individual girls to Christ but to allow the members to build up the Grail Movement themselves. Women were encouraged, always each to her own ability, to creatively compose activities, study, and work which might benefit a community.[122]

The Grail's Relation to the Liturgical Movement

The Grail, initially slow in development, rapidly expanded both within Holland and internationally, with three houses and thousands of members in Berlin and two houses in London, along with burgeoning missionary activities in Dutch settlements in the East Indies. Part of the Grail's rapid expansion undoubtedly came from its orientation to youth, and to young women specifically. Youth movements were common, attracting members to groups from the nonconfessional

---

[120] Boland, "The Grail Movement," 293.

[121] Ibid., 296.

[122] Boland notes, "Here the possibilities are endless, from the distribution of the Grail paper or the organizing of the sports, to providing music for the plays or studying the Youth Movements of other countries. Every activity is valuable, because we are all prone to take a special interest in a thing which we ourselves are creating. Moreover, independence and a capacity to stand alone being the qualities most admired today, girls readily respond to an appeal for initiative on their part, rather than dumb acquiescence in a cut-and-dried program imposed upon them. So they themselves think out schemes for spreading the Grail and the value of their cooperation is shown by the growth of the enrolled members in little more than four years to the remarkable total of 15,000, a number daily increasing" (Boland, 294).

Boy Scouts, to the Catholic Jocistes (Jeunesse Ouvrière Chrétienne or Union of Young Christian Workers) of Belgium or the Neudeutschland of Germany, to political groups such as the Balilla of Italy, to the explicitly anti-Christian Komsomol, the Communist League of Youth.[123] A review of the early history of the Grail Movement reveals how it meshed with an increasing trend for Catholics to identify modernism and its social ills as an entity which could be answered by an active Catholicism, from the hierarchy to the lay apostolate, women included. But, was this spirit of the Grail a spirit in common with the liturgical movement? Neither the Women of Nazareth/the Grail Movement nor their director, van Ginneken, make mention of the liturgical movement which rustled around them in Germany, France, and the Low Countries. Yet, these women did relate themselves to the call to Catholic Action and the responsibility of the lay apostolate to expand the kingdom of God. Interestingly, a 1941 article in *Orate Fratres* by Robert B. Heywood of the University of Chicago, titled "The Spirit of the Grail," explored the "ambiguous position" in which those Catholics cognizant of both the liturgical movement and the call to Catholic Action might find themselves, for the Catholic might be confronted "with action which seems . . . to have only the remotest and vaguest associations with the larger and fuller world-view of the liturgy."[124] Yet, as Heywood elaborated, what was essential to Catholic Action was the participation of the lay person in the apostolate—and this apostolic action flowed from "the abundance of the Christian life," that is, that "being" must come before "doing"; before one might think of the liturgical movement, one must *be* liturgical oneself.[125] As Heywood concluded, "If we remember this essential relationship between Catholic action and *lived* Christianity, if we remember the integral correlation between prayer-life and active-life, then there is no danger that we will fall into what spiritual

---

[123] Boland, 289. Pope Pius X had recently written, in "On the Sacred Heart" (*Caritate Christi*; 1932), "It is, indeed, a powerful inspiration of the Holy Spirit which is now passing over all the earth, drawing especially the souls of the young to the highest Christian ideals, raising them above human respect, rendering them ready for every sacrifice, even the most heroic" (quoted in Boland, 289).

[124] Robert B. Heywood, "The Spirit of the Grail," *Orate Fratres* 15, no. 8 (1941): 360.

[125] Ibid., 360–61. See also Jacques Maritain, *Scholasticism and Politics* (New York: Macmillan Co., 1940) 198; Dom Theodore Wesseling, *Liturgy and Life* (New York: Longmans & Green, 1938), 119.

writers have called the 'heresy of good works.'"[126] The relation of Catholic Action and the liturgical life for Heywood was clear:

> [If] we are seriously interested in the lay apostolate our works will flow from, be permeated with a fully lived Christian, liturgical life: our works could not, then, lack the true spirit of the apostolate. Then our penetrations into the profane and secular worlds will be rightly directed, for we will go with a vital knowledge of what the '"conversion of the world" really means.[127]

The Grail Movement was paradigmatic of this impulse—their *raison d'être* being the work of the lay apostolate. Heywood observed that the ethos of the Grail should be taken as a model for the work of the lay apostolate in America: "Throughout, they seem to be enlivened with a living appreciation of liturgical life and an active awareness of the real meaning of the lay apostolate. For them the 'conversion of the world' is no vagary."[128]

By the time Heywood wrote for *Orate Fratres* in 1941, the Grail had expanded from the very small group of Dutch women called the Women of Nazareth among working girls and women between 1921 and 1928 to reimaging themselves (at the ultimatum of their bishop) as the Grail movement, with a refocused emphasis on the young Catholic girls of the lay apostolate. And, within eight years, they had spread to England, Scotland, and Australia (where they were known, in these English-speaking countries, as "Ladies of the Grail"). By 1937, the Grail Movement in Holland alone had fifteen thousand members. While the numbers themselves were impressive, admitted Heywood, it was the Spirit of the Grail which was most compelling. The amazing growth was not only from the hands of a few Dutch women (core members and founders), but from the Grail's encouragement of thousands of young women to flourish with all the vigor of youth in not only "activities," sports, games, or meetings but in *identity*:

> Every man—and especially youth—in our time longs for some kind of world-view that will unify the twisted extremes of our civilization.

---

[126] Heywood, "The Spirit of the Grail," 361.
[127] Ibid.
[128] Ibid.

And so, in all their work, the Ladies of the Grail seek to recreate the only spirit which can be such a unifying force, the spirit of the cross.[129]

The uncompromising nature of the Grail women as they combated complacency and mediocrity—from their own sphere as lay Catholic women—impressed Heywood, who noted that they derived this spirit, the "joyous spirit of the cross," from an understanding of the Mass, a spirit of sacrifice, and a conscious self-sacrifice in their daily lives. The pinning of the Grail to an understanding of the Mass did not appear to be fabrication on Heywood's part; as an English Grail member wrote in 1938:

> The secret of the apostolate is an understanding of the Mass, of our being offered up with Christ. For once we understand it and act upon it, we have the clue to the redemptive power of all our efforts, even the slightest. Through offering ourselves with Christ we are being changed from something insignificant and worthless to something divine and redemptive.[130]

The young woman's understanding of the Grail's apostolate might be a model for all Catholic apostolates. Yet, Grail members could fully ensconce themselves, for a time at least, in the fullest living of this apostolate, through studying, singing, praying, and living the Mass and, in a most striking and public way, extending this experience to others through their dramatic reenactments of the Church's feasts in the liturgical year, such as their spectacular enactments of Pentecost or All Saints Day.[131]

---

[129] Ibid., 362. Of course, Heywood ironically began his evaluation of the Grail Women by noting that "every man" desires peace in civilization.

[130] Anonymous, *Grail Magazine* 5, no. 2 (February 1938), n.p. Quoted in Heywood, 363.

[131] Heywood noted that on All Saints day in 1936, hundreds of Grail members in Holland marched in a procession carrying lighted lanterns, each symbolizing a different saint: "Then the whole city became aware of what the Church means when she sings at the Mass for that feast: 'Let us rejoice in the Lord, celebrating a festival day in honor of the sayings, at whose solemnity, the angels rejoice and give praise to the son of God.'" Wryly, Heywood noted that this interpretive dancing might be a "Shattering, upsetting thought to the conventional and to the purist, perhaps, but then anyone who has not completely lost sight of the Middle Ages will not be too disturbed. Besides, the Ladies of the Grail are not particularly concerned about 'upsetting' people. In fact, we

Finally, Heywood remarked on the unity of the European Grail Movement—where no Grail member ever acted as an isolated individual—and how each one's talent was developed for the common good. "Most simply," Heywood concluded, "this kind of activity is a practical realization of the basic doctrine of the unity of man in the mystical body. . . . It need hardly be said that this spirit of the unity of all Christians in the mystical body is the very essence of the liturgy; it is the spirit which flows from the Mass."[132] A commitment to daily meditation and prayer placed Catholic spirituality at the forefront of life as a woman of the Grail. An interest not only in collective training of young women in "supernatural and in natural things" but in training each member of the body according to her particular gifts and talents ensured that the Grail, like the Church, would be infused with "a great diversity of human character and personality."[133] The spirit of the Grail so effectively penetrated the secular world because of the very conscious effort by its members to act as members of the lay apostolate and as *women* for the conversion of the world from *within* the world.

Despite Heywood's (who was an American) evaluation of the European Grail Movement, it is unclear whether the founders of the Grail believed or even considered themselves to be acting in a spirit in concert with the liturgical movement burgeoning in the Low Countries, Germany, France, or Austria. It did, however, explicitly share an interest in the lay apostolate's action and formation in the Mystical Body of Christ for the reforming of their world to Christ. As Heywood indicated, the spirit of the Grail was readily identified as consonant with the American liturgical movement and quickly found a home there in the summer of 1940 after its suppression in most of Nazi-occupied Europe. Lydwine van Kersbergen and Joan Overboss, founders of the American Grail movement, along with a number of Grail members, became actively involved in the annual National Liturgical Weeks as early as 1942. They found that the ethos of women's activity in the lay

---

have long been timid and reserved, influenced by the Reformation and by Puritanism. Some Grail methods will be outside the quiet, apologist mind of the 'siege period'" (Heywood, "The Spirit of the Grail," 363–64).

[132] Ibid., 365. Interestingly, when the American *Liturgical Arts* magazine recommended *The Grail Magazine* as potentially of interest to its readers, it described the society as bearing "a considerable resemblance to our Girl Scouts, with the exception that it is exclusively Catholic" (*Liturgical Arts Quarterly* 5, no. 2 (1936): 40).

[133] Vance, 30.

apostolate naturally meshed with the ethos of the American liturgical movement, because it centered on social reform and re-Christianizing life which both rejected a selfish individualism and embraced a mentality that all work might be praise of God, that is, that all aspects of life could be understood as liturgical.[134]

CONCLUSION

Move to the American Liturgical Movement

This chapter summarizes some prominent features of the social, theological, and historical context of the European landscape out of which the liturgical movement arose, noting that women are not absent from this narrative, contrary to normative historical accounts. Identifying the frequency with which women and theological questions regarding women and the liturgy were part of the European liturgical movement provides both context and a contrast for the

---

[134] At the National Liturgical Week held at St. Meinrad Abbey in 1942, Joan Overboss of the Grail, which was, at that point, centered in Libertyville, Illinois (prior to permanent settling in Loveland, Ohio, in 1943), after exile from occupied Holland, reflected on how all aspects of life, even suffering—or especially women's suffering—could be converted into joy, and the particular character of modern American women whom she had seen enter the Grail: "[W]omen in a very special way [are] being made to bear suffering and to bear it as a great joy. If we women would always do what is expected of us in this matter, and realize how very fortunate we are when we are made to carry our cross, sometimes even a very heavy one, I think we would make a great contribution to the praise of God. At least, to view our suffering in this light would be a start in presenting suffering as something very beautiful. Our experience as Ladies of the Grail with the young women in America is that once they discover the beauty of suffering, all this, of course, in union with Christ's suffering, their whole lives seem to change. We have never very many of them who say that it has [not] given them an entirely different outlook on life. Formerly they were accustomed always to try to escape the difficult things of life, believing that in doing so they would find happiness. Instead, they found that they were not happy at all; whereas once they really understood how everything that happens, not only the beautiful things, but also the hard things, could be made an act of praise to God, they really found happiness and peace. I only wish, as I look over this audience, that we could have many more young women participating in this wonderful event here at St. Meinrad's." Discussion following "Praise in Sacrifice and Sacrament," *1942 Liturgical Week Proceedings* (Newark, NJ: Benedictine Liturgical Conference, 1943), 64.

uniqueness of the American scene. Löhr provides insight into the conversations held by women (lay and religious) in Europe, and she herself was influential for American readers of the liturgical movement. Her work served both the academy of liturgical studies and as a source for liturgically based spirituality. Meanwhile, the European Grail Movement illustrates the emergence of lay activity, interest in women's Christian identity, and provides an example of how the liturgical movement intersected with the aims of Catholic Action. While American women were interested in reading liturgical theology, they tended to express this interest through development of practical strategies for understanding the liturgy, such as how to use the breviary or how to read Latin. In the same way, while some American lay women were attracted by the possibilities of "Christian Womanhood," such topics are seized upon not by independent women writers but by American clerics and male religious or become subject matter for organizations under ecclesial supervision, such as the National Council of Catholic Women.

The next chapter turns to the sociocultural context of American Roman Catholic women in the era leading up to the formal reception of the liturgical movement, again, through the advocacy of a Benedictine, Virgil Michel, at the liturgical center of Saint John's Abbey in Collegeville, Minnesota. Women's concerns and activities in American society and as Christian activists (either as Protestant or Catholic) tended to coincide with the trajectory of American liturgical reform, that is, its interest in social reform, an appropriation of intellectual Catholicism, cementing of Catholic identity, and an interest in well-crafted arts as a venue for properly orienting the human spirit. The coincidence of women activists and the tenets of the liturgical movement is especially curious as, often, Catholics and particularly Catholic women sought to distance themselves from the "protestant" tendencies of their Christian sisters involved in reforms, whether in the vein of American Progressivism or the so-called feminism of the "New Woman."[135] Though the liturgical movement was, historically, a Catholic movement, Protestant congregations shared many of the

---

[135] See Kathleen Sprows Cummings, *New Women of the Old Faith: Gender and American Catholicism in the Progressive Era* (Chapel Hill: The University of North Carolina Press, 2009), 8.

same pastoral problems that Catholics experienced.[136] The particular experiences of Protestant women of varying denominations in liturgical reform have yet to be explored. But for Roman Catholics, the contextualization of lay women's involvement in the liturgical movement within the contours of American society provides the necessary landscape for interpreting the particular involvement of women and how women's involvement and identity changed throughout the liturgical movement.

[136] John Fenwick and Bryan Spinks, "The Anglican Church and the Liturgical Movement I," in *Worship in Transition: The Liturgical Movement in the Twentieth Century* (New York: Continuum, 1995), 37. See also P. Edwall, E. Hayman, and W. D. Maxwell, eds., *Ways of Worship* (London: SCM Press, 1951).

Chapter 2

The Burgeoning American Liturgical Movement: The Catholic Response to the Modern World (c. 1926–38)

INTRODUCTION

The Liturgical Movement Emigrates to America

Like much of the Roman Catholic population, the liturgical movement emigrated to America. The early twentieth-century parish was full of immigrants, and the communal identity afforded by the Church remained one of the spiritual and emotional mainstays of transplanted and often marginalized populations.[1] At the peak of immigration in the late nineteenth century, congregations remained tightly tied to French, Slovak, Polish, Italian, or German ethnic heritages and their ethnic parishes, even if the retention of these identities required building a Polish church across the street from its Irish neighbor.[2] As the twentieth century progressed, a complex and thriving political and social atmosphere had inspired both an intense desire for Catholics to identify as truly American and, second, to combat the perception that their population was composed solely of poorly educated and nonprogressive immigrants by promoting an active intellectual life.[3] An effort to construct and sustain Catholic identity inspired a thriving network of religiously associated professional social workers, by both lay orga-

---

[1] See, for example, Robert Orsi, "Toward an Inner History of Immigration," in *The Madonna of 115th Street* (New Haven, CT: Yale University Press, 1985), 150–62; and Jay Dolan, *The American Catholic Experience: A History from Colonial Times to the Present* (Garden City, NY: Doubleday, 1985).

[2] In South Bend, Indiana, St. Hedwig's Parish, founded by Polish immigrants in 1877, was built *across the street* from St. Patrick's Parish, founded in 1858 by Irish immigrants. The two congregations were combined in 2001.

[3] James T. Fisher, *Communion of Immigrants: A History of Catholics in America* (New York: Oxford University Press, 2000).

nizations and religious communities, particularly on the urban fronts, in order to care for Catholics in all areas of life.[4] On the structural level, Catholic charities and organizations pooled resources to found schools, set up recreational centers, and advocate for the marginalized and impoverished, particularly among those vulnerable new (and often Catholic) immigrants. And, in a more social way, Catholic organizations and clubs and Catholic media proliferated, serving not only as a resource and protectorate of the flock but as combatants against the lure of "degenerate" recreational activities, threats of communism, and "Protestant" worldliness.[5]

The liturgical movement thus arrived on an already robust scene of Catholic Action, Catholic intellectual life and arts, and Catholic structures, from hospitals to schools to charitable organizations, which supported a Catholic life. The American liturgical movement became a natural focus for men and women who were interested in greater spiritual understanding, intellectual grasp, and active realization of their faith as Roman Catholics in any of these venues. In part, these women and men were inspired to adopt the liturgical movement as a natural response to the needs of modern American Roman Catholicism by papal inspiration (i.e., Pius X's *motu proprio*) and by the intellectual trends of their time (e.g., the Oxford Movement, historical theology).[6] They were also driven by a concern for what was increasingly regarded as rampant secularism: the social evils of industrialism,

---

[4] For a discussion of the intersection of Catholicism and American society, see David J. O'Brien, *American Catholics and Social Reform: The New Deal Years* (New York: Oxford University Press, 1968).

[5] See, among others, Aaron Abell, "Preparing for Social Action: 1880-1920," in *The American Apostolate: American Catholics in the Twentieth Century*, ed. Leo R. Ward (Westminster, MD: Newman Press, 1952), 11-28.

[6] In mid-nineteenth century England, the "Oxford Movement" developed parallel to the "liturgical movement" on the Continent, which described those scholars, many from Oxford, whose interest in church history and patristics paired with a desire to reclaim medieval styles of grand ritual and neo-Gothicism in liturgical practice. Sometimes referred to as Tractarians (after the series of publications *Tracts for the Times*, between 1833–41), the Oxford Movement sought to intellectually and ritually support the "re-Christianization" of society and culture. See André Haquin, "The Liturgical Movement and Catholic Ritual Revision," in *The Oxford History of Christian Worship*, ed. Geoffrey Wainwright and Karen Westerfield Tucker (Oxford: Oxford University Press, 2006), 697.

capitalism, and the relative usury of modern society which stripped the individual of freedom, creativity, pride in one's work, in short, all the vitality intended for human life. Thus, those Catholics already interested in reform—from social action to education to the arts—found the ethos of the liturgical movement and its theological underpinnings in the Mystical Body easy to integrate. In fact, the distinctiveness of the American liturgical movement is often identified by its integration with the American scene of social action.[7] Much like the Social Gospel Movement, largely led by lay Protestant men and women, the liturgical movement was the Catholic answer to reaching into the social concerns of society.[8] The liturgical movement was quickly identified as the proper venue for a sacramentally informed or *Catholic* response to the modern world.

While American women social reformers are more frequently identified as Protestant or secular, American Catholic lay women were involved in social reform from the early nineteenth century into the mid-twentieth, in causes ranging from temperance to suffrage (and anti-suffrage), involvement as settlement house workers, union organizers, school teachers, and writers and editors of Catholic publications.[9] However, non-religious lay women did not enter reform groups in large numbers until the last quarter of the nineteenth century. Prior to this time, women religious were caretakers of the poor and needy; nuns, who would undergo their own process of professionalization in tandem with the Progressive era, primarily sustained programs of nursing, education, and social agencies with inexpensive labor.[10] Meanwhile, Catholic women were encouraged to be private nurses,

[7] Godfrey Diekmann, "Is There a Distinct American Contribution to the Liturgical Renewal?" *Worship* 45, no. 10 (1971): 578–87; Gerald Ellard, "The Liturgical Movement: in and for America," *The Catholic Mind* 31 (1933): 61–76; and Ellard, "The American Scene, 1926–51," *Orate Fratres* 25, no. 11/12 (1951): 500–8.

[8] For some background on the role of the laity in nineteenth and twentieth century Protestantism, see "Lay Movements," in *The Encyclopedia of Christianity*, ed. Erwin Fahlbusch et al., vol. 2 (Grand Rapids, MI: Eerdmans, 2001).

[9] Deborah A. Skok, "The Historiography of Catholic Laywomen and Progressive Era Reform," *U.S. Catholic Historian* 26, no. 1 (2008): 4.

[10] Debra Campbell, "Reformers and Activists," in *American Catholic Women: A Historical Exploration*, ed. Karen Kennelly (New York: Macmillan Publishing Company, 1989), 154–55. See also Kathleen Sprows Cummings, *New Women*

teachers, and reformers for their own families. As the *Mirror of True Womanhood*, a popular volume written for Catholic lay women, instructed, the Catholic woman was the indisputable life force for her family:

> O woman, within that world which is your home and kingdom, your face is to light up and brighten and beautify all things, and your heart is to be the source of that vital fire and strength without which the father can be no true father, the brother no true brother, the sister no true sister,—since all have to learn from you how to love, how to labor lovingly, how to be forgetful of self, and mindful only of the welfare of others.[11]

Catholic women's service should find its seat and home within her domestic domain; her first service was not to the street but to the poor who came to her door.[12]

With the increasing public face of Catholic identity, Catholic women's groups became more acceptable and common, often in parallel to existing men's groups. These groups, such as the Daughters of Isabella or the Catholic Daughters of America, were usually composed of more mobile or socially advantaged women, not working class and not necessarily professionals, and were more readily able to take on charitable causes in a somewhat controlled context. But, with the shifting nature of women's role in society, the activity of late nineteenth-century women became increasingly independent and, as Margaret Mary McGuinness suggests, the activity of late nineteenth-century women pioneered the professionalization of Catholic social workers, as well as served as a precursor to the centralization of Catholic charities in the twentieth century.[13]

---

of the Old Faith: Gender and American Catholicism in the Progressive Era (Chapel Hill: The University of North Carolina Press, 2009), 9.

[11] Bernard O'Reilly, *The Mirror of True Womanhood: A Book of Instruction for Women in the World* (New York: Peter F. Collier, 1878), 8.

[12] See Debra Campbell, "'I Can't Imagine Our Lady on an Outdoor Platform': Women in the Catholic Street Propaganda Movement," *U.S. Catholic Historian* 26, no. 1 (2008): 103–14.

[13] Margaret Mary McGuinness, "Response to Reform: An Historical Interpretation of the Catholic Settlement Movement, 1897–1915," (PhD diss., Union Theological Seminary, 1985).

American Lay Women and Social Change

This evolution in lay women's opportunity and suitability to promote social change was due to several factors, as Catholic historian Debra Campbell suggests: the growth of labor unions, the arrival of new immigrants from southern and eastern Europe, and the increase in social status of middle-class Catholics from Irish and western European backgrounds all had significant effect in transforming the social makeup of the American Catholic woman.[14] Not only this, but the rapid increase in Catholic organizations from the Sodality of Our Lady to the Knights of Columbus encouraged a group identity for Catholics which had not been as cohesive in the previous century. Rather than clinging to a more defensive bulwark mentality and private faith, Catholic lay persons became more interested in publically organizing and advocating for means of Catholic identity. This took place not only in the blossoming of parallel social agencies, hospitals, and the parochial school system but also in the particular advocacy of Catholic lay women in protecting and advocating stability and sanctity in the community and in the Catholic home.

In some ways, this was a response to a tension between advocates of "Americanization," those more liberal persons who wished the Catholic Church to quickly assimilate itself and its largely immigrant population to American Protestant culture, and conservative Catholics, who wanted to keep close ties with an ethnic past. "Liberals," as Campbell indicates, tended to have more contact with non-Catholic reformers and were more inclined to become involved with the Progressives who advocated economic and social justice, ending poverty and discrimination by social aid. "Conservatives," meanwhile, often saw "protestantizing" social agencies as attempting to steal away young, poor, immigrant Catholics and tended to promote the more traditional Catholic attitude—that corporal works of mercy were the responsibility of well-off individuals who were within the private sector, or religious sisters who were the public face of the Church.[15]

Yet, women continued to fill the parish with lifeblood, sustaining charities, works of mercy, study clubs, altar and rosary societies, and the like with intensive labor and planning, most often on a volunteer

---

[14] Campbell, "Reformers and Activists," 159.
[15] Ibid., 159–60.

basis.[16] By 1920, in an attempt to construct some accountability and order (or control), the Roman Catholic hierarchy acknowledged women's potential to serve the Church and reform society by establishing official channels for this effort, particularly through the National Catholic Welfare Conference's establishment of the National Council of Catholic Women (hereafter NCCW). The new Catholic women's organization served both to unify Catholic women and to better implement episcopal interests. The NCCW, therefore, took up political activities in concert with the viewpoints of the National Council of Catholic Bishops (hereafter NCCB). For example, the NCCW worked to improve the status of women through their support of equal pay for equal work, adequate working conditions for women, nondiscriminatory immigration laws, and improved healthcare, but resoundly rejected "feminism," which they identified as the proponing of "unnatural" goals for women, veering women away from their natural realm, the home.[17]

[16] Mary Jo Weaver, "From Immigrants to Emigrants: Women in the Parish," in *New Catholic Women: A Contemporary Challenge to Traditional Religious Authority*, 2nd ed. (Bloomington: Indiana University Press, 1995), 37. See also Florence R. Rosenberg and Edward M. Sullivan, *Women and Ministry: A Survey of the Experience of Roman Catholic Women in the United States* (Washington, DC: Center for Applied Research in the Apostolate, 1980), 175. Miss Teresa R. O'Donohue, president of the League of Catholic Women, witnessed to the variedness and the intensity of "women's work" in a letter to Father John J. Burke of the National Catholic Welfare Conference [hereafter NCWC] on March 1, 1920. Since the First World War, "100 girls have been given comfortable lodgings, and a luncheon room serves 125 girls a day." Rosenberg's list of the organizations with which the League (in 1920, post-War) worked included the American Red Cross, the Division of Foods and Markets, the Medical Department of the U.S. Government, the Knights of Columbus, the American Fund for Devastated France, the National League for Women's Service, and the War Camp Community Service. Teresa R. O'Donohue to John J. Burke, March 1, 1920, National Council of Catholic Women [hereafter cited as NCCW] 76/19, The American Catholic History Research Center and University Archives, Catholic University of America, Washington, DC [hereafter cited as ACUA].

[17] Mary Jo Weaver, "Ordination, Collective Power, and Sisterhood," in *New Catholic Women*, 2nd ed. (Bloomington: Indiana University Press, 1995), 119. See also Esther MacCarthy, "Catholic Women and War: The National Council of Catholic Women, 1919–1946," *Peace and Change* 5 (1978): 23–32.

The NCCW was founded under the direction of the National Catholic Welfare Conference in the hope of offsetting the aggressive objectives of the "feminists" who supported such political campaigns as the Equal Rights

American Women in the Early Liturgical Movement

The emerging landscape for American women's involvement in the realization and promotion of Catholic life occurs immediately prior to the liturgical movement's inception in the United States. Because of the liturgical movement's very integration with any number of its contemporary Catholic social movements, American women's involvement in the spiritual and social renewal of the liturgical movement was a natural extension of their work and interests as Roman Catholic women. Indeed, American women were active from the first years of *Orate Fratres* and even before its beginning in 1926, contributing within the first numbers of the journal. Some of the early activists were American Roman Catholic women whose primary involvement was in the scene of Catholic social action and advocacy of a Catholic intellectual life, in common with the attempts to inspire and uplift American Catholic culture during the end of the Progressive era. Their interest in liturgical renewal flowed, very naturally, from their interest in restoring a Christian spirit within society, advocating for the Church's attention to the marginalized, and fostering a more engaging Catholic intellectual life in the face of a society which often saw Catholics as poor, marginal, or ignorant. The very tenets of the liturgical movement, if one draws upon the common themes of active participation, the Church's potential as renewing modern society, and the necessary trajectory of the eucharistic experience from the individual member of the Body of Christ into the world, render it quite sensible that these women, already actively involved in faith-informed social action and intellectual development, should have naturally found a home in the pages of *Orate Fratres* and in the earliest conversations within the liturgical movement in America.

One of the unifying characteristics of some of the most prominent women involved with the liturgical movement at its onset on the American front was their stage in life—middle-aged by twenty-first-

---

amendment. In the 1920s, NCCW members, including executive secretary Agnes G. Regan, testified before congressional committees that the Equal Rights Amendment would remove protection from working women and endanger the family, undermining morality, marriage, and motherhood. James J. Kenneally, "A Question of Equality," in *American Catholic Women: A Historical Exploration*, ed. Karen Kennelly, The Bicentennial History of the Catholic Church in America, ser. ed. Christopher J. Kauffman (New York: Macmillan Publishing Company, 1989), 141.

century standards, but quickly approaching elderly by the social standards of the 1920s. These professional women had already been actively involved in their particular spheres for a number of years; thus they were already experts in their first rounds of contact with other activists in the liturgical sphere and ready suspects for Virgil Michel's expeditious garnering of like-minded, intellectual, and resourceful contacts in his crafting of the national "organ" of the liturgical movement, *Orate Fratres*. In short, both the intellectual side of the liturgical movement (emphasis on learning Latin, using texts of the breviary and missal, studying the liturgy via new theological books or reading journals such as *Orate Fratres*) and its social-political awareness (interest in the liturgy's ability to form the person to act as a positive force in the world, helping the hungry, the needy, those afflicted), bespeak both a more experienced, educated population of women and a population with some privilege.

As discussed above, American women bore only a half consonance with their European sisters. On the one hand, some of the chief advocates and most publically/nationally involved women were, like their European counterparts, highly educated, professional women who were very much academically minded. In contrast to Europeans, however, most of these earliest women advocates did not hold academically based careers. The most significant contrast in which the American women involved in the liturgical movement differ from their European parents was with regard to inscribing the liturgy with terms of Catholic womanhood, or inscribing Catholic womanhood in liturgical reflection. American women who self-identified as members of the liturgical movement, especially in its earliest stages, tended to contribute in more concrete ways through promoting liturgical practices, while reflections on Catholic womanhood in America tended to be from the pens of clerics, most famously from Virgil Michel. Michel's interest in the subject of liturgy was clearly in concert with his exposure to European liturgical movement writers who found the role of women in Church and society to be a particularly absorbing subject.

This chapter considers how the professionalization of women and the increased organizational power for Catholic women's groups intersected with the growth and organization of the American liturgical movement. First, in the professional sphere, two particular women, Justine B. Ward (1879–1975) and Ellen Gates Starr (1859–1940), were advocates of learning, liturgical activity, and, particularly, active *witnessing* of their own gifts or venues of liturgical involvement and of *teaching* or *modeling* this involvement to others. Second, liturgical activity by women was not limited to the professionals, and a wide variety of other women involved in the liturgical movement appears in letters and occasional articles published in *Orate Fratres*. The large and increasingly organized Catholic women's groups, including independent groups such as the Daughters of Isabella and the Catholic Daughters of America, as well as groups organized by the NCCB, the NCCW, appropriated the liturgical movement in their own ways, taking the study of the liturgy as the antidote to modern evils.

JUSTINE BAYARD WARD AND THE REFORM OF LITURGICAL MUSIC

Early Education and Inspiration

As Pierre Combe concluded in his study of Justine B. Ward, among her most distinctive features was her "acute sense of liturgical prayer."[18] He concluded his history of her association with the Solesmes Movement from 1920 until her death in 1975 by observing:

> She fully understood the spirituality of Gregorian chant, its value as prayer; she used her talent as an educator, and spared no effort to make children appreciate this, in the hope of reaching all Christians through them. We saw that this was, from the very beginning, her only objective and that she remained faithful to it. For her, liturgy was the most effective means of sanctification.[19]

Justine Bayard Cutting was born on August 7, 1879, in Morristown, New Jersey, to William Bayard Cutting and Olivia Peyton Murray, members of the New York "aristocracy," of the Guilded Age and of the Episcopalian Church. Her father, heir to financial success through the railroad industry and other businesses, devoted much energy to philanthropic organizations and the arts, while her mother attended to New York through social circles. At the time of William Bayard Cutting's death in 1912, his estate totaled over ten million dollars, an immense sum at the time.[20] Justine was educated at home, which

---

[18] Pierre Combe, *Justine Ward and Solesmes* (Washington, DC: The Catholic University of America Press, 1987), 31.

[19] Ibid.

[20] Francis Brancaleone, "Justine Ward and the Fostering of an American Solesmes Chant Tradition," *Sacred Music* 136, no. 3 (2009): 6–26. See also

was usual for "well-to-do" young women and, though she went to school from 1893 to 1897, she did not receive a diploma; her musical interests drove her greatly, but to study in Europe (the necessary step for a young woman of good standing) was not possible for the young Justine. Instead, she took private lessons in composition, orchestration, harmony, counterpoint, and form from Hermann Hans Wetzler in New York. Though she did study Renaissance music, she did not receive formal training in pedagogy, vocal music, or choral training, the areas in which she would excel, until she went to Solesmes in 1920. In 1901, at age twenty-two, Justine Bayard married George Cabot Ward (1876–1936), attorney and amateur musician, but the marriage was annulled ten years later. Justine B. Ward remained independently wealthy.[21]

At the time of her reception into Roman Catholicism from the Episcopal Church in 1904, Ward was twenty-five years old and quickly identified the music of the Church as the location in which she wished to spend her musical energy and financial resources. She attributed her desire to affect a permanent reform of church music to the inspiring *motu proprio* of Pius X, *Tra le sollecitudini*, in 1903. As she recalled on the twenty-fifth anniversary of this document: "I was not a Catholic yet but this papal document made a profound impression on me and I had already promised myself that when I was received into the Catholic Church I would work for this good cause."[22] Ward began, between 1905 and 1910, to write articles for national reviews, particularly the *Atlantic Monthly*, in which she promoted the development of church music and routinely expressed frustration with the inferior quality of Catholic "musiquette" as she called it and the incomprehension among her fellow Catholics of the call for reformed religious music which Pius X had issued.[23] It was also during this period that Ward began to

---

Richard R. Bunbury, *Justine Ward and the Genesis of the Ward Method of Music Education* (PhD diss., University of Massachusetts at Amherst, 2001); Georgiana Pell Curtis and Benedict Elder, "Justine Ward," *The American Catholic Who's Who* (Washington, DC: National Catholic News Service, 1938–1939); Gabriel M. Steinschulte, *Die Ward-Bewegung* (Regensburg: G. Bosse, 1979).

[21] See Catherine Dower, "Patrons of the Arts, The Wards: Justine and George, Symbolic Illusions," in *Cum Angelis Canere* (St. Paul, MN: Catholic Church Music Associates, 1990), 145–79.

[22] Justine B. Ward to Dom Mocquereau, Nov. 22, 1928. See Combe, 1.

[23] J. Kelly, "La Réforme grégorienne aux Etats-Unis," *Revue Grégorienne* (1920), 69; and L.P. Manzetti, "Echoes of the Gregorian Congress," *Cathedral Choir* (1920), 114.

develop her program for teaching chant to children, what would later be internationally known as the Ward Method of School Music. Inspired by her first chant tutor, John Young, SJ,[24] and influenced by Fr. Thomas E. Shields's pedagogy,[25] she organized this material into a series of books designed for children in parochial schools.[26] Her success led to an invitation from the Sisters College of Catholic University of America to teach, beginning in 1910. She remained at Catholic University until she, assisted by Mother Georgia Stevens, RSCJ (1871–1946), left to found the Pius X Institute of Liturgical Music in New York at Manhattanville Academy. Headed by Ward and Mother Stevens and staffed by sisters of the Sacred Heart, the academy sought to assist teachers in learning how to relay both the musical and spiritual aspects of liturgical music to their students.[27]

[24] John Young had been experimenting teaching chant to the boys and men of his choir at St. Francis Xavier Church in New York; he had worked out a system in which children could read Gregorian notation through numbers.

[25] See Paul Marx, *Virgil Michel and the Liturgical Movement* (Collegeville, MN: Liturgical Press, 1954), 79. In 1910, Ward met Shields who already had considerable fame for his development of new teaching methods for primary grades in Catholic schools. During a meal at which both Shields and Ward were in attendance, he asked her for her opinion of the music in his course. She duly gave him her opinion that it was quite worthless! For this reason, Shields invited her to oversee the preparation of a practical method for teaching music to children in his manuals, that which became known as the Ward Method. As Ward later recalled, "Together—he for the pedagogy and I for the music—we prepared a practical method of music for children in Catholic schools. From the start, this method was directed toward Gregorian chant." Quoted in Combe, 2.

[26] See Marx, 79. Helpfully, after the appeal of Pius X in 1903 to restore the use of chant, the second and third Plenary Councils of Baltimore determined that chant could best be restored by teaching it to children, as the trained children of the day would be the singing congregations of the next, an ecclesial position which further affirmed her efforts.

[27] Combe, 2. Other sisters were deeply involved in this work, both during and after Ward's term as director. Josephine Morgan, RSCJ, a musician who also had studied Gregorian chant at Solesmes, was director of the Pius X School of Liturgical Music from 1951–1969. She taught music at Manhattanville College for forty-three years. See Kathleen Hughes, ed., *How Firm a Foundation: Voices of the Early Liturgical Movement* (Chicago: Liturgy Training Publications, 1990), 190.

Contact with Liturgical Pioneers

The Pius X Institute's training of teachers was successful to the point that Justine Ward had opportunity to organize an International Congress of Gregorian Chant (the first one had been in Arezzo, Italy, in 1882), along with other teachers of chant, in 1920. This Congress allowed one of the most influential experiences for Ward's musical development, for it afforded the opportunity to meet Dom André Mocquereau, OSB (1849–1930), choirmaster of Solesmes, whose shared interest in the essential integrated nature of chant and liturgical prayer solidified her own. Both Ward and Mocquereau believed that Gregorian chant might be used to encourage children to pray the prayers of the Church in liturgical worship and that chant could train future cantors and congregation members who would form the praying, singing assemblies of the future.[28] She invited Mocquereau to direct the singing at the Congress, which began their lifelong correspondence. In a letter from Ward to Mocquereau on May 25, 1920, she described why reforming music by working with young people was so important for the liturgy:

> I have been trying for a long time to express the deep gratitude and the joy which is in all our American hearts because you are honoring us by crossing the sea to come and guide our first steps on the liturgical way and to encourage our love, very young still, for the sacred chant of the Church. But words are so cold and so commonplace—I need beautiful neums to express this to you. . . . You will not expect perfection, will you? because I would not want you to be disillusioned—but you will find much goodwill and even some enthusiasm, especially among the nuns—and the future is in their hands. They will pass the beautiful flame on to the children—they are doing it already—and this is our promise for the future. You will perhaps see 5,000 children who will come to the Congress. These little ones will please you, I truly believe. As His Holiness Pius X said, "Children will set a good example." There is among them none of the personal vanity which is so obvious, unfortunately, among the older Congress members. Worshipers are suffering . . . but all this suffering of the body and the spirit is probably necessary in order to make a work of God. . . . You are going to open a whole world of beauty for us, dear Dom Mocquereau; we have never known liturgy in America—it is ignored rather than neglected. It has to be created here.[29]

[28] Combe, 2.

[29] Letter from Justine B. Ward to Dom Mocquereau, March 25, 1920. See Combe, 3–4. See also a brochure by Justine B. Ward, "A Response to the Call of

The efforts of the Congress did not, as Mocquereau had enthusiastically concluded, "convert all of America to Gregorian chant," or, as the *Catholic News* on June 5, 1920, described the event with a story headline, "The Silence of the Catholic Church Broken after Centuries."[30] Yet, as Virgil Michel's biographer, Paul Marx, suggested—as was the case with many tendrils of the liturgical movement—the "silence" was intermittently broken. The teaching of children was successful in some areas, as is attested by the numerous "Liturgical Briefs" reporting on the successful teaching, reception, and participation in liturgical singing into the mid-1930s.[31] It was apparent that a grasping of chant's intrinsic nature as prayer was best conveyed among small groups.[32]

Study at Solesmes: Sung Prayer

Following the success of the Congress among its participants, at her first opportunity, Ward went to France to study under Mocquereau, where she stayed through 1921 and 1922. At last free to study more intensely, she was deeply influenced by the Benedictines' care in method, execution, and artistry and the profound spiritual gravity of the Solesmes schola.[33] As she wrote in reflection of her impressions of the monks, a letter which was soon published in *Revue Grégorienne*:

Pius X," ed. Blanche M. Kelly (New York: Pius X Institute of Liturgical Music, 1922).

[30] Marx describes a rather spectacular realization of the success of the Pius X School and the Ward Method, which took place at the Gregorian Congress held in New York on June 1–3, 1920. During this meeting, the gathered conference-goers sang Vespers, Compline, and high Masses congregationally, attended lectures on liturgical subjects, and perused exhibitions. The "high Mass" at St. Patrick's Cathedral was buoyed by a choir of 5,000 children, directed by Dom André Mocquereau, who enthused: "I realized that my dream had come true, and that through the medium of the children of America the great heritage of congregational singing will be restored to the Church" (Marx, 79n27).

[31] See, for example, "Liturgical Briefs," *Orate Fratres* 1, no. 3 (1927): 95–96; "Liturgical Briefs," *Orate Fratres* 1, no. 7 (1927): 224; "Liturgical Briefs," *Orate Fratres* 2, no. 12 (1928): 384; "Liturgical Briefs," *Orate Fratres* 3, no. 8 (1929): 252; "Liturgical Briefs," *Orate Fratres* 4, no. 9–10 (1930): 426; "Liturgical Briefs," *Orate Fratres* 5, no. 10 (1931): 487; "Liturgical Briefs," *Orate Fratres* 7, no. 6 (1933): 282; and "Liturgical Briefs," *Orate Fratres* 9, no. 3 (1935): 126.

[32] Combe, 5.

[33] Ibid., 6–13.

The scientific aspect of the work, the analysis and comparison of the manuscripts, is something extremely interesting and impressive. The extraordinary care given to the study of the smallest questions and the eager and graceful manner in which the monks explain the slightest details of their work, make a lasting impression. But even if there were no scientific element at the basis of this work, the beauty of the result would be enough to conquer the listeners, and I doubt that anyone with the slightest artistic sense could possibly stay for a while at Quarr Abbey without being converted to the method of the monks of Solesmes.[34]

In addition to her musicality, she also developed a deep affiliation with the monastic life, known to her through her extensive study and time spent at Solesmes, and became a Benedictine oblate in 1921.[35] Not only was she influenced by the quality of chant, but Ward also became increasingly interested in the liturgy during this time. At the advice of Mocquereau, Ward had become familiar with the liturgical work of Prosper Guéranger. Guéranger had described the liturgy as Christ's prayer continued in the Church, rendered present throughout the drama of the liturgical year, and transforming the faithful into an image of Christ. Within the liturgy, poetry had its own role to play in drama, spinning the mysteries of the Old and New Testament and the reality of Christ through a medium most suited for the praise of God—music.[36] Thus, Ward believed that the study of chant had to be unified with a grasp of its intrinsic liturgical character—that its form as musical art could not be divorced from its function as liturgical language. As she attested to her mentor, Mocquereau: "I do not want to talk about Sacred Music or Liturgical Music any more. It seems that we should rather talk about *sung prayer*."[37]

[34] Ibid., 9.

[35] Ibid., 131–32. As Combe describes, Justine B. Ward's attachment to the spiritual life at the heart of the monastic community of Solesmes is revealed in her letters to Mocquereau, as she writes about being "wrenched" away from Solesmes (June 13, 1923), being "out of place" when she is not there (March 10, 1924) of her "yearning" for Solesmes (March 12, 1929), and her "being uprooted" (October 1, 1929).

[36] Prosper Guéranger, *Institutions liturgiques*, vol. 4 (Paris: Société Génerale de Librairie Catholique, 1885), 305.

[37] Letter from Justine B. Ward to Dom Mocquereau, January 23, 1929. See Combe, 132.

Contact with Virgil Michel and Work for Orate Fratres

On May 10, 1925, after continued activity and study in France and Rome, and the success of the Pius X School according to her method (including a blessing by Pope Pius XI), Justine Ward received her first inquiry from Virgil Michel about his wish for her involvement with his forthcoming publication, to which she responded:

> The Review is a splendid idea and I like very much the proposed title, *"Orate Fratres."* It would be a beautiful thing if we could develop through this review the close connection between the liturgy itself and its living voice—the Chant—and go more deeply into this than is possible in any review which exists at present. I think there is much unexplored ground here.[38]

Ward had been interested in incorporating the liturgy into her summer school at the Pius X Institute in a more intentional manner and told Michel that she had "always felt that our school was incomplete because of its absence" and hoped to incorporate a liturgy course into the general training for music as well. She concluded by telling Michel that "I feel sure that by uniting our forces we will accomplish wonders for the object which we all have at heart."[39] And, likewise, since the third number of *Orate Fratres*, Virgil Michel had included notes about the Ward Method in his "Liturgical Briefs" section, praising the success with which the method had been used in the parochial schools of the Archdiocese of St. Paul, Minnesota, for the summers of 1921 through 1924, by a graduate of the Pius X School of Music.[40]

In turn, after Michel's contact, Justine Ward invited Michel to lecture at the St. Pius X summer school and encouraged his plans for the upcoming *Orate Fratres*. Michel did give a course of lectures on the liturgy of the Church at the Pius X Institute of Liturgical Music in the summer of 1926. Described as "an added feature of the growing work of that institute," the lectures emphasized the spiritual aspects of the liturgy, "in order to furnish the true basis for the work on the chant," which, Michel complimented, had been taught "so splendidly by the Institute for a number of years."[41]

---

[38] Justine B. Ward to Virgil Michel, May 10, 1925, The Virgil Michel Papers Z 28: 6, SJAA.

[39] Ibid.

[40] "Liturgical Briefs," *Orate Fratres* 1, no. 3 (1927): 95–96.

[41] Ibid., 96.

At the point of Ward's incorporation with the mainstream liturgical movement and her collaboration with Virgil Michel, thirteen thousand teachers of chant had studied with her, mostly men and women of the religious orders, but also laypersons. In her view, uniting the "efforts for the apostolate of the liturgy and of the chant" would enrich the church musicians' formation far more than what could be given from a musical standpoint alone.[42] She saw the development and promotion of chant as absolutely inseparable from the development and promotion of the liturgy. Wanting to link her work as closely as possible with the liturgical movement, she assured Michel of her readiness to "contribute according to my small capacity" and her hope to "link up the movement for the development of liturgical music with the whole movement in favor of the liturgy."[43]

Though Justine Ward did accept Virgil Michel's invitation to become one of the editor contributors of *Orate Fratres* and remained on the editorial board until 1933, she had been reluctant to do so, due to pressures of her work with the Pius X School and, after her departure from the school in 1931, with the continued development of liturgical music.[44] She assured him that her reluctance to be a more regular

[42] Justine B. Ward to Virgil Michel, May 10, 1925, The Virgil Michel Papers Z 28: 6, SJAA. Other women, such as college student Marie Scanlon, class of 1928, of Marywood College in Scranton, Pennsylvania, also believed in the importance of linking musical liturgical performance with love of the liturgy. In *The Catholic Choirmaster*, she reported on the liturgical work of Marywood College, where the girls all were taught hymnody, chant, the Divine Office, and where each girl had her own missal: "Each Marywood girl is expected to keep within herself the light which is given her, but to pass it on to other souls. God grant that [graduates of other Catholic colleges] can obey the command, 'Go and teach all nations' in respect to a keen appreciation of Catholic liturgy." Marie Scanlon, "Letter to the Editor," *The Catholic Choirmaster* 12, no. 4 (1926): 128–29.

[43] Justine B. Ward to Virgil Michel, January 23, 1926, The Virgil Michel Papers Z 28: 6, SJAA. ". . . I feel doubtful whether I ought to accept your very kind invitation to be one of the Editorial Contributors because I am so terribly pressed with other work that it would be impossible to make a definite promise to write 5 or 6 articles a year. I can see that you must have such definite assurances before it would be safe for you to start publication, and while I hope to be able to contribute frequently, I should not dare to promise. For this reason do not you think it would be better to let me be an occasional contributor?"

[44] The original editorial board was carefully crafted to include women (Justine B. Ward and Mother Mary Ellerker, OSD) and lay people (Justine

contributor to *Orate Fratres* was out of concern for her not being able to fulfill the implied obligation of five or six articles a year.[45] While Ward had been repeatedly invited to write multiple articles for *Orate Fratres*, time simply did not permit her to do so (she even returned an honorarium, because she felt she was so remiss in her work),[46] and she found it impossible to balance the administrative and teaching ends of the chant movement with regular contributions to *Orate Fratres*.[47] In the

---

B. Ward and Donald Attwater); for more information on the earliest board members, see Kathleen Hughes, *The Monk's Tale: A Biography of Godfrey Diekmann* (Collegeville, MN: Liturgical Press, 1991), 144–45n12; and Marx, *Virgil Michel and the Liturgical Movement*, 106–36.

[45] Justine B. Ward to Virgil Michel, February 7, 1926, The Virgil Michel Papers Z 28: 6, SJAA.

[46] "You are not at all in my debt but quite the contrary since I am very much in arrears with the regular articles that I was supposed to write for you, and it is a joy to do the little I am able to do; so I am returning my check; you will find good use for it." Justine B. Ward to Virgil Michel, March 22, 1930, The Virgil Michel Papers Z 28: 6, SJAA.

[47] Justine B. Ward to Virgil Michel, May 15, 1929, The Virgil Michel Papers Z 28: 6, SJAA. She continued to apologize for the lack of articles contributed in the first years of *Orate Fratres*'s circulation, sheepishly writing: "I am ashamed to write always with an apology on my lips, but I know that you can understand better than anyone how crowded one can be, with a Summer School on one's hands. . . . It has been simply impossible to find a minute to write an article for the *Orate Fratres*, but I always keep up the good intention and try to forget the place that is *paved* with the latter! Some day, somehow, I will send you an article." Justine B. Ward to Virgil Michel, July 18, 1929, The Virgil Michel Papers Z 28: 6, SJAA.

In lieu of her long-delayed writing, Ward offered to send in a number of "casual reports" about the progress of the apostolate of the chant in various places, its use in schools, dioceses, and among particular segments of the population. While Michel expressed interest in using reports on the progress of the chant among different groups, he wished for longer articles and suggested that Ward invite another person present at the school (a Miss McKenzie, whom he had long been attempting to convince to write) to submit them if Ward found herself unable to do so, an idea to which she assented. Justine B. Ward to Virgil Michel, January 15, 1930, The Virgil Michel Papers Z 28: 6, SJAA. ". . . the work is really growing so fast that mere report of its progress now could fill a page or two in the Orate Fratres almost monthly if you should so desire." Virgil Michel to Justine B. Ward, January 21, 1930, The Virgil Michel Papers Z 28: 6, SJAA; Justine B. Ward to Virgil Michel, January 24, 1930, The Virgil Michel Papers Z 28: 6, SJAA.

end, Ward submitted only two articles to *Orate Fratres* for publication: "Winged Words," which appeared in 1927, and an article on the death of her friend and mentor, Dom André Mocquereau, in 1930.[48]

Reflections on Liturgical Music

Of these two contributions on liturgical music which appeared in *Orate Fratres*, the first contribution, "Winged Words," which she described as "quite popular in character,"[49] aptly summarized her philosophy of liturgical chant, emphasizing the "mysterious power" of music and how the Church, from its earliest time, chose to organize liturgy by taking this "mighty force" and making it "an intrinsic part of her worship—bone of its bone, flesh of its flesh."[50] Thus, music became not a powerful magic charm but a prayer. But not all music was incorporated into worship—only that music which would provide "that *appropriate feeling* which will enable the faithful to assimilate her doctrines," namely, Gregorian chant. Justine Ward attended to that which animated a text, for words alone were not enough. Words needed art to vivify them, to allow them to penetrate the inmost parts of the soul; as Pius X wrote, "*Vivificare et fecundare*—to make alive and faithful." A chanted text "reaches us not by the spoken word alone, but with the penetrating power, the transforming force of melody, of words that wing their way to God in song."[51]

Ward explained in this article how she had "frequent opportunity" to observe the "formative effect" of Gregorian chant upon all ages and its "infallible power to bring about a vigorous renewal of the Christian spirit."[52] She concluded "Winged Words" by recalling that transforming the Christian, beginning with children, was surely possible and could be expected through the application of good teaching. She stressed that:

> Unless we could expect such results, the insistence of the Holy See
> upon a certain type of music and no other would be inexplicable. The

[48] Justine B. Ward, "Winged Words," *Orate Fratres* 1, no. 4 (1927): 109–12; Justine B. Ward, "Dom André Mocquereau of Solesmes," *Orate Fratres* 4, no. 5 (1930): 199–207.

[49] Justine B. Ward to Virgil Michel, September 3, 1926, The Virgil Michel Papers Z 28: 6, SJAA.

[50] Ward, "Winged Words," 109.

[51] Ibid., 110.

[52] Ibid., 110–11.

desire of the Church that *the people should take an active part in the litur-gical singing* would be pointless unless that singing were one of the essential ingredients of a full Catholic life, unless its vivifying influence were like oxygen to the body, required by each of us, whether rich or poor, talented or not—winged words of eternal life.[53]

Ward saw educating the faithful in the medium of chant, the preferred form of music for the Catholic Church, as the most practical and beneficial way to aid the faithful in actively participating in liturgical prayer.

The Ward Method, Resources for Liturgical Chant, and the Liturgical Arts Society

Though Ward was unable to write more frequently, *Orate Fratres* faithfully noted her work and the progress of the Pius X School and other chant-related services and workshops in the "Liturgical Briefs" section until the ninth volume of *Orate Fratres* in 1935. For example, *Orate Fratres* gave Ward's new edition of her textbook for children, *Music: First Year,* high reviews in December 1932 and praised the con-tinuing success of the Ward Method:

> The unpedagogical methods of a hundred years ago are completely abandoned. . . . [O]n the contrary, there is pedagogy and psychology, there is the unfailing devotedness of a loving and genial teacher, there is a resourcefulness that cannot be surpassed. . . . Twenty years of practi-cal application in the schools of America, of France, and of Italy have proved conclusively that the "Ward Method" is doing wonders, that it captivates the child's mind and heart and brings forth the sweetest music. The Eucharistic era has led the little children to the Communion railing to receive their Lord even daily, and behold, the Lover of innocent hearts has opened up for His beloved ones a paradise of sacred song.[54]

The restoration of chant, a communal action of prayer, was likened to the restoration of frequent Communion, an increasingly common prac-tice among the Catholic faithful.[55]

---

[53] Ibid., 112.

[54] G.H., Review of *Music: First Year,* by Justine B. Ward, *Orate Fratres* 8, no. 2 (1933): 94.

[55] See Joseph Dougherty, *From Altar-Throne to Table: The Campaign for Frequent Holy Communion in the Catholic Church,* ATLA Monograph Series, no. 50 (Lanham, MD: Scarecrow Press, 2010).

One of the issues with which Ward was concerned was how a love for the liturgy could be stifled by tripping up over mere technicalities. While she had experienced children who enjoyed singing and teachers who were increasingly open to developing chant as part of their musical programs, she found that the lack of accessible, fundamental resources and texts with regard not to the *music* but to its rubrical application in the *liturgy* was one of the biggest issues holding back the liturgical movement:

> Our children *can sing* what the Church requires—they love to do so—
> the teachers are beginning to be interested, and everything is in favor
> of a rapid growth—but then fear and diffidence crop up, for with a
> love of the liturgy comes also a desire not to do the wrong thing. It is
> all so simple if the choir master could have absolutely clear directions
> on these purely technical points. Don't you think, dear Father, that this
> is well within the field of *Orate Fratres*? Do help us if you can![56]

Among her requests for practical sources were an *ordo* for Vespers on Sundays; instructions as to who was to sing (cantor, choir, clergy) what parts of items, such as the Litany of the Saints, the Benediction, the daily hours, etc.; and other questions both of her own and which other people had directed to her. She admitted that, even though she and some of the other questioners could *read Latin*, they simply could not discover official, authoritative answers to these simple rubrical questions for the correct use of chant.[57]

Another of the sustaining projects of Ward's post–Pius X Institute years was the overseeing of recordings of Gregorian chant. One of her earliest projects was completed in 1930, with the Victor Company, in which she produced a collection containing the whole ordinary of the Mass on four phonograph records, a project with which she was quite

---

[56] Justine B. Ward to Virgil Michel, September 15, 1926, The Virgil Michel Papers Z 28: 6, SJAA.

[57] Ibid. "Again, there is much confusion (particularly among the clergy) about *who* is to sing the Litany of the Saints! We believe that it should be sung by the *choir*, (Cantors vs. Choir) but often have much difficulty in keeping the clergy silent as they consider this their prerogative! . . . These and a number of questions, all quite simple in themselves, need clearing up. Most people (including the writer!) do not know where to look them up for an official pronouncement. . . . I do really think that technicalities such as these are holding back the movement more than anything else."

satisfied.[58] Finally, while Ward was unable to contribute as frequently to *Orate Fratres* as had originally been hoped, she shifted her attention toward promoting liturgical chant through the Liturgical Arts Society (hereafter LAS).[59] On the musical side of the arts, the LAS formed the Liturgical Arts Schola Cantorum, an all-male choir, in 1934, whom Ward would hear numerous times throughout its tenure. As always, Ward was exacting about the manner in which chant was performed and was duly critical of what she viewed as the new Schola Cantorum's more lackluster efforts.[60]

[58] Justine B. Ward to Virgil Michel, February 13, 1930. The Virgil Michel Papers Z 28: 6, SJAA. Coincidentally, Michel had just written Ward the previous week in February 1930 to inquire whether a phonograph recording project was something in which she would be interested in producing. Michel thought the creation of phonograph records would be helpful in learning Gregorian chant; to his knowledge in early 1930, very few recordings existed, and it would be most helpful to the movement if the St. Pius X School might arrange with a record company to produce some. He was sure that the time was "ripe" and the records demonstrating how Gregorian chant should be rendered would "make a good sale." Virgil Michel to Justine B. Ward, February 8, 1930, The Virgil Michel Papers Z 28: 6, SJAA.

[59] Ward would also contribute significantly to drawing the Liturgical Arts Society (hereafter LAS) out of debt at the end of the 1930s. In November 1937, the LAS had debts of $22,982.92 and assets of only $659.64. See Susan White, *Art, Architecture, and Liturgical Reform: the Liturgical Arts Society (1928–1972)*, (New York: Pueblo Publishing, 1990), 56.

[60] Justine B. Ward wrote in a letter to Maurice Lavanoux on June 21, 1941, regarding the Schola Cantorum, which she heard on Pentecost in New York: "You know I like your idea and am thoroughly with you as regards the plan, but the performance was *not* what it should be if it is to incite others to love and practice the liturgical chant. I will talk to you about this some time. Please don't think I am trying to discourage you, for I should rather say nothing at all than do that. But it really should be done *better*. The chant must have the correct *form* in its phrasing and rhythm, it must be correct as to *pitch* in order to be true *art* which alone can move the heart to sanctity. If it lacks these fundamental things, it becomes a torture. It affects the musician just as it would affect an architect to see a building the proportions of which were absurd and the material truqué. You who stand for sane and healthy ideals in art must stand for them in music too! I know you DO in principle, but the practice is not up to the principle." Justine B. Ward to Maurice Lavanoux, June 21, 1941, Liturgical Arts Society Records [hereafter cited as CLIT] 19/3, University of Notre Dame Archives, Notre Dame, IN [hereafter cited as UNDA].

Her relationship with the LAS was primarily as a benefactress and adviser; she was unable to directly oversee the musical articles which LAS had begun to include in its *Liturgical Arts Quarterly*, which she felt were in sore need of careful editing. She believed that the LAS should include articles "wider than architecture,"[61] suggested a number of graduates of the Pontifical Institute at Rome who she thought might serve well as musical advisers,[62] and offered additional names for corporate membership in LAS.[63]

By the 1940s, the pressures upon Ward's involvement in liturgical music reform and her ability to be involved with the various arms of the liturgical movement were made clear by a series of correspondence with Maurice Lavanoux, executive secretary of the LAS. Lavanoux, due to the struggling financial situation of the LAS, had continued to petition Ward for additional support. She replied:

> I am terribly sorry, but you must not count too much on me for financial support (apart from what I have very gladly done in the past) because, as you know, I am carrying the burden of the musical reform not only in America, but in other lands—practically alone. The better things get, musically, the heavier the expense—and I suppose it will be so in the future too. I have to keep up a faculty of trained people to carry through and keep in close touch with the work. It is the only way to get anything permanent done. That means I cannot do as much as I would like for other movements—even those that are closely associated with ours.[64]

[61] "[I]n order to have [articles on music] up to the standard of what the Liturgical Arts has been publishing hitherto, you ought to have a really competent musical editor or associate editor who would go over these articles and cut out inaccuracies—and also give a sense that the same high standard of taste prevails in the musical policy as in the architectural and decorative policy. It may need some time, obviously, to work this out, especially just now when the Review needs so many things to keep going at all." Justine B. Ward to Maurice Lavanoux, March 22, 1939, CLIT 17/6, UNDA; Letter from Maurice Lavanoux to Justine B. Ward, August 29, 1939, CLIT 17/6, UNDA.

[62] Including Rev. Robert Brennan, Rev. Theodore Joseph Kush, Rev. Giovanni di Dio Oldegeering, Rev. John Edward Ronan, and Rev. Fr. Bernier, SJ. Justine B. Ward to Maurice Lavanoux, March 22, 1939, CLIT 17/6, UNDA.

[63] Justine B. Ward to Maurice Lavanoux, March 22, 1939, CLIT 17/6, UNDA.

[64] Justine B. Ward to Maurice Lavanoux, July 31, 1941, CLIT 19/3, UNDA. Lavanoux had convinced Justine B. Ward to make loans to the LAS (of $1000, with the condition that it was matched by four other donors, for a total of

Ward's self-perception that she was carrying out musical reform "practically alone" is fascinating, as is her intent to get something "permanent" done. While Ward was not the only person interested in liturgical music (as the presence of *Caecilia*, *The Catholic Choirmaster*, the continuing Pius X School, and the inclusion of occasional articles on music in *Orate Fratres* suggests), she did strongly believe that only particular methods (hers, informed by Shields and Mocquereau) were appropriate and frequently found it difficult to combine forces with other teachers of liturgical music. Indeed, the intensity of her commitment, and her self-assurance as to how her schools should be run, unfortunately led to her eventual disassociation from her own Pius X Institute and her cofounder and friend, Mother Stevens.[65] Ward had resigned from the school in 1931, and the abbot of Solesmes, in support of Ward, refused to send monks to Manhattanville following her resignation. Though course offerings at the Pius X School during the summer featured many of the best-known liturgical pioneers—including Virgil Michel, Martin Hellriegel, Reynold Hillenbrand, Hans Anscar Reinhold, Gerald Ellard, SJ, and Godfrey Diekmann, OSB—Stevens insisted that the school keep music, not liturgy, as its primary focus, even rejecting Virgil Michel's offer in 1935 to lodge at Manhattanville to afford students greater opportunity for informal discussions.[66]

$5000) and personal loans. A series of correspondence between 1941 (the point at which a personal loan was made to Lavanoux) and 1946 indicates a growing frustration on the part of Ward with the management of the LAS. See Letter from Justine B. Ward to Maurice Lavanoux, September 12, 1941, CLIT 16/23, UNDA; and Letter from Justine B. Ward to Maurice Lavanoux, November 22, 1946, CLIT 16/23, UNDA.

[65] See Catherine A. Carroll, *A History of the Pius X School of Liturgical Music, 1916–1969* (St. Louis, MO: Society of the Sacred Heart, 1989), 37–56.

[66] Stevens wrote: "It would be quite impossible for the students to give any extra time to you as you suggest because they are here for the music and find it extremely difficult to get in the necessary assignments, so that we would not be able to have the extra conferences and talks, deeply as I regret this. . . . We shall always hope to have lectures on the Liturgy but this School, as you know, is primarily for the Chant and people who come here come for that purpose. I have found it absolutely necessary, for the sake of the students, to concentrate on the musical side during the six weeks of the summer school." Letter to Virgil Michel from Mother Georgia Stevens, 27 December 1935, The Virgil Michel Papers Z 27: 6, SJAA. See Pecklers, *The Unread Vision*, 269–73, for a short history of Justine B. Ward and the Pius X Institute.

Ward's Contribution to Reform of Catholic Arts

As is evident from the scope of her work in liturgical reform, Justine Ward was very much at the heart of the liturgical movement's aims for reform of Catholic arts. Because she was in a position of privilege, both in terms of her monetary status as benefactress and her education and opportunities for international exposure, Ward had significant presence on the liturgical landscape. She earnestly sought to do something "permanent" with regard to church music reform and was deeply disappointed with the near-rejection of congregational chant singing following the Second Vatican Council.[67] More recently, a resurging interest in Gregorian chant has prompted a renewed interest in her work. In 2007, the Church Music Association of America decided to reissue Ward's *Advanced Studies in Gregorian Chant* (1949) as well as her four-volume set of music for teaching children in primary schools.[68] Ward died in her home in Washington, DC, in 1975.

ANGEL OF THE STRIKERS, HERALD OF THE LITURGY: ELLEN GATES STARR

Early Education and Religious Background

The second lay, non-religious writer to appear in *Orate Fratres* is social worker, artisan, and Benedictine oblate Ellen Gates Starr (1859–1940) of Chicago, Illinois. As others have noted in reflecting on the life and work of Starr, for the cofounder of Hull-House, one of the most significant women-initiated social work projects in the twentieth century and one of the most influential social developments during the Progressive Era, Ellen Gates Starr is all but invisible in the landscape of American social history.[69] Starr was born in 1859 to Caleb and

[67] Anthony Ruff, *Sacred Music and Liturgical Reform: Treasures and Transformations* (Chicago: Hillenbrand Books, 2007), 223.

[68] Justine B. Ward and Elizabeth Ward Perkins, *Music First Year* (Washington, DC: Catholic Education Press, 1914); Justine B. Ward and Elizabeth Ward Perkins, *Music Second Year* (Washington, DC: Catholic Education Press, 1916); Justine B. Ward, *Music Third Year* (Washington, DC: Catholic Education Press, 1919); and Justine B. Ward and André Mocquereau, *Music Fourth Year* (Washington, DC: Catholic Education Press, 1923).

[69] Mary Jo Deegan and Ana-Maria Wahl, "Introduction," in *On Art, Labor, and Religion*, ed. Mary Jo Deegan and Ana-Maria Wahl (New Brunswick, NJ: Transaction Publishers, 2003), 1. A short biography of Ellen Gates Starr is contained in Allen F. Davis's entry in *Notable American Women*, ed. Edward T.

Susan Starr in Laona, Illinois, where her parents had moved in 1855 to be farmers.[70] A descendant of New England Puritans (first arriving in New England in 1634), Starr's immediate upbringing was "mildly Unitarian"; she described her parents as having given her "no instruction in religion beyond teaching me the Our Father and a few informal, childish petitions."[71] Her aunt, Eliza Allen Starr, who went west with Ellen's parents, was her most important teacher. After Eliza Allen had moved to Illinois with the family in 1855, Eliza Allen established a painting studio in Chicago and soon became established as an artist, teacher, and lecturer. Following Eliza Allen's reception into Catholicism, she promoted the arts in her Chicago Catholic community and, by the late 1870s, had begun her work for Christian art which made her known nationwide.[72] Both her Catholic affiliation and her interest in the arts would influence Ellen Gates Starr.

When Starr was eighteen, her father turned to pharmacy business in 1877 after lack of success as a farmer, and she went to Rockford Seminary where she formed a fast relationship with Jane Addams

---

James (Cambridge, MA: Belknap Press of Harvard University Press, 1971), 351–53; some dissertations which focus on Starr include those of Jennifer Lynne Bosch, "The Life of Ellen Gates Starr, 1854–1940," (PhD diss., Miami University, 1990); and Bruce Robert Kahler, "Art and Life: The Arts and Crafts Movement in Chicago, 1897–1910," (PhD diss., Purdue University, 1986).

[70] Starr's early exposure to politics and socialist theory came through her father who, from his poor experience as an Illinois landowner, became interested in socialism, attending local Grange meetings in the 1870s, railing at "middle men, manufacturers, merchants" who burdened Illinois farmers with unfair taxes, and expressing anger at a centralized government which put "wealth in the hands of a favored few; poverty, ignorance, oppression and degradation for the laboring many." Quoted in Victoria Bissell Brown, *The Education of Jane Addams* (Philadelphia: University of Pennsylvania Press, 2004), 76–77.

[71] Ellen Gates Starr, *A Bypath into the Great Roadway*, (Chicago: Ralph Fletcher Seymour, 1926; (reprinted from *Catholic World,* May and June 1924), 3. She added her parents' response to her early attempts to read the Bible: "I was never urged to read the Bible, and when I began to do so of my own motion, my father seemed a good deal amused by my comments. I recall his saying that he always felt a curiosity as to how the Scriptures would impress a quite unbiased mind; and he seemed to feel that the opportunity for gratification was at hand." Starr, "A Bypath into the Great Roadway," quoted in *On Art, Labor, and Religion*, 168.

[72] See Brown, *The Education of Jane Addams*, 77.

(1860–1935), with whom she would be closely associated in the Settlement House Movement in the coming decades.[73] Unfortunately, Starr left school due to financial reasons and moved to Chicago where she became a schoolteacher at Miss Caroline Kirkland's private school.[74] While living in Chicago and finding in herself "rudiments of spiritual craving," she decided upon "a trial of the Episcopal Church," which she joined, being baptized and confirmed at the age of twenty-five (1884).[75] The priest of that church, Father Huntington, impressed Starr with his "deep concern for justice to the workers" during the 1889 dock strike which occurred in London. Later, he prompted Starr's interest in, as she described, "the welfare of my soul," and she claimed his influence led her "steadily toward the Catholic faith."[76]

Shocking and Independent: Self-Employment and the Arts and Crafts Movement

Ellen Gates Starr's American youth coincided with a significant shift for middle- and upper-class women in terms of education and employment.[77] Starr herself worked hard to support herself, without

---

[73] For more on the nature of the relationship between Starr and Addams, see Louise W. Knight, *Jane Addams: Spirit in Action* (New York: W. W. Norton, 2010), 59–60, 84–85; Brown, *The Education of Jane Addams*, 11.

[74] Brown, *The Education of Jane Addams*, 75.

[75] In "Bypath to the Great Roadway," Starr retrospectively described her conversion to "Anglo-Catholicism" as that which prepared her for her conversion to Roman Catholicism. See Brown, *The Education of Jane Addams*, 139n67.

A more evangelical form of religion never had much draw for Starr and she recalled some feeling of freedom or advantage of mind when she first met other young people at Rockford Seminary. Upon her move from Rockford Seminary to Chicago, she began attending Unitarian services, as she felt "going to church on Sunday appealed to my New England sense of decorum." She found in these services only "mild intellectual enjoyment" and described them as "spiritual only in a very vague and somewhat sentimental way," attributes for which she had not great patience. See Ellen Gates Starr, "A Bypath into the Great Roadway," in *On Art, Labor, and Religion*, 168.

[76] Ellen Gates Starr, "A Bypath into the Great Roadway," in *On Art, Labor, and Religion*, 169. Her exposure to the Catholic faith, notwithstanding her Unitarian upbringing, had begun in her association with her Aunt Eliza Allen Starr, in whom Ellen Gates Starr had been "accustomed from earliest childhood to observe Catholic devotion."

[77] Educational opportunities abounded in New England with the founding of women's colleges: Vassar (1851), Smith (1872), Wellesley (1875) and Bryn

help from her family. Not only did she provoke the usual social standards, but both her financial stress and her fearless personality prompted her to defy some traditionally Victorian sensibilities regarding presentation of self. As historians Mary Jo Deegan and Ana-Maria Wahl describe, Starr's dress was eccentric; for example, she wore only lavender for some time, colors which were associated with mourning and the women's movement, and was frequently identified by her oversized, hand-me-down men's trench coat.[78]

Contemporary to expanding horizons for women's education was the advent of an important avenue for women's employment in the burgeoning European Arts and Crafts industry, which proved significant for Starr, who found both the aesthetic and social implications of the Arts and Crafts Movement attractive and coincident with her spiritual convictions.[79] The goals of the Arts and Crafts Movement included a revival of handcrafted goods, the creation of more satisfying working conditions, and the promotion of simple, uncluttered houses and interiors through a unification of all art forms. As art historian Wendy Kaplan summarizes, its driving factors were "simplicity," "utility,"

Mawr (1886), and coeducational possibilities at Cornell, Harvard, and other state universities. See Steven L. Piott, "Jane Addams and the Settlement House Idea," in *American Reformers 1870–1920: Progressives in Word and Deed* (Lanham, MD: Rowman & Littlefield Publishers, 2006), 91–107.

[78] Deegan and Wahl, "Introduction," *On Art, Labor, and Religion*, 10. Gioia Diliberto, biographer of Jane Addams, describes Starr as follows: "For years she wore a fraying raincoat that had belonged to an elderly machinist who frequented Hull-House events. The man, a bachelor named Mr. Dodge, left all his possessions and $3,000 to Ellen when he died—a token of his gratitude for Ellen's help in finding him suitable chess partners. Wearing 'Mr. Dodge,' as Ellen referred to her raincoat, and a small hat with a purple veil streaming out behind her, she strode purposefully through the neighborhood, shocking many with her outspokenness." Gioia Diliberto, *A Useful Woman* (New York: Charles Scribner's Sons, 1999), 167.

[79] In 1861, designer William Morris (1834–1896) began employing his daughters, wife, and female friends in his home design business in order to handle the designing and manufacturing (particularly embroidery) of his various craftworks. The reputable Morris's employment of women "set the seal of respectability on women's employment" for the Arts & Crafts Movement. See Irene Cockroft, *New Dawn Women: Women in the Arts & Crafts and Suffrage Movements at the Dawn of the 20th Century* (Compton, Guilford: Watts Gallery, 2005), 5.

and the "democratization of art."[80] Such goals, interestingly, were not unlike the reforming aims of the liturgical movement. The Arts and Crafts Movement was socially progressive in that it promoted the industry and education of women, but the movement was more profoundly formed by a social philosophy in which craftsmen and craftswomen would be uplifted from soulless, repetitive factory work devoid of creativity and thought.[81] The Arts and Crafts Movement was taken up as a response to economic change and social conditions,[82] and its success was due to the involvement of a moneyed middle class interested in its expanded role in society and committed to promoting workforce welfare.[83]

The Social Implications of the Arts and Crafts Movement and the Settlement House Movement

The social implications of the Arts and Crafts were lived out in its close association with the Settlement House Movement,[84] and it is this

[80] Wendy Kaplan, *The Arts & Crafts Movement in Europe and America: Design for the Modern World, 1880–1920* (New York: Thames & Hudson, 2004), 143, 146.

[81] One of the most influential figures was John Ruskin, who described in an important essay, "The Nature of Gothic (1853)," that factory work was, in fact, dehumanizing and socially deconstructive in which "workers" were turned into thoughtless cogs, separate from the rest of the meaningful, thoughtful "gentlemen" of society: "the workman ought often to be thinking, and the thinker often to be working, and both should be gentlemen, in the best sense." See John Ruskin, "The Nature of Gothic," in *The Lamp of Beauty: Writings on Art by John Ruskin*, ed. Joan Evans (Ithaca, NY: Cornell University Press, 1980), 236; see also Arthur Astor Carey, "The Past Year and Its Lessons," *Handicraft* 1, no. 1 (1902): 3–27; and Denman Waldo Ross, "The Arts and Crafts: A Diagnosis," *Handicraft* 1, no. 10 (1903): 229–43.

[82] Elizabeth Cumming and Wendy Kaplan, *The Arts and Crafts Movement* (New York: Thames and Hudson, 1991), 19.

[83] Cumming and Kaplan, 19. Ironically, William Morris eventually concluded that his hopes for a restoration of joy in craftship was simply "ministering to the swinish luxury of the rich," as the labor-intensive, handcrafted wares were often beyond the means of the poor men and women he hoped to benefit.

[84] The Settlement House Movement was concerned with welfare of the worker and sought to divert leisure hours spent on drinking or gambling to woodcarving and metalworking, not only occupying free time but also providing aesthetic stimulation and beauty for the home. Toynbee Hall of London's East End is perhaps the most famous and provides another important American link, as this is the settlement house which Jane Addams and Ellen

connection which interested Starr most greatly. She had joined her friend Jane Addams for a European tour, which included a visit to Toynbee Hall of London. From their experience there, the two women were convinced that they must begin a similar project in their home of Chicago. Shortly afterward, Addams and Starr opened Hull-House on Halstead Street in Chicago in September 1889. Starr was surprised at the public's positive perception of the project and was affirmed in her conviction that class divisions would be destroyed by real relationships forged between them:

> I had no idea in my most sanguine moments that people were going to take it up as they do. . . . The thing is in the air. . . . [P]eople are coming to the conclusion that if anything is to be done toward tearing down these walls . . . between the classes . . . it must be done by actual contact and done voluntarily from the top.[85]

To effect this tearing down of walls, Starr sought to bring culture and beauty to the poor immigrants served at Hull-House, as well as to wider Chicago. To aid this effort, she founded the Chicago Public School Art Society in 1894 and the Chicago Society of Arts and Crafts in 1897 and, after training with Cobden-Sanderson on a return trip to London, established a hand bookbindery at Hull-House in 1898.[86] At the bindery, she trained apprentices, established an arts and crafts "business and school" which lasted until 1919, and held a summer workshop for Hull-House residents and neighbors in 1900.[87] Aside

---

Gates Starr visited on their European tour during the winter and spring of 1888 and inspired them to open Hull-House the following year.

[85] Brown, *The Education of Jane Addams*, 213.

[86] Kaplan, 154–55.

[87] Deegan and Wahl, 23. See George M. R. Twose, "The Coffee-Room at Hull House," *House Beautiful* 7 (January 1900): 107–9; Ellen Gates Starr, "Hull-House Bookbindery," *Commons* 47 (June 30, 1900): 5–6; Ellen Gates Starr, "The Renaissance of Handicraft," *International Socialist Review* 2 (February 1902): 570–74; Walter Rice, "Miss Starr's Bookbinding," *House Beautiful* 12 (June 1902): 11–14; "The Handicraft of Bookbinding [Article 1]," *Industrial Art Magazine* 2 (March 1915): 102–7; Ellen Gates Starr, "The Handicraft of Bookbinding [Article 2]," *Industrial Art Magazine* 4 (September 1916): 104–6; Ellen Gates Starr, "Bookbinding [Article 3]," *Industrial Art Magazine* 4 (November 1916): 198–200; Ellen Gates Starr, "Bookbinding [Article 4]: Tooling and Finishing," *Industrial Art Magazine* 5 (March 1916): 97–103.

from the chief business of the bookbindery, which led her to significant contributions to Arts and Crafts–related organizations in Chicago,
Starr also organized other cultural events for Hull-House residents
and visitors.[88] Drawing on her experience as a schoolteacher, Starr held
classes on Dante and Browning for many years.[89]

Starr and Labor Reform

Despite these efforts, pressing systemic issues of sweatshop labor,
factory conditions, inadequate schools, and awful sanitary conditions
surfaced as the most vital issues for Settlement House workers, including Starr, to address. Starr took these matters strongly to heart, taking
her fearless personality to the picket lines. As a friend witnessed: "Miss
Starr is picketing and passionately longing to be arrested. I do hope it
will be over when I get [to Hull-House], Miss Starr is so difficult when
she is striking."[90] In the early 1910s through the 1920s, Starr frequently
protested for the rights of workers and regularly confronted bullying
police officers, either on the pavement or while being trundled off to
jail. Having become more committed to socialism in light of degrading
work conditions and the brutality with which strikers were treated in
her experiences with the garment workers' strike in 1910 in Chicago,
Starr worked in writing for and organizing the strikers, proving instru-
mental in "swinging public sympathy toward the strikers."[91]

Starr and the Liturgical Movement

Ellen Gates Starr's background in social work was very much in line
with the social impulse described by Virgil Michel in his work. Her
spiritual quest, which she detailed in "Bypath to the Great Roadway,"
revealed that, as she began experiencing the liturgical prayers of the
breviary and missal, the same convictions she held about finely

---

[88] Starr was involved with the Chicago Public School Art Society, cofounded
the Chicago Arts and Crafts Society in 1897, and was a leading figure in the
British Association of Arts and Crafts. See Deegan and Wahl, "Introduction,"
On Arts, Labor, and Religion, 1–35.

[89] Jane Addams, "Socialized Education," in *Twenty Years at Hull-House*, ed.
Victoria Bissell Brown, The Bedford Series in History and Culture (Boston:
Bedford / St. Martins', 1999), 199.

[90] See Barbara Sicherman, *Alice Hamilton: A Life in Letters* (Cambridge, MA:
Harvard University Press, 1983), 174.

[91] Deegan and Wahl, 26.

crafted art held for finely crafted liturgical prayer.[92] Never one for in-action, she sought to change how the faithful used liturgical prayer. She had been a Catholic for only a few years when she first contacted Virgil Michel in January 1927. Starr had met Michel's sister, Mary Elea-nore Michel, a sister of St. Joseph who was studying at the University of Chicago, who suggested that her brother, Virgil Michel, would very much be interested in seeing Ellen Gates Starr's "little apology," "A Bypath into the Great Roadway." This article detailed her move from "Anglo-Catholicism" to Roman Catholicism. Starr wrote to Michel, "If you do me the honor to read *The Bypath*, you will see why I am much interested in *Orate Fratres* and also that I am more or less of a Bene-dictine . . . !"[93] She also sent him a book of the stations which she had edited, titled *The Way of the Cross: Devotions on the Progress of Our Lord Jesus*, in 1926.[94] Starr's reflection on her "conversion" experience ap-peared in two articles in *Catholic World* in 1926 and was typical of her meditative and artistic style in describing her spiritual quest. The ar-ticles, indeed, interested Michel, and he included a note about them in the "Liturgical Briefs," describing Starr's "interesting account" of her

[92] In "A Bypath to the Great Roadway," Ellen Gates Starr described how, after her aunt Eliza Allen Starr's death, she received Eliza Allen's breviary, rosary, crucifixes, and other devotional objects, pictures, and books, including Prosper Guéranger's *Liturgical Year*. Ellen Gates related: "While I was assisting [Eliza Allen] in nursing her during her last illness, she had referred to *The Liturgical Year* in a way which arrested my attention, and I fell to reading it, and for several years went through the seasons with it, laying thus a fairly solid liturgical foundation, from which I passed on to the habitual use of the Breviary and Missal, constantly adding to the days, both festivals and fasts, on which it became necessary for me to assist at the offices of the Roman Catholic Church because I could not find them at all in my own 'branch of the Catholic Church' [Anglo-Catholics self-identified as one of "three branches" of the Catholic Church], or found them so impoverished and incomplete as to give no delectation." Ellen Gates Starr, "A Bypath into the Great Roadway," quoted in Deegan and Wahl, 170–71.
[93] Ellen Gates Starr to Virgil Michel, January 32, 1927. The Virgil Michel Papers Z 28: 1, SJAA.
[94] Alfeo Faggi and Pádraic Colum, *The Way of the Cross: Devotions on the Progress of Our Lord Jesus*, ed. Ellen Gates Starr (Chicago: Ralph Fletcher Seymour, 1926); see Ellen Gates Starr Papers [hereafter cited as EGSP] 18/3, Sophia Smith Collection, Smith College, Northampton, Massachusetts.

journey to Catholicism.[95] Though Starr was a "convert," she had long been aware of and used the Roman Catholic Breviary as a book of devotion "in preference to all others,"[96] making use of a "beautiful translation" by John Patrick Chrichton-Stuart (1900).[97] She admitted her inability to master the Latin of the hymns, despite her enjoyment of the "sonorous Latin of the Psalter, and of the Mass."[98] But Starr could not fathom why any "intelligent and literate Catholic" would not "prefer the breviary to the many somewhat flabby popular books of devotion (if one may say so) in common use."[99] Like Justine Ward, Starr saw immense potential in the resources already available to Catholics, who simply needed to learn how to access them.

Correspondence and Work for Orate Fratres

As soon as their correspondence began, Starr and Michel continued a healthy flow of exchanges with regard to advertising, perpetrating, and expressing the liturgical movement, sending books, manuscripts, and names of friends and acquaintances whom they wished to involve in the movement. Michel also recognized the potential Starr had, already an experienced and reflective writer, to be a contributor to *Orate Fratres*. His first response to her in late winter of 1927 included a copy of *My Sacrifice and Yours* and an invitation for Starr to compose

---

[95] "For years Miss Starr had been attached to the liturgy of the Church by strong bonds of sympathy and appeal; and this appreciation gave her soul needed rest until she had entered the fold." Virgil Michel, "Liturgical Briefs," *Orate Fratres* 1, no. 7 (1927): 223.

[96] Ellen Gates Starr, "The Delights of the Breviary," *Orate Fratres* 1, no.8 (1927): 263.

[97] John Patrick Chrichton-Stuart, Marquess of Bute, *A Form of Prayers Following the Church Office, for the Use of Catholics Unable to Hear Mass upon Sundays and Holidays* (London: Burns & Oates, 1900). Though she claimed to be no scholar in Latin, she used the Latin breviary, occasionally going back to the "Bute" English translation "either from affectionate habit or from slothfulness" and for its use of John Cardinal Newman's translations of hymns, which she found "a perfect literary as well as devotional delectation." Both practices she recommended to other Catholics: "To those who use the Latin breviary privately but find the Latin hymns not a spontaneous expression, I would suggest supplementing these delightful English versions." Starr, "The Delights of the Breviary," 268.

[98] Starr, "The Delights of the Breviary," 263.

[99] Ibid.

an article titled "The Delights of the Breviary."[100] The goal of the article would be to inspire popular use of the breviary, affirming that the breviary was accessible to more of the apostolate as a rich resource for spirituality and formation in the Faith.[101] Always speedy to act, she responded in March 1927 that she had already begun "The Delights of the Breviary" and was enjoying it greatly. "It is very good of you," she wrote Michel, "to let me collaborate in any smallest way in the work of extending the knowledge and love of the Liturgy."[102] She specifically included the subtitle "From the Point of View of a Laywoman," to further underline the universality of the Church's prayer to all of the lay apostolate. Not only had she begun her article, but she had apparently finished with *My Sacrifice and Yours*, for she had already lent it out to a "good Jesuit pastor" in "service of the Liturgical Movement."[103]

Having once begun her direct contact with the liturgical movement's center at Collegeville, Starr quickly saw the liturgical movement as a powerful force in the Church:

[100] "I am already beginning on the 'Delights of the Breviary' and enjoying it greatly. It is very good of you to let me collaborate in any smallest way in the work of extending knowledge and love of the Liturgy. So do not hesitate to make use of my small capacity in that direction or to make any suggestions about the use of it. I would rather go, as soon as I am well, into the Breviary article. I will send you some of it so that you may see whether I am in the right track for what you want before I put it into final form." Ellen Gates Starr to Virgil Michel, March 18, 1927, The Virgil Michel Papers Z 28: 1, SJAA.

[101] Starr wrote, "The wonder is that they [the missal and breviary] should ever have fallen into disuse. Nothing can take the place of these great universal prayers of the Church, the prayers of the Mass and the Divine Office. One has only to know them to find them indispensable. And alas, how few of the laity know them!" Starr, "The Delights of the Breviary," 263.

[102] Ellen Gates Starr to Virgil Michel, March 18, 1927, The Virgil Michel Papers Z 28: 1, SJAA.

[103] Ibid. In 1927, during her correspondence with Virgil Michel regarding her upcoming article on the "Delights of the Breviary" which would appear in the June issue of the first volume of *Orate Fratres*, she writes "As you can see, I had a good time write [sic] it, and it's perhaps too long. . . . I should be refractory about omitting the call to true Christians and . . . if you think my lecture to the Reverend clergy about endless sermons out of place, I will take that out." Ellen Gates Starr to Virgil Michel, April 2, 1927, The Virgil Michel Papers Z 28: 1, SJAA.

The liturgical movement in the Church has much to accomplish, directly and indirectly. The liturgy restored in its full beauty and perfection, and a congregation of the faithful trained to its use, all that is incongruous with it will gradually come to be felt as such, and in due time brought into harmony. One of the fruits, we may hope, will be the development of a true ecclesiastical art.[104]

Her experience of liturgical worship, "the most august of dramas,"[105] caused her continual frustration, both before and after her joining of the Catholic Church, with the apparent unconsciousness of the worshipers about what was happening on the altar. Most Catholics seemed not at all aware of their privilege, even simply to "hear" the Mass. They simply prayed *during* Mass.[106] As she related to Michel, Starr once asked her "good and very devout" laundress what people *did* during Mass; the laundress responded, "Oh, some of 'em stands and some of 'em sits."[107]

Devotions or the Liturgy?

Aside from annoyance over the general noncomprehension of the goings-on at Mass, Starr had definite opinions about the use of devotions. She noted that the Church had, on the one hand, given "great latitude" to various devotions that the faithful followed—enough devotions for an endless variety of "tastes, temperaments, and capacities." Some minds preferred "unvaried repetition," such as the rosary, but for those who were inclined "to contemplate a subject under richly varied aspects," there was the liturgy.[108] She firmly believed that this

---

[104] Ellen Gates Starr, "On the Feast of the Assumption: Reflections on Some Breviary Texts," *Orate Fratres* 1, no. 10 (1927): 300. She included a note about "the reasonableness of this hope" being realized in this article, giving the example of St. Thomas the Apostle Parish in Chicago. Ellen Gates Starr, "On the Feast of the Assumption," 300n1.

[105] Ellen Gates Starr, "The Liturgy of Palm Sunday and Holy Saturday," *Sponsa Regis* (1937): 151.

[106] Ellen Gates Starr, "Praying the Mass Aside from Mass," *The Sentinel* (1934): 64.

[107] Ellen Gates Starr to Virgil Michel, November 27, 1935, The Virgil Michel Papers Z 28: 1, SJAA.

[108] Starr, "Praying the Mass Aside from Mass," 64. She added, "The writer cannot help feeling that Saint Dominic himself never intended his devotion to supplant the liturgy."

more serious food of the liturgy was readily attainable, and the faithful only needed encouragement and direction in order to draw upon the Mass itself as a form of prayer and meditation.[109] Indeed, the faithful should seek to strip themselves of the mind-set in which Mass was attended "from necessity, custom, or any lesser motive" and resist the well-worn temptation to simply follow the liturgy or pray individually.[110] To pray, missal in hand, "with mind, heart and soul, truly 'assisting,'" would be a return to the earliest days of the Church and the liturgy's growth, "so fervently wished and prayed for by Pius X."[111] But the first step to this end was "to know and understand the liturgy, to become truly at home in it." By an intellectual grasp, a "love of [the liturgy] is then sure to develop."[112]

This "being at home" in the Mass in a way which integrated spirit, mind, and body in worship was what Ellen Gates Starr defined as liturgical. Assisting at Mass in a liturgical manner, praying in a liturgical way, and living in a liturgical life called attention to the words and their rich theological meanings and to participation in the powerful symbolic action intended by the rituals. She encouraged grasping of the words through use of the breviary and missal, her most frequent subjects of instruction and critique, and firmly believed that knowledge of the Church's prayer not only formed the individual's corporate faith life but fed the need for individual prayer and contemplation so sought after by the faithful. Indeed, intellectual engagement with the Church's prayer would quickly become fodder for spontaneous, devotional patterns of prayer, words of the Office spinning out of one's mouth as readily as an *Ave*: "If one knows it [e.g., a canticle] 'by heart'—literally by heart rather than by rote (for it is not necessary to have all the *opera* in exact succession to enjoy them)—one finds oneself ejaculating parts of it."[113]

<hr />

[109] Ibid., 64–65.

[110] Starr, "The Liturgy of Palm Sunday and Holy Saturday," 157.

[111] Ibid.

[112] Ibid.

[113] Starr, "Praying the Mass Aside from Mass," 66. "At daybreak and in the night: 'O ye light and darkness, bless ye the Lord: O ye sun and moon, O ye stars of heaven, praise Him and magnify Him forever.' In springtime how often one may exclaim, *Benedictite universa germinantia in terra Domino*—(Bless the Lord, all things that spring forth upon the earth.)—When flocks of birds pass over one, coming and going in their migration: *Benedicite omnes volucres*

A First Writer for the Breviary

Starr was, in fact, one of the first writers for *Orate Fratres* who dealt with the subject of the breviary, another reason why Virgil Michel was quite keen for her work. In correspondence regarding her first two articles, on the "Delights of the Breviary" and the "Assumption," which followed soon afterward, Michel wrote that her conclusions about the Divine Office of the Assumption might "express what seems understood and ordinary to you. But I am of the opinion that some of your most ordinary contacts with the Breviary will be as a revelation to many persons—not excluding the clergy by any means."[114] It is curious to consider that so few people had expertise with the breviary that Ellen Gates Starr, herself a rather new Catholic and self-taught reader of liturgical texts, was actually on the cutting edge of the renewed use of liturgical prayer.

As expressed in "The Delights of the Breviary," Starr's own use of the breviary had become for her "a kind of spiritual journal," and she recorded her experiences of both the "high" and the "desert" days in the margins of her breviary. When she returned to her notes as she followed the Office, she found it "enriched with the memory of blessings of other years."[115] Such textual engagement (and the very willingness of the reader to scratch ink pen to paper) allowed the breviary to be lifted from the abstract and become personalized, serving as a record of a pilgrimage in life and faith.[116] But, the journal of the breviary could serve

---

coeli Domino—(Bless the Lord, all ye fowls of the air.)—Birds of the air lend themselves naturally to praise."

[114] Letter from Virgil Michel to Ellen Gates Starr, April 1, 1927, EGSP 5/10, Sophia Smith Collection. In planning the appearance of the series of articles she eventually composed for *Orate Fratres*, Michel continued: "So far we have not said a word in our articles about the Breviary. Father Busch is preparing an excellent introductory series, of which the first is now in our hands. It seems to me that your general article will be doubly effective after the topic has been introduced by Father Busch's article. It will be a sort of confirmation of what he says; or a direct answer to the questions the uninitiated might ask after reading his article—and how many of us are not really uninitiated? I am delighted with your kind willingness to assist at the general work."

[115] Starr, "The Delights of the Breviary," 264.

[116] Ibid. Starr's practice of attending to the shrines of Europe resonates with a wider practice by mobile Catholic women. See Jenny Franchot, *Roads to Rome: The Antebellum Protestant Encounter with Catholicism* (Berkeley: University of California Press, 1994).

not only retrospectively but also as a message of hope for the future, particularly during wartime.[117] The breviary was no more irrelevant to current events than it was abstract, and its lessons, verses, and psalms offered poignant insight in skilled and thoughtful language. In short, the qualities of excellently crafted, inspirational, and justice-inspired reading were, for an audience of increasingly educated Catholics, laudable characteristics. As Starr concluded, these were her own "observations and applications" of the breviary and might not be particularly important; however, interacting with the breviary did illustrate how "the beautiful and inspiring matter of the liturgy becomes, by frequent use, an expression of one's daily life and experience."[118] She added that relating one's own "feeble religious and emotional life" to the depth and breadth of the thought of the Church's saints and doctors, allowed one to lift the self, at least momentarily, "out of its narrow, temporal existence, into harmony with the great Catholic life of the Church."[119]

Starr composed four additional articles for *Orate Fratres* during the late 1920s, including more reflections on breviary texts and illustrations of their accessibility and edification for the lay person. Like Justine Ward, Starr also returned an honorarium Michel sent to her for her work, claiming she was glad to "make this small contribution to the liturgical movement."[120]

Improving Aesthetics and Understanding, Bringing the Breviary Near

For Starr, the liturgical experience tightly intertwined with the aesthetic. She compared the contrast of the beautiful and sublime texts of the breviary with the "sentimentality" fostered by so many devotional books to the contrast of the mosaics of the early Christians and the "mechanically produced" popular religious arts.[121] Text and craft both

[117] "There are many dates of the war period in my margins," she added, and the "Strong and dignified language, with a sense of perspective and the long view, afford an assuagement of one's baffled feelings and tried faith." Starr, "The Delights of the Breviary," 265.

[118] Ibid., 267.

[119] Ibid.

[120] Ellen Gates Starr to Virgil Michel, May 31, 1927, The Virgil Michel Papers Z 28: 1, SJAA.

[121] "The constant reading of the breviary and use of the missal, the classic prayer books of the Church, would be an almost sure corrective of the tendency to sentimentality, fostered by many modern devotional books, and naturally reflected in popular so-called religious art. Who could read often

served as bearers of meaning, but the comprehensibility of meaning was highly dependent on the quality of the material. In her article on the Assumption breviary texts, she described the texts' choice in "more solemn imagery," which led the faithful away from "sentimentality and oversoftness" and provided a richer source for contemplating Mary and the Church:

> The Church is our mother, as our Lady is. But neither is a weak sentimental mother. The breviary offers for contemplation passages . . . which suggest a mental image of the holy Mother differing widely from those cultivated by many popular prayer books; a picture of strength, of wisdom, of solemnity.[122]

Just as with finely crafted goods, finely tuned words drawn from rich sources of the early Church and couched in imaginative poetry could capture and form the minds and hearts of their beholders.[123] Thus, Starr saw the renewed understanding, comprehension, and participation of the laity in the liturgy as impetus for multiple venues of reform, including those structural and aesthetic. Encouraging the laity to become actors in the wider scope of the "drama" of the liturgy through use of texts was compelling, as witnessed by letters she received. With delight, Starr informed Virgil Michel that a woman, who later became a subscriber to *Orate Fratres*, from South Amherst, Massachusetts, "cared for my little Breviary articles" and that this reader had "given them away right and left," including one to William Henry Cardinal O'Connell.[124] In another instance, a reader of *Orate Fratres* wrote to Starr confessing that, until he had read her articles, the breviary "was a term practically unknown" to him, but now he was "not a little envious" of her "infinite pleasure and satisfaction" in praying the prayer of the Church and inquired about editions she might recommend.[125]

---

such language as that ascribed to our Lady . . . and not find a lack in the usual shrine statues of her, practically all alike, mechanically reproduced, and from models of no original value." Starr, "Feast of the Assumption," *Orate Fratres* 1, no. 10 (1927): 299.

[122] Ibid., 297.

[123] Ibid.

[124] Ellen Gates Starr to Virgil Michel, October, 21, 1928, The Virgil Michel Papers Z 28: 1, SJAA.

[125] "Walter" to Ellen Gates Starr, April 15, 1928, The Virgil Michel Papers Z 28: 1, SJAA.

The author of the letter admitted his inability to focus on prayer exhaustively or even intelligently but that, even in his "ignorance," he read her reflections "with great interest and appreciation."[126] He concluded, praising Starr for bringing the breviary closer to the laity than he had ever realized it could be: "I respond to [your reflections on the breviary] because you are so absolutely reasonable and impartial and above all because you perceive and emphasize the human element in it that is close to us as human beings. In other words, you bring it near."[127]

Disconnect between Ritual Action and Ritual Meaning

Aside from the inattention or lack of comprehension about the textual elements of worship, Starr also found the disintegration of ritual action and meaning in her contemporary experience of Roman Catholic eucharistic liturgies to be insupportable, a concern similar to that of Justine Ward. In a 1929 article which appeared in *The Abbey Chronicle*, titled "A Few Trials of a Happy Convert," Starr related how she felt "pained and scandalized" by the "almost universal practice" of collecting money during the most solemn part of the Mass. "Why," she asked, "is it necessary that a money box be thrust before one's face immediately before or immediately after the words of Consecration?"[128] She offered some alternative moments for the collection, for even the

[126] Ibid.

[127] Ibid.

[128] Ellen Gates Starr, "A Few Trials of a Happy Convert," *The Abbey Chronicle* 3, no. 2 (March 1929): 1. She provided an anecdote of her experience of this most inopportune yet, perhaps, efficient practice: "On one occasion I was permitted by her non-Catholic mother to take to Mass with me a very lovely little girl who had adopted certain devout Catholic practices quite of her own motion. I asked the mother if she was willing that I should make any explanations. Having received her consent I told the child what I could of Catholics' belief about the Mass. Her eyes full of awe and wonder, she whispered, when she heard the Sanctus bell, 'Is the most solemn part coming now?' And as I assented, at that precise moment every one about us began fumbling in pockets or purses, and the inevitable money box punctually arrived, the transaction being achieved just in time for the Elevation. One can scarce refrain from calling to mind the money changers in the temple. 'Why do they do that?' murmured my little companion. What could or can one answer to that natural question? I throw myself and my fellow sufferers on the compassion of the guardians and governors of Holy Church."

Credo or the sermon would be a better time than the elevation for the congregants to be distracted.

Similarly, Starr expressed concern over the disconnect between ritual action and corporate understanding (even on the part of the homilist) of the eucharistic ritual. She related a certain church which she had attended where two priests were present, one preaching and one presiding: "It is difficult to describe my amazement," she recalled, "when the priest who was preaching said, 'We will kneel a moment for the Elevation.'" Somewhat confused, Starr realized that the priest at the altar had been proceeding with the Mass, to which the congregation was "giving no heed," their attention being upon the sermon. Even more disturbing for her, the preacher had, at one point, said something which provoked the congregation to laughter, quite oblivious to the sacrifice of the Mass occurring before their eyes. Starr concluded, "I did not rise from my knees after the Elevation, but continued to make acts of reparation. And I have never since ventured to trust myself in that church."[129]

Spreading the Gospel of Liturgical Reform

Starr was concerned with the "intelligent use" of the missal, promoting it whenever possible. Spreading knowledge of the Church's prayer gave her "intense satisfaction," and she bemoaned the "common excessive in dualism or separation as installed in the prayers" people said during Mass, that this separatism, she saw, "resulted in mediocrity and vagary in private devotions" and a lack of understanding of the Mass "as true public and corporate prayer of all the faithful made one in Christ."[130] Starr, however, was wary of loving the liturgy as an end in itself and not as a means to cultivating a responsible moral life.[131] Appreciative of the breadth and coverage of *Orate Fratres*, she

[129] Ibid.

[130] Ellen Gates Starr to Virgil Michel, June 10, 1929, The Virgil Michel Papers Z 28: 1, SJAA. Lay interest in the use of the breviary would be organized in the League of the Divine Office. See, for example, "League of the Divine Office," in "The Apostolate," *Orate Fratres* 12, no. 2 (1937): 88, in which Miss Florence Breen, codirector of the St. Joseph Center of New York, succeeded in sparking interest in the Breviary in the far-off state of Colorado. *Orate Fratres* reported that the St. Joseph Center advertised in newspapers and periodicals, held conferences, and disseminated pamphlets and prayer books around the country.

[131] In writing to Virgil Michel about a young man who was interested in the Church and liturgy, she wished that she knew how to inspire in him a "moral

encouraged others to subscribe, such as Miss Dickenson, a young woman about whom she wrote to Virgil Michel in early 1929.[132] She did not hesitate to send Michel the contacts of persons who might be interested in the movement, in his writing, or in subscribing to *Orate Fratres*[133] and was happy to send others her extra copies of *Orate Fratres* which she culled from Michel.[134]

Her own reading of *Orate Fratres* was frequent and appraising, having begun with the earliest numbers of the first volume; in her correspondence with Michel, she noted her approval of the magazine and its sections.[135] An experienced bookbinder, she even praised Michel for

---

religious responsibility" and to help him toward "steps to the sacramental life." She complained that he "plays about with the Church" and that, while he "loves the liturgy," he felt he could resist authority and be a "libertine" if he wished. Ellen Gates Starr to Virgil Michel, Feast of SS. Peter and Paul, 1927, The Virgil Michel Papers Z 28: 1, SJAA.

[132] Ellen Gates Starr to Virgil Michel, January 31, 1929, The Virgil Michel Papers Z 28: 1, SJAA.

[133] Ellen Gates Starr to Virgil Michel, July 13, 1927, The Virgil Michel Papers Z 28: 1, SJAA; Ellen Gates Starr to Virgil Michel, October 21, 1928, The Virgil Michel Papers Z 28: 1, SJAA.

[134] Ellen Gates Starr to Virgil Michel, January 1, 1928, The Virgil Michel Papers Z 28: 1, SJAA. "Thank you for sending me *My Sacrifice and Yours*, and the numbers of *Orate Fratres* which I am disseminating with care, some to the clergy and some to laity (Fr. Busch sent me some). . . . I gave one . . . to a young teacher of economics who is a lapsed Catholic, but is manifesting an interest in the Church again. He confessed to being an ignorant Catholic, and said that he was sometimes asked things (when people knew he had been born a Catholic) that he couldn't answer. He wanted things on the Mass. So I gave him all these things to begin in, and he took down the name of Fr. Adrian Fortescue's *History of the Mass*, . . . the Breviary, and Msgr. Duchesne's *Early Christian Church*. He is a student; and if he begins to *study* the Catholic Church and Religion, he may come out somewhere." Ellen Gates Starr to Virgil Michel, January 1, 1928, The Virgil Michel Papers Z 28: 1, SJAA.

Virgil Michel wrote to Ellen Gates Starr, regarding the letter of Miss Dickenson's which Ellen Gates Starr had enclosed, "You are conducting an apostolate all your own and you will get your reward some day!" Letter from Virgil Michel to Ellen Gates Starr, January 31, 1929, The Virgil Michel Papers Z 28: 1, SJAA.

[135] Ellen Gates Starr to Virgil Michel, March 5, 1929, The Virgil Michel Papers Z 28: 1, SJAA.

Orate Fratres' well-proportioned margins.[136] Aside from their more literary-based correspondence, Starr, at times, served as a sort of on-the-ground resource for Michel, reporting the goings-on of parishes where she attended and how (or if) congregations were interacting with the liturgy.[137] Continually, her acquaintances and meetings prompted her to vouch for Michel's journal.[138] She even kept Michel in touch with her international liturgical travels; when she visited the Cathedral at Milan, Italy, she attempted to secure a missal before Mass so she might study the Ambrosian Rite.[139]

Aside from her work for *Orate Fratres*, while she was still living in Chicago, Starr was involved with the Chicago Calvert Club, along with Sara B. O'Neill and other notable Catholic Chicagoans, giving occasional lectures. On April 11, 1929, Starr was invited to speak to the Calvert Club about "anything" with regard to liturgy; in her usual straightforward way, she informed Virgil Michel, "I shall begin with a general view on the deplorable ignorance of Catholics about the Mass."[140] Starr took speeches such as this one as opportunities to advertise *Orate Fratres*, and, in writing Michel about her speech, assured

---

[136] Ellen Gates Starr to Virgil Michel, May 31, 1927, The Virgil Michel Papers Z 28: 1, SJAA.

[137] For example, in March 1927 she wrote to Michel, "I do observe with encouragement that a number of people in the congregation at St. Thomas's have Missals and use them." Ellen Gates Starr to Virgil Michel, March 1927, The Virgil Michel Papers Z 28: 1, SJAA.

[138] She described sending a married woman a Breviary pamphlet, a number of *Orate Fratres* issues, the *Tre Ore* pamphlet, and "several other things," and concluded that she "strongly urged upon her subscribing for *Orate Fratres*." Ellen Gates Starr to Virgil Michel, June 10, 1929, The Virgil Michel Papers Z 28: 1, SJAA.

[139] She asked a priest whom she met in the church and, "politely and evidently in haste," he said that he regretted it was a holiday and all the shops closed. Unsatisfied, she proceeded to storm the sacristy where she respectfully convinced "a deaf and dull old sacristan" to allow her to look at the Ambrosian rite. Ellen Gates Starr to Virgil Michel, April 8, 1929, The Virgil Michel Papers Z 28: 1, SJAA.

[140] Sara B. O'Neill, who had been under the instruction of some religious and "may be ready to begin in the Breviary" had been supportive of this endeavor, and there were even some priests "who probably need to be urged to do something about their poor languishing flocks" with regard to knowledge of the liturgy. "I shall try not to offend," she wryly noted. Ellen Gates Starr to Virgil Michel, March 13, 1929, The Virgil Michel Papers Z 28: 1, SJAA.

him she would do her best to improve the "circulations of the Liturgical Press" and expressed her suspicion that Miss O'Neill would also successfully sell some of the publications at the event.[141]

As one who had become Catholic as an adult, Starr was acutely aware of the need for good catechesis. She was routinely surprised by the wealth of the liturgical life of which the average educated Catholic was completely unaware. In a letter to Virgil Michel in April 1929, Starr related how a young woman, born Catholic, had come to Hull-House to consult her. The young woman had become "very restless and troubled" and wanted to "know more about the Faith and liturgy."[142] The young woman, not knowing how to discover more, appealed to an Anglican friend, a "last resort" which Starr thought "Pathetic." In Starr's mind, it was tragic that "so little and so *little teaching*, too," was given to young Catholics, aside from the penny catechism: "I wonder what they do all those years that they are under instruction—So you see, I *need* things to work with."[143] Starr reasoned, "I shall advise this young woman, when she comes, to take in *Orate Fratres*." Starr told Michel that the young woman was not alone in her frustration and that she had given the same advice to a new Catholic in Pittsburgh, observing: "Converts have more to go on, usually; for they wouldn't be converts if they hadn't already done something towards it."[144] Starr knew well that, despite the laudable efforts of some sisters, not all school-age Catholic children were being cultivated in liturgical study, evidenced by a characteristically spicy run-in with a religious sister *en route* to Mass in January 1930:

> I have railed formally and privately about doing the rosary at Mass
> for years—ever since I became a Catholic. I even arise or depart from

[141] Ellen Gates Starr to Virgil Michel, March 13, 1929, The Virgil Michel Papers Z 28: 1, SJAA. For this event, Starr requested that the Liturgical Press send some twenty-five copies of *My Sacrifice and Yours*, a book she had already read, as Michel had sent her a copy two years prior, along with several pamphlets which the Liturgical Press was in the habit of putting together, including her own article "Reflections on the Breviary" and Fr. William Busch's "Principal Parts of the Mass." Ellen Gates Starr to Virgil Michel, April 6, 1929, The Virgil Michel Papers Z 28: 1, SJAA.

[142] Ellen Gates Starr to Virgil Michel, January 31, 1929, The Virgil Michel Papers Z 28: 1, SJAA.

[143] Ibid.

[144] Ibid.

a church when I see they are about to do it. I even told a sister, leading her flock into church, while I was going in [that I was going to leave if they started praying the rosary.] "You aren't going to miss Mass!" she said, in a horror, struck tone. "*No*, I'm going to find a church where I shall *not* miss Mass." May some idea *aside* from that of a hyper-irritated *elderly* lay woman have permeated her intelligence.[145]

Again, Starr never missed an opportunity for a pointed comment.

Starr's Contribution to the Liturgical Movement

Though Starr was effective as a writer, lecturer, and proponent of the liturgy, her writing appears only five times in *Orate Fratres* and, occasionally, in the less scholarly magazine *Sponsa Regis*. An unfortunate part of Starr's biography was her struggle with physical pain and regular hospital stays, culminating in a botched spinal operation which left her paralyzed in 1929.[146] Virgil Michel continued to contact Starr through the end of January 1930, wondering, "How about a Breviary article some time? Would it be too taxing for you?"[147] Starr had, by this time, moved to Suffern, New York, away from Hull-House and to the much different atmosphere of the Convent of the Holy Child.[148] As noted above, despite the natural connection of the liturgical movement with social action, more secular institutions, including Starr's former situation at Hull-House, ultimately did not successfully become citadels of the movement.[149] By moving to Holy Child, Starr chose a new institution in which she could more clearly live out her spiritual identity as a Roman Catholic, as well as have access to medical attention.

With this move, after 1930, Starr lost contact with the liturgical movement as Virgil Michel, her main contact, also suffered a severe

[145] Ellen Gates Starr to Virgil Michel, January 20, 1930, The Virgil Michel Papers Z 28: 1, SJAA.

[146] Ellen Gates Starr to Virgil Michel, August 5, 1929, The Virgil Michel Papers Z 28: 1, SJAA.

[147] Virgil Michel to Ellen Gates Starr, August, 21, 1929, The Virgil Michel Papers Z 28: 1, SJAA.

[148] For a more complete story of Ellen Gates Starr's move to Holy Child, see Jennifer Lynne Bosch, "Strong Soul, Frail Body, 1920–1940," in "The Life of Ellen Gates Starr, 1859–1940" (PhD diss., Miami University, 1990), 151–73.

[149] Despite the fact that some "religious" or "prayer" activity did take place at Hull-House, at least, Starr ultimately found it lacking in spiritual substance. Some American settlement houses made religion a more central part of their services.

breakdown in health.[150] It was not until 1935 that Starr wrote to him again. After an article she had written for the *Catholic World* was rejected as "too liturgical," she thought of *Orate Fratres*, the only liturgical magazine.[151] Her manuscript was, however, "too long and too simple for *Orate Fratres*," and she indicated that she was not surprised and wondered if the ordinary parish congregation member "may have advanced liturgically since I stepped out of the world but I wonder if very safely."[152] She chose to send her work to *Sponsa Regis*, which Virgil Michel advised was "all right" but that its readers were not "by any means . . . in the habit of using the missal intelligently." He invited her again, "Do you think that you would want to try your hand at a short article for *Orate Fratres* that is not so simple or introductory, on any liturgical topic—say, for instance, 'The Laity and the Breviary'?"[153] But she responded on January 14, 1936, that this sounded very similar to what she had done seven years before and was not sure she could do much better than that. In lieu of this, she suggested that her last public lecture at the Calvert Club might be a good subject for an article and included her notes.[154] These, unfortunately, did not appear; it is likely that Virgil Michel was unable to work with her further before his own health declined rapidly. Starr herself would die two years after Michel, in Suffern, New York, in 1940.

[150] Michel's exhausting pace had worn out both his eyes and nerves so that, despite the warnings of his superiors in 1930 against overtaxing himself, by late April his eyes had completely failed and he was near nervous collapse. Unable to even fulfill his daily obligation of saying the Office, Michel was assigned to the Native American missions in northern Minnesota. He was completely disconnected from the liturgical movement, save for some correspondence with Sr. Jane Marie Murray, OP, and Sr. Estelle Hackett, OP, who were working on the Christ-Life Series. He returned to Collegeville, reluctantly, to serve as dean in 1933. Marx, *Virgil Michel and the Liturgical Movement*, 161–65.

[151] Ellen Gates Starr to Virgil Michel, October 24, 1935, The Virgil Michel Papers Z 28: 1, SJAA.

[152] Ellen Gates Starr to Virgil Michel, November 27, 1935, The Virgil Michel Papers Z 28: 1, SJAA.

[153] Virgil Michel to Ellen Gates Starr, December 8, 1935, The Virgil Michel Papers Z 28: 1, SJAA.

[154] Ellen Gates Starr to Virgil Michel, January 14, 1936, The Virgil Michel Papers Z 28: 1, SJAA.

Starr's privilege as an educated, skilled, and independent trades-woman offered her the freedom to engage in social and political action issues of her day and in her community. Her study and practice of the liturgy led her to astute observations on the quality of popular piety in relation to the formal worship of the Church. Some of Starr's observations with regard to Requiem Masses, individual devotions during the liturgy, and the social responsibility of the Christian not only meshed with the "organ" of the liturgical movement but anticipated the issues which would become pertinent for liturgical reformers.[155] Starr, like so many of her liturgically minded peers and successors, was a woman who integrated her life, work, and faith with both individual and corporate action.

CATECHISTS, WRITERS, AND STUDENTS, WOMEN IN *ORATE FRATRES* COMMENTING ON THE LITURGY

Young Women and the Study of the Liturgy

The witness of Justine Ward and Ellen Gates Starr suggests three pathways for lay women's liturgical interest during this period: the connection of liturgy and social responsibility, the importance of finely and carefully crafted liturgical arts as appropriately reflecting the depth of liturgical prayer, and the necessity of catechesis through and about the liturgy. Many women addressed these themes through articles and letters written to *Orate Fratres* during the earliest years of the liturgical movement. Their writing and interest reflect the increasing population of women who established forums for action, entertainment, and education, all designed to incorporate the goals of the liturgical movement. For example, with regard to liturgy and social responsibility, women like Elizabeth Tobin reflected on the potential of liturgical participation as profoundly social. As a senior student of Saint Mary's College of Notre Dame, Indiana, she submitted a short article to *Orate Fratres*, in which she claimed:

> To some it may seem an overstatement to suggest as a remedy for present day industrial evils active participation in the holy Sacrifice of the Mass. Yet it is a fact that the one real hope for the cure of the diseases afflicting the body economic is just that. Teach the people not

---

[155] For example, Ellen Gates Starr, "A Few Trials of Happy Convert," 33–34; and Ellen Gates Starr, "Settlements and the Church's Duty," *Publications of the Church of Social Action*, no. 28 (1896), EGSP 19/5, Sophia Smith Collection.

only to love the Mass but to participate in it by use of the Missal. An industrial system where justice, peace, and charity reign will be the result. This is the thesis we wish to establish by a diagnosis of the industrial ills.[156]

Drawing on Pope Leo XIII's (1810–1903) social encyclical on labor, *Rerum Novarum*, of 1891, Tobin concluded that the moral, economic, and social evils generated by labor practices could only be reformed by the reformation of an individual. Instead of looking to structural change alone, individuals must first "suffer a renewal of religious life"; only a spiritual renewal could provide the proper ground for social reform. In order to illustrate her point, Tobin drew on several texts from the liturgy which illustrated "lessons of justice," summarizing:

> With such a spirit of justice and peace gained from the liturgy, what may the world hope for charity? Love is a lesson taught in each epistle and gospel. . . . Exaggerated individualism, which is so prevalent today, is a form of selfishness entirely separated from the Christian ideal of love one's neighbor.[157]

Tobin's example is not isolated, though somewhat unique for her position as a young college student. The activity of lay women with regard to social justice would become much more visible with the advocacy of the Catholic Worker Movement, founded by Dorothy Day, Catherine de Hueck Doherty of Friendship House, the American Grail Movement, and the work of Catholic Worker artist Ade Bethune.

Aside from an interest in the liturgy's potential for social renewal, a growing advocacy for the liturgical arts was fostered among persons convinced that the power of finely crafted arts could tend the spirit to God. This caught the imagination of young women, such as Kathleen Burns, a student of Marygrove College of Detroit, Michigan, who wrote about the possibilities for liturgy as a subject for learning literature in "Liturgy and the College English Class," which appeared in *Orate Fratres* in 1928.[158] Burns was actually inspired by the breviary articles of Ellen Gates Starr, in which Starr drew attention to the strik-

---

[156] Elizabeth Tobin, "The Liturgy: A Remedy for Industrial Evils," *Orate Fratres* 3, no. 12 (1929): 389.

[157] Ibid., 391.

[158] Kathleen Burns, "Liturgy and the College English Class," *Orate Fratres* 2, no. 11 (1928): 214–19.

ing power of metaphor in liturgical poetry. In her own article, Burns suggested that:

> It would surely help to further the liturgical apostolate, as well as the apostolate of Catholic literature, if the students in the English classes of Catholic colleges were encouraged to look to the missal for literary inspiration, and particularly for poetic inspiration.[159]

Burns recommended that a study of the "poetry of Mary Magdalen" or "the rite of benediction" might give rise to contemplation of the world stirred by purest emotions—which she listed as love, grief, patriotism, religion, and nature—and gave several examples to illustrate her point (likely of her own composition). In turn, newly composed poetry, inspired by texts and themes of the liturgy, could have "a spiritualizing influence upon the mind of the writer," forming her eyes and heart to see God in all works. Burns concluded, "It would be, if consistently developed, a Christianizing force in the field of contemporary poetry, now so largely materialistic, and would so forward the central idea of the liturgical movement, *Instaurare omnia in Christo*, for it would reestablish poetry in Christ."[160]

In other artistic realms during this early period, lay women sought creative outlets for the liturgy in the dramatic. Cecilia Young, writing in March 1933 for *Orate Fratres*, described how a group of young people in the cathedral parish of Holy Name in Chicago organized a dramatic club, the Chicago Cathedral Players, in order to "stage playlets that are calculated to convey to its patrons a deeper liturgical understanding of the more prominent feasts and seasons of the ecclesiastical year."[161] Aside from this aim, Young described a secondary motive, which was to provide "wholesome recreation and stimulation to the morale" for parishioners who suffered from the evils of economic depression, with special efforts being made to "reach the lonely,

---

[159] Ibid., 214. "Much has been said of the poetic liturgy of the Church, but very little of the liturgical poetry which is its outgrowth. By liturgical poetry is not meant poetry which is a part of the liturgy as, for example, the 'Dies Irae,' but poetry which is the result of the writer's meditation on the liturgical texts, and of his finding reflections of liturgical themes in the beauties of nature and the experiences of the human heart."

[160] Ibid., 219.

[161] Cecilia Young, "Liturgical Drama Movement," *Orate Fratres* 7, no. 5 (1933): 226.

down-hearted people of the district."[162] The plays were in the style of a medieval mystery play, well-advertised, and were well attended by people from "various strata" of the city.[163] For example, a nativity play, staged on Christmas Eve, and an Epiphany play about the three magi were both "praiseworthy" undertakings and produced, as Young concluded, their intended effects: "Christian encouragement and cheer for the poor and depressed, a strengthening of the faith and spirit of players and visitors as a fitting preparation for the feasts to be celebrated on the following days."[164] Both Burns and Young placed liturgical knowledge and participation, creativity, and spiritual nourishment in stark contrast to those less wholesome cultural norms pervading modern society, and all three young women (Tobin, Burns, and Young) saw the liturgy and the liturgical movement as a means for renewing society.

Women and the Liturgical Arts

Aside from Justine Ward, other lay women also worked to promote liturgical music, such as Wanda Birder, a graduate of the Minneapolis School of Music, who encouraged education in liturgical music. Along with her husband, Cecil Birder, Wanda Birder conducted a monthlong music course in St. James Parish of Aitkin, Minnesota, with a view toward better church singing in a generally rural parish culture.[165]

---

[162] Ibid.

[163] "The large stage of the parish hall was divided into two sections, each Mystery being presented on its own stage in the ancient custom by alternating casts of thirty-six players, all appearing in medieval costumes, designed and prepared by the members of the group under the direction of the writer. A genuine simplicity and devotion was the outstanding characteristic of the entire performance and setting, the greatest respect and interest was noted in the large audience that was composed by people from various strata of the city's population." Cecilia Young, "Liturgical Drama Movement," 226–27.

[164] Ibid., 227.

[165] "Mr. Birder conducted classes in the physiology of the voice, voice placing, sight reading, choir directing, polyphonic music and plain chant, using the junior and senior choirs of the parish for demonstration purposes. Mrs. Birder gave lessons in pipe organ, piano, sight reading, harmony, and ear training. On three evenings of each week special work was done in choir organization, singing, and directing. The entire course for the month was free for the members of the parish, while externals were charged the small sum of ten dollars." "Liturgical Briefs," *Orate Fratres* 4, no. 11 (1930): 475.

Interestingly, those who advocated for liturgical education in *Orate Fratres* did not stress that liturgical music should be sung by only boys or men. Due to shifting diocesan policies in the United States, liturgical musicians could develop children's choirs which included both boys and girls, or adult choirs which also included women.[166] The inclusion of women and girls in parish choirs where an all-male choir "was not possible" became the officially adopted regulation by the Diocese of Baltimore in 1930 and was followed by the adoption of like measures by the Dioceses of Indianapolis, St. Louis, Cincinnati, Cleveland, Pittsburgh, Rochester, Newark, and San Francisco by 1935.[167] In a rare example from the American Southwest, Eleanor Tracy of Santa Barbara, California, witnessed another example of teaching children chant and its powerful effect. She related her visit in December 1934 to the town of Las Cruces, New Mexico, where she happened upon what she expected to be a quiet Mass at which she resigned herself to saying a few rosaries. However, she related to *Orate Fratres*:

> [T]o my joy and amazement I heard high and clear the voices of children intoning "Da pacem Domine. . . ." A High Mass, and the Proper as well as the Ordinary chant all most beautifully and reverently rendered. And by whom? School children, chiefly Mexican, a choir of them standing in the front pews and led by a young woman who did not seem to be over twenty. It was a contrast to Mass in a large city just the week before, and if this perfection can be achieved in a town set in our last Western spaces, why not everywhere?[168]

Tracy's example of liturgical chant is particularly interesting because she witnessed young, Latino/a children experiencing the "best" form

---

[166] For example, "Liturgical Briefs," *Orate Fratres* 5, no. 5 (1931): 245–46, which noted that the Diocese of Baltimore had revised its Regulations of the Archdiocesan Commission of Music, including the note that "Women are allowed, by special dispensation for the United States, to sing in church where an all-male choir is not possible," and "In every school there should be a children's choir of both boys and girls." Other articles included the encouragement of the study of sacred music in all-girls' schools, such as the Catholic Girls' High School in Los Angeles, California, in which a course in sacred music was inaugurated. See "Liturgical Briefs," *Orate Fratres* 4, no. 3 (1930): 137.

[167] "Liturgical Briefs," *Orate Fratres* 9, no. 9 (1935): 422.

[168] Eleanor Tracy, "Perfection in New Mexico," in "The Apostolate," *Orate Fratres* 9, no. 2 (1934): 91.

of liturgical worship (an uncommon example from a largely midwestern liturgical movement). Her example also suggests, however, that, despite the cultural context, Gregorian liturgical chant was viewed to be normative for Catholic music and how little inculturation, which would become one of the strains of the Second Vatican Council, was operative in the liturgical movement. Catholic culture was often an imported force: the extent to which liturgy reflected culture was constantly a point in tension.[169]

All the liturgical arts, of course, were promoted in various liturgical art associations and publications, including the Catholic Art Association and the aforementioned LAS. The *Liturgical Arts Quarterly*, begun in 1931 and following the establishment of the LAS in 1928, included examples of women's art from its first volume, including E. Charlton Fortune, California impressionist-turned-liturgical adviser and frequent correspondent of Maurice Lavanoux.[170] The *Liturgical Arts Quarterly* also enjoined Hildreth Meière to serve as one of its directors, as Meière was interested in the ability of art to function in service of reli-

---

[169] "Liturgy and culture" was one of Virgil Michel's interests; yet "culture" was usually understood as that which was "secular," something which the liturgy must come to reform and change. See Virgil Michel, "The Liturgy and Catholic Life," *Orate Fratres* 13, no. 7 (1939): 304. This article, published posthumously, draws from a manuscript upon which Michel was working at his death, titled "Liturgy and Christian Culture." See The Virgil Michel Papers Z 34: 3, SJAA. The book was published as Virgil Michel, *The Social Question: Essays on Capitalism and Christianity*, ed. Robert L. Spaeth (Collegeville, MN: Saint John's University Office of Academic Affairs, 1987). See also See Paul Marx, "Liturgy and Culture," in *Virgil Michel and the Liturgical Movement* (Collegeville, MN: Liturgical Press, 1954), 255–97.

[170] For more information on women's contributions to liturgical art, see Rebecca Berru Davis, "Women Artists of the Liturgical Movement: The Contributions of E. Charlton Fortune, Sr. Helene O'Connor, OP, and Ade Bethune," (PhD diss., Graduate Theological Union, 2011). Davis's research in the *Liturgical Arts Society* journal, the *Liturgical Arts Quarterly* (hereafter *LAQ*) yielded more than two hundred women artists who were included and advertised in its pages, including Elsa Schmid, featured in Hildreth Meière's "A Modern Way of the Cross in Mosaic," *LAQ* 1, no. 1 (1931): 34–37; Edith Morton Eustis, "Eighteenth Century Catholic Stone Carvings in New Mexico," *LAQ* 1, no. 3 (1932): 112–15; and Hazel Clere, featured in Leopold Araud's article "The Church of the Most Precious Blood (in Astoria, Long Island, NY)," *LAQ* 1, no. 4 (1932): 146–47.

gion. Finally, the *Liturgical Arts Quarterly* reviewed liturgical artists, including lay women, such as German-born mosaic artist Elsa Schmid.[171]

Lay Women, Liturgical Catechesis, and the Use of the Breviary

With regard to catechesis, explaining the accessibility of the breviary to the laity and affirming the lay person's "ability to plumb liturgical depths" was taken up by other laywomen contributors to *Orate Fratres*, such as Grace Schutte of St. Paul, Minnesota. In 1933, her article, "The Divine Office and the Laity," took up the banner which Ellen Gates Starr had touted by asking, "Would you like to participate to a fuller degree in the official life of the Church?"[172] Grace Schutte urged her readers:

> You have already become a very active member of the Mystical Body of Christ if you not merely attend Mass but actually follow the Mass prayers with the aid of the Missal, for you are offering in a proper manner the Church's one great Sacrifice. To prolong throughout the day the splendor and radiance of this glorious morning Sacrifice, I would urge the recitation of some part at least of the Church's Hour Prayers or the Divine Office.[173]

---

[171] See Hildreth Meière, "A Modern Way of the Cross in Mosaic," *LAQ* 1, no. 1 (1931): 35–37. Meière reviewed the recent work of Elsa Schmid, who had completed a set of Stations of the Cross in New York City: "The layman in art will of course approach these panels [of Elsa Schmid] with a very different point of view from that of the amateur of mosaics, and he will be quite justified in demanding first, 'Are they good religious art? Do they serve their fundamental purpose of bringing home to the worshipper the awful drama of the Passion?' The answer is unquestionably, 'Yes.' Here, throughout, is an intensity of emotion which expresses love and tenderness, sorrow and suffering, dignity and death, because these things have been truly felt by the artist, not merely depicted. Here is a directness of attack, a paring down of each episode to its essentials, which calls to mind the power of the Christian primitives; while the clarity, vibrance, and rareness of the color is a purely modern contribution. The pious can look on these Stations and suffer with the suffering Lord as they will never be moved to by the lifeless, if elaborate, illustrations which hang in so many churches; and those who are sensitive to artistic beauty—and who, after all, is not?—will feel that added sense of worship and of awe which is art's function to give in the service of religion." Meière, 36.

[172] Grace Schutte, "The Divine Office and the Liturgy," *Orate Fratres* 7, no. 11 (1933): 492.

[173] Ibid.

While Schutte admitted that the suggestion of the Office for the laity was startling and the breviary quite distant from the likes of the lay folk, she hoped that, by describing her own entrance to the life of liturgical prayer, she would be "destroying this false notion" and inviting others to familiarize themselves with this way of being the Mystical Body. Schutte described her entrance into using the breviary, which was at the suggestion of a priest "with faith" in her ability, and described how very much impressed she was by the "beauty and propriety" of the psalms and prayers as she began to recite Compline daily. She realized, as she continued month by month, that she could add more of the day hours and assured her readers that she was able to find time in her daily schedule, even with an eight-hour working day.[174]

Grace Schutte stressed that one of the greatest values of liturgical prayer—such as the Office—was its ability to draw one out of "private religious enthusiasm" which could be inconstant, based on "vacillating personal feelings," which allowed prayer to be controlled by emotions rather than faith.[175] She found that recitation of daily liturgical prayer drew one closer with the members of the Mystical Body:

> One feels a stronger bond of union with other members of the Mystical Body of Christ, for when we join in the Church's official prayers, we are raised above the sphere of the personal. Liturgical prayers are universal in their scope—they are truly Catholic. We no longer pray for ourselves alone, but we are offering homage and presenting petitions to God in the name of all those who are united to us in the mystical union of Christ and His Church.[176]

Like many others of her fellow writers preaching the liturgical life, she was sorry to claim that "too many of us of the laity . . . are merely existing in the peripheral zone of the treasury of our Catholic faith," and

---

[174] "The Office seems to lend an edge to private prayers. What is more, I seem to find more time for my private devotions, such as meditations, rosary, particular examens, etc. The necessity of setting aside a definite period every day for the recitation of the Office has forced me to arrange a daily schedule and, somehow, daily schedules have a way of helping us to utilize many moments hitherto wasted upon trifles." Schutte, "The Divine Office and the Liturgy," 494.

[175] Ibid., 494–95.

[176] Ibid., 494.

she encouraged other lay persons like herself to realize their Catholic lives to the fullest.[177]

In fact, as Ellen Gates Starr had suspected in 1935, more lay people and readers of *Orate Fratres* had become familiar with the breviary. By the latter part of the 1930s, use of the breviary among lay folk had become somewhat more common, evidenced by movements such as the formation of the League of the Divine Office and an increase in persons writing about the breviary not only in *Orate Fratres* but also in Catholic diocesan weeklies.[178] Lay people, meanwhile, noted the need for a simplified version, such as Miss M. E. J., who wrote in "The Apostolate" section of *Orate Fratres* in December 1936:

> No doubt as an individual I make many mistakes, but go right on in any case, as it is such an outlet for the soul in her desire for praise and adoration, in its truly liturgical form. I think a small book, even in pamphlet form, with simple explanation, for the proper recitation of divine office in its many details—in English—would be must helpful to souls not perfectly familiar with Latin.[179]

Miss M. E. J. had rightly identified a need, as, also in 1936, Rodolphe Hoornaert and William Busch published *The Breviary and the Laity*, a

---

[177] Ibid., 495.

[178] For example, *Orate Fratres* reports that, in 1937, Miss Marie Shields Halvey contributed a series of articles on the recitation of the Divine Office by lay people to a number of diocesan weeklies. "League of the Divine Office," in "The Apostolate," *Orate Fratres* 12, no. 2 (1937): 88. See also, Miss G. of New York, who wrote to the editor in November 1937, who, while she was not a member of the League of the Divine Office, was associated with the Dominicans as a tertiary and prayed the breviary every day: "I have never sent in my name for the League of the Divine Office because, being a Dominican tertiary, I use their breviary: I have used it about twelve years now, and it is the core of my spiritual life, a source of inspiration every day." "From an Old Friend," in "The Apostolate," *Orate Fratres* 12, no. 1 (1937): 42.

[179] Miss M. E. J., "In Answer to a Circular" (Virgil Michel had sent inquiries to those who had dropped subscriptions; Miss M. E. J., like numerous others, had to drop her subscription "reluctantly" owing to her reduced income), "The Apostolate," *Orate Fratres* 11, no. 2 (1936): 91. Miss M. E. J. continued: "Living the liturgical life in union with the Church interiorly reacts on one's daily life in every aspect and certainly brings with it peace which the world cannot give and which surpasses all understanding, even in the world of one who has because of circumstances to live in the world rather than in the cloister."

Popular Liturgical Library pamphlet which was the product of work done by seminarians in their course of study on the breviary.[180] The pamphlet both prompted interest in lay use of the breviary and affirmed those who were interested in praying the Divine Office that lay people certainly had the ability to do so. Likewise, shortly afterward, in 1941, Liturgical Press issued the first edition of *A Short Breviary*, "an unofficial adaption, primarily by abridgement, rearrangement, and translation, of Breviarium monasticum," for use by religious and the laity.[181] This version went through two more editions, in 1954 and 1962. Lay women continued to make use of the breviary in private and public,[182] ask for better, cheaper editions, and report their use of the breviary to *Orate Fratres* as the liturgical movement unfolded.[183]

[180] Rodolphe Hoonaert and William Busch, *The Breviary and the Laity*, Popular Liturgical Library, ser. 1, no. 7 (Collegeville, MN: Liturgical Press, 1936).

[181] William George Heidt, *A Short Breviary: for Religious and Laity* (Collegeville, MN: Liturgical Press, 1941).

[182] In 1937, Elizabeth Nash of New York City described how she and two other women gathered for Sunday Vespers in a New York public park. Searching for a place to sit, they spotted a Pierce-Arrow, "with a long running board . . . and upon this we descended almost as one woman and with but one thought." Nash wrote: "Vespers in this day when your city church knows it not and one must needs say it alone or perhaps occasionally in company with a few others . . . is doubtlessly offered up in many seemingly unlikely places. But we three contend that never, anywhere, have the concluding lines of the office—the little versicle following our Lady's anthem—been rendered with more genuine meaning and fervor than that with which we rendered them." Elizabeth Nash, "'Et Cum Fratribus nostris absentibus,'" in "The Apostolate," *Orate Fratres* 12, no. 1 (1937): 38–39.

[183] Miss M. C. of Long Island, New York, wrote the editor in November 1937: "It is essential that the Catholic faithful become better acquainted with the liturgy in all its aspects. But I doubt whether many of the clergy have informed themselves about the breviary in its relation to the laity. When I sent to you for my copy of the *Breviary and the Laity*, you enclosed a copy of *Orate Fratres*, which is the most comprehensive publication (Catholic) I have ever come across; and when I return to our home parish I shall try to interest the pastor in the periodical and in what it stands for. Catholic people are eager, but they must be shown the way. Most Catholic publications are too high-priced for the average person. After all, it is souls, and not money, that count before God." Miss M. C., "Laity and the Liturgy," in "The Apostolate," *Orate Fratres* 12, no. 2 (1937): 43.

Catechesis for children was also an issue grappled with by Catholic lay women, such as Dona Madigan of Laramie, Wyoming, who identified herself "among that happy throng of catechists."[184] She also expressed distress over an "appalling lack" of "a workable knowledge of their religion among Catholics."[185] Also one who had become Catholic as an adult, Madigan spent many years teaching young children, preparing them for the sacraments. She reported to *Orate Fratres* that she had recently added the teaching of girls in confirmation years and had conducted religious instruction in a Catholic women's club, which included liturgical study. She admitted that, being a new Catholic, she might "expect too much" of her fellow Catholics and observed that, while she found *Orate Fratres* a wonderful help in applying the liturgy to daily life, she felt that, "strange as it seems, many supposedly intelligent Catholics do not appear to understand."[186] Madigan believed that religion "must be interwoven" closely with life and that, for herself, *Orate Fratres* had helped her:

> For myself, the Mass has always meant much; but I feel, after studying the liturgy and reading the *Orate Fratres*, that I was poor indeed before, and now rich indeed; for it has helped weave into a perfect pattern my life. Now I live liturgically.[187]

But, she urged the editor that Catholics needed proper instruction and intelligent and willing women and men to teach. Catholics must also have more simplicity if the rich contents of *Orate Fratres* were to reach more of the faithful:

[184] Dona Madigan, "Problems of a Convert Catechist," in "The Apostolate," *Orate Fratres* 7, no. 9 (1933): 424.

[185] Ibid. "Indifference is the stumbling-block for all advancement, no matter which branch of work is attempted. No one seems to comprehend the tragedy of the little ones' going week in and week out without proper instruction. Worship must have cooperation at home, in order to accomplish anything in the one hour a week we have to teach. We need intelligent and willing men and women to teach; not the ones who give their time and not their heart and soul, for without the spirit the effort is fruitless." Dona Madigan, "Problems of a Convert Catechist," 425.

[186] Ibid., 425.

[187] Ibid.

More instruction of the laity, less play of words from which only the few gain inspiration. More urging to study the Mass, for Catholics do not know the Mass; if they did, they could not make the mistakes they do.[188]

Madigan astutely pointed out the perennial problem of the liturgical movement, despite its best efforts to become more popular or accessible to lay folk. The liturgical movement was continuously, from its beginning, in danger of being too intellectual, abstract, or complicated for the average lay Catholic to understand or follow.

As the example of Madigan also suggests, the education of children was another subject frequented by lay, non-religious women. While children's religious education was often the realm of religious sisters and, indeed, religious sisters frequently were among the most enthusiastic about the liturgy as a source for education, lay women also served as catechists and "concerned citizens" with regard to the state of children's education. Teaching children the liturgy also took place within children's clubs led or organized by women; even a group of Girl Scouts in New York City who, under the direction of Miss Mabel Shannon, prepared, printed, and recited Vespers for the Feast of All Saints in 1937.[189] In other cases, women found *Orate Fratres* a source for self-education, such as Helen M. Calpin of St. Louis, Missouri, who wrote, in addition to renewing her subscription, "I look forward to every issue and, for me, it has been a liberal education in many things relating to our holy Faith."[190] Some, who became involved in study clubs, were surprised how few Catholics took advantage of resources which were available to them. Rose E. Haus, who attended a study club at the Convent of Cenacle in New York, wrote with surprise that what her group studied "seems to be absolutely new to ninety-nine per cent of the members, although they might be classed as the more intelligent Catholic girls and are from all parts of New York."[191] Even though resources for learning the liturgy, faith, and Catholic Action were available, convincing Catholics to make use of them was another task.

[188] Ibid.

[189] Mabel Shannon, "League of the Divine Office," in "The Apostolate," *Orate Fratres* 12, no. 2 (1937): 88.

[190] Helen M. Calpin, "An Education in the Faith," in "The Apostolate," *Orate Fratres* 7, no. 4 (1933): 187.

[191] Rose E. Haus, "A Friend Writes," in "The Apostolate," *Orate Fratres* 8, no. 6 (1934): 284.

Women's Study Clubs, the NCCW, and Other Catholic Women's Groups

Finally, while the full-length articles by readily recognizable personas, or even one-time article writers, readily reveal some of the lay women proponents of the liturgical movement, one must also ask to what extent liturgical interest permeated the less public or more anonymous women who sat in pews, attended church functions, and met with fellow Catholic women in social settings. As suggested by some of the college students' descriptions of artistic endeavors or catechists citing good material, liturgical issues and questions were a subject of study among women's groups, frequented the magazine pages of popular Catholic journals, and crept into the various Catholic women's groups and study clubs popular within parishes. The editorial column of *Orate Fratres* encouraged both men and women in the pursuit of their interest in liturgical matters, affirming that neither were lay persons who expressed a keen interest in things liturgical alone, nor were they lesser members of the Mystical Body. Indeed, the hierarchy vested with the sacrament of orders and spiritual powers were there "for the people," and lay readers should not feel "a touch of reserve in expressing their interest in the liturgy, as if they were trespassing on forbidden ground."[192]

While the women discussed thus far do not tend to identify with the more gendered approach to women's role in the liturgical life, as had been the case in Europe, women in study clubs or national Catholic women's groups often did take up the banner, or at least were exposed to the banner, of women's special role in the Mystical Body of Christ. The role of Christian women was an interest of Virgil Michel's, who, at an address given at a joint meeting of the Central Verein of America and the Catholic Women's Union during the national convention in St. Cloud, Minnesota, in August 1928, stressed that one of the most powerful ways to transform and strengthen the Christian in sacramental assimilation with Christ, and displace selfish individualism, paganism, egotism, and self-deification, was through the Christian woman:

> We are thus in crying need of a renewal in Christ, of a return to a
> deeper understanding of the ideals of Christianity, of a fuller submission of the souls of men to the action of divine grace as enacted in the

---

[192] Virgil Michel, "Only a Layman," *Orate Fratres* 1, no. 11 (1927): 346.

life of the Church of God. How is that to be brought about? What is one of the most powerful natural means of bringing souls of men into contact with these channels of grace, of disposing them towards this contact? The answer is WOMAN![193]

Michel described the Christian woman as a "natural sacrament" in the world, an "external sign of inner grace" which radiated goodness, compelling the "most debased of men" to goodness by inviting them to drink deeply of the "fountain of the true Christian spirit, the life of the Church."[194] Instead of appealing to the "lower nature of man,"[195] woman must, in fact, become "another Christ," burning with the zeal of the early Christians and the Spirit of Christ, as she united her heart in the one true Sacrifice eternal of the Altar.[196] Such language reveals a strongly gendered understanding of the Church and its members; women are both likened to the "Church," as a natural sacrament in the world, and urged to become "another Christ."

Michel was clearly drawing upon the wave of theological commentary prevalent among German and Austrian theologians regarding women's roles in the liturgical life, including women liturgical authors. He noted, without naming her, that a "woman in Austria" (actually, Frau Dr. Hieronimi) wrote of the liturgical movement:

There is much talk today of a liturgical movement, of a renewal of our holy liturgy and of the necessity to bring it back into close contact with the faithful. What can we women do as our share in the solution of this burning question? Is there not an apostolate here that literally cries for the co-operation of us women? The spiritual energies work with great-

[193] Virgil Michel, "The Liturgy and Catholic Women," *Orate Fratres* 3, no. 9 (1929): 274.

[194] Ibid.

[195] Virgil Michel, *The Liturgical Movement and the Catholic Woman*, Popular Liturgical Library Series (Collegeville: Liturgical Press, 1959), 9. This work is a pamphlet form of the address Michel had given in August 1928 to a joint meeting of the Central Verein of America and the Catholic Women's Union and reprinted in part in *Orate Fratres* 3, no. 9 (1928): 270–79. While, in the pre-World War II period, very few were writing about women's self-realization with regard to the liturgy, this became an increasingly popular subject in the Second World War Period and into the 1950s; the Liturgical Press, recalling Michel's earlier work, thought it timely to republish his thoughts on the liturgy and Catholic women in pamphlet form.

[196] Michel, "The Liturgy and Catholic Women," 274–75.

est efficacy in the family. The family, taught and inspired by its priestess, the mother, must become the cradle unto a new liturgical life.[197]

As did Hieronimi, Michel stressed that woman was "everywhere a great power for good," but her "greatest possibilities lie in the home":

> Unless the mother has the proper influence over the child, leads it on properly towards God, the further agencies of school and social center, can only partly undo the evil done so early to the child. The mother must be the first to instill into the heart of the child, not only the general truth of the fatherhood of God, Creator of all, but the still more wonderful truths of the birth of Christ on earth, of His continuation in the Church, the sublime truths of our Redemption as they continue to be living realities in all souls that beat in harmony with the pulse of the Church: The duty of praying with the Church as a part of the Church, and the duty of living out in daily life the truths prayed, as shining models to the world of the resplendent truth of Christ.[198]

Again, in this early period, women's gender and its role in liturgical renewal was often described by men. Even those more popular journals, such as *Altar and Home*, were produced and contributed to almost exclusively by male religious.[199] Interestingly, Virgil Michel even explicitly noted that the woman who was wife and mother would act as an inspiration not only to her family but to "the woman worker in the world" with whom she dealt, especially the social worker, the nurse, the religious sister, the teacher, the woman lawyer, or the doctor.[200]

There were varying degrees of engagement with the liturgical/theological description of women offered by Michel, filtered from a

---

[197] Hieronimi, "Wie lehre ich mein Kind mit der Kirche beten?" *Bibel und Liturgie* 2 (July 1928): 346–47. The image of woman as priest or priestess of her home can be found in this earlier literature, such as Norbert Stenta, "Lebensweihe durch die Liturgie," *Lebe mit der Kirche* 7, no. 31 (1935): 26–30; and Norbert Stenta, "Volksliturgie und Lebensweihe," *Bibel und Liturgie* (1932/1933): 33–37, 60–63, 78–81, 102–5, 130–33, 193–96, 236–39, 345–49, 402–6, 444–49. See also Teresa Berger, *Liturgie und Frauenseele: Die liturgische Bewegung aus der Sicht der Frauenforschung* (Stuttgart: Verlag W. Kohlhammer, 1993), 73–93.

[198] Michel, "The Liturgy and Catholic Women," 275–76.

[199] *Altar and Home*, for example, was begun in 1934 by the monks of Conception Abbey, Conception, Missouri.

[200] Michel, "The Liturgy and Catholic Women," 276.

wider European theological network. Professional women (and the more frequent contributors to *Orate Fratres*) did not tend to engage the vocational potential of the wife/mother to live the liturgical life and thus deeply affect those within her influence. The responsibility/duty of Christian women to live the liturgical life and thus re-Christianize their families and communities does appear, however, to appeal to women within a wider sector of American Catholics, particularly in the plethora of study clubs, which emerged in the latter 1920s and into the 1930s, for both men and women who agreed to study the liturgy.

While this conclusion does not accurately blanket all women (some women's study clubs were based in communities or parishes that had contact with other leaders in the liturgical movement and thus were more aware of broader aspects of liturgical renewal), it is evident that some women's groups identified the study of the liturgy as a way to live authentic Catholic Christian lives which would combat the evils of secularism (or Protestantism) which beleaguered their families. The study clubs formed by women were a recurring line item in the "Apostolate" and the "Liturgical Briefs" sections of *Orate Fratres* during the late 1920s and early 1930s. Catholic women's clubs or societies, increasingly popular as a desire to solidify Catholic identity grew in the twentieth century, wrote to *Orate Fratres* to describe the work they were doing to study the liturgy. For example, Miss Agnes G. Grant of Janesville, Wisconsin, wrote to the Liturgical Press in 1927 to describe the activity of her Catholic Women's Club:

> There are about twenty in our group, which we call the St. Therese Study Group. We meet every other week at the homes of members, at 7:30 in the evening, and open with prayer. The leader gives a sort of—shall I say lecture?—on a few chapters of the text book in review at each meeting—the cycles, the divisions of the Liturgical Year, etc., for the benefit of newcomers—then we take our Missals and assemble the Mass of the next Sunday. Last meeting we took the first Sunday of Lent. Then we read a chapter in the Autobiography of St. Therese— and if the hour is not too late, we discuss current events, religious and secular. It is gratifying to see the serious interest, in fact enthusiasm, with which the meetings are attended. There is so *much* to learn, it seems very difficult to choose.[201]

---

[201] "The Apostolate," *Orate Fratres* 1, no. 6 (1927): 188.

Grant concluded by asking Michel to recommend good materials for her St. Therese Study Group to read together. In response to such an invitation, Michel described a long list of general material available for liturgical clubs, especially the pamphlets of the Popular Liturgical Library and articles in *Orate Fratres*, aside from, of course, the supreme source of the missal. Aside from his own magazine, Michel listed a long trail of publications, including *The Acolyte, America, American Ecclesiastical Review, Catholic Educational Review, Fortnightly Review, The Homiletic and Pastoral Review, The Placidian, Caecilia, The Catholic Educational Association Bulletin, Catholic Educational Review,* and *Emmanuel*; all of these journals contained articles addressing the liturgical movement, the liturgical apostolate, the use of the breviary and missal, or strategies men and women might employ to be brought closer to Christ via the liturgy. Such variety gives a sense of how widely the subject of liturgy was discussed within Catholic periodical literature in the late 1920s.[202] Concurrently, Catholic newspapers began to more frequently include explanations or "little lessons" on ceremonies and ceremonial items for their readers. This was somewhat critically viewed, as there was a tension over using liturgical things or the liturgy as means of instruction but still squashing them into an outmoded box of devotionalism so railed against by the proponents of the liturgical movement.[203]

National Women's Organizations and the Liturgy

As noted above, the Catholic Church developed a massive infrastructure of social charities and agencies in the first part of the twentieth century. Once limited to parish-based activities or "ladies' auxiliaries" to men's organizations, women began establishing their

[202] Ibid., 188–190.
[203] See "The Apostolate," *Orate Fratres* 3, no. 8 (1929): 253: "Some of our Catholic newspapers are happily beginning to insert explanations or 'little lessons' on ceremonies and ceremonial paraphernalia for the instruction of their readers. In this matter, however, it is by no means an unmitigated good or a means of true instruction, if everything connected with Catholic worship—e.g., the different parts of the altar equipment—is interpreted as referring to some aspect of the Passion of our Lord, to the different moments of his suffering, etc. So much of this sort of thing is not at all traditional in the best sense of the term. It dates rather from those centuries in which the liturgical sense was declining or had been lost entirely, and certainly is no means for making 'the true Christian spirit flourish again.'"

own national organizations. Lay women experienced a challenging tension between cultivating professionalism and authority, necessitated by the new roles available to and, on several fronts, necessary for them to assume. At the same time, women lived in an effort to preserve an ideal of womanhood presented to them (by themselves as inheritors of a Catholic viewpoint on womanhood and from their ecclesial leaders) as normative. Thus, women often needed to accept hierarchical authority readily and keep the centrality of their Catholic values at the fore of every quest, even if they acted in a society and culture which increasingly privileged public and professional roles for women.[204]

One of the most significant ventures on the part of organized Catholic women with regard to the liturgical movement came in November 1929 during the ninth annual convention of the NCCW, which voted that every local Catholic women's club would study the liturgy during that year. The NCCW's president, Mary Graham Hawks, spoke of women's responsibility to "make Christ known" and to do this effectively by knowing "the mind of the Church"; this was in line with Catholic Action, which she described as a "work of apologetics—the apologetics of example."[205] She continued:

[204] L. E. Hartmann-Ting, "The National Catholic School of Social Service: Redefining Catholic Womanhood through the Professionalization of Social Work during the Interwar Years," *U.S. Catholic Historian* 16, no. 1 (2008): 103. See also Elizabeth McKeown, "The National Bishop's Conference: An Analysis of Its Origins," *Catholic Historical Review* 66 (October 1980): 565–83; Elizabeth McKeown, *War and Welfare: American Catholics and World War One* (New York: Garland Publishing, 1988); and Kathleen Sprows Cummings, "Not the 'New Woman?': Irish American Women and the Creation of a Useable Past, 1890–1900," *U.S. Catholic Historian* 19, no. 1 (Winter 2001): 37–52.

[205] Mary G. Hawks, "NCCW Monthly Message to Affiliated Organizations, No. 97," November 1929, National Catholic Welfare Conference / United States Catholic Conference, National Council of Catholic Women [hereafter cited as NCWC/USCC, NCCW] 63, ACUA. See also "Liturgical Briefs," *Orate Fratres* 9, no. 9 (1935): 423, which reported that Hawks, in the May issue of *Catholic Action* (1935), showed how the study of the Mass was appropriate and meaningful for individuals or groups "especially in view of the present universal unrest and threat of war." She wrote that Mass prayers were concerned with peace "not as a beautiful ideal or theory but as a practical outcome."

If indeed, our activities as Catholics must "make Christ known," we must act as Christ would act. How can we hope to do this? . . . Now, the only way we have of knowing a person's mind is to study his words and his actions. The official language and actions of the Church are called the Liturgy.[206]

The NCCW thus saw the study of the liturgy as a natural resource for "learning" how to unite women's lives with the papal initiative of Catholic Action. This connection was in concert with other groups who tied the liturgy with effecting Catholic Action, such as a note in the *Orate Fratres* "Apostolate" section in July 1930, which claimed that the study of the liturgy would be the prominent topic at two national Sodalist conventions (one for students and one for women), as well as a subject of journals of organizations, like *The Queen's Work* of the Catholic Sodalities of America.[207]

Two years earlier, in 1927, national president Mrs. Arthur F. (Mary) Mullen had described the NCCW's purpose as a responsible answer to the needs of the world:

We came not as of ourselves but in response to a call from our leaders in the Church, a call to service for God, for country, for humanity. A great national program was presented to us, a program which demanded faith, idealism, devotion. That progress had and still has but one end in view—the restoration of the reign of Christ the King. It proposes a great spiritual campaign, a campaigning which requires

---

[206] Hawks, "NCCW Monthly Message to Affiliated Organizations, No. 97," November 1929, NCWC/USCC, NCCW 63, ACUA.

[207] The program for these events notes that: "The two chief subjects for discussions at the conventions will be Personal Sanctification and the Lay Apostolate. The discussions on personal holiness will center about the liturgy, especially about the Mass and Communion. Emphasis will be laid upon closer participation in the Mass and better understanding of it, on the use of the Missal, on the general priesthood, and on the liturgy as the source of Catholic Action." Virgil Michel, "The Apostolate," *Orate Fratres* 4, nos. 9–10 (1930): 426.

The Queen's Work was a magazine devoted to Catholicism, charmingly self-described as "an illustrated monthly for the home." A magazine of Catholic activities, it was owned and published by the Jesuit Fathers, St. Louis, Missouri, and served as the official organ of the Sodalities in America. NCWC/USCC, NCCW 17/19, ACUA.

intelligent thought, definite action, but material resources as well, if it is to be affective.[208]

The NCCW was, from its origin, interested in study and action, but the topics of its study clubs were more specifically social or moral, without reference to the liturgy as a source for inspiration.[209]

Following the decision of the NCCW to study the liturgy (much to the delight of Virgil Michel, who included this announcement in the December 1929 section of "The Apostolate"[210]), the NCCW issued instructions in its "Monthly Message to Affiliated Organizations," describing the object of study and available resources. Topics addressed as potential for study included the study of the purpose of Advent, the objective being union with Christ through participation in the life of the Church, and a comparison of the "Incarnation or Christmas" cycle with the "Redemption or Easter" cycle.[211] Aside from focus on the liturgical year, the "Monthly Message" also included more general outlines for study of the Mass and Catholic Action, including one for women who had already used the earlier study club outline on the Mass or who were familiar with the missal and a version for beginners. As for the Mass, discussion questions included a consideration of ritual actions,[212]

[208] Mrs. Arthur F. Mullen, "Address to the 7th Annual Convention of the NCCW," 1927, p. 2, NCWC/USCC, NCCW 76/19, ACUA.

[209] Topics included, for example, Mexico, Education, Cooperation with Racial Groups, Industrial Problems, Literature, and Field work. See Mullen, "Address to the 7th Annual Convention of the NCCW," 1927, pp. 7–9, NCWC/USCC, NCCW 76/19, ACUA.

[210] "A news item from Washington announced that the National Council of Catholic Women would make the liturgy of the Church the official program of study for its members during the coming year. Once our Catholic mothers are steeped in 'the true Christian spirit,' as derived from the 'primary and indispensable source', we shall not have to wait for the grade school period, or even later, to have our Catholic children learn something of the high privilege and dignity to which every member of the Mystic Body is called through Christ." "The Apostolate," *Orate Fratres* 4, no. 2 (1929): 89.

[211] "National Council of Catholic Women Monthly Message to Affiliated Organizations, No. 98," December 1929, NCWC/USCC, NCCW 63, ACUA.

[212] One suggestion was: "Discuss why sign of cross [is an] act of prep[aration] for mass." "National Council of Catholic Women Monthly Message to Affiliated Organizations, No. 98," December 1929, NCWC/USCC, NCCW 63, ACUA.

questions about characters of the ministers,[213] and encouragement to use liturgical texts as springboards for discussion.[214]

The nationwide goal to study the liturgy seemed to be somewhat successful, as the NCCW "Monthly Message," issued in September 1930, reported in an article, "Liturgy, Living with Mother Church," that it was accomplishing its goal to study the liturgy set at its ninth annual convention.[215] The "Monthly Message" praised the "Benedictine Fathers" who had aided Catholic women in the supply of resources and pamphlets and urged all women to procure a missal and use it during the study of and attendance at Mass. The article encouraged Catholics to *assist at* rather than *attend* Mass and reminded readers that any local diocesan paper "no doubt carries three helpful features sent out weekly by the NCWC Press Service: Sunday's Liturgy, Masses for the Week, Catholic Customs and Symbols."[216]

Interest on the part of the NCCW in studying the liturgy was reaffirmed at its twelfth annual convention held in Charleston, South Carolina, in October 1932. At this meeting, aside from studies of social life, education, and missionary activities, time was set apart for those interested in the liturgy. *Orate Fratres* reported that, during the 1932 annual convention, the NCCW held a demonstration of the liturgy and

---

[213] An instruction reads: ". . . the server at mass represents the congregation; show how this signifies that though the priest alone consecrates, the congregation joins in the Mass as a joint offering and joint prayer." "National Council of Catholic Women Monthly Message to Affiliated Organizations, No. 98," December 1929, NCWC/USCC, NCCW 63, ACUA.

[214] For example, "The priest says he will 'go unto the altar of God'; the response is, 'to God who giveth joy to my youth.' Discuss what the joy of the youth means in terms of innocence, faith, obedience, health and strength of body, interest in doing things, kindness, fervor of affection towards God and one's family and friends, the hope and determination to 'make something of myself,' willingness to make sacrifices, unselfishness, honesty in confronting facts, dreams of great accomplishments." "National Council of Catholic Women Monthly Message to Affiliated Organizations, No. 98," December 1929, NCWC/USCC, NCCW 63, ACUA.

[215] It reported, "A wide correspondence with the National Headquarters showing interest in the Liturgy; and giving evidence of earnest study on the part of certain groups. At the present time of the NCWC Study Club outlines those pertaining to the Liturgy have the widest distribution." "Volume of 1930," NCWC/USCC, NCCW 63, ACUA.

[216] Ibid.

various aids for its study. Mrs. A. F. Adelman of Newark, New Jersey, conducted the demonstration, which included an introduction and explanation of the *Leaflet Missal*.[217] During the convention, Miss Miriam Marks of the "Parish Federation" described the effectiveness of the study club programs:

> To be vitalizing, the subject for study must be of general interest. As the central act of Catholic worship is the sacrifice of the Mass—which Christ left to all men—a study of it makes a widespread appeal. Through study groups, understanding and appreciation of the Mass are increased; as we learn more of its infinite meaning, we are incited to express actively our devotions to our Savior. A greater unity or purpose is created when all organizations are simultaneously experiencing this spiritual growth.[218]

From the information received from the secretaries of local organizations of Catholic women, an "appreciable number" chose to become "intimately acquainted" with the Mass and the Liturgy through the use of the Liturgical Press Study Club outline, *The Eucharistic Sacrifice*. To demonstrate the widespread interest in liturgical renewal in America, *Orate Fratres* listed, among the correspondence it received, Butte and Great Falls, Montana; Albert Lea and Faribault, Minnesota; Milwaukee, Wisconsin; Belleville, Illinois; San Francisco, California; Austin, Texas; Rochester, New York; and the Hawaiian Islands.[219] Within the Diocese of Great Falls, Montana, the first convention of the Great Falls Diocesan Council of Catholic Women determined that "within each parish was established an altar society, with a subcommittee on the sanctuary, and at least one study club studying the Mass."[220] According to the frequent correspondence concerning study clubs, whether they were under the auspices of the NCCW or other

---

[217] "Catholic Women Are Studying the Liturgy," in "The Apostolate," *Orate Fratres* 7, no. 1 (1932): 30; Catholic Church, *Leaflet Missal* (Chicago: Lawrence N. Daleiden, 1931).

[218] Miriam Marks, quoted in "Catholic Women Are Studying the Liturgy," in "The Apostolate," *Orate Fratres* 7, no. 1 (1932): 30–31.

[219] Ibid. Liturgical subjects were also presented at state Councils of Catholic Women, such as that of Minnesota, held in St. Paul, October 26–27, 1932, at which Rev. Joseph Lord spoke on "German Young People and the Liturgical Movement." "Liturgical Briefs," *Orate Fratres* 7, no. 2 (1932): 88.

[220] Quoted in "The Apostolate," *Orate Fratres* 7, no. 3 (1933): 134.

organized national women's groups or not, the women who made the effort to write in to *Orate Fratres*, at least, acknowledged that study of the liturgy had helped them in their understanding and love of the liturgy and that this had been instilled in other members of their groups, inspiring others to purchase missals.[221]

Characteristics and Success of Study Clubs

Two characteristics about Catholic women's study clubs depart from the general trend of the more professional women discussed above (Justine B. Ward and Ellen Gates Starr). Unlike the women writers for *Orate Fratres*, the NCCW women were encouraged to read "The Liturgy and Catholic Women," which was not the subject of women who *wrote*. The interpretation of Catholic womanhood and a Catholic woman in the more traditional sense (of wife and mother) was a theme which would not be engaged in a more comprehensive way by the liturgical movement until the period surrounding the Second World War. Second, the interpretation of learning the liturgy so as to become active, spiritually informed members of the lay apostolate sometimes had the added sentiment "in order to make converts." While the mainstream liturgical movement did have an underpinning motive of reforming society with liturgy as the answer to modern evils, other liturgical movement advocates sometimes appear to reduce the transformative power of the liturgy to "making converts." Taking the liturgy into life became associated with a fierce construction of Catholic identity for many Catholics.[222]

---

[221] For example, Agnes M. Marceron of Washington, DC, reported: "With a greater knowledge of the Mass, the members were instilled with a greater love and a deeper understanding of the beauty and value of the holy sacrifice. Realizing the beauty of the prayers and wishing to assist at Mass in the very best manner, many of the club members have ordered Missals." Agnes M. Marceron of Washington, DC, "Study Club on the Mass," in "The Apostolate," *Orate Fratres* 7, no. 12 (1933): 570.

[222] For example, in an article describing the value of shrines in the home, Mrs. John Bell Hood wrote, "Can you—and you—and you refuse the opportunity to bring ONE soul back to Christ? If every family brought just one soul back to God—what a conquest! Is not this united Catholic Action, so desired by our Holy Father? So pleasing to God?" Mrs. John Bell Hood, "Shrines in the Home," *NCCW Monthly Message* 17, no. 2 (December 1937), NCWC/USCC NCCW 64, ACUA. While incorporating spaces for familial prayer in the home, and the wider objective of living an apostolic life were

It is also interesting to ask *why* Study Clubs seemed to "take off" so well during this period.[223] It is hard to imagine, as Mrs. D. M. Walsh, diocesan chair on study clubs for the NCCW in Springfield, Illinois, reported, that a study club focusing on *The Eucharistic Sacrifice*, published by Liturgical Press, was formed *in every parish in Springfield*.

---

constant for both members of the liturgical movement and groups such as the NCCW, the apostolic life was usually cast in more "conquest" terms by these national groups.

[223] For example, the Catholic Action Committee of Women of the Diocese of Wichita, Kansas, numbered eighty-three study clubs which completed a course on the externals of the Mass using *Altar and Sanctuary*. "Liturgical Briefs," *Orate Fratres* 7, no. 8 (1933): 374. See also Mrs. John W. Clendenin (Executive Secretary of the Catholic Action Committee of Women, Wichita, Kansas), "Study-Club Accomplishments," in "The Apostolate," *Orate Fratres* 7, no. 11 (1933): 523. Clendenin noted that she hoped to prepare a carefully revised edition of *Altar and Sanctuary* (issued by the Wichita Catholic Action Committee of Women), of which the first edition of two-thousand copies was sold out. See also "Liturgical Briefs," *Orate Fratres* 8, no. 3 (1934): 136; and "Liturgical Briefs," *Orate Fratres* 9, no. 9 (1935): 422 which reported: "Mrs. Angela A. Clendenin of Wichita, Kans., well known for her work in the development of religious study clubs, and the author of several study club booklets on the liturgy, has been awarded the papal medal '*Pro Ecclesia et Pontiface.*'"

In *Orate Fratres* 8, no. 2 (1933): 86, a "Liturgical Brief" reported that the "multiplication of liturgical study clubs is going on apace," with biweekly programs in Fargo, North Dakota, in its Orestes Brownson Study Circle, during which half an hour was devoted to an aspect of the Mass and another fifteen minutes to the missal; in Litchfield, Illinois, members of the Sodality studied the Mass; and one which met at Mundelein College, in Mundelein, Illinois, and was run by the Ciscora, the Catholic youth organization of Chicago high schools and colleges.

Also at Mundelein College for Women, in 1936, Charlotte Wilcox, Student Press Representative of Chicago, Illinois, wrote about the program the liturgical committee of the Sodality presented in "Symposium on the Ceremonies of Holy Week." She described the rituals of the week and how members of the college glee club contributed in singing some of the antiphons and sequences in Gregorian chant. She claimed, "A most appreciative audience received the symposium, and commented extensively upon its value and timeliness," concluding that the members of the Sodality felt they should pass on the suggestion to other groups desirous of a Lenten program. Charlotte Wilcox, "Sodalists' Liturgical Activities," in "The Apostolate," *Orate Fratres* 10, no. 5 (1936): 235.

Walsh reported that the pamphlets, because they were inexpensive, could be provided to "every girl" and that, through the "enthusiasm and advertizing of these young people, several groups of older ladies asked for help in getting started."[224] It seems that the success of the study clubs was often driven by the younger women of any given parish, and some observed that the "new generation" of young Catholics demanded activity, a sentiment echoed by other organized women's groups expressing Catholic Action, including the Daughters of Isabella and the Catholic Daughters of America. A growing middle-class populace with greater access to education, coupled with increased educational opportunities for women in particular, added to the more overt assertion on the part of American Catholics to publically claim and evangelize their faith. In turn, this intensified the involvement of Catholics (both men and women) in groups which studied the principles of faith, touted the Catholic responsibility to recognize their membership in Christ's Mystical Body, and urged other Catholics to take part in converting the world.[225] Interestingly, just as the NCCW had ratified the study of liturgy in 1929, the National Council of Catholic Men likewise turned its attention to the liturgy as a source of Catholic Action, encouraging liturgical participation and study of the missal and providing pamphlets on the aims of the liturgical movement.[226]

[224] Mrs. D. M. Walsh, "Study Club Activity," in "The Apostolate," *Orate Fratres* 7, no. 6 (1933): 275–76. She continued, "*The Eucharistic Sacrifice* is the most popular subject in this diocese. 'Every beginning is weak,' is certainly true of the study club movement. We must start with something useful, interesting, something that doesn't require too much time and yet is instructive and worthwhile. The Liturgical Press has given us an outline on the Mass."

[225] Ibid., 276–77. The report of the Des Moines Diocesan Council of Catholic Women, appearing in the May 1933 issue of *Catholic Action*, reported that the "interest of young women who will so soon be our leaders" was especially significant. "Liturgical Brief," in "The Apostolate," *Orate Fratres* 7, no. 8 (1933): 273.

[226] "The Apostolate," *Orate Fratres* 7, no. 3 (1933): 134. The sentiments for action on the part of the Catholic Daughters were somewhat more violent than the mainstream liturgical movement: "The need for concerted Catholic action is obvious to any serious observer. Irreligion is sweeping over our land like a dust storm, and only a well informed and instructed Catholic laity can stem the rising tide of subversive movements which threatens to wreck our civilization. . . . The world today needs and awaits Catholic women ready

Aside from the NCCW, other Catholic women's groups organized liturgical study clubs, such as the Catholic Daughters of America, whose "vice state regent," Mrs. Ella Cancey, established one such club at the parish of Saints Peter and Paul Church in Naperville, Illinois.[227] Likewise, the Catholic Daughters of America's "Court of St. Catherine" of Dunkirk, New York, "enthusiastically adopted" the *Saint Andrew Missal* for "their co-offering of the holy sacrifice."[228] In this court (a name for any local group of Catholic Daughters), the women attended lectures on the priesthood of the laity, the co-offering of the holy sacrifice, and the use of the missal.[229] An even more ambitious campaign was proposed by the Catholic Daughters in 1935 at their convention held in Seattle, Washington. They planned a "novel program to insure at least the minimum" of "active participation of the laity in the divine Mysteries."[230] The program would include swamping "automobile service stations, railroad stations, bus terminals, airports, hotels, and other public gathering places" with "cards setting forth the names and addresses of nearby Catholic churches together with their schedule of Masses for Sundays and holy-days."[231] The Daughters of Isabella, another women's group founded in the late nineteenth century, also

---

to assume dignified authoritative leadership in our social order. The time is past when Catholics of this or any other nation, can honestly pretend that apparently unrelated outbursts against the Church are merely local incidents. There is too much painful evidence from unhappy lands where Catholics have been deprived of their God given rights to deny the fact that our enemies are highly organized. The presentation of the well defined ideals and objectives of the Catholic Daughters of America, acting in consonance with the program of Catholic Action as outlined by our Most Reverend Bishops, should prove an incentive to Catholic women and girls to join hands in the 'participation of the laity in the apostolate of the Hierarchy' for the salvation of America from the throes of the Red menace." "Untitled," *Women's Voice* 23, no. 5 (1938): p. 1, Catholic Daughters of America 7 / Folder titled "Women's Voice," ACUA.

[227] "Liturgical Briefs," *Orate Fratres* 7, no. 5 (1933): 233.

[228] "Liturgical Briefs," *Orate Fratres* 7, no. 8 (1933): 373.

[229] *Orate Fratres* remarked that the Catholic Daughters had thus "laid the foundations from which this successful Court will further pursue its studies of the holy Mass in view of greater grace and blessing for their zealous apostolate." "Liturgical Briefs," *Orate Fratres* 7, no. 8 (1933): 373.

[230] "Liturgical Briefs," *Orate Fratres* 9, no. 10 (1935): 472.

[231] Ibid.

reported its completion of studies on the liturgy among the women of the Isabella Study Club in Meriden, Connecticut.[232]

Oftentimes, the groups in which Catholic women met to discuss the liturgical apostolate were highly integrated with other avenues within the liturgical movement and in the wider context of advancing, educating, or developing American Catholicism.[233] The Catholic Forum of Pittsburgh, Pennsylvania, for example, under the direction of Mrs. Paul D. Wright, used both *Orate Fratres* and *Liturgical Arts Quarterly* as springboards for discussion of the ceremonies of the Church, the daily missal, and Church music reform and, in addition to this, maintained a membership in the Calvert Associates (the Catholic book club of which Ellen Gates Starr was also a member in the Chicago chapter).[234] In a more independent setting, Catholics of Los Angeles, California, "interested in the Liturgical Apostolate and scholastic philosophy" were invited to a bimonthly meeting at the home of Sarah I. and Julia T. Metcalf.[235]

[232] "Liturgical Briefs," *Orate Fratres* 7, no. 9 (1933): 420.

[233] Rose E. Haus of New York City wrote to the editor of *Orate Fratres* in 1934, encouraging the liturgical movement and its aims: "The Liturgical Movement does move very slowly, but so do its contemporaries—the retreat movement, Father Lord's efforts for the Children of Mary Sodalities, and the efforts to improve methods of teaching Christian Doctrine. The success of each of these movements will be of benefit to the others. . . ." Rose E. Haus, "A Friend Writes," in "The Apostolate," *Orate Fratres* 8, no. 6 (1934): 284.

[234] "Liturgical Briefs," *Orate Fratres* 7, no. 6 (1933): 282. See also Mrs. R. A. Byrne, of Pittsburgh, Pennsylvania, who in 1936 was the president of Catholic Forum. She reported that their program's liturgical efforts continued, particularly within the realm of learning the musical parts of the Mass in unaccompanied Gregorian chant: "Our devotion to this effort and its evident success would indicate that it is not beyond the ability of any average lay person or group to sing the musical service of the Church acceptably and correctly. We wish with all our hearts that we might communicate our love and enthusiasm for the study of the liturgy to all around us. We feel honored and blessed for this great privilege we enjoy, and sincerely hope that our effort may prove an incentive to others. We wish to thank you for past favors and to assure you that we derive much instruction and inspiration from your magazine." Mrs. R. A. Byrne, "Liturgy and the Laity," in "The Apostolate," *Orate Fratres* 10, no. 6 (1936): 280.

[235] Classes studied papal pronouncements and liturgical scholars such as Prosper Guéranger and Columba Marmion; special classes were conducted by Mr. Everett R. Harman, one of the founders of the Liturgical Arts Society,

Despite the plethora of interest among college students, young women, and mothers, some of its most active members were middle-aged or elderly by their contemporaries' standards. For example, Justine B. Ward was forty-five and Ellen Gates Starr was sixty-five when they first came in contact with the organized liturgical movement on the American scene. Other evidence exists within the published correspondence of *Orate Fratres* that women had been interested in things liturgical for a significant time *before* the movement began in the United States. In 1933, Kate E. Sartori of Le Mars, Iowa, wrote that she was seventy-five years old and had been interested in "learning everything" she could about the liturgy of the Church for the past *forty years*.[236] She even had advice for the editor, encouraging him to publish a short article on the *Ordo* so that people might know where to buy and how to use this useful resource, "so that they may have the great advantage of praying the same Mass as the priest at the altar is saying."[237] She also offered to tell the members of her ladies' aid society about *Orate Fratres*, take copies of the magazine there, and encourage those interested to subscribe. Another subscriber, "Miss G." of New York City, wrote to the editor in Advent of 1937:

---

and the group also formed a small circulating library. "Liturgical Briefs," *Orate Fratres* 9, no. 10 (1935): 472.

[236] Emphasis author's. Kate E. Sartori, who noted that all her children and grandchildren also learned to use the Missal "as soon as they were old enough to manage it" related: "I have been very much interested for forty years in learning everything I could about the liturgy of the Church. I have used a Missal for forty years, but have used the diocesan *Ordo* only for about ten years. A few instructions from our Rev. Pastor enabled me to read it without trouble. I use it for my Missal and the divine Office. When I first used the Missal I found a great deal of inspiration and information in Dom Geruangér's [sic] great work *The Liturgical Year*. My pastor at that time had that set of books, and as the different liturgical seasons came around he would pick out for me the proper volume to read. And for a number of years I studied it that way. That was forty-five years ago. Since then I have been on the lookout for anything I thought would help me to a better understanding of the liturgy. Now, you can see why I appreciate your magazine *Orate Fratres*. I should like to see it in every home." Kate E. Sartori, "Not a Newcomer," in "The Apostolate," *Orate Fratres* 7, no. 7 (1933): 329.

[237] Ibid.

I should like to add my appreciation of your review to all the others you are receiving. I am an old subscriber, old in years as well as in my relations with your work. I should love to take a two years' subscription, but the enclosed two dollars are all that I have and I do not know if there will ever be any more. Anyhow, *Orate Fratres* will come to me for another year.[238]

Even with few resources, Miss G. sought to continue her subscription. Other older women pursued liturgical study by founding liturgical study groups. Agnes L. Struble of Minneapolis, Minnesota, related how the Incarnation Study Club, run by her mother, had been studying the liturgy for the past three years (since 1930) but initially found it quite daunting: "The suggestion to study the liturgy came from one of our own members. The subject seemed so difficult, so remote, we scarcely knew how to begin."[239] Struble explained that her mother, "who has been a student of the liturgy for nearly forty years," helped the Study Club begin a study of the liturgical apostolate by use of the materials and outlines made available by *Orate Fratres*. The group, composed of about twenty members, met twice a month in the homes of members, all of whom secured copies of a missal, such as the *St. Andrew Missal*. Struble also expressed gratitude to *Orate Fratres* for providing the outlines to the group, otherwise they might "still be groping in the dark."[240] Struble concluded that, in the group her mother coordinated, "We feel we are accomplishing the purpose of our study, namely, to discover how to participate actively in the holy sacrifice of the Mass so that we may hear Mass with intelligent devotion."[241]

---

[238] Miss G., "From an Old Friend," in "The Apostolate," *Orate Fratres* 12, no. 1 (1937): 42.

[239] Agnes L. Struble, "Liturgical Study Club Activity," in "The Apostolate," *Orate Fratres* 7, no. 10 (1933): 474.

[240] Ibid. "May I express to the Liturgical Press our very great appreciation of these helpful outlines, as well as our thanks and appreciation of their kind generosity which has made it possible for us to provide ourselves at so small a cost with the necessary outlines, books, and pamphlets with which to pursue this course."

[241] Ibid., 474–75. Struble explained the history of the group: "During the first year we learned something of the need for the Liturgical Movement, its aim or purpose, and something of the Papal pronouncements regarding the Movement. We came to realize that in our humble way we were heeding the wishes and commands of the Holy Father. This gave us courage to go on with

CONCLUSION

Preparing for the Next Stage of the Liturgical Movement

This chapter focused on three spheres of lay women's involvement in the early stages of the liturgical movement, from the public work, writing, and organization of Justine B. Ward and Ellen Gates Starr to the more privately circulated work of Catholic women's study clubs. First, Justine B. Ward and the development of chant and Ellen Gates Starr and her interests in the breviary provide examples of two leading women writers and liturgical advocates. Ward had the ability and resources to realize active participation through music—and communicated this energy to liturgical musicians across the United States and beyond. Starr, though her background was strongly socially oriented with her involvement in labor strikes and advocacy for immigrants, contributed most directly to the liturgical movement through exposing the spiritual wealth of the breviary to the laity. Interestingly, she did not discuss directly the social aspects of the liturgy in the Roman Catholic context, though she did speak of the churches' duty in social reform, from the Anglican viewpoint, in her article "Settlements and the Church's Duty." Her writing for *Orate Fratres* and *Sponsa Regis* took up the problem of the Arts and Crafts Movement, which focused on the need for well-crafted goods (i.e., liturgical prayers) which would lift up the souls who used and made them (i.e., read and prayed the breviary).

Second, developing a sense of the range and number of women interested in or exposed to the liturgical movement, particularly in its newest stages, provides a fascinating window into the social history of the liturgical movement. One finds young college women interested in seeing prayer in poetry, or taking up Virgil Michel's proposal of the liturgy as a solution for social evils, women who find creative avenues for realizing the liturgy in the arts, and women who identify as devotees of the liturgy for decades. Finally, in a different appropriation of the liturgical movement's methods of education and familiarization with the liturgy, Catholic women's associations frequently focused on the liturgy as a means for promoting a "conversion" of the world. In these cases, while such organizations had a public face, the bulk of

---

the study of the Eucharistic Sacrifice. This year we are following your outline on the liturgical Year. In connection with this outline, we have found *Living with the Church*, by Dom Otto Haering, OSB, very helpful." Struble, "Liturgical Study Club Activity," 474.

such liturgical study would occur on the local level, often in private living rooms.

In all cases, women's increased education, mobility, and organizational powers enabled women to become learners and advocates of liturgical study. At the same time, such study was contingent on certain conditions and necessitated both time and resources to consistently pursue such activities, especially during the Great Depression. Some examples even explicitly reveal some privilege, for example, among the number of women who self-identified as college-educated. And the liturgical movement was also not universally successful across regions and cultural backgrounds. Though examples of women interested in liturgy come from throughout the United States, the majority come from the midwest or the eastern half of the country. At the same time, few women self-identified as minorities, though women occasionally discussed *encounters* with minorities, suggesting a certain homogeneity among liturgical advocates. Again, though the liturgical movement was successful in particular places, its success was not universal. Finally, though study clubs and sodalities do appear to be successful to some extent, the fragmentation of such groups, and the many competing groups often existing within one parish, made wide-sweeping change difficult to coordinate, whether in coordinating social services or in promoting the use of the missal during Mass.[242]

Despite these difficulties, many American Catholics, and American Catholic lay women, saw the liturgical spiritual renewal as an excellent and authentically Catholic answer to the needs of the modern world. At the same time, women enjoyed increased social opportunities to

---

[242] Debra Campbell critiques large organizations under the Church umbrella as unable to realize the radical social implications of the theology of the Mystical Body, developing contemporaneously to them, or to experience the social solidarity suggested by the doctrine of the Mystical Body. This is due, she suggests, to the restrictions on freedom which women's organizations had previously experienced, and that the very size or fragmentation of such groups (i.e., the many different types of groups, multiple groups within a parish, not to mention multiple parishes in a diocese, etc.) made intimate social connections impractical. She notes that, by the 1930s, "it became apparent that church organizations and agencies to train social workers or administer poor relief did not strike at the heart of America's social and economic ills, nor did they satisfy the growing need for a deeper sense of social solidarity and lay spirituality apparent within the increasingly educated, upwardly mobile Catholic population." Campbell, "Reformers and Activists," 175.

study, teach, and take active roles in society; they saw doing so as contributing to the larger goals of Catholic Action and as an opportunity to evangelize. These objectives, all supported by the liturgical movement, paired well with several developments which would transform American Catholicism, including the Catholic Intellectual Movement, fresh from Europe; radical Catholic Social Activism, which promoted social regeneration in dramatic ways; and Catholic Action, the participation of the laity in the activity of the hierarchy.

Chapter 3

The Lay Apostolate Enters the Liturgical Movement: Catholic Intellectual Life, Social Regeneration, and Lay Initiative (c. 1930–40)

INTRODUCTION

The Relation of Catholic Action and the Liturgical Movement

Historian Jay Dolan writes that the American Catholic laity "entered a new era in the late 1920s, an age in which the responsibilities of the people in the pews were taken increasingly seriously, or at least discussed with growing frequency under the rubric of the lay apostolate and Catholic Action."[1] Pius XI (1857–1939) spoke of the need for Catholic Action in 1922, asking the laity to commit themselves to the task of restoring the secular world to Christ,[2] and the constant stream promoting lay activity in converting the world dovetailed with the efforts of liturgical renewal. Virgil Michel's syllogism perfectly reflected the synthesis of the social responsibility of the Catholic (the Catholic's responsibility to bring Christ to the world) with formation in the liturgy. One could only draw "all things to Christ" by committing the self to Christ in the sacrament of the Mass, and lay people had just as much responsibility to actively "assist" at Mass as the priest had responsibility to actively preside. To this effect, the liturgical movement and Catholic Action were tightly intertwined, and this was readily

---

[1] Jay Dolan et al., *Transforming Parish Ministry: The Changing Roles of Catholic Clergy, Laity, and Women Religious* (New York: Crossroad, 1989), 222.

[2] For the development and assessment of Catholic Action, see Martin Quigley, Jr. and Edward M. Connors, eds., *Catholic Action in Practice: Family Life, Education, International Life* (New York: Random House, 1963); Jim Cunningham, "Specialized Catholic Action," in *The American Apostolate: American Catholics in the Twentieth Century*, ed. Leo Richard Ward (Westminster, MD: Newman Press, 1952): 47–65.

recognized. As Leo R. Ward, CSC (1893–1984), described in 1959, when reflecting on contemporary Catholic lay movements, the liturgical renewal in America was but "a drop in the bucket," but he determined that it was the most *universal* recent religious development within Catholic lay movements: "It is far from swallowing up other developments, but something of it is almost sure to be induced in others, such as the Legion of Mary or Grailville or any expression of Catholic Action."[3]

A distinction between "mainstream" Catholic Action and the liturgical movement had to do with its organization. Formal Catholic Action would be overseen by Church hierarchy with its various groups, from the National Council of Catholic Women and the National Council of Catholic Men, to the Christian Family Movement, serving as conduits to convey the Church's teaching to laypersons.[4] The liturgical movement, on the other hand, was not organized under ecclesial auspices, even though it sought approval from its very beginning. The independence of the liturgical movement heightened its need for lay initiative. And, while the liturgical movement is often referenced in thanks to the clergy who promoted liturgical revival, the way in which the liturgical life was desired, sought, studied, and acted upon can only reveal the volition with which lay people actively participated. The success with which missals were purchased off the shelves, the rising subscriptions to *Orate Fratres*, and the very fact that so many lay groups associated with Catholic Action were involving liturgical prayer as part of their group structure reveals the extent to which the liturgical revival was just as much in the hands of lay persons and in the hands of women.[5]

[3] Leo R. Ward, "Living the Liturgy," in *Catholic Life, Catholic Life, U.S.A.: Contemporary Lay Movements* (St. Louis, MO: B. Herder Book, 1959), 10.

[4] In a recent dissertation, Kathleen Carlton Johnson discusses the differences between Church-promoted Catholic Action organizations and "radical" lay-sponsored movements. See Johnson, "Radical Social Activism, Lay Catholic Women and American Feminism 1920–1960," (PhD diss., University of South Africa, 2006).

[5] The suggestions or liturgical frustrations which women readers sent in to Virgil Michel reveal the frequency of their interaction with the latest editions of liturgical texts. For example, Mrs. J. S. M. of New York wrote to Virgil Michel to praise the *Day Hours of the Church*, published by Burns, Oates, and Washbourne, yet indicated that the book could never be widely used by layfolk because it would need some sort of calendar suited to them. She noted that "The Missal directory put out by Lohmann Co., St. Paul, Minn., has

For example, the volition to learn the liturgical movement was dramatically witnessed by the performance of liturgical prayer at a large annual meeting of Catholic societies, such as the one Leo R. Ward described as having occurred at a recent annual meeting of archdiocesan Catholic women. At the meeting, "without any rehearsal the women recited the people's plea for mercy in the *Kyrie*, their hymn of praise in the *Gloria*, their canticle of thanks in the Preface, their family prayer in the Our Father, and their testimony of faith in the Lamb of God," a feat of active participation which apparently surprised and pleased the presiding archbishop. The archbishop concluded, "The active participation of 1,100 women in this morning's glorious Mass was a magnificent demonstration of woman's place in the Mystical Body of Christ."[6] It can be presumed that the archbishop placed a high value on the knowledge these women displayed in the heart of their faith, the Mass, which they attested to through their active participation in the liturgy.

The Catholic Intellectual Revival and Catholic Social Action

Aside from its intersection with Catholic Action, the interwar period also saw the development of the Catholic Intellectual Revival, which was closely associated with liturgical study and social regeneration. Following the condemnation of Modernism in 1907 (*Lamentabili Sane*, Syllabus Condemning the Errors of the Modernists), which led to narrowly prescribed limits on matters of doctrine, Catholic scholarship found its inspiration in the reappropriation of St. Thomas. This Thomistic revival provided a fresh approach for Catholic scholarship around the world, prompting Catholic scholars to move away from the manual tradition and return to original sources. For Catholics, natural law served as a bridge between Catholic philosophy and "Protestant" rationalism of the Enlightenment. The new Catholic intellectual scene enabled the Catholic perspective to agree, due to both natural reason and supernatural revelation, that all humans had unalienable rights, and the purpose of government was to protect these rights, providing

---

opened up the Missal perfectly to a large group of my immediate friends, and I feel sure that the Day Hours will find much greater appreciation if one knew how to use the book." "Liturgy of the Layfolk," in "The Apostolate," *Orate Fratres* 9, no. 7 (1935): 334.

[6] Quoted in Leo Ward, "Living the Liturgy," 23. On the other hand, the women might have been able to successfully recite such prayers based on rote repetition, not study.

a springboard for Catholic and, increasingly, lay Catholic inclusion in early social justice movements which blossomed in the late 1910s and 1920s.[7] With the influence of neo-Thomism and Catholic philosophical and cultural vision which had burst on the European stage, American Catholics sought to impart the best of this thought, including the "doctrine" of the Mystical Body, which would become the watchword for the liturgical movement and the laity's ownership over the project of converting the world.[8]

This chapter and the next focus on some of the key women involved with movements interconnected with the liturgical movement, focusing on increased lay initiative in the Catholic Intellectual Movement, the development of Catholic literature and art, and the women involved with Catholic social groups such as the Catholic Worker and Friendship House. This period offers a bridge between some of the earliest advocates, discussed in the previous chapter, and their understanding of the liturgical movement in terms of responsibility to become informed, participating Catholics in order to promote spiritual and moral development, and the women of the next generation of American Catholics, who became involved in the movement and were more profoundly influenced by the theology of the Mystical Body of Christ.

More specifically, this chapter will consider Maisie Ward (1889–1975) of the Catholic Evidence Guild and American Catholic publishing house Sheed & Ward; the bookseller and Catholic Library Movement advocate Sara B. O'Neill (1869–1954) and her successor, Nina Polcyn Moore (1914–2006); Dorothy Day (1897–1980) of the Catholic Worker Movement; Catherine de Hueck Doherty (1896–1985) of the Friendship House Movement; and several examples of concurrent trends among American women, witnessed in the pages of *Orate Fratres* during the interwar period.

MAISIE WARD: THEOLOGIAN, PREACHER, PUBLISHER

Early Life and Influences

Maisie Ward stood (on a soapbox) at the very heart of the Catholic intellectual movement which supported and fueled the American

[7] Dolan, *Transforming Parish Ministry*, 24–25.

[8] See Margaret Mary Reher, "The Path to Pluralism, 1920–1985," in *Catholic Intellectual Life in America: A Historical Study of Persons and Movements*, Makers of the Catholic Community Series, ed. Christopher J. Kauffman (New York: Macmillan Publishing Company, 1989): 114–41.

liturgical movement. Born in 1889 in England, Maisie was the eldest of five children of Wilfrid Ward, a prominent Catholic biographer and editor of the *Dublin Review*, and Josephine Ward, a Catholic novelist. As biographer Dana Greene described, Maisie's childhood was "lived in the insular world of nineteenth century English Catholicism" which was both highly intellectual, in the midst of the Oxford Movement, and very interested in liturgical practice.[9] Through her father, Maisie Ward knew leading figures of the Oxford Movement, including Henry Cardinal Newman, G. K. Chesterton, and Robert Browning. But, despite Ward's informal education and attendance at private schools, a university education was still difficult for women to obtain in the first decades of the twentieth century in England.[10]

While a Catholic woman could not independently attend Oxford lectures, she could more easily join a growing core of lay Catholic apologists defending the faith in public open-air lectures.[11] One which quickly became the most prominent was run by the Catholic Evidence Guild, launched in 1918 in the Diocese of Westminster, England, a

[9] See Dana Greene, "Maisie Ward as 'Theologian,'" in *Women and Theology*, The Annual Publication of the College Theology Society, vol. 40, ed. Mary Ann Hinsdale and Phyllis H. Kaminski (Maryknoll: Orbis Books, 1994), 51. Maisie Ward would later reflect, in an article which appeared in *Life of the Spirit* in 1961, that she could "hardly remember, from the time I could read, being unable to find my places in a missal." Maisie Ward, "Changes in the Liturgy: Cri de Coeur," *Life of the Spirit* 16, no. 183 (October 1961): 128.

[10] "Cambridge University was oriented toward mathematics and science and did not admit women. London University allowed women to matriculate, but it was too secular for a Catholic woman to attend. To go to university meant to attend Oxford, where at least Catholics had some connection. Women attended Oxford lectures in the first decades of this century, but a chaperon had to accompany them and they could not enroll in a degree-granting program." Dana Greene, *The Living of Maisie Ward* (Notre Dame: University of Notre Dame Press, 1997), 36.

[11] Open-air lectures were a popular way for speakers and performers to provide entertainment, culture, and news (or propaganda) to the public before the advent of radio. Catherine de Hueck also worked on a lecture circuit, but for the Chautauqua League. See Janet Wilson James, "Women in American Religious History: An Overview," in *Women in American Religion*, ed. Janet Wilson James et al. (Philadelphia: University of Pennsylvania Press, 1980), 1; and Debra Campbell, "'I Can't Imagine Our Lady on an Outdoor Platform': Women in the Catholic Street Propaganda Movement," *U.S. Catholic Historian* 26, no. 1 (2008): 103–14.

movement established after the war by Vernon Redwood, a lay man from New Zealand who wanted to counter inflammatory anti-Catholic speakers in Hyde Park of London.[12] The Guild speakers were volunteers, including teachers, typists, bus conductors, nurses, scientists, housemaids, and professors. Ward, who had no profession, joined the movement in 1919 and was quickly able to devote much time to the Guild, assuming a role as organizer and trainer of new recruits. While Ward had been more associated with the upper-class in her family life, her exposure to the Guild quickly introduced her to working-class and professional people and alerted her to their spiritual acumen. She would later reflect that association within the Guild allowed her to appreciate faithful theological reflection "in the minds of everyday laboring people who never have the opportunity to reflect upon the theology or spirituality that comes trickling down to them through the hierarchy and clergy."[13] Ward felt that her responsibility as a Guild member was to make Catholic teachings come alive for her outdoor audiences. Confident in the ability of lay persons to effectively (and accurately) teach fellow Catholics, she was continually annoyed with clergy and hierarchy who were nervous about Catholic street preachers.[14]

Maisie Ward and Frank Sheed

Maisie Ward married fellow Guild member Frank Sheed (1897–1981), a young law student of Australian heritage, in 1926 when she was thirty-seven, and she continued to lecture in tandem with her husband on topics related to Catholic theology, history, and social ac-

---

[12] For a history of the Catholic Evidence Guild, see Maisie Ward, *Unfinished Business* (New York: Sheed and Ward, 1964); Frank J. Sheed, *The Church and I* (Garden City, NY: Doubleday, 1974); Henry J. Brown, *The Catholic Evidence Movement* (London: Burnes, Oates and Washbourne, 1921); and Campbell, "I Can't Imagine Our Lady," 110.

[13] Debra Campbell, "The Gleanings of a Laywoman's Ministry: Maisie Ward as Preacher, Publisher and Social Activist" (Colby College, 1985), General Print Collection [hereafter cited as PGEN] 103/4549, University of Notre Dame Archives [hereafter cited as UNDA]; see also, Debra Campbell, "Gleanings of a Laywoman's Ministry: Maisie Ward as Preacher, Publisher and Social Activist," *The Month* 258 (August–September 1987): 313–17.

[14] She came to agree with her husband, Frank Sheed, who claimed to have met priests "who [were] more afraid of the laity than of the Communists" (Frank Sheed, *The Church and I*, 2nd ed. [Garden City, NY: Doubleday, 1985], 283.)

tion. As Ward wrote in *Born Catholics*, "two children [Rosemary, 1927, and Wilfrid, 1930] and the firm of Sheed & Ward are a result of their union."[15] At the time of Sheed & Ward's establishment, there was no Catholic publisher exclusively dedicated to Catholic materials or geared to an audience composed of cleric *and* lay persons. Sheed & Ward's opening was, according to one description, "a daring attempt to launch a Catholic publishing firm that did not sell rosaries, medals, and statues to balance its budget."[16] As Frank Sheed would describe, the firm (which first opened in London but moved to New York in 1933) aimed to serve Catholics by hitting them "just above the middle of a brow" which was, as Sheed noted, "not a congested area."[17] Maisie Ward, as vice president of the company, worked in a variety of roles, including selecting, editing, and translating manuscripts, cultivating authors, drawing up contracts, and occasionally dealing in financial matters. Though women working in journalism and publishing were not unique, the public only gradually realized that "Ward" was a "Mrs.," as evidenced by an era-typical jingle which appeared in a comic column in the *Daily Express* during the early years of Sheed & Ward: "When I am in my direst need, I seek the help of Mr. Sheed. But much prefer when I am bored, the company of Mr. Ward."[18]

Public Lectures and the Move to America

Sheed & Ward continued to expand, and in early 1929, when Frank Sheed had an opportunity for a lecture tour in the United States, Maisie Ward went with him, where she found the warmth and eagerness of the audiences appealing. Both Ward and Sheed believed they were contributing to something greater; speaking at Catholic colleges and high schools, Newman Centers, communion breakfasts, and parish gatherings, they visited states across the country, including New York, Illinois, Minnesota, and Oklahoma. The lectures invigorated Ward:

[15] Maisie Ward, "Maisie Ward," in *Born Catholics*, ed. Frank J. Sheed (New York: Sheed & Ward, 1954), 123. The Ward of "Sheed and Ward" was initially supposed to be Maisie's brother, Leo. However, due to his lack of business acumen and poor health, it quickly became evident that he was not up to the work and that Maisie could competently take up the task. See Greene, *The Living of Maisie Ward*, 64–65.

[16] Campbell, PGEN 103/4549, UNDA.

[17] Sheed, *The Church and I*, 87.

[18] Greene, *The Living of Maisie Ward*, 73; Ward, *Unfinished Business*, 203.

[A] long space without a lecture leaves me played out. Lecturing can be tiring but not to lecture can be utterly exhausting; the details of the day pile up into a dusty heap of depression. The only alleviation is writing—or reading in preparation for a book. Writing, too is a form of expression—but lecturing is more: it is an exchange of ideas, a meeting of minds, a friendly clash of personalities. In short, it is life.[19]

Her identity as a woman lecturer was not totally unique, as numerous women were involved in "street-preaching" during the era. Nevertheless, women on the public platform were still somewhat surprising to audiences.[20]

The Sheed and Ward's lecture travels to the United States convinced them to open a New York office in 1933. Though an expansion of one's business in the midst of the Depression was risky indeed, the move to America was auspicious. While the Catholic intellectual revival in England had reached a standstill, despite its terrific outpouring of Catholic literature, the small number of Catholics and the distinctive history of the Catholic Church of England prevented the Church from reaching into the systems of education, the press, and the like, which would expand readership. Nevertheless, even during the Depression, American Catholics proved to be an eager audience.[21] The market for Catholic books was ready, with very few publishers dealing in Catholic materials, and a burgeoning American Catholic audience interested in study clubs, Catholic libraries, Catholic education, and Catholic identity fueled an intellectual revival.[22]

[19] Ward, *Unfinished Business*, 142.

[20] A letter from a college woman named Mary Kate sent to Maisie Ward, from Trinity College in Washington, DC, November 6, 1935, reveals this tension regarding gender and public speaking: "Your lecture at Illchester impressed the dear nuns profoundly, and their enthusiasm has been communicated to their sisters at Trinity to such an extent that I think that even the unpardonable crime of being a woman would never be held against you again." Mary Kate to Maisie Ward, November 6, 1935, Sheed and Ward Family Papers [hereafter cited as CSWD] 5/05, UNDA.

[21] See Greene, *The Living of Maisie Ward*, 86.

[22] Bruce Publishing Company and Newman opened in the 1930s, along with Prentice Hall and McGraw-Hill, adding Catholic lines during this time. See Greene, *The Living of Maisie Ward*, 85.

Liturgical Movement and the Lay Apostolate

Maisie Ward's example reveals how the increasing initiative and responsibility taken up by Catholic laity intersected with the liturgical movement. Reporting to *Orate Fratres* in 1949 regarding a recent conference in Northhamptonshire, England, concerned with "the modern problems of the apostolate," Ward claimed that there was "nothing of which Catholics are becoming more keenly aware today than their union with other Catholics all over the world in the Mystical Body of Christ."[23] Ward was surprised at how many efforts were working together in tandem to "win the world to Christ." A complex network of the liturgy, intellectual societies such as the Catholic Evidence Guild, and "a very ardent intensification of lay spirituality and of Catholic home life" were all needed to form a profound spiritual and liturgical life for the Catholic.[24] She saw the lay apostolate as slowly gaining momentum, slowly understanding what the relation of Christ's Mystical Body to the outside world might be, and slowly realizing its own responsibility.

Reflecting on her experience in liturgical prayer, Ward noted that in "nothing was the lack of a Catholic mind more manifest in my youth than in our attitude towards the Mass," thinking of it as mere machinery for producing communion.[25] But as her understanding of theology and the liturgy developed, she came to describe participation in the Mass as an integral component of Catholic understanding and source of strength that poured into each day lived. She was in accord with proponents of the liturgical movement with regard to how, in liturgical practice, this understanding might be achieved:

> There is no better way for bringing understanding of the Action of Mass, of what is happening at the altar, than for the priest to dialogue the words with the people as he stands facing them at one of those low and narrow altars that in France are now so often placed in the center of the church.[26]

[23] Maisie Ward, "Problems of the Apostolate," *Orate Fratres* 24, no. 1 (1949): 28.

[24] Ibid.

[25] Maisie Ward, "Maisie Ward," in *Born Catholic*, 143.

[26] Ibid. Mary Sparks of South Bend, Indiana, describes how, when she and her husband lived in Paris in the 1940s, their parish priest turned toward the congregation and said Mass in dialogue fashion, with great success. Mary Sparks, interview with the author, May 20, 2010, South Bend, Indiana.

Ward's understanding of Catholic life and liturgy also connected to her concern for social justice, another defining strain of the early-to-interwar period liturgical movement. In her later years, she sought to provide better social services in India and low-income housing in England, and she advocated for the Catholic Worker, though she was not always at one with Dorothy Day's methods.[27] Maisie Ward saw liturgical renewal as walking hand-in-hand with movements for social justice, with groups everywhere choosing to live in voluntary poverty so that the Mystical Body of Christ might be realized.[28] These groups made the Mass and the Divine Office the "food of an intense Catholic life."[29]

In the United States, Maisie Ward served as an important liaison between the latest in intellectual thought, Catholic Action, the liturgical movement and American colleges. The first theology program for lay Catholics, begun under the initiative of Mother Mary Madeleva Wolff, CSC (1887–1964), of Saint Mary's College at Notre Dame in 1944, was a frequent stop for Maisie Ward.[30] During Madeleva Wolff's tenure at Saint Mary's, rarely a year went by when either Maisie or Frank or both made a visit to Saint Mary's and Notre Dame, keeping

[27] Ward was critical of Dorothy Day's arrests (often prompted by antiwar demonstrations) which seemed to increase with Day's years: "She herself is doing more to spoil her own great work than all the opposition by Conservative elements could ever do. The initial impulse to a real alteration in Catholic social thinking came from Peter Maurin and Dorothy: I used to believe chiefly from her but I am beginning to wonder. . . . Later on came the Catholic Interracial Movement, the Family Movement, the Grail. All these and many small groups, many families owe so much to the Worker, but for years now Dorothy herself has dragged one red herring after another across her own path: First extreme pacifism, then an almost Jansenist view of the spiritual life, then 'Christian anarchism' have filled the paper, crowding out of course the original spending presentment of the workers' needs natural and supernatural, the picture of what is being done and can be done to inspire and teach, as well as to clothe and house." Ward, "Journal," p. 17, CSWD 13/19, UNDA.

[28] Her understanding of the Mystical Body is apparent in *This Burning Heat* (New York: Sheed & Ward, 1941), which she wrote in response to the Second World War, and the connection between the Mystical Body and activism is explained in *Be Not Solicitous*, ed. Maisie Ward, (New York: Sheed & Ward, 1953).

[29] Ward, "Journal," p. 8, CSWD 13/19, UNDA.

[30] Gail Porter Mandell, *Madeleva: A Biography* (Albany: State University of New York Press, 1997).

both schools' faculties and students informed of the latest works in the Catholic intellectual world.[31] Not only a go-between for students and books, Ward herself was a respected writer. She authored twenty-nine books and oversaw the publishing of the most prominent Catholic English Revivalists, including G. K. Chesterton, Hilaire Belloc, C. C. Martindale, Ronald Knox, Christopher Dawson, and E. I. Watkin. Sheed & Ward published all the major new theological works in English for American audiences, both during the liturgical movement and into the years following the Second Vatican Council, including Gregory Baum, Edward Schillebeeckx, Hans Urs von Balthasar, Jean Danielou, Karl Rahner, Avery Dulles, and Joseph Ratzinger.[32] Ward was also a thorough, though rather overly sympathetic, biographer and was best known for her biographies, particularly those of G. K. Chesterton, Henry Cardinal Newman, Robert Browning, and her own extensive family history (in three volumes).[33] Ward's subjects also included the lives and activity of women, ranging from Catherine of Sienna to Caryll Houselander.

---

[31] Ibid., 166.

[32] Dolores Elis Brien, in "The Catholic Revival Revisited," claims that "Maisie Ward, perhaps more than anyone, brought to our attention the heroic efforts of the French clergy and laity to revitalize the faith in that country. French thinkers and activists, such as Abbe Godin, Abbe Michonneau, Henry Perrin, Jacques Loew, Yves de Montcheuil, Jean Danielou, Yves Congar, Henri de Lubac, and Cardinal Célestin Suhard, had a profound influence on me." Brien, "The Catholic Revival Revisited," *Commonweal* (December 21, 1979): 714–16.

[33] *Gilbert Keith Chesterton* (New York: Sheed & Ward, 1943); *Young Mr. Newman* (New York: Sheed & Ward, 1948); *Robert Browning and His World: The Private Face—1812–1861*, vol. 1, and *Robert Browning and His World: Two Robert Brownings?* vol. 2 (New York: Holt, Rinehart and Winston, 1967, 1969); *Caryll Houselander: The Divine Eccentric* (New York: Sheed & Ward, 1962); *The Wilfrid Wards and the Transition: The Nineteenth Century* and *The Wilfrid Wards and the Transition: Insurrection versus Resurrection* (London: Sheed & Ward, 1934, 1937). While her work as a biographer was extensive and thorough, Maisie Ward was criticized of being too sympathetic toward her subjects and therefore uncritical. Graham Greene, in a review of her biography of Chesterton, wrote : "Mrs. Ward is too fond of her subject and too close to it to reduce her material into a portrait for strangers." Graham Greene, *Collected Essays* (London: Bodley Head, 1969), 135.

Tracing the Trajectory of the Liturgical Movement
into the Catholic Family Life

At the height of the Catholic Intellectual Movement, Ward served as a speaker-publisher-writer who fueled the efforts of liturgical pioneers to educate the faithful and learn the liturgy. As the liturgical movement shifted from larger goals of social reform to interest in promoting liturgy in the family in the post–Second World War era, however, Ward also moved her energies to this strain of the liturgical movement. Among her efforts in this vein was the collection of essays considering marriage, spirituality, and the family, in *Be Not Solicitous: Sidelights on the Providence of God and the Catholic Family* (1953). Ward wished to advocate that responsibility for physical, economic, and spiritual care should rest not on the individual family alone but on all the families which together made up the Church, Christ's body.[34] With regard to the state of the Catholic family and the liturgical life, Maisie Ward astutely observed:

> It was the weakness of nineteenth-century social and religious work that it always groups the objects of its attention by age and by sex. Today we still see this in the structure of our parishes: men's clubs, women's clubs, boys' clubs, girls' clubs. Children of Mary, Knights of Columbus, Men's Communion Day, Children's Mass. The family has been split today, not only by its enemies the Communists but by its friends the Catholics.[35]

The experience of splitting up one's family was widespread, as Mary Sparks, parishioner of St. Joseph Parish in South Bend, Indiana, related about her experience as a young wife and mother in Wakefield, Massachusetts: "We went to Mass, but children had to go downstairs for children's mass; you never got to go to Church with family: Mom to early Mass, dad to the 8:30 Mass!"[36] The Mystical Body, as Ward described, was not located in the individual family, nor was it supported by gendered divisions. Rather, a model of integrated family life best reflected the aims of the Mystical Body and provided a ground for liturgical formation.

[34] Maisie Ward, "Plea for the Family," in *Be Not Solicitous*, ed. Maisie Ward (New York: Sheed & Ward, 1953), 37.

[35] Ibid., 9.

[36] Mary Sparks, interview with the author, May 20, 2010, South Bend, Indiana.

Ward evaluated that there was a drive, in the 1950s, for Catholics to rediscover "the fullness and richness of the supernatural community, through exploring all that is contained in the Christian idea of marriage and family life."[37] Hence, the development of family life study groups, Cana conferences, retreats for married couples, the Catholic Rural Life Movement, the Christian Family Movement, and the "Liturgical Revival" were all increasingly centered on the family.[38] Her insight, that is, that families composed of lay persons had volition in promoting and living a Christian life, coincided with her belief in the importance of lay initiative, formed by her experience and leadership work with the Catholic Evidence Guild. She strongly believed in the ability of all, even children, to have theological insight and to acutely appreciate the liturgy. In July 1955, she recorded a story in her journal which she had been told about two children:

> I was told of two children aged around eight and ten who were furious at being taken to churches, one where the rosary was going on during Mass, the other where the congregation was simply silent. "This isn't a bit like Mass" was the reaction of both—for the priest who teaches them to answer teaches them too what the Mass means, and even near-babies begin to demand a real participation.[39]

Nor was an active understanding of faith limited to the most educated Catholics. Forums which invited lay participation and reflection were crucial for drawing all into active lives of faith. In a Catholic Evidence Guild meeting (upon which she was reflecting in 1955), she once saw a young, somewhat unkempt but recently baptized boy stand up. In front of the crowd, he began, slowly and surely, to describe what it meant for God to create the world. Grasping how significant the young boy's insight was, Ward concluded that it was "a great strength of the Guild" to discover "insight where it is seldom dug out—for [insight] lies deep, in so many whose education stopped at fourteen."[40] Children and adults alike were designed for the Mystical Body of Christ.

[37] Ward, "Plea for the Family," 12.
[38] Ibid.
[39] Ward, "Journal," p. 7, CSWD 13/19, UNDA.
[40] Ibid., p. 6.

Closer to the days of the Council, Maisie Ward provides an interesting perspective on the development of liturgical reform and lay initiative as the liturgical movement entered a new phase of reform with Church-wide restoration of Holy Week services. Following the restored Easter Vigil (1951) and Holy Week (1955), Ward actually took umbrage to the assumption that Holy Week had only been "given back" to the laity,[41] claiming that she and not a few others could say the Easter Vigil liturgy, for example, "almost by heart, so long had we been devoted to it."[42] Unlike some of her contemporaries who reflected on the liturgical movement on the eve of the Second Vatican Council, Ward interpreted the liturgical movement as strongly at the hest of lay persons:

> I think it is sometimes too lightly assumed that the liturgy for the laity only started of recent years. . . . The liturgical movement may have been a revolution for the laity of the rosary-at-mass variety, but there are many others who were already doing all they could to participate, and longing to be allowed to do more.[43]

In considering the development of the liturgical movement, Ward pointed to Pius X's influence upon the liturgical movement, in his restoring of early and frequent Communion and urging congregational singing, but observed that his invitation for "real lay participation in the central act of the liturgy was only very slowly accepted."[44] That is, while frequent Communion did begin, it seldom took its proper place in the Mass.[45] Congregational singing fared somewhat better but still

---

[41] See Anne C. McGuire, "The Reform of Holy Week, 1951–1969: Process, Problems, and Possibilities" (PhD diss., University of Notre Dame, 2001); "The Restoration of the Holy Week Order," translation of *"Liturgicus Hebdomadae Sanctae Ordo Instauratur,"* in *The New Liturgy: A Documentation, 1903–1965,* ed. Kevin Seasoltz (New York: Herder and Herder, 1966), 211; "Liturgy of Holy Week: Palm Sunday, Holy Thursday, Good Friday, Easter Vigil, and Easter Mass," *Jubilee* 3 (1956): 2–24.

[42] Ward, "Cri de Coeur," 128.

[43] Ibid.

[44] Ibid., 129.

[45] Ibid. Ward continued: "Frequent communion did begin at once; but in Italy itself and most other European countries this meant, as I well remember, a priest rushing to the Blessed Sacrament chapel every half hour, in some

remained "a rarity."[46] Aware that the liturgical movement "began" in different countries under different circumstances, she evaluated that, in Belgium, the real movement began with Lambert Beauduin's directing of the dialogue Mass and the use of the missal and the publishing of *La Piété de L'Église* (1914). Likewise, in the same year, she marked the beginning of the German movement as taking place at a meeting of lay people at Maria Laach who, under the direction of Ildefons Herwegen, focused their discussion on the liturgy as the center of life. Ward described:

> The Abbey could not fail in itself to give a deep inspiration, the Abbot's presence to insure wise guidance—but I love to think that it was a group of laymen—doctors, lawyers, university professors—who were at the heart of the German movement for a greater lay participation.[47]

Both instances depended on lay participation. Ward felt quite certain that the value of liturgical studies and theological reflection would only be evidenced by practical development at the parish level. In short, success in pastoral application was "one chief test of liturgical

---

churches even every time anyone chose to ring a bell, and distributing communion with no relation to the masses going on at perhaps half a dozen altars in the larger churches. In small churches communion was given out before and after—but seldom in its proper place in the mass." See also Joseph Dougherty, in *From Altar-Throne to Table: The Campaign for Frequent Holy Communion in the Catholic Church*, who draws a distinction between "devotional Communion," or "Communion-on-demand," and "liturgical communion." Communion, disjunct from the Mass, lost its proper relation in the liturgical realization of salvation history in the Eucharist. See Dougherty, *From Altar-Throne to Table*, ATLA Monograph Series, no. 50 (Lanham, MD: The Scarecrow Press, 2010): 197–204. See also Joseph Kramp, "A Religio-Psychological Attitude toward the Eucharist," *Orate Fratres* 4 (1930): 514–21, here at 516: "No connection between the Mass and Communion is recognized other than that Mass affords the opportunity to communicate. But one can communicate at all times; it is possible even by an act of the soul, for adoration excels everything and unites everything into one. It is remarkable that the popular opinion obtains that the recitation of the Rosary during a Mass has more value than outside of Mass; while Communion is rather received before Mass than during it."

[46] Ward, "Cri de Coeur," 129.
[47] Ibid.

development."[48] How would liturgical change be deemed successful? For Ward, positive liturgical changes would be manifest in empirical modes which facilitated active participation:

> If it is our sacrifice we must know what is happening and take part in it. The words at the altar should be audible. What mass is being said should be announced, especially if the Proper is not being read in the vernacular. If at all possible we should be able to *see*. For this, modern churches are far better than gothic, with their pillars; an altar at which the priest faces the people far better than one at which his back is turned to them. The dialogue [Mass] has done more to make the mass understood than anything else in my lifetime; and wherever it is adopted it has swept away such nineteenth century practices as the rosary said aloud at mass, or (even more distressing) the novenas that prevailed in so many American churches—"For this relief much thanks."[49]

Interestingly, Ward expressed some reserve about some colleagues or "the little handful of people who may be called the pundits of the liturgical movement," who when anything was "changed or dropped cry out that this is only a beginning."[50] Ward reflected on the danger in changing liturgical practice from a very human standpoint: "Our nerves are kept in a constant state of jitters by the threat that we are going to lose things which mean very much to us, which are immensely helpful to the fullness of our mass, but which are under relentless attack—an attack sometimes delivered by rather unfair methods."[51] She referred to, for example, the last Gospel of John, which she saw as explaining why the Mass had become central for worship of the Creator: "'The word was made flesh and dwelt amongst us—and we saw his glory.' What better words than these can sound in our ears as we leave the place of our sacrifice to take the message of salvation into the world?"[52]

[48] Ibid., 130.
[49] Ibid.
[50] Ibid., 131.
[51] Ibid., 131–32.
[52] Ibid., 133. A priest, with whom Ward was arguing, suggested to her that, if she found these parts of the Mass which were under fire so valuable, perhaps she could recite them by herself in her bedroom? Ward sighed that this response was "strangely to miss the point."

Ward concluded that the "eager questing of today" was a sign that Catholics were no longer "living on the intellect of a former age" but were experiencing an awakening, a good.[53] This prospect could, however, be a dangerous one:

> [O]ur eyes unaccustomed to the light, the immense flood of information, historical, scriptural, theological, may dazzle our mental vision. And I have read enough history to know that if one side of a doctrine has been under-emphasized, the reassertion of the forgotten element may lead to unbalance in the opposite direction.[54]

Her comment was astute, anticipating revisions of the Roman Rite which the Church of the twenty-first century has experienced. Forty years following the liturgical reforms of the Second Vatican Council, which Ward was first beginning to experience at this time, have witnessed a pendulous swing from that which is "progressive" in twenty-first-century standards to that which is described as "traditional."[55] Ward emphasized the need for balance: liturgical development should draw on the Church's many-sided advances in theological and socially oriented thought and action, but, at the same time, liturgical change needed to be sensitive to the pastoral needs of the people in order to be effective and lasting.[56]

[53] Ibid., 136.

[54] Ibid.

[55] For some discussion of the revision of the Roman Rite for English-speaking Catholics, see Keith F. Pecklers, *The Genius of the Roman Rite: On the Reception and Implementation of the New Missal* (Collegeville, MN: Liturgical Press, 2010); and John Baldovin, Mary Collins, Joanne Pierce, and Edward Foley, eds., *A Commentary on the Order of Mass of the Roman Missal* (Collegeville, MN: Liturgical Press, 2011).

[56] Ward was frustrated by well-meaning "reformers" who remained oblivious to the people's practice of prayer. She related some experiences with "liturgically minded" priests attempting to "improve" the liturgical experience of unsuspecting congregations during the opening rites: "What I feel an unfair method is that these [prayers] are said by the priest who disapproves of them in a hurried whisper ('as if', said a Jesuit friend of mine, 'they were dirty words'). Or again, in one church I know, while the priest and server whisper the opening prayers, hymns are sung to drown them. The remainder of the mass is then dialogued. In a church where the full dialogue is the custom, a visiting priest of this persuasion will whisper the *Confiteor* so low as to make it impossible for the congregation to join in. If you talk to him afterwards he first

Maisie Ward's Later Life

Maisie Ward, through her multifaceted and long career, significantly developed the literary and theological tools of the liturgical movement, both through her work with her husband and their publishing business and through her work as a lecturer among American Catholics. The apex of the Sheed & Ward's publishing career was in the 1950s, fueling the Catholic intellectual revival by reprinting classic Catholic literature and encouraging new Catholic writers. The Sheed & Ward business also helped launch other print media which represented the view of the lay apostolate, such as *Integrity*.[57] Yet, aside from her continual writing, editing, and researching, Ward added other social projects to her agenda, particularly the Catholic Housing Aid Society, founded in 1956, which sought to enable impoverished Catholics in Ireland to secure housing.[58] By the early 1960s, however, both Sheed and Ward began to wish for some withdrawal from their busy lives; with anxieties regarding the changing attitude of Catholics following the Second Vatican Council, the decline of the dynamic Catholic Evidence Guild, and the overwhelming need for public housing (as experienced through the Catholic Housing Aid Society), Sheed and Ward decided to transfer control of their publishing business.[59]

Though Sheed & Ward book sales remained steady throughout the Second Vatican Council, they began to decline as numbers of religious women and priests dwindled, one of the largest audiences. In addition, fewer students signing up for religious courses in colleges also depleted book sales. After the Sheed and Ward's withdrawal from the company, they divided their time between England, Australia, and

---

alleges that his concern is pastoral—the people dialogue better if they begin with the *Kyrie eleison*. But anyone could tell him that they do it better in *this* church anyhow if allowed to start in their usual way with the prayers at the foot of the altar." Ward, "Cri de Coeur," 131–32.

[57] Greene, *The Living of Maisie Ward*, 144.

[58] Ibid., 161–63.

[59] Maisie Ward and Frank Sheed were concerned with what they saw as "chaos" arising in the Church following the Council. One year after the Council closed, Frank Sheed recalled, "I remember a conversation we had just before I left San Antonio. Twenty things have come my way since to confirm my view that chaos is staring us in the face," including a "priest in Australia who in the pulpit took a rosary apart and flung pieces into the congregation with the remark 'That's the end of that nonsense.' . . ." Frank Sheed to Bishop Stephen Leven, August 8, 1966, CSWD 1/14, UNDA.

America; they continued to travel and continued involvement with international aid, including both Ireland and India. In 1970, however, Frank Sheed was called back to Sheed & Ward, with which they had had little business contact for the past eight years and suddenly found himself scrambling in an attempt to keep the company solvent. The Sheed and Wards decided to move back to the New York area, finding a tiny apartment in Jersey City, and the publishing business finally sold in 1973 to Universal Press Syndicate.[60] Ward completed her final book, *To and Fro on the Earth*, a chronicle of "a new world being born from the old," in 1973.[61] Maisie Ward died in New York on January 28, 1975; Frank Sheed died in 1981.

SARA B. O'NEILL OF ST. BENET'S LIBRARY AND BOOKSHOP OF CHICAGO

Early Life and Influences

Maisie Ward's involvement with the liturgical movement was multi-faceted and spanned its entirety, from early days and connections with the burgeoning Catholic intellectual revival to its close during the cultural changes of the 1960s. Yet, during its zenith in the pre-Conciliar period, the Catholic intellectual renaissance was buoyed by other parallel literary movements, which also supported the study of the liturgy. One of these was the Catholic Library Movement, fostered by librarians and publishers. Not immediately apparent to twenty-first-century eyes, the relationship of the Catholic Library Movement and the liturgical movement as supporting one another was well recognized. For example, the Catholic Literature Congress, held at Denver November 24–26, 1933, advocated radio talks, conferences, and study clubs which would familiarize the laity with the liturgy of the Church. Catholic schools of all levels, meanwhile, were encouraged to augment their liturgical programs by offering formal courses on the liturgy and encouraging students to purchase Catholic texts (published by Sheed & Ward, for example). Advocating liturgical books, or books about

---

[60] Biographer Dana Greene describes the difficult nature of this move, and the utilitarian lifestyle Sheed and Ward kept, from simple surroundings to public transportation. Ward found the 1970s a difficult stage, full of hopelessness: "a despair wailing through literature and drama, smothered temporarily by drink or drugs but a despair from which suicide offers itself to many as the only exit." Quoted in Dana Greene, *The Living of Maisie Ward*, 197.

[61] Greene, *The Living of Maisie Ward*, 198–203.

liturgy, was considered important for the advancement of liturgy but was also viewed as one of the "chief means towards the revival of Catholic literature in the United States."[62]

Sara B. O'Neill was a chief character in the midwestern scene of Catholic intellectual life, as founder of an (and perhaps the most) influential Catholic bookshop in Chicago during the prime of the liturgical movement. Interestingly, as an early reader of the liturgical journal *Orate Fratres*, O'Neill first became associated with the mainstream liturgical movement by reading Ellen Gates Starr's "Reflections on the Breviary" in 1927. O'Neill was inspired immediately to send in her subscription to *Orate Fratres*.[63] O'Neill's interest in Starr's work on the breviary began a long involvement with other persons in the liturgical movement, as O'Neill's St. Benet Bookshop became not only a place to purchase the newest theological and liturgical texts but a meeting place both for formal meetings of the Chicago Calvert Club (of which both Starr and O'Neill were members) and for more informal meetings of liturgically interested persons. The bookshop also frequently served as a space for liturgical leadership and prayer. O'Neill would serve as a mainstay of the liturgical movement in Chicago, frequently hosting events and advertising for the Liturgical Press at Collegeville.[64]

Born in 1869, Sara B. O'Neill's experience, devoting her lifetime to the Catholic Library Movement, fits neatly both with the benefits to the liturgical movement proffered by the new educational experiences afforded to women and with the desire to cultivate Catholic intellectual life and participation. O'Neill related her account of the founding of this cornerstone of Catholic bookstores:

[62] "The Apostolate," *Orate Fratres* 8, no. 4 (1934): 182.

[63] Ellen Gates Starr wrote to Virgil Michel: "Miss O'Neill said she had sent [her subscription]. She is a Benedictine oblate; I will put in her pretty little card, in case you haven't seen it, though it is rather vainglorious of me." O'Neill's card read: "From my heart I thank you for your beautiful and most inspiring 'Reflexions on the Breviary' which thrill my soul with spiritual delight. My first practical re-action after the initial reading was to send my immediate subscription to Orate Fratres. I will re-read them many times and bless your goodness always. Sincerely, Sara B. O'Neill, Obl., O.S.B." Sara B. O'Neill to Ellen Gates Starr, n.d. [1927?], The Virgil Michel Papers Z 28: 1, St. John's Abbey Archives [hereafter cited as SJAA].

[64] For additional background on St. Benet's, see Margery Frisbie, *An Alley in Chicago: The Life and Legacy of Monsignor John Egan* (Evanston, IL: Sheed & Ward, 2002).

My burning desire for a good, big convenient Catholic Library in Chicago dated from my college days (probably before you or any of your readers were born!), when after graduating from the Public Schools I entered Northwestern University.[65]

At the time of her attendance at Northwestern in 1885, she claimed, there was not one Catholic college for women in the entire country.[66] She became a school teacher when her father died during her third year at Northwestern and remained in the Chicago public school system for thirty-five years. Not forgetting her dream of a Catholic library, she took a course in library science at the University of Chicago, noting that the Benedictines "saved Christian and pagan learning in the Middle ages," and pledged that St. Benedict would be the patron of her library.[67]

Beginning a Library

O'Neill talked of a library week after week to the Calvert Club, a Chicago Catholic group active during the early twentieth century. At one meeting in 1924, the editor of *Catholic New World*, the Chicago archdiocesan paper, overheard her and wrote a story which was also printed in *Publisher's Weekly*, a journal of book trade. Soon, postal workers were staggering up her steps loaded down with catalogues and other advertising matter from book publishers. In her sister's parlor, then, with a large stock of books on hand, O'Neill established credit with publishers. In the parlor window, she hung a placard, "Sara B. O'Neill, Book-dealer for the Chicago Calvert Club," announcing that she would be at home Tuesdays, afternoon and evening, and

[65] "As We See It," *This Week in Chicago: the Magazine of Chicago* (1951), The Nina Polcyn Moore Collection [hereafter cited as CPOL] 1/18, UNDA.

[66] At Northwestern University, O'Neill was the only Catholic in the Liberal Arts Department and, she joked, if there had been a Newman club, she would have been the whole club, officers and members rolled into one! "Open Letter to the Grail," in *The Grail* 13, no. 5 (May 1950): 16–25, CPOL 1/18, UNDA.

[67] Bob Senser, "Library in the Marketplace," *The Catholic Digest: The Golden Thread of Catholic Thought* 11, no. 2 (1947): 32, condensed from *Today* (November 1946), CPOL 1/18, UNDA. Benedictine influence inspired O'Neill's pilgrimage to Monte Cassino in Italy in 1902, during which she was received as a Benedictine oblate at that ancient monastery, the same monastery to which Ellen Gates Starr made three pilgrimages.

serve tea.[68] On her first Tuesday, she had a "whole houseful" arrive for the novelty and took in fifty-six dollars, but the next Tuesday, nobody came. Nevertheless, George N. Shuster of *Commonweal* continued to print her "absurd announcement" gratuitously in his Catholic weekly, which afforded her sporadic success. O'Neill wryly evaluated that "people would rather have their clothes torn off in a crowded department store than enter a private home to buy books, even with the enticement of tea and cookies."[69]

In 1931, Fr. Timothy Rowan, moderator for Chicago's Archdiocesan Council of Catholic Women, offered a corner of the fourteenth floor of the McCormick Building, on VanBuren and Michigan in Chicago, and O'Neill's "Calvert Renting Library" opened on October 31, 1931, carrying about 250 books and "about the same number of dollars."[70] O'Neill found it very difficult to carry on the library and meet its expenses and was frustrated by the Archdiocese of Chicago's lack of support for this "very Cinderella of all Chicago Libraries." She and her storekeepers had barely enough to pay office expenses, paid for books from private donations, and charged only three cents a day for book rentals and ten cents for tea during Saturday afternoon *causeries*. In 1933, the archdiocese and library parted ways, but O'Neill and two friends decided to keep it running. The principal benefactors, two Protestant men who managed the McCormick building, gave the women two years of donated space, until a paying tenant would force the library to move.[71] In 1937, O'Neill incorporated the library and changed its name from Calvert to Benet, the Anglicized form of Benedict.[72] O'Neill recalled those

[68] "As We See It," p. 12, CPOL 1/18, UNDA.

[69] Ibid.

[70] Ibid., 13. "When the clocks struck noon that day, six women and a priest-moderator knelt down and recited the *Angelus*. Later they went to work on their library, 250 books in the corner of the office of the Archdiocesan Council of Catholic Women." Bob Senser, "Library in the Marketplace," p. 32, CPOL 1/18, UNDA.

[71] O'Neill described them as "two good Protestant men," Philip Peck and Mr. Curtis. "As We See It," p. 13, CPOL 1/18, UNDA.

[72] O'Neill noted that becoming independent from the Calvert Club was "a subtle way of making it known that, if anyone wanted to die and leave us some money or make us a substantial gift without dying, it was all right with the State of Illinois and likewise with us. It must have been a little too subtle. No one took the hint and there was neither legacy nor gift." "As We See It," p. 2, CPOL 1/18, UNDA; see also Senser, "Library in the Marketplace," p. 33,

earliest years, observing, "we had really little to encourage us except our enthusiasm, which fortunately was of the Irish brand that thrives on defeat."[73]

O'Neill, the Chicago Switchboard for the Liturgical Life

Though the library's start was slow, O'Neill brought extensive aptitude and determination to the project which eventually secured its success. Extensive study and travel had afforded her a knowledge of the latest in Catholic intellectual life and, particularly, liturgical subjects in both Europe and the United States. Her familiarity with several foreign languages aided her European travels and observations of liturgical renewal in European monasteries, to which she made numerous visits. Like her friends Frank Sheed and Maisie Ward, she was concerned with the lack of dissemination of Catholic literature and theology among the Catholic faithful and chose, as a member of the lay apostolate, to act upon it. O'Neill's knowledge allowed her to operate as a veritable switchboard for the latest in the liturgical life in the Chicago area, knowing all the major figures in the developing Catholicism of the 1930s and its new progressive voice.[74] In Keith Pecklers' evaluation of the liturgical movement, he describes O'Neill as "more educated and informed than most American clergy at the time," a claim supported by her challenges to priests and her intensive study of Catholic theology and liturgical literature, both in the United States and Europe.[75]

Despite her savvy and ability, however, after the Second World War began, the library's success began to falter. By the summer of 1942, its patrons were at an all-time low. Following two days when no one crossed its threshold at all, save O'Neill and her two companion librarians, O'Neill announced on its "birthday," October 31, to the twenty-five or so guests gathered on the fourteenth floor of the skyscraper, that she thought it would be the last such celebration. Word

---

CPOL 1/18, UNDA. The name "Benet" was chosen, as O'Neill later related, with two objects in mind: first, as an opportunity to tell of the Benedictine order, and, second, it saved several dollars off the price of gilt-lettered signs on the windows. "Open Letter to the Grail," pp. 16–25, CPOL 1/18, UNDA.

[73] "As We See It," p. 13, CPOL 1/18, UNDA.

[74] See Keith F. Pecklers, *The Unread Vision: The Liturgical Movement in the United States of America: 1926–1955* (Collegeville, MN: Liturgical Press, 1998), 202.

[75] Ibid.

of St. Benet's trouble reached Bishop Bernard James Sheil (1888–1969), auxiliary bishop of Chicago, however, and he invited the shop to serve as part of the empiric Sheil School of Social Studies in the Archdiocese of Chicago.[76] At the time of the merger in 1943, the St. Benet Library and Bookshop included more than six thousand volumes and forty periodicals, with a free circulating library and reading room.[77] Nina Polcyn, a Catholic Worker from Milwaukee, joined this network in 1943 when she, at the age of twenty-nine, was invited along with two other women to become part of the staff of the Sheil School of Social Studies, teaching classes in the school and working for O'Neill.[78]

[76] Senser, "Library in the Marketplace," p. 33, CPOL 1/18, UNDA. O'Neill's reaction to Bishop Sheil's invitation was somewhat vague and tongue-in-cheek, as she related how Bishop Sheil approached the St. Benet Bookshop for incorporation as part of the Catholic Youth Organization-sponsored Sheil School of Social Studies: "The King, Bishop Sheil, decided that, after letting the young son box and bowl for a number of years, a school, the Sheil School of Social Studies, would be a good thing for Young Prince, CYO . . . and who would help but Cinderella, with his studies . . . and a new place would be situated on the ground floor . . . [with] two full time librarians. . . . With all her happy heart the mother consented, making only one condition—that the name 'St. Benet' should never be changed. To this his Excellent Majesty smilingly agreed and the work on the new palace (39 E. Congress St) began immediately." "As We See It," p. 14, CPOL 1/18, UNDA.

The Sheil School of Social Studies noted how Pope Pius XI had instructed, "It is of the utmost importance to foster a program of social education." "Chicago CYO Bulletin," p. 35, CPOL 1/18, UNDA. In response to this directive, Sheil authorized the establishment of the CYO Educational Department in 1942. Since that time, developing efforts to fill its purpose, "the presentation of the social teachings of the Church in application to modern problems" led to a program of courses, lecture series, and forums which dealt with problems of social order, race, religious prejudice, war, politics, and peace. During 1946, the school offered 161 courses; class hours attended numbered 36,894, with a weekly average of 1,054. Facilities included three classrooms and three offices on the sixth floor of the Congress Bank Building.

[77] The St. Benet's Bookshop moved temporarily to the new Catholic Youth Organization building on East Congress Street, but city construction of the Congress Highway required a final relocation to 506 South Wabash Avenue, where the shop remained through later owners and past the Second Vatican Council. "Chicago CYO Bulletin," p. 37, CPOL 1/18, UNDA.

[78] See also Dan Herr, "The Gentle Firebrand," *U.S. Catholic* (1964): 12, CPOL 1/18, UNDA.

Intersection with the Liturgical Movement

With the help of a move from the basement of the Sheil School to the street level, the improved location and advertisement helped St. Benet's popularity to soar, attracting prominent Catholic men and women. Articles and reviews regarding the St. Benet's Bookshop revealed its industriousness. As Bob Senser of *Today* wrote in an article titled "Library in the Market Place," "Scenes of heated discussion are common before the window of St. Benet library on E. Congress St. in Chicago."[79] Senser speculated that, if a microphone were concealed outside the shop window, it would pick up some prize arguments on white supremacy, world peace, labor, and divorce. In short, he described, "The St. Benet library serves as intellectual powerhouse not only for individual Catholics (and some non-Catholics) but also for Catholic movements."[80] The library became more properly like a bookstore and sold some of the most important journals and newspapers on liturgical matters, social regeneration, and Catholic Action, including *Orate Fratres*, *The Catholic Worker*, and *The Commonweal*.[81] In a quick turnaround from its near demise in 1942, by 1947 the library's books were overflowing from the shelves and its philosophy and theology

[79] Senser, "Library in the Marketplace," p. 31, CPOL 1/18, UNDA. At the time of Senser's writing, O'Neill was seventy-seven years of age, and he described her as a "fervent preacher of the ideals of St. Benedict, especially his emphasis on the family as the basic unit of society." St. Benet's, Senser noted, was not stuck among beautiful elm trees with robins but was "thriving near gray skyscrapers and noisy 'L' trains on the fringe of Chicago's Loop," thus attracting persons to whom a conventional library seemed forbidding.

[80] Ibid. The Sheil School's influence upon "an amorphous group of Chicago young people" in the mid-1940s to 1950s was "incalculable." With the home base of St. Benet's Bookshop, "religion became brilliantly alive for the first time" and the voices of John Courtney Murray, Maisie Ward, H.A. Reinhold, Jerome Kerwin, Frank Sheed, Karl Stern, and Jacques Maritain were frequently heard. St. Benet's Bookshop was alternately described as an information center, a gathering place for young apostles, a must-stop for Catholic intellectuals passing through the city, and a salon on Saturday afternoons when tea or wine and crackers were served—and a bottle of Benedictine was reserved for very special guests.

[81] Pecklers notes that the St. Benet's Bookshop was, in fact, the only place in Chicago from which *The Commonweal* could be procured in the 1940s. See Pecklers, 203.

collection was considered one of the most complete in Chicago.[82] Visitors to Sara B. O'Neill's shop included "more bishops and monsignors than she could name," along with international visitors (Dom Albert Hammenstede of Maria Laach and Dom Mauro Inguanez, librarian of Monte Cassino Abbey), American liturgical movement activists (Frank Sheed, Maisie Ward, Godfrey Diekmann, H. A. Reinhold), and renowned scholars (including Jacques Maritain).[83] All these and many young Catholics attended the events hosted by the bookshop, with the latest in theology inspiring conversations which fueled their Catholic faith. This faithful and intellectual pursuit was attended by a network of friendships "formed and sealed for life and eternity" and supported by the regular weekly recitation or chanting of Compline at the close of work on Saturday afternoon.[84] At the bookshop, O'Neill's influence formed a community:

> Every Saturday afternoon members of the "family" gather to nourish their bodies and souls. For their bodies they sip tea and munch cookies. For their souls they partake in a much neglected art, conversation, and wind up the week's business by reciting Compline, official night prayer of the Church. In other words, this is a place not shackled by the strict definition of a library, a building devoted to a collection of books. From friendships made at the library wedding bells have rung for half a dozen couples. The religious vocations fostered by Miss O'Neill and the library are beyond tabulation.[85]

[82] "After 15 years of existence the library now has spread through three ordinary stores. Its books are so numerous that some no longer have room on the shelves. Its philosophy and theology collection, boasting the 22-volume *Summa Theologica* in English, is one of the most complete in Chicago. And all these can be borrowed free for two weeks after payment of a 25-cent registration fee." Senser, "Library in the Marketplace," p. 33, CPOL 1/18, UNDA.

[83] "Open Letter to the Grail," p. 25, CPOL 1/18, UNDA.

[84] Ibid., p. 24, CPOL 1/18, UNDA.

[85] Senser, "Library in the Marketplace," p. 32, CPOL 1/18, UNDA. O'Neill affirmed: "Almost from the beginning we have served tea every Saturday afternoon, combined with what one boy called 'untrammeled conversation' (not just gossip), quite informal, usually suggested by the books or by some important Catholic news. This has been a lovely feature of St. Benet's." "Open Letter to the Grail," p. 23, CPOL 1/18, UNDA. Senser added in his article, "Library in the Marketplace," "This magic is wrought by a white-haired woman with an integrated personality the like of which is seldom matched

As with Maisie Ward, O'Neill's development of the Catholic intellectual life was coterminous with the development of the liturgical life. As a seminarian recalled one of these afternoon tea sessions in the library, "Miss O'Neill gives us tea and talks with us,—and the next thing we know we're in the monastery with a choir book in our hands."[86]

Until her death in January 1954, O'Neill's love of the liturgy had taken her to each of the National Liturgical Weeks (save 1953 in Grand Rapids, Michigan).[87] During the National Liturgical Weeks, she advocated for lay use of the Psalter, relating the difficulties she had in convincing publishers (including Frank Sheed) to issue it in a cheap and readily available version.[88] She was greatly concerned that Catholics, especially those who seldom opened a Bible (let alone the Old Testament) would never be exposed to the psalms, "the very cream of the Old Testament, and the very core of the Divine Office," and used opportunities during the discussions at the National Liturgical Weeks

---

by laymen. Convinced of her vocation as a single person, she realizes that her job is basically the same as those with vocations to the religious or married life—saving her own soul and those of others. Despite her age, she manages to begin every day with Mass and Communion. As a member of the League of the Divine Office, she says part of the Office daily, and recommends this practice to others." Senser, "Library in the Marketplace," p. 32, CPOL 1/18 UNDA.

[86] *Saint Benet's Booknotes* (1954), CPOL 1/22, UNDA. *Saint Benet's Booknotes* was an occasional bulletin from the St. Benet Library and Bookshop, on 506 S. Wabash Avenue.

[87] In fact, the officers of the Liturgical Conference sent her a telegram telling her she was missed. *Saint Benet's Booknotes* (1954), CPOL 1/22, UNDA.

[88] "I have been wanting to say something about the psalms ever since it was intimated this afternoon that we can't praise God until we get into the habit of using God's prayerbook. For some years I have been trying to get people interested in the Psalter. You will hardly believe me when I tell you that educated people, many of them from Catholic schools, do not even know what the Psalter is, and I don't believe they all know that it begins with a 'P.' For years I have been importuning various publishers, trying to get them to print a cheap and new translation of the Psalter. One of them was my friend, Mr. Frank Sheed, and his answer was: 'No, Miss O'Neill, I don't think the Psalter would ever be a seller.' He had not lost his sense of humor, even though his London shop had just been bombed out of existence, so I forgave him the pun." "Discussion," in *1942 Liturgical Week Proceedings* (Newark, NJ: Benedictine Liturgical Conference, 1943): 75.

to voice her attack on those with power to advocate (including the editors of *Orate Fratres*).[89]

In these instances, O'Neill offered her own example of St. Benet's Bookshop, with its weekly recitation of Compline, as an example of the ability of the faithful to pray the Divine Office. In a discussion at the National Liturgical Week in 1940, O'Neill described:

> I am the one who has the tea parties in the library. We have all classes of piety and liturgicalness at the library and I generally, at 5:30, invite the godless ones to get out if they don't want to sing Compline. A number of them, particularly two very fine individuals, simply will not say it because we have been saying it in the Latin and their particular hobby is that it should be said in the vernacular. So, we compromise and satisfy the laity. We have been saying the Psalms in English, but we most liturgical ones insist upon singing the Latin hymns and the *Nunc dimittis*. By the way, Mary Perkins was the one who first showed us how beautiful the canticle is when it is sung.[90]

The issue of the vernacular is also interesting here, as O'Neill simply dismissed those objectors as "unliturgical." This, again, reflects how emphasis in liturgical renewal was not placed upon the medium of the liturgy but on an intellectual effort to study and appreciate the present form, learn it, and participate in it. As her words reflect, O'Neill devoted her life to ensuring intellectual participation and spiritual desire for the sacraments, the Mass, and the Divine Office. Beginning in tandem with the earliest days of the liturgical movement and directly influenced by its core members, O'Neill certainly deserves to be remembered as a "vigorous pioneer in the liturgical movement in this country."[91]

---

[89] "So I want to beg everyone here who has anything to do with a printing press to do something to help me get a cheap edition of the Psalter, which is the very cream of the Old Testament, and the very core of the Divine Office; so that it can be distributed in our Catholic schools that they may learn to love it and use it for their prayers." "Discussion," *1942 Liturgical Week Proceedings*, 76.

[90] "Discussion," in *1940 Liturgical Week Proceedings* (Newark, NJ: Benedictine Liturgical Conference, 1941): 159. After Compline, many of the group walked across the street to eat dinner together in the Congress hotel; Nina Polcyn Moore reflected, "Customers must have thought they had entered something crazy. [H. A.] Reinhold felt it [Compline in the bookshop] was inappropriate." See Pecklers, 204.

[91] *Saint Benet's Booknotes* (1954), CPOL 1/22, UNDA. Even months before her death in January 1954, O'Neill wrote to the editor of *Orate Fratres* when

NINA POLCYN MOORE AND THE NEXT GENERATION OF LITURGICAL ADVOCATES

Beginnings at the Worker

Fortunately, the St. Benet Bookshop's role in the liturgical movement did not die with the death of Sara B. O'Neill in 1954. As noted above, ten years prior, in 1943, the bookshop's management had been given to a young woman from Milwaukee, Wisconsin, Nina Polcyn (pronounced "Pole-tsin"). Born in 1914 to "very poor" Polish parents, Polcyn's mother worked at the notions counter in a store and her father, a socialist, worked as a railroad switchman. As a young person, Polcyn participated in summer classes where Jesuits from St. Louis came to speak about baptism, Eucharist, and other topics, providing a unique education in Catholic formation.[92] Also important for her development, Polcyn was introduced to *The Catholic Worker* paper by Franklyn Kennedy, a priest who was a graduate student in journalism at Marquette University and editor of the Milwaukee diocesan paper. He was an early subscriber to the *Worker* and brought copies to be distributed to the Catholic Instruction League at St. Matthew's in 1934, where Nina Polcyn was attending religious instruction. Polcyn attended Marquette University and, upon graduating in 1935, went to New York City to stay at the Catholic Worker for a month.[93] There, she formed a

---

she felt that certain important liturgical books, such as Msgr. Frey's *My Daily Psalm Book*, were "sadly neglected" by the liturgical journal when it should have hailed the new volume "with crashing cymbals and trumpets of joy!" "An Ideal Psalm Book," in "The Apostolate," *Orate Fratres* 27, no. 6 (1953): 328. Godfrey Diekmann responded to O'Neill's note: "The Editor crashed cymbals enthusiastically when the Psalm Book was published (cf. *Orate Fratres* 22, no. 2 (1947): 95), but perhaps didn't blow the trumpet of joy as sostenuto as the book warrants. He therefore hopes that publishing this letter, by America's most vigorous (though most senior) lay apostle of the psalter, will serve to re-focus attention on the merits of Msgr. Frey's important contribution to the liturgical revival." Editor, "Editor's Note," in "The Apostolate," *Orate Fratres* 27, no. 6 (1953): 330.

[92] Marilyn McKinley Parrish, "Seeking Authenticity: Women and Learning in the Catholic Worker Movement" (EdD thesis, College of Education, Pennsylvania State University, 2004), p. 144, Thesis and Dissertations Printed Material 5/04, UNDA.

[93] Ibid., 145.

friendship with Dorothy Day which would last throughout her life.[94] Inspired by the Catholic Worker of New York, Polcyn returned to Milwaukee and formed a core of supporters to open a new house of hospitality; it moved several times but remained open for four years until issues related to management of the house and the war caused it to close.

Contact with Sara B. O'Neill

Nina Polcyn originally came to know Sara B. O'Neill through Catholic Worker circles on her visits to Chicago and at the gatherings of "*The Commonweal* Catholics," as they were called, which met at St. Benet's. Polcyn lived at the Catholic Worker in Milwaukee from 1937 to 1941, at which point she reported that O'Neill herself called with an invitation to come assist at St. Benet's, along with Margaret Blaser.[95] These two women moved to Chicago, where Blaser was to work as an accountant, and Polcyn was to teach in the Sheil School and work in the bookshop.[96] Within a few months, over two thousand adults attended evening classes on topics including liturgy, science, mathematics, women in wartime, and race. Polcyn also organized speakers for the School of Social Studies' Friday night Forums.[97] As witnessed above, at the end of each Saturday, Polcyn and Blaser joined O'Neill in hosting Compline. Again, because the shop was in "the Loop," it was convenient for Saturday shoppers and office workers at the end of a day.

Polcyn's Contribution to the Liturgical Movement

While Polcyn was very much influenced by the Catholic Worker movement and the need for Catholic social action, she was also deeply interested in religious education, an articulate laity, and religious art. Polcyn also initiated new practices in the shop during her tenure as manager. While Polcyn was interested in including liturgical art in the

[94] Polcyn would bail Day from jail when Day was incarcerated in the 1950s, and travel with Day on a three-week trip to Poland, the Soviet Union, and Romania during the 1970s. Parrish, 147.

[95] Catherine de Hueck had influenced Bishop Sheil and claimed it had been her suggestion to open the school. See "Sheil School Opens Doors," *New World* (January 22, 1943).

[96] See Pecklers, 203, where he describes an interview with Nina Polcyn Moore.

[97] Once, when the speaker was Maisie Ward, the Forum had to be held in a boxing ring because so many people came to hear her. Parrish, 147.

bookshop's merchandise, O'Neill was skeptical. In O'Neill's usual vociferous way, she told Polcyn, "There'll be too much 'kitsch' and you'll burn with Benzinger."[98] Polcyn's selection of high-quality liturgical art, however, somewhat assuaged O'Neill. Polcyn was, in fact, interested in purchasing art which reflected the best in liturgical thought. As an article praising the bookshop's new merchandise described, "Good religious art, as she sees it, must be motivated by the spirit of the liturgy. The materials must be good and the artist must use them with integrity. There must be a feeling of awe, of majesty about the work. And, above all, an aura of mystery that will trigger the imagination."[99]

In fact, Nina Polcyn's sensibilities were remarkably similar to Ellen Gates Starr's but were marked by the freedom of a different generation. While Polcyn certainly shared in the liturgical movement's mission which her predecessors began, she offered an excellent example of women with new opportunities for professionalism, mobility, and education and how they adopted the work ethic of the liturgical movement's ideas for promoting spiritual understanding, worship experience, and the integration of these into the public sphere. Polcyn chose a route more similar to that of forewomen in the professional side of the liturgical movement, with activity in concert with those women in Catholic social action and a sensibility for the arts.

By the 1940s, however, Polcyn's work was no longer as anomalous as that of her predecessors. In fact, similar bookshops existed throughout the United States, including The Paraclete Bookshop, on the upper east side of New York City, founded by Elizabeth Sullivan on October 2, 1942. Sullivan was also a regular participant in the annual Liturgical Weeks, becoming president of the Liturgical Conference. Like St. Benet's, the Paraclete was also established with the desire to become an educational center for New Yorkers involved with the liturgical movement, such as those at the Catholic Worker.[100] The American Grail likewise had its own bookshops, such as the Junipero Serra Bookshop in San Francisco. The Junipero Serra also hosted roundtable discussions,

<hr />

[98] Nina Polcyn Moore, Interview with Keith Pecklers. See Pecklers, 205. See also Joanna Weber, "The Sacred in Art: Introducing Father Marie-Alain Couturier's Aesthetic," *Worship* 69 (1995): 243–62. Weber describes "kitsch" as "watered-down sentimentality, devoid of any truth, a conglomeration." Weber, 249.

[99] Herr, "Firebrand," *U.S. Catholic* (April 1964): 11.

[100] See Pecklers, 206, in which he interviews Robert Rambusch.

including topics such as renewal within the American Church, and the liturgical movement.[101] Nearly all of these bookstores were run by lay women.[102]

After O'Neill's death and the dissolution of the Sheil School in 1955, Nina Polcyn continued as manager of the shop but began to shift the focus and objective of the shop according to changing needs. In 1958, the shop moved from its Congress Street location to become a next-door neighbor to De Paul University. In this stage of the shop's existence, Polcyn observed that the Catholic literary scene had changed drastically since the shop's inception in 1932. Once unique as a Catholic library, St. Benet's now had to compete with a plethora of bookstores which were willing to supply the demand of a growing body of Catholic readers of rich Catholic literature and theology. St. Benet's needed to respond to a new demand which was, in Polcyn's opinion, the same intensive and informed "merchandizing in Catholic art that once was necessary in Catholic publishing."[103]

Polcyn worked as manager of St. Benet's bookstore for thirty years, from 1943 to 1973. During this time, the shop continued to be influential among Chicago young people and was even included as a field trip destination, as Mary Ann Hinsdale, IHM, relates in her essay, *Women Shaping Theology*.[104] Polcyn ended her involvement in 1973 when she married Thomas Eugene Moore, a former college classmate and a

[101] Ibid., 206–7.

[102] I am grateful to Catherine Osborne, PhD candidate at Fordham University, for this note.

[103] "'Is Honest Art Pretty Art?' St Benet's Shop—DePaul's new neighbour," *De Paul: The University Newsmagazine* 9, no. 3 (1958): p. 14, CPOL 1/18, UNDA.

[104] Mary Ann Hinsdale, interview with author, February 19, 2010, Boston, Massachusetts. See also Mary Ann Hinsdale, *Women Shaping Theology*, 2004 Madeleva Lecture in Spirituality (New York: Paulist Press, 2006): 17. "The nuns who were responsible for introducing me and my high school friends to the Summer School of Catholic Action (in Chicago) also introduced us to a fabulous bookstore, St. Benet's Library and Bookshop, just around the corner from the Conrad Hilton Hotel where the SSCA was held. On Saturday afternoons during the school year, after finishing our 'research' at the downtown Chicago Public Library, my friends and I would amble over to St. Benet's on Wabash Avenue. At the time, I had no idea that the owner, Nina Polcyn Moore, was a friend of Dorothy Day and Msgr. Jack Egan. All I knew was that her store was a spiritual gold mine. It was where I discovered Thomas Merton's *Seven Storey Mountain*, Michel Quoist's *Prayers*, and modern-

widower with five children, and moved to Sauk Center, Michigan. In August of that year, Polcyn Moore sold the shop to Joan Burke and Isabelle Weltzer. The two women had been designing and constructing clergy vestments for ten years and planned to incorporate this business into St. Benet's line of fine liturgical art, books, cards, and jewelry. The shop, however, was not viable. It closed in August 1977 and its space was consumed by the De Paul University Law School.[105] More than ten years after her husband Thomas's death in 1995, Nina Polcyn Moore died in her home in 2006 at the age of ninety-two.

DOROTHY DAY AND THE CATHOLIC WORKER MOVEMENT

Early Life and Influences

Nina Polcyn Moore intersects two realms of the movements which coexisted with and were influenced by the liturgical movement, having participated in both the Catholic intellectual revival and the Catholic Worker Movement. The Catholic Worker Movement calls Dorothy Day to the forefront and, though Day's contribution to Catholicism has been well-documented, her intersection with the liturgical movement is a necessary portion of a history of lay women's involvement and provides a compelling example of how the liturgical movement strove to fuel a true reform of society. The Catholic Worker Movement began during a meeting of Peter Maurin (1877–1949) and Dorothy Day on December 8, 1932, the feast of the Immaculate Conception. They founded *The Catholic Worker* newspaper and the movement the following year in 1933, in order to coordinate a radical Catholic renewal of society. Influenced by the philosophy of personalism, which emphasized the dignity of the human person along with an intense appreciation of each individual's freedom and responsibility, the Catholic Worker Movement challenged the seeping priority of economics and dehumanization which plagued society in the midst of the Great Depression. Characterized by historian Mel Piehl as "a decentralized anarchist movement," the Catholic Worker Movement was, in some ways, an extension of the person of Dorothy Day: "She was at once thoroughly modern and deeply traditional, socially

___

day holy cards from Argus Communications with neat sayings from Teilhard de Chardin, Peter Maurin, and Leon Bloy."

[105] *St. Benet's Booknotes*, CPOL 1/22, UNDA. A personal pilgrimage by the author has verified this.

committed yet uninterested in power, devoted to ideas yet absorbed by elemental concerns, ambitious yet unassuming, completely American and Catholic to her fingertips."[106] One of the most distinctive features of this radical Catholic social movement was its emphasis on integrating the core of the Church's prayer, the Office, and the Mass with the Church's social action.[107]

Day was born in 1897 in New York where her father was a newspaper editor. The family, including Dorothy, her two older brothers, and her baby sister, moved to California when she was a little girl, where they lived until the 1906 San Francisco earthquake destroyed her father's newspaper plant and the family moved to Chicago. They lived a difficult existence in a six-room flat, where the child Dorothy took her share of housework until her father secured a new editorial position.[108] Her father insisted on her reading "good books" which included Scott, Hugo, Dickens, Stevenson, Cooper, and Poe. Her childhood was full of brief but deep impressions of religion and God, culminating in her election to be baptized in the Episcopal Church at the age of twelve.[109] While she had deep religious interest, she was confounded by the disconnect between the direction to love the poor given in the gospel and the way in which the workers, the poor, and the destitute were looked upon as shiftless and worthless, deserving of their lot.[110] Day went to the University of Illinois and, during her tenure there, she became convinced that religion was for the weak: "In my youthful arrogance, in my feeling that I was one of the strong, I felt then for the first time that religion was something I must ruthlessly

---

[106] Mel Piehl, *Breaking Bread: The Catholic Worker and the Origin of Catholic Radicalism in America* (Philadelphia: Temple University Press, 1982), x.

[107] Ibid., xii.

[108] "Without knowing it, I had imbibed a 'philosophy of work,' enjoying the creative aspect of it as well as getting satisfaction from a hard and necessary job well done." Dorothy Day, *The Long Loneliness* (1952; repr., San Francisco: Harper & Row Publishers, 1997), 24.

[109] Day, *The Long Loneliness*, 29.

[110] "I did not see anyone taking off his coat and giving it to the poor. I didn't see anyone having a banquet and calling in the lame, the halt and the blind. And those who were doing it, like the Salvation Army, did not appeal to me. I wanted, though I did not know it then, a synthesis. I wanted life and I wanted the abundant life. I wanted it for others too. . . . I wanted everyone to be kind." Day, *The Long Loneliness*, 39.

cut out of my life."[111] Day became involved with radical secular movements protesting the evils of society and associated herself with the Socialist Party. In her eyes, the Marxists seemed to be "the only people in America committed to improving the conditions of the poor and the victims of bourgeois capitalism."[112]

Disillusionment and Move to Catholicism

In her twenties, Day lived the bohemian life of a Greenwich intellectual in New York as an increasingly well-known journalist and essayist, befriending writers such as Eugene O'Neill, Agnes Boulton, John Dos Passos, and Malcolm Cowley. Yet her life as a radical secular activist was a life of painful separation, floundering, and cultural fragmentation: "mind from body, theory from practice, work from labor, intellect from spirit, knowledge from morals, the individual from the community."[113] She became thoroughly disillusioned with secular political interests as a field for an authentic way of life:[114]

> If I could have felt that communism was the answer to my desire for
> a cause, a motive, a way to walk in, I would have remained as I was.
> But I felt that only faith in Christ could give the answer. The Sermon on
> the Mount answered all the questions as to how to love God and one's
> brother.[115]

Her decade of broken and tumultuous relationships concluded with the birth of her daughter, Tamar Teresa. Day, at the age of thirty, entered the Catholic Church and had her daughter baptized. Dorothy Day fully immersed herself in the teaching, authority, and liturgical life of the Church. In grateful joy, she "turned to God and became a Catholic":

---

[111] Dorothy Day, *From Union Square to Rome* (Silver Spring, MD: Preservation of the Faith Press, 1938), 46–47.

[112] Day, *The Long Loneliness*, 63.

[113] Keith Morton and John Saltmarsh, "A Cultural Context for Understanding Dorothy Day's Social and Political Thought," in *Dorothy Day and the Catholic Worker Movement: Centenary Essays*, Marquette Studies in Theology, no. 32., ed. William J. Thorn et al. (Milwaukee: Marquette University Press, 2001), 234–35, 237.

[114] Dorothy Day described this experience in the rare early autobiography, *The Eleventh Virgin*, of which she attempted to remove all copies in circulation.

[115] Day, *The Long Loneliness*, 141.

I could worship, adore, praise, and thank Him in the company of others. It is difficult to do that without a ritual, without a body with which to love and move, love and praise. I found faith. I became a member of the Mystical Body of Christ.[116]

She received a *St. Andrew Missal*, books by Karl Adam, and Richard Challoner's book of meditations so that she might "learn to follow the seasons of the Church, the saints of the day, and have the doctrinal instruction containing many quotations from the Fathers of the Church."[117]

While her religious convictions were deep, so too was her critique of contemporary American Christianity. Though her decade of radical life had left her spiritually lacking, she continued to look on the radical movement as morally superior to the Church's response to the frightful needs of the poor and issues of social justice: "The Marxists, the IWW's, who looked on religion as the opiate of the people, were the ones who were eager to sacrifice themselves, thus doing without the good things of the world which they were fighting to obtain for their brothers."[118]

Beginning of the Catholic Worker, a Catholic Response to Social Evils

Peter Maurin first contacted Dorothy Day to invite her, as an accomplished newspaperwoman, to start a newspaper to accompany the fledgling Catholic Worker Movement. George Shuster, an editor of *Commonweal* who had worked with Day, had suggested her as editor. *The Catholic Worker* was presented as an alternative labor newspaper to the Communist *Daily Worker*, which advocated violent class struggle.[119] As historians of the Worker Movement, Mark and Louise Zwick

---

[116] Ibid., 10.

[117] See Mark and Louise Zwick, *The Catholic Worker Movement: Intellectual and Spiritual Origins* (Mahwah, NJ: Paulist Press, 2005), 10; and Day, *The Long Loneliness*, 152.

[118] Day, *The Long Loneliness*, 63. See also Piehl, 16–17.

[119] At the time of the printing of the first issue, twenty-five percent of Americans were out of work. The first issue of twenty-five hundred copies was printed by Paulist Press for fifty-seven dollars. See Zwick and Zwick, 22–23. Dorothy related: "Many times we have been asked why we spoke of Catholic workers, and so named the paper. Of course it was not only because we who were in charge of the work, who edited the paper, were all Catholics, but also because we wished to influence Catholics. They were our own, and we reacted

relate that people who "read about hospitality in the newspaper arrived to receive it," and the farms, the Houses of Hospitality, and the bread and soup lines followed.[120] At first, only Day, Maurin, and Day's elder brother John were able to help. But within three or four months, the circulation of *The Catholic Worker* was 2,500; by the end of one year it grew to 100,000, and by 1926 its circulation was 150,000.[121] As the Catholic Worker Houses of Hospitality grew up in other cities outside of New York, each one was independent, loosely associated with the movement in New York City. The Catholic Worker was and remains a lay movement without official status in the Church and without formally organized leadership.[122]

Intersection of the Worker with the Liturgical Movement

Virgil Michel first learned of *The Catholic Worker* and reported on it in the April 1934 issue of *Orate Fratres*. He noted with "genuine satisfaction" that this "veritable godsend in our time of social disintegration and unrest" had appeared:

> The friend of the Liturgical Movement will be agreeably surprised to note that the editors of the paper [*The Catholic Worker*] have caught the spirit of the Church's liturgy and admirably link up their restatement of the Church's social doctrines with the inner life of the Church. They have come to realize that the doctrine of the Mystical Body of Christ is the focal point for all efforts at curing the ills of human society. *The Catholic Worker* is an excellent apology of the Liturgical Revival and its efforts to bring the liturgy into the lives of *all* Catholics. "The liturgy of the Church is the prayer of the Church. The religious life of the people and the economic life of the people ought to be one" (*The Catholic Worker* of February 1). We heartily recommend this courageous little paper to our readers.[123]

---

sharply to the accusation that when it came to private morality the Catholics shone but when it came to social and political morality, they were often consciousless." Day, *The Long Loneliness*, 210.

[120] Zwick and Zwick, 25.

[121] Day, *The Long Loneliness*, 182. The paper sold at a penny a copy; Day sought to develop bulk subscriptions at Catholic schools and parishes. Many parishes, Zwick and Zwick note, received five hundred copies, and one Catholic high school received three thousand copies. Zwick and Zwick, 25.

[122] See Zwick and Zwick, 19.

[123] Virgil Michel, "The Apostolate," *Orate Fratres* 8, no. 6 (1934): 277.

One of the most important aspects of the Catholic Worker Movement was its emphasis on scholarship and faith as the foundation for its existence as a work of mercy, a conviction shared by Peter Maurin and Dorothy Day. As Zwick and Zwick observe, a study of the Catholic Worker Movement might cause one to wonder "where these two people who were committed to voluntary poverty were able to obtain the books to read for their scholarship."[124] One source for books was Michel himself, who had secured permission from his abbot to send the editors of *The Catholic Worker* free copies of all the books issued from Liturgical Press. So appeared *The Catholic Worker* editors' own "Letter to the Editor" following the *gratis* slew of books:

> We are overwhelmed with gratitude at your generosity in sending to us the entire list of publications of the Liturgical Press. They arrived this morning, and the office staff has been sitting around ever since devouring them eagerly and profitably. Nearly all our friends who are interested in social justice from a Catholic point of view, from the very beginning of the paper, have been people equally interested in the Liturgical Movement—a fact which rather surprised us at first, as we hadn't realized that the relation between the two was so widely appreciated. But by now we are well accustomed to having most of the all-day discussions in our office come around eventually to the doctrine of the Mystical Body of Christ. So you can imagine the eagerness with which your donations will be seized upon by the many people who make use of the all-too-meager facilities of our office and library.[125]

As the relationship between Day and Michel developed, he continued to send new books to Day to be reviewed by *The Catholic Worker*[126] and began faithfully including the Worker in *Orate Fratres's* "Apostolate" section.[127]

The spirituality of the Benedictines deeply influenced the Catholic Worker Movement, including its hospitality, liturgical prayer, and

---

[124] Zwick and Zwick, 28–29.

[125] The Editors, "From *The Catholic Worker*," in "The Apostolate," *Orate Fratres* 8, no. 6 (1934): 284.

[126] Paul Marx, *Virgil Michel and the Liturgical Movement* (Collegeville, MN: Liturgical Press, 1957), 374.

[127] For example, a lecture by Rev. John Corbett on "Bringing the Mass to the Masses," and another by Maurice Lavanoux concerned "The Crafts of the Church," in "The Apostolate," *Orate Fratres* 8, no. 7 (1934): 330.

manual labor. These elements, combined with an emphasis on scholarship, formed the "rule" of the Catholic Worker, if it had a rule. As Peter Maurin would describe, Houses of Hospitality would exemplify Christian charity by combining "Cult, Culture, and Learning," which he translated as "Liturgy, Learning, and Agriculture."[128] As Stanley Vishnewski, a longtime Catholic Worker described, "From the Benedictines we got the ideal of Hospitality—Guest Houses—Farming Communes—Liturgical Prayer. Take these away and there is very little left in the Catholic Worker program."[129] Maurin presented an "ideal integration" of a life of work and prayer borrowing the Rule of St. Benedict:

> The motto of St. Benedict was
> *Laborare et Orare*, Labor and Pray.
> Labor and prayer ought to be combined;
> labor ought to be a prayer.
> The liturgy of the Church
> is the prayer of the Church.
> The religious life of the people
> and the economic life of the people
> ought to be one.[130]

While, as Zwick and Zwick note, Maurin brought Benedictine spirituality to the Catholic Worker, Day had long been reading Benedictine writers prior to her reception into the Church.[131] Meanwhile, through Michel, the Worker was closely associated with the Benedictines of St. John's Abbey in Minnesota. Day herself became an oblate with the English Benedictine congregation at Portsmouth Abbey at which Ade

---

[128] See Zwick and Zwick, 42–57. The three prongs of this program, as Peter Maurin envisioned it, were very closely and intentionally related to monasticism and, particularly, the Irish monks. Day herself, both of her own initiative and by the persuasion of Maurin, read the desert fathers extensively.

[129] Brigid O'Shea Merriman, *Searching for Christ: The Spirituality of Dorothy Day* (Notre Dame, IN: University of Notre Dame Press, 1994), 107n98.

[130] See Zwick and Zwick, 54.

[131] "I read *En Route, The Oblate, The Cathedral*, and it was these books which made me feel that I too could be at home in the Catholic Church. . . . They acquainted me with what went on there. . . . I felt the age, the antiquity of the Mass, and here to find in Huysmans' detailed instructions in regard to rubrics, all the complicated ritual, was a great joy to me, so that I went more often to the Cathedral." Day, *The Long Loneliness*, 107.

Bethune (1914–2002), the Catholic Worker artist, would also become an oblate. Influenced by author and *Orate Fratres* contributor Helene Iswolsky, who encouraged Day's interest in Eastern Catholicism and liturgy, Dorothy Day forged contacts with the Benedictine monks of St. Procopius Abbey in Lisle, Illinois. In April 1955 she shifted her oblature to that of St. Procopius.[132]

A common conviction that Catholics could be formed in the Mystical Body of Christ by liturgical participation in the Divine Office, the Mass, and the sacraments knit the Catholic Worker and the liturgical movement tightly together. A comparison of the Catholic Worker Movement and Virgil Michel's social writings reveals striking similarities. Both warned that mere speech about social transformation would accomplish nothing, and an authentic conversion of the world must be actively practiced in lives of sacrifice and in daily living. Michel wrote: "What the early Christians thus did at the altar of God, in the central act of Christian worship, they also lived out in their daily lives."[133] Michel also emphasized that the liturgy provided the source for renewing the social order, describing the liturgy as "the ordinary school of the development of the true Christian, and the very qualities and outlook it develops in him are also those that make for the best realization of a genuine Christian culture."[134] The "doctrine" of the Mystical Body allowed the Church to be understood as an organism, one in which each member had responsibility to work and love for the other, not as

[132] In her April 1957 column in the *Catholic Worker*, Day related: "Now I am a professed oblate of the St. Procopius family, and have been for the last two years, which means that I am a member of the Benedictine community at Lisle [in Illinois]. . . . My special love for St. Procopius is because its special function is to pray for the reunion of Rome and the Eastern Church. Their monks can offer Mass in the Eastern or Roman rite and when Fr. Chrysostom came to give us retreats at Maryfarm, we sang the liturgy of St. John Chrysostom." Day was also a longtime friend of the Trappist monastery at Gethsemani in Kentucky. There, she established her relationship with Thomas Merton, whose writings were often published in *The Catholic Worker* and whose books were reviewed. Zwick and Zwick, 56–57; see also Merriman, *Searching for Christ*, 213–14; and Dorothy Day, "On P," *Catholic Worker* 21 (December 1954): 2, 6.

[133] Virgil Michel, "The Cooperative Movement and the Liturgical Movement," in *Orate Fratres* 14, no. 4 (1940): 155. A number of Michel's writings were published posthumously, including this.

[134] Virgil Michel, "Christian Culture," in *Orate Fratres* 13, no. 7 (1939): 303.

an organization bounded by ecclesial structure. The dynamic understanding of Church life and liturgical participation stood in stark contrast to the general understanding of liturgy, which had been on the external forms of worship.

Throughout the tenure of the liturgical movement, Day continued to intersect with it and its activists, with varying degrees of success. The intellectual edge of the liturgical movement was attractive to Workers, but finding accessible ways to practice the liturgy, such as praying Compline together, was often difficult. As evidenced by the Catholic Worker Farms, Day and other Workers were very interested in the shift of the liturgical movement toward promoting holistic living, such as was modeled by the Grail Movement and paralleled by the National Catholic Rural Life Movement. Yet, the Farms proved difficult to coordinate and sustain. As with the liturgical movement at large, some instances of Worker initiatives were more successful than others, and some disconnect existed between theory/ideals and practice.

A dynamic and complex leader, Dorothy Day, her life, and her work have been well documented, and the course of her long involvement as a faithful Roman Catholic and social activist produced an immense volume of writings and lectures. Her serious realization of the Gospel paired with an equally serious reverence for the liturgy, the Eucharist, and the Mass as formation in the Mystical Body of Christ.[135] Day died in New York in 1980 and is currently under consideration for canonization.

EVALUATING THE INTEGRATION OF SOCIAL REGENERATION AND THE LITURGICAL MOVEMENT

Social Reconstruction and Liturgical Activity

The examples of Dorothy Day and Maisie Ward move the liturgical movement at the hands of women into a somewhat different sphere. While the work of Justine B. Ward, Ellen Gates Starr, and Sara B. O'Neill certainly coincided with the values of intellectual

---

[135] Catholic Workers like to tell the story of how, after the celebration of Mass in a New York House of Hospitality, Day was horrified that the coffee mug, which had been used as an impromptu chalice, would simply be put back on the shelf to be filled with coffee. Instead, Day took the cup out to the backyard and buried it. See, for example, Catholic Worker Jim Forest, who relays the story in *The Road to Emmaus: Pilgrimage as a Way of Life* (Maryknoll, NY: Orbis Books, 2007), 167.

participation, spiritual edification, catechesis, and understanding and fine art elevating the soul, their most direct work in the liturgical movement remained on the form attached to liturgical performance. Justine Ward was interested in the quality of spiritual edification offered by the proper understanding of chant and how this properly executed chant might further the Church's worship. Starr, though she was heavily involved in social reform, found her liturgical outlet in the rendition of the psalms, in learning Latin, and in understanding the breviary as a source for prayer and contemplation. Starr is particularly fascinating because, though she had the very same concerns for labor and the creation of fine handcrafts and art as did Nina Polcyn Moore, Dorothy Day, and, later, Ade Bethune, Starr's liturgical writing remained more on the intellectual understanding of the psalms rather than Catholic renditions of a radical social regeneration. This distinction is perhaps even more interesting because Starr had written about the Church's responsibility for social regeneration before she became a Catholic.[136] In fact, even though Starr *lived* in and *founded* Hull-House, she ultimately left Hull-House because she found it unable to sustain her spiritual quest for the liturgy.

In contrast, these women of a slightly later generation took the liturgical movement to a more radically practical level, more fully integrating the theological notion of the Mystical Body in their understanding of liturgical worship and its necessary implications for social regeneration. For Day, along with Michel and Maurin, the Body of Christ's worship could not be separated from the Church's teachings on service to the poor, most recently reiterated in Pius XI's On Reconstruction of the Social Order (*Quadragesimo Anno*) of 1931. For example, in October 1934, *The Catholic Worker* reported, "The illness of hate, injustice, disunion, prejudice, class war, greed, nationalism, and war weaken this Mystical Body . . . just as the prayers and sacrifices of countless of the faithful strengthen it."[137] Likewise, in 1933, Day wrote, "We feel that it is very necessary to connect the liturgical movement with the social justice movement. . . . Each one gives vitality to the other."[138]

---

[136] Ellen Gates Starr, "Settlements and the Church's Duty," *Publications of the Church of Social Action*, no. 28 (Boston: Church Social Union, 1896).

[137] See *The Catholic Worker* 2 (October 1934), 3.

[138] Dorothy Day to Father Henry Borgmann, December 30, 1933, The Catholic Worker Papers, W-2, Marquette University Archives. For an excellent discussion of the interrelation of Day, Michel, and Maurin, see Zwick and

For many, Catholic liturgical activity and social reconstruction was an increasingly natural connection. As Norman McKenna of New York City and an editor of Catholic and labor publications, wrote:

> Of all groups in the Catholic body in America, those devoted to social reconstruction should be the first to appreciate the value of the liturgical movement. Several of them do; others proceed without reference to the corporate worship of the Church. When the liturgical movement is more generally and properly valued by Christian reconstructionists in this country the Catholic social movement will advance with the impetus of a renewed Christian spirit.[139]

Some years later, Godfrey Diekmann (1908–2002) took up an issue of the Chicago *Catholic Worker* paper, which devoted its leading article and a further full page to explaining how all Catholic activity must have its roots in the liturgical life or else be sterile. Diekmann noted the problem of separating liturgical devotion from popular devotion:

> The liturgy is the worship of, by, and for a people, the people of God, the entire people, hierarchy and laity. Hence only the liturgy can, strictly speaking, be *popular* devotion; and the usual terminology which speaks of private devotions adds "popular" in contradistinction to "liturgical" is a heavy and unfortunate handicap against the liturgical movement. The only way to overcome it is gradually to make the liturgy "popular" also in the derived sense of the word, *i.e.*, familiar to and esteemed by all. To make it such is ultimately the big task of the liturgical renascence.[140]

Diekmann, like Day, Michel, and Maurin, saw the radical meaning of what a "popular" liturgical revival would be. Again, the liturgical movement struggled, somewhat ironically, to be truly "popular."

The Context of the Catholic Worker and Social Reconstruction
Historians of Catholicism regularly identify the Catholic Worker movement as significant in the broadening landscape of American

---

Zwick, "The Liturgical Movement and the Catholic Worker," in *The Catholic Worker Movement: Intellectual and Spiritual Origins*, 58–74.

[139] Norman McKenna, "The Liturgy and Reconstruction," *Orate Fratres* 12, no. 8 (1938): 337–38.

[140] Godfrey Diekmann, "The Apostolate," *Orate Fratres* 15, no. 1 (1940): 43.

Catholicism during the early to mid-twentieth century. Notably, Mel Piehl describes the Catholic Worker Movement as one of the first efforts by Catholics of the post-Reformation era to advocate a radical social gospel effort like that of their Protestant brothers and sisters.[141] While the "Social Gospel" was alive and well during the Progressive era, Catholic movements such as the Worker did not evolve until American Catholicism itself had matured. As a recent dissertation by Marilyn McKinley Parrish concludes, those involved in the Catholic Worker Movement were commonly involved in a "rich and complex environment of learning" within this Catholic social movement.[142] This "complex" culture was part of a broader environment of American Catholicism of the 1930s and 1940s which was consciously developing a counterculture to that of "mainstream" Protestant America. This Catholicism was reinforced by parishes, clubs, Catholic schools, and organizations and fueled by record numbers of vocations to the priestly and religious life, most of all by thousands of religious sisters. The Catholic Worker Movement was, perhaps, an extreme version of a countercultural movement, allowing a more radical Catholicism to emerge. Specifically for the development of American Catholic women, Parrish describes that these social movements were particularly important locales for women. In the decades prior to the 1930s, expectations for women limited their involvement in Church, aside from the convent or involvement in benevolent associations, altar societies, or Sodalities. Evolving Catholic culture increasingly provided opportunities for women to learn, teach, and practice their faith as lay persons both formally and informally.[143]

Spin-Offs of the Catholic Worker and Related Projects

Some other groups and publications "spun off" of the Worker, not all as successful at integrating liturgy and social responsibility. A short-lived literary outgrowth of the *Catholic Worker* was the periodical *Liturgy and Sociology*, issued by the Campion Propaganda Committee of New York and edited by Dorothy Weston (later, Coddington; 1912–66) and Albert Thomas Coddington (1906–69).[144] The movement and sub-

---

[141] See Piehl, *Breaking Bread*, 95.

[142] Parrish, 292.

[143] Ibid., 305.

[144] Virgil Michel reported on this magazine in the context of Christian reconstruction in "Christian Reconstruction Cells," in "The Apostolate," *Orate Fratres* 9, no. 4 (1937): 179–82.

sequent publication began as a rather militant offshoot of the Boston and New York Catholic Worker houses. In 1934 and 1935, Coddington and Weston engaged in street confrontations with pro-Nazi support-ers, accruing some anger and minor violence toward other Catholic Workers. Though first impressed by their adamancy against Nazism, Day ceased to support the "Campionites" and no longer reported on their activities in the Catholic Worker, as she believed that they were actually inciting more violence. The Campionites had assumed that in-tense piety and social concern would require an equally intense attack on the status quo. In addition to the Coddington's pressing Day to oust some of the "bums, deadbeats, and freeloaders" by limiting those who could participate in the soup-line operation (and a failed attempt to re-move Day and take over the Catholic Worker paper), Tom and Dorothy Coddington and followers left by the end of 1936 to begin their own movement and journal, which was published for three years.[145] Using "Prayer-Action-Sacrifice" as their guiding word, the periodical studied the liturgy, the social encyclicals, and the more militant activities of Catholic Action which the Catholic Worker would not embrace. After her marriage, Dorothy Coddington's writing would appear in Orate Fratres in a much less confrontational form, focusing on the family and the teaching of psalms to children.[146] Dorothy Weston Coddington also worked at Time magazine from 1942 to 1944, authored Glory to God in 1951, and worked as editor of medical and educational publications for many years.[147]

[145] See Piehl, 123–24. As Pecklers notes, extensive correspondence in the St. John's Abbey archives reveals that Michel attempted to mediate the dispute between the Campionites and Day, acting as a friend to both. The Campionites identified as a lay group: "We are a lay group. . . . This means that we do not accept priests or clerics in major orders, or religious as active members, but only as advisors, spiritual directors or teachers. We feel that the initiative should come from the layman and the laywoman and that much of the Campion action can only be done by laypeople." "Campion Pamphlet No. 1: The Organization, Development, and Aims of the Campion," (1936), The Catholic Worker Collection, W-9, Marquette University Archives. See also Pecklers, 113–14.

[146] For example, Dorothy Coddington, "Let Those Who Can, Do," Orate Fratres 19, no. 10 (1947): 433–39; and Coddington, "Teaching Psalms to Children," Orate Fratres 23, no. 9 (1947): 403–8.

[147] See Kathleen Hughes, ed. How Firm a Foundation: Voices of the Early Liturgical Movement, (Chicago: Liturgy Training Publications, 1990), 72.

Also finding resonance with other persons and groups was Day's own acumen for finding the arts and scholarship as food for developing a relationship with God. For Dorothy Day, as biographer Robert Coles relates, literature and art were no "mere occasions for aesthetic satisfaction of self-enhancing erudition."[148] Art and literature gave her inspiration for contemplating the poor and helped her to take up the wisdom of other hearts who evoked contemplation and compassion for the poor. Her favorite writers included Dostoevsky, Dickens, and Tolstoy, and she favored the art of Van Gogh and Daumier, who painted the poor and the workers.[149] Day also had a "friendship" with the saints and was concerned that they be authentically and humanly depicted:

> There are . . . the lives of the saints, but they are too often written as though they were not in this world. We have seldom been given the saints as they really were, as they affected the lives of their times. We get them generally, only in their own writings. But instead of that strong meat we are too generally given the pap of hagiographical writing.[150]

[148] Robert Coles, "Introduction" to Dorothy Day, *The Long Loneliness* (1952; repr., San Francisco: Harper & Row Publishers, 199), 5.

[149] Ibid., 4–5.

[150] Dorothy Day, *On Pilgrimage* (New York: Curtis Books, 1972), 90. Day frequently promoted good hagiography and the need for contemporary saints through comments, articles, and book reviews which appeared in *Catholic Worker* [in this note, hereafter *CW*]. For example, "NBTW," *CW* 11 (March 1944): 1; Raymond Larsson, "The Fruits of Wonders in the Lives of the Saints," *CW* 17 (March 1951): 3, 8; Dorothy Day, "The Race of Heroes and Saints," *CW* 18 (January 1953): 1, 7–8; Pat Jordan, "Thomas More: God's Loyal Servant," *CW* 41 (February 1975): 8; Review of Margaret T. Monro, *A Book of Unlikely Saints* (New York: Longmans, Green, 1943), in *CW* 10 (December 1943): 7. Day's only full-length biography of a saint, *Therese*, considered St. Thérèse of Lisieux, recently canonized, in 1927. Day, *Therese* (Notre Dame, IN: Fides Publishers Association, 1960). Day found much resonance with Philip Neri and Francis of Assisi but was attracted to feminine models of sainthood. For example, she wrote of Teresa of Avila: "She was a mystic and a practical woman, a recluse and a traveler. She liked to read novels when she was a young girl, and she wore a bright red dress when she entered the convent. Once . . . when she was crossing over a stream, she was thrown from her donkey. The story goes that the Lord said to her, 'That is how I treat my friends,' and she replied, 'That is why you have so few of them.'" See Piehl, 19.

Day's interest in understanding the saints as true and human persons, not milky and ungraspable inaccessible ideals, resonated with Ade Bethune's own depiction of the saints, famously carved, colored, and blazoned throughout her media, and in the pages of *The Catholic Worker*. Bethune's work was first advertised in *Orate Fratres* in December 1936.[151] Also interested in the witness of the saints for modern Catholic life, Dr. Mary Elizabeth Walsh (1905–87), associate of Msgr. Paul Hanly Furfey (1896–1992) in the Department of Sociology at The Catholic University of America, authored *The Saints and Social Work* in 1936. First written as a doctoral dissertation, Walsh examined social workers who died between 1835 and 1936 and delved into the differences between Catholic social work and secular social work. Walsh concluded that Catholic Worker's lives, being grounded in prayer and sacraments, not merely professionalism, allowed them to delve into the true spirit of Christianity by connecting the spirituality of the liturgy to charity.[152]

The Liturgy as School of Instruction

For the reformers of the interwar period, the liturgy had the potential to serve as a universal school of service, instruction, and love. This was exactly the medicine required to alleviate the problems of the modern world, and certainly for modern Americans. The strain was repeatedly addressed by reformers, including H. A. Reinhold (1897–1968), who urged American Catholics to allow their parish life[153] to flow into work for the poor:

[151] "The Apostolate," *Orate Fratres* 11, no. 2 (1936): 87: "Readers of the *Catholic Worker* are acquainted with the work of Ade Bethune, some of whose illustrations appear in each issue. Done in excellent wood-cut technique, they constitute a distinct and wholesome contribution to religious art in this country. About twenty of them are now procurable separately, in slightly larger than holy picture size, and should find a wide sale. Some of them might well be used for Christmas greeting cards, or for First Mass cards. The address of the artist is 114 East 90th Street, New York City."

[152] See Virgil Michel, Review of *The Saints and Social Work*, by Mary Elizabeth Walsh, *Orate Fratres* 11, no. 8 (1937): 335. Mary Elizabeth Walsh, *The Saints and Social Work* (Silver Spring, MD: The Preservation of the Faith, 1936).

[153] See also Virgil Michel, "The Parish, Cell of Christian Life," *Orate Fratres* 11, no. 10 (1937): 433–40; originally given as a lecture at the Central Verein at St. John's Institute for Social Study in March 1937.

For the true revival of liturgical piety and its re-integration into Christian lives I know no better way than this "*missio*" of neighborly love. If the floods of living water, descending from the altar into the parish, spilled over into a house for pilgrims (whom we call hoboes) and guests, for wanderers and the poor, would that not be a sermon from the roofs and housetops? A rectory basement, an old school, a barn will do for a beginning.[154]

He believed that the greatest beneficiaries would be, not the poor, but those priests and parish members who served the poor.

This attitude was expressed by both those observing the Catholic Worker and the Workers themselves. Catholic Worker Will Woods related, in an anecdote about Dorothy Day in "Mass-Hands," about how she advised a group seeking to start a new House of Hospitality:

If you and your group are attending Mass as often as possible—attending it devoutly and attentively—and offering all your activities of the eternal Father in union with the sacrifice of His divine Son on the cross and on the altar, then your work will be a success, no matter how great a failure it may be in the eyes of the world. And, if you're not going to do it in that spirit, I advise you not to start the work at all. Leave it to the state agencies and the Protestant Missions. They can probably do it as efficiently as you can. Remember always, the MASS IS THE WORK![155]

Though the connection of the liturgy and social regeneration had, apparently, strong bonds, the center simply failed to hold. The question as to why the liturgical movement failed to retain this Catholic social motivation has been summed up by one contemporary Catholic Worker in the following statement: "Virgil Michel died."[156] Fascinat-

[154] H. A. Reinhold, "House of God and House of Hospitality," *Orate Fratres* 14, no. 2 (1939): 78.

[155] Will Woods, "Mass-Hands," *Orate Fratres* 16, no. 7 (1942): 321. Woods continued, noting that "It remained for Adé Bethune in her inimitable way to render this maxim into slang by telling us 'The Mass is the Works!'—pointing out that it is Christ in the Mass who performs the works of mercy, when they are rightly done, using the workers as His agents. Effective workers in Houses of Hospitality are Mass-hands!" Woods, "Mass-Hands," 321–22.

[156] Sheila McCarthy, PhD candidate at the University of Notre Dame, related this opinion to the author. In Day's tribute to Virgil Michel, "Fellow Worker in Christ," Day wrote that Father Virgil was "a dear friend and advisor," and

ingly, even a few years after Michel's death, a writer to the editor lamented the lack of a "social slant" to the articles included in *Orate Fratres*, evaluating that, to his practical mind, *Orate Fratres* had begun to keep liturgy "up in the vague stratosphere of the abstract and theoretical" and was getting nowhere.[157] The tension between scholarly and socially oriented articles continued, despite the fact that persons such as Day, Maurin, Michel, and Maisie Ward had sought to integrate them. As Keith Pecklers suggests, the slackening of the social edge may have been due not simply to the "over-intellectualism" of the liturgical movement but to a theological shift during the Second Vatican Council. Godfrey Diekmann felt that the move from the Mystical Body of Christ theology had distinctly different ramifications than the adopted language of the "People of God," as would be described by the Constitution on the Sacred Liturgy (*Sacrosanctum Concilium*).[158] In any

---

likened him to Peter Maurin, "friendly in a simple way" who spoke directly of what filled his mind: "He was at home with everyone, anywhere. He could sit down at a table in a tenement house kitchen, or under an apple tree at the farm, and talk of St. Thomas and today with whoever was at hand. He never noticed whether people were scholars or workers, he never watched to see whether they understood or not. He had such faith in people, faith in their intelligence and spiritual capacities, that he always gave the very best he had generously and openheartedly. . . . He was so simple that he did not care whether he was giving of his wisdom to two or three or to an audience of hundreds." Dorothy Day, "Fellow Worker in Christ," *Orate Fratres* 13, no. 2 (1938): 139. She related that Father Virgil was never disheartened by scorn or lack of enthusiasm for his intensity.

[157] S. C., "Letter to the Editor," *Orate Fratres* 14, no. 5 (1940): 234.

[158] In a letter to Keith Pecklers, October 17, 1994, Godfrey Diekmann wrote: "It seems to me that at the *heart* of the entire liturgical movement in the U.S. was the doctrine of the mystical body of Christ. We had a Virgil Michel Symposium (national) here 2 or 3 years ago. *Every one* of the speakers had independently come to the same conclusion. The liturgical movement was a *spiritual*, life-shaping apostolate. They were heady, exciting days, because they meant an ever deepening and widening discovery of the dimensions of our life in Christ. The doctrine of the mystical body itself was a 'new' discovery— more or less looked at with suspicion by the general stream of Catholic thinking, until Pius XII's encyclical in the early 40s gave it respectability! I'm not kidding. And it was the doctrine of the mystical body lived out in *pastoral liturgy*, especially the *Missa recitata*, that largely occasioned the (I can only say) new (recovered) insights about *Christology* and *Ecclesiology*, which found expression in the liturgical document ('Mediator Dei') and then in subsequent

case, though there were continual attempts to integrate liturgy and social work, the relationship was at its height when Virgil Michel and Dorothy Day were in touch, with Michel being very much interested in everything the Catholic Workers were doing, making them feel, as Day would relate, "that we were working with him."[159]

Influence of the Catholic Worker in the Liturgical Movement

As Maisie Ward would have evaluated, one of the outgrowths of the Catholic Worker was the influence that was felt on the parish level, within those very study clubs on the liturgy which had become so popular. In a remarkable witness to changing social history, Genevieve M. Casey, member of a liturgical club at a Catholic women's college in "the vicinity" of St. Paul (College of St. Catherine's), related an occasion when a young white woman arrived of an evening, accompanied by a young black woman, to a general college lecture on moral law. Casey recounted:

> In this group, the black girl was accepted as casually and kindly as her white companion. Several persons nodded to her and called her by name. She took part in the discussion and after the program left laughing and talking with a group of white girls. There was no hint of condescension or strain. The black girl was one of us.[160]

What is remarkable about this account is Casey's next comment:

---

ones." Quoted in Pecklers, *The Unread Vision*, 284; Keith Pecklers, conversation with the author, January 2011, San Francisco, California.

[159] Dorothy Day, "Fellow Worker in Christ," 140. The Catholic Worker community was deeply saddened by his death, for, through friendship and constant vigilance about the doings of the Worker, the pulse of the liturgical movement kept in close contact with it. Day reflected, "When we received word of his death we were all overcome, saddened at our own loss of a friend, and overwhelmed at the loss of a great teacher. We got out his letters from the files and went through them, and though Ade Bethune comfortingly talked of his being closer to us than ever, the very thought that we would not get one of his hurried and interested letters again made us miserable. He never said very much, just sending us encouragement and letting us know what he was doing." Day, "Fellow Worker in Christ," 140.

[160] Genevieve M. Casey, "The Liturgy as the Solution of the Negro Problem," in "The Apostolate," *Orate Fratres* 11, no. 8 (1937): 370.

Three months ago this could have hardly happened. If a negro had been asked into a study club, the group would automatically have disintegrated. The young woman who entered the hall with a black companion would immediately have been branded as queer or worse, and become more or less a social outcast. At that time, when we thought of negroes at all, we considered them as a definitely inferior people.[161]

Casey identified the acceptance of the black woman at the lecture as due to the exposure of the campus community to the discussions at the liturgical club, during which several black women were invited to attend. Throughout the winter of 1936–37, the group met each Sunday to discuss articles on the liturgy and its implications, drawing articles from *Orate Fratres, Liturgy and Sociology,* and *The Catholic Worker.* Paul Furfey's *Fire on the Earth* (1936) and Mary Walsh's *Saints and Social Work* were reviewed, and a number of priests, including Virgil Michel, Paul Bussard, and William Busch, came to lecture to the group. Casey recounted that:

As we acquired new realizations of what the liturgy means in the life of the mystical body of Christ, our discussion was centered always, whether explicitly or not, on the problem of what *we* could do to live Christ more completely, and of how *we* could share our God-gift of appreciation of the liturgy with others.[162]

Their talk focused on how *The Catholic Worker* staff in New York City was "living the liturgy" and how social Catholicism "could overcome such evils as war, class hatred, unequal distribution of wealth, interracial prejudice, the totalitarian state."[163] Casey attested that the group's study led them to discover their black companions "as other Christs," and that their contact with them led them to appreciation and respect, evidenced by the community's immensely altered attitude with respect to the inclusion of African Americans in social settings.[164]

---

[161] Ibid.

[162] Ibid.

[163] Ibid., 370–71.

[164] The witness of Genevieve Casey also presents some problematic issues; again, the liturgical movement rarely appears in the context of minority groups. And, as Noel Terranova, of the doctoral program in Liturgical Studies at the University of Notre Dame, has observed, the language employed speaks

CATHERINE DE HUECK DOHERTY, THE LITURGY, AND THE INTERRACIAL MOVEMENT

Early Life and Influences, the Foundation of Friendship House

The example of Genevieve Casey in *Orate Fratres* considering liturgy's teaching potential for racial integration leads attention to (Baroness) Catherine de Hueck Doherty and her development of an interracially attentive apostolate. De Hueck was more briefly explicitly connected with the liturgical movement, though she moved in circles with those who were more readily connected, including Dorothy Day, the Sheed and Wards, and Nina Polcyn Moore.[165] Catherine Kolyschine was born in western Russia in 1896 to an aristocratic family, where her life was complicated and intensely spiritual, beginning as a privileged member of the Russian aristocracy with sundry religious devotions. Though she was exposed to the Russian Orthodox liturgy, her father was Polish and a Byzantine Catholic, thus she was raised as a Catholic. At the age of fifteen, she was married to Baron Boris de Hueck, which began a long and troubled marriage that eventually ended in divorce. During the turbulent years of Russia's early twentieth century, de Hueck lived through great suffering, hunger, and bloodshed as a nurse in World War I on the Russian front and, later, as a refugee and prisoner during the Bolshevik Revolution of 1917. De Hueck saw horrific things and the destruction of the people and Church of her country under the opium of the Communists. Her experience left her with a persistent, driving urge to serve the lowly and the poor. Once she escaped her homeland and arrived in North America, she became a dynamic lecturer against the "reds" and a spokeswoman for the need for Christian love, traveling the Chautauqua lecture circuit.

Yet, lecturing did not suffice, and de Hueck realized her vision by electing to live in voluntary poverty, developing a series of homes for the poorest immigrants in society. The original house was founded as "Friendship House" in Toronto, Ontario, in 1932, but de Hueck moved to inner-city New York's Harlem in 1937 to establish an apostolate

---

of "us" and "them," and rings with a certain "benevolent acceptance" that the white women did not "mind" the black women coming to join them.

[165] A dissertation by Andrew Schoenberger of the Pontifical Gregorian University, titled "Go in Peace to Love and Serve the Lord: A Study of the Liturgical Theology of Catherine De Hueck Doherty," under the direction of Keith Pecklers, develops more fully Catherine de Hueck Doherty's contribution to the liturgical movement.

which ministered to African American men, women, and children. Beginning with a staff of nine men and women and thirty to forty occasional volunteers (including a visit by Thomas Merton), success in Harlem prompted the founding of similar houses and farms in Chicago, Washington, DC, Portland (Oregon), and Los Angeles. After her marriage in 1943 to Eddie Doherty, a successful Chicago reporter, Catherine de Hueck Doherty set up residence in Toronto again, establishing a rural community for both lay and priests to gather for prayer and work.[166] Throughout her career, which soared and tumbled, she came into contact with Auxiliary Bishop Sheil of Chicago and urged him to develop the Sheil School of Social Studies, so as to present a Catholic alternative to the development of Communist adult education at the time.[167] According to de Hueck, it was through her own influence that Nina Polcyn Moore was encouraged to move from the Catholic Worker in Milwaukee and come to work in Chicago.[168]

[166] Lorene Hanley Duquin, *They Called Her the Baroness: The Life of Catherine de Hueck Doherty* (New York: Alba House, 1995), 233–63. Madonna House was located in Combermere, near Montreal, in Ontario, Canada. The Madonna House was distinct in its administration from Friendship House, USA, with which Catherine de Hueck Doherty had increasingly little to do after the 1950s.

[167] De Hueck was greatly concerned that, while the Christian Churches stood by, the Communists lured away poor immigrants (much like the Catholics of 1920s Progressive Chicago were concerned the Catholics were being lured away by the Protestants): "There he finds a warm welcome, a good free entertainment, and mischievous propaganda sapping slowly but surely his spiritual strength. Yet, when he turns to his own, they know him not. There are no parish halls open to welcome him any time of the day or evening. There are no recreational activities to cheer him up; no intellectual endeavors are made to explain the bewildering situation of our days. . . . There are no study hours to strengthen his faith against a new kind of unknown-to-him, seemingly logical reasoning." Catherine de Hueck Doherty, "Report on Communistic Activities in Toronto, Canada, in Relation to the Catholic Church," Archives of the Catholic Archdiocese of Toronto. See Duquin, 121–30.

[168] According to Duquin's biography of Catherine de Hueck Doherty, de Hueck Doherty met with Sheil and convinced him to organize a counter program of adult education to the Communistic efforts. Nina Polcyn Moore recalled, "She wrote out a whole plan and she convinced Bishop Sheil to sponsor it. When we came there, we discovered we were totally ill-equipped to run such a thing! But that was part of her grand scheme, you know. She thought a little piety substituted for a vast body of knowledge. That was just

De Hueck's theological emphases coincided with that of the liturgical movement of the 1930s: taking seriously the responsibility of the Mystical Body of Christ to be formed in the Eucharist, allowing the meaning of the sacrament to permeate the heart and mind, and inspiring the pouring out of the self as Christ to the world. De Hueck had only limited conversation with Virgil Michel shortly before his death, revealed by a series of letters exchanged after de Hueck visited Saint John's Abbey. De Hueck, impressed with the work and hospitality of Michel and the monks at Saint John's, asked for their prayers and for a free year's subscription to *Orate Fratres*.[169] Michel graciously responded in the affirmative. During their brief correspondence up to the time of Michel's death in 1938, he and de Hueck discussed her present work with Russian immigrants in Toronto. She had been long desirous of a reconciliation between Rome and the East and had a profound concern for the people of Russia having no place to pray:

> I acknowledge frankly, that I had a long range vision of getting slowly to work on them and reconcile them with Rome (with the grace of God naturally). Years passed and things have progressed, 4 of the Russian men are regularly attending a Catholic Jesuit study club[;] they have learned much and are leaveners of others, now slowly with the help of one of them who already has joined the Church about 7 years ago and two that are getting there[;] we work on the priest and the breaking down of foolish historical prejudice, we have succeeded thank God, in one point, there is a general study Club on the Encyclicals of the POPE in progress at the Russian Church now. But it is an uphill battle, the people are so poor, and the catholics of Toronto so prejudiced and

---

her method of operation. It was a rich adventure." Lorene Hanley Duquin, interview with Nina Polcyn Moore. See Duquin, 203–4.

[169] Letter from Catherine de Hueck Doherty to Virgil Michel, December 20, 1937, The Virgil Michel Papers Z: 24, 4, SJAA. She continued: "It was such a great joy to meet you, and I was really happy to see you, the fathers and the home of Orate Fratres." She asked for a free subscription for one year: "Perhaps you think this is selfish, but I bind mine and love having them. If it is impossible let me know and I will try to scrape the money up. Thank you again for your hospitality and the lovely time I had up at your place. Please pray for us." See also Virgil Michel to Catherine de Hueck Doherty, January 6, 1938, The Virgil Michel Papers Z: 24, 4, SJAA.

ignorant, and the Anglican Church as everywhere else, is courting them with material help.[170]

De Hueck concluded by inquiring if Michel, the "saintly editor" of *Orate Fratres*, might convince some Benedictine sisters to make some vestments for the new Orthodox Church she helped to found in Toronto. She confessed that she had not often met someone who understood her so well and wrote a theological reflection on "seeing Christ so vividly amongst us."[171] Michel invited her to revise her writing and submit it to *Orate Fratres*. She responded by enclosing an article which was published as "I Saw Christ Today," to which she attached the vehement explanation in a letter to Michel:

> [E]veryone [sic] of the scenes described are TRUE. I saw them with my own eyes. And seeing I wept, and weeping I looked into my heart

[170] Letter from Catherine de Hueck Doherty to Virgil Michel, January 13, 1938, The Virgil Michel Papers Z: 24, 4, SJAA. De Hueck's letters were often full of exuberance which sometimes resulted in unconventional capitalizations and run-on sentences.

[171] "And then blame yourself—it is not always that one meets people like you, somehow, I would not be afraid to confide to you some of the crazy ideas and notions that eternally drift thru my head. [You seem to understand] what prompts them? It is that strange fire that burns in my heart and will not be put out, I can't rest ever, something prompts me on, ever on. . . . For perhaps due to my Slavic imagination, I can see Christ so vividly amongst us. . . . Walking our streets standing gaunt and tired on the many corners of many streets of many cities, I see Him in the patient women in the slums, the dispirited men, the undernourished children. Bound and smitten in the hearts of the Communists, covered with spittle in those of our modern pagans. . . . And it hurts father! What we need today is thousands of Damiens to nurse leprose souls, right here and not in far away Molokai . . . and millions of Veronicas to wipe the bloody face of Christ in His poor. . . ." Letter from Catherine de Hueck Doherty to Virgil Michel, January 13, 1938, The Virgil Michel Papers Z: 24, 4, SJAA.

Regarding the request for vestments, in a letter from Virgil Michel to Catherine de Hueck Doherty, January 17, 1938, he advised her to ask the sisters directly and claimed to be impressed with her Slavic imagination, as she called it, and thought it "could be expanded into a very nice article for Orate Fratres it seems to me. How about trying it some time (2,000 to 2,5000 words) connecting the ideas up with the Mass and Calvary?" The Virgil Michel Papers Z: 24, 4, SJAA.

and found it wanting. . . . And wended my way to Church and Mass, since then, life has been different. A day without Mass and Communion . . . is an empty lost day. I am rich now, for He has filled me, unworthy as I am with the wealth of His love.[172]

Michel was pleased with the article and thought it "should go into O.F. even if it does not touch upon the liturgy until in the last page or so."[173] The article had the character of her famous Chautauqua lectures: descriptive, enticing, and emotional stories about poverty-stricken men and women of all ages and races. She concluded by affirming that all must "take full part" in Mass and Communion; only this would let Christians "every day walk about with Christ in our hearts. *Ite Missa est!* Let us go forth in Christ! There is only one way of changing the world and that is to start with ourselves. There is so little time. Let us start now!"[174]

The two continued to correspond over the following year, and de Hueck, at least in her letters to Michel, more explicitly noted that she started "with the Liturgy" in teaching Christians what it was to be in the Mystical Body.[175] Michel was duly impressed with the variety of works organized by Friendship House of Harlem and found de Hueck's discussion of "the brotherhood of man under the Fatherhood of God" to have potential for a sociological perspective on the liturgy. He characteristically encouraged her with her work and invited her to

[172] Catherine de Hueck Doherty to Virgil Michel, January 25, 1938, The Virgil Michel Papers Z: 24, 4, SJAA.

[173] Virgil Michel to Catherine de Hueck Doherty, January 31, 1938, The Virgil Michel Papers Z: 24, 4, SJAA.

[174] Catherine de Hueck Doherty, "I Saw Christ Today," *Orate Fratres* 12, no. 7 (1938): 310.

[175] Catherine de Hueck Doherty wrote to Virgil Michel: "But how about the Mystical Body of Christ, why don't the white R. C. obey the teachings of Christ, is it not an empty word then and why should we not listen to the Communists who preach and practice the Brotherhood of men, since the other Brotherhood of men under the Fatherhood of God is just a mockery that only hurts with each repetition. So when they see someone living here in the heart of harlem as it were, no white people within four blocks, this bitterness recedes a little." Catherine de Hueck Doherty to Virgil Michel, March 30, 1938, letter dated March 30, 1938 , The Virgil Michel Papers Z: 24, 4, SJAA.

submit more writing to *Orate Fratres*.[176] This was five months before his death.[177]

Friendship House Participants and the National Liturgical Weeks

While Catherine de Hueck Doherty did not contribute again to *Orate Fratres*, other members of the Friendship House organization did appear at National Liturgical Weeks. For example, Ann Harrigan, who had long assumed leadership over Friendship House in Chicago, attended Msgr. Joseph P. Morrison's lecture titled "The Spirit of Sacrifice in Christian Society: The Racial Problem" on October 14 at the National Liturgical Week held in 1943. In the discussion following Morrison's lecture, Harrigan raised examples of racial tension, such as a Catholic college which had recently begun refusing enrollment to black students for fear of causing "scandal" to the white. She asked, "How about the scandal that was given to those who might have been literal followers of the doctrine of the Mystical Body?"[178] The "interracial problem," as it was called, was a practical ground in which the formation which liturgical pioneers championed should be made manifest. The "comfortability" of living a culturally and racially homogenous liturgical life was challenged by advocates of Friendship

---

[176] Letter from Virgil Michel to Catherine de Hueck Doherty, June 22, 1938, The Virgil Michel Papers Z: 24, 4, SJAA. He continued: "Just live the liturgy, as I am sure you do, and you will realize the need of sharing in Christ's Calvaries to have a share also in his resurrections. As soon as you get a few good ideas on liturgy and sociology in relation to your work, put them down on paper and let us have a look at them. The worst we can do is return the manuscript, and the best, accept it for O.F. So why not try?"

[177] Godfrey Diekmann to Catherine de Hueck Doherty, November 26, 1938, The Virgil Michel Papers Z: 24, 4, SJAA. Diekmann wrote: "Dear Baroness: Father Virgil died this morning. May his parousia have been a blessed one: Proprior est nostra salus quam cum credidimus. He was sick only a week. Pleurisy developed into lobar pneumonia, and a system poisoned by a streptococcus infection hastened the end. We recommend his soul to your prayers and those of your negro friends, that the good Lord whom he served so intensely may be unto him a merciful Judge; also for the flourishing of the liturgical renewal and the rechristianization of society, for which he labored so ardently."

[178] Ann Harrigan, "Discussion," *1943 Liturgical Week Proceedings* (Ferdinand, IN: Liturgical Conference, 1944): 119.

House, thus making its workers valuable conversation partners during this period of racial unrest and liturgical development.

Through its newspaper, *The Catholic Interracialist*, and its study clubs, Friendship House would be influential in networking Catholic women's involvement in civil rights protests through the 1950s and 1960s. Some women, such as Monica Durkin, who sold her Cleveland insurance company to run a Friendship House farm in rural Wisconsin, the aforementioned Ann Harrigan (an English teacher from Brooklyn),[179] and Ellen Tarry (a successful African American reporter from New York),[180] had left professional careers to run Friendship House in Chicago and would find full-time vocations in this realization of the lay apostolate. Historian Karen Kennelly, CSJ, describes Friendship House and the Catholic Worker Movement, along with the Grail Movement, as transformative of the social vision of the American Catholic community. Each movement, without outwardly denying the more centralized attempts at social reform by Church hierarchy, modeled a radical alternative vision of the Mystical Body's unity which was fueling theological conversation. Importantly, both Friendship House and the Catholic Worker Movement, as well as the Grail, realized this model in small communities.[181]

Catherine de Hueck Doherty, like Dorothy Day, contributed much in terms of writing and lecturing; she was also deeply interested in exposing Western Christians to the best in Eastern spirituality, detailed in her book, *Poustinia: Christian Spirituality of the East for Western Man* (1974). And, the Madonna House of Toronto is still active today.

---

[179] Duquin, 171.

[180] Ellen Tarry reflected on the power of the message of Catherine de Hueck Doherty and the Mystical Body of Christ after listening to her at a Newman Club in New York City in 1938: "I would catch phrases like 'the Fatherhood of God, and the Brotherhood of man,' or 'the Negro and the Mystical Body,' which indicated much more depth than I had attributed to these youngsters. . . . Then the Baroness talked about 'Christ in the Negro' and along with all the others in the room I came under the spell of Catherine de Hueck. I had entered the room a Doubting Thomas and left as an ardent disciple." Tarry's reflection reveals both the magnetism of Catherine de Hueck Doherty and the powerful call of her message. Ellen Tarry, *The Third Door: The Autobiography of an American Negro Woman* (Tuscaloosa: University of Alabama Press, 1992), 144.

[181] Debra Campbell, "Reformers and Activists," in *American Catholic Women: A Historical Exploration*, ed. Karen Kennelly (New York: Macmillan, 1989), 175–76.

De Hueck, who died in 1985, is also a candidate for canonization and was declared a "Servant of God" by John Paul II in 2000, the first step toward beatification.[182]

CONCLUSION

In the 1930s, the liturgical movement gained momentum as it plunged fully into the scene of Catholic Action and intersected with lay-led movements such as the Catholic Intellectual Revival, the Catholic Library Movement, and social movements such as the Catholic Worker and Friendship House. Some key characters, such as Maisie Ward, Sara B. O'Neill, Nina Polcyn Moore, Dorothy Day, and Catherine de Hueck Doherty, give some sense of the multiplicity of ways in which lay initiative was realized in the period prior to the Second World War. In each case, the liturgy was seen as a touchstone for reviving a true Catholic spirit, one which would take seriously the implications of the Mystical Body, being formed by liturgical prayer and participation, and bringing this new spirit into the world. Thus, a broader swath of American Catholic laity, equipped with Catholic education, literature, and awareness of social responsibility, as modeled by groups like the Catholic Worker and Friendship House, were ready to enter the liturgical movement.

[182] See, for example, http://www.catherinedoherty.org. Some biographies exist of de Hueck, including Duquin's *They Called her the Baroness,* and Emile Briere's *Katia: A Personal Vision of Catherine de Hueck Doherty* (Sherbrooke, Quebec: Éditions Pauline, 1988); alongside her own reflections on her life, such as *I Live on an Island* (Notre Dame, IN: University of Notre Dame Press, 1979); *Fragments of My Life* (Notre Dame, IN: University of Notre Dame Press, 1979); and *My Heart and I: Interior Conversations, 1952–1959* (Petersham, MA: St. Bede's Publications, 1987).

Chapter 4

Joining Liturgy and Life:
The Liturgical Movement in Labor, the Arts,
and Lifestyles (c. 1933–45)

INTRODUCTION

In the Midst of Catholic Action

From the beginning of the liturgical movement in America, its character had been marked by a desire for social change. Taking the social encyclicals of Leo XIII (*Rerum Novarum*) and Pius XI (*Quadragesimo Anno*) in one hand and the latest in Catholic theology in the other, pioneers of the liturgical movement looked to the liturgical celebration of the Eucharist as the ground for forming people in the true Christian spirit. The Mystical Body of Christ, assembled in and shaped by liturgical celebration, would be the response to patterns of destruction and hatred, as well as lethargy and despair.[1] As seen in the previous chapters, new infrastructure in the form of booksellers, library associations, and study clubs made the liturgical movement more accessible. Liturgical writers found many avenues to explain how the liturgy served as the most direct experience of the Mystical Body of Christ and how all the faithful were called to liturgical participation. Journals such as *Commonweal* and the liturgical movement's *Orate Fratres* were among the first national venues for lay people to interact with and speak about their Catholic faith, while organized programs of Catholic Action encouraged lay people to take an active part in bringing their faith to life in the world.[2] Meanwhile, still more Catholics took the

---

[1] Virgil Michel, "The Liturgy the Basis of Social Regeneration," *Orate Fratres* 9, no. 12 (1935): 545.

[2] See Gary MacEoin, "Lay Movements in the United States before Vatican II," in *America* 165 (August 3–10, 1991): 61–65; and Mary Jo Weaver, "Still Feisty at Fifty: The Grailville Lay Apostolate for Women," *U.S. Catholic Historian* 2, no. 4 (Fall 1993): 3–12.

188

"doctrine of the Mystical Body" even more seriously, responding to the intense social problems of the Depression era, from unemployment to the threat of godless Communism. Groups like the Catholic Worker and Friendship House emerged, independent from ecclesial oversight, in the hopes of putting to practice the doctrine of the Mystical Body of Christ which emphasized the dignity of each person in the Church as a member of a united, just society.[3]

The Continuing Development of the Liturgical Movement

In a radical alternative to patterns of individualistic piety and limited social outreach, an increasingly mobile and educated Catholic population found the invitation to activity attractive. The liturgical movement called people to corporate prayer which did not end in piety but extended through time and space, involving the whole of life and asking that this life be attentive to the needs of the world. As Msgr. William Busch wrote:

> Prayer not only implores and honors God, it also educates mankind. This is especially true of liturgical prayer. The liturgy well understood will show us the meaning of the Christian religion in all its scope. The *lex orandi* will help us to know the *lex credendi* and the *lex agendi*. We shall be conscious once more of our social solidarity in Christ. We shall see a transformation of social life, agricultural, industrial and political. If this is too much to hope for Christian nations, then the outlook of the modern world is dark indeed.[4]

Attempting to reestablish the necessary connection between liturgy, life, and social action recalled the maxim of Prosper of Aquitaine (c. fifth century): *ut legem credendi lex statuat supplicandi* (often shortened to *lex credendi, lex orandi*), the law of prayer grounds the law of belief. Twentieth-century liturgical reformers added *lex agendi* (later, *lex vivendi*) to this axiom, stressing the end of prayer and belief as a holistic, liturgical life.

To achieve this end, the liturgical movement intertwined the promotion of liturgical renewal with its surrounding social and cultural contexts, sometimes with explicit continuity, and sometimes with

---

[3] Alden V. Brown, *The Grail Movement and American Catholicism, 1940–1975*, Notre Dame Studies in American Catholicism (Notre Dame, IN: University of Notre Dame Press, 1989), 20.

[4] William Busch, "Liturgy and Farm Relief," *Catholic Rural Life* 8 (April 1930): 2.

intentional contrast. The media for liturgical renewal, including the arts, integration of lifestyle, and a desire for social justice, were propelled by evolving cultural technologies as the liturgical movement moved into the latter 1930s and early 1940s. The revolution in design, for example, from rococo to art deco, influenced liturgical arts which were "simple" and "clean," modes which artist Ade Bethune would adopt. And, increased access to education, literacy, and technological means of collecting and reproducing information (from inexpensively produced missals to phonograph records of liturgical music) added to the numbers of people who could even be exposed to elements of the liturgical movement. On the other hand, the advent of mass-produced commercial products for the construction of the Hollywood image of femininity fueled the American Grail's desire to offer an alternative model for Christian womanhood. In short, as liturgical historian Michael Woods, SJ, describes, the liturgy's "interface with culture and culture's role in contributing to a just society" significantly defined the approach of liturgical pioneers.[5] Such interface of liturgy and culture is certainly evidenced by the complex histories of the reformers, particularly lay women, who were often involved in multiple arenas of liturgical teaching, reform, and practice.

Finding Labor, Art, and Lifestyles in the Liturgical Movement
    While the previous chapter dealt with the liturgical movement as it intersected with the intellectual realm and the more radical environs of the increasingly active lay apostolate, this chapter collects some threads from the previous decade and launches into the Second World War period by focusing on the intersection of the liturgical movement with labor, the arts, and lifestyles. Examining this landscape reveals the great interest being focused on integrating a Catholic, liturgical life with all realms of human activity: from work, to creative craftship and art, to family life. Two principal examples illustrate this phenomenon: the work of artist Marie Adélaïde de Bethune, usually referred to as "Ade [ah-day] Bethune," and the American Grail Movement. Bethune provides an example of a liturgical pioneer who intersects multiple fronts, having begun her direct work with the liturgical movement as a

---

[5] Michael J. Woods, *Cultivating Soil and Soul: Twentieth-Century Catholic Agrarians Embrace the Liturgical Movement* (Collegeville, MN: Liturgical Press, 2009), xix; see also Kevin Irwin, *Models of the Eucharist* (Mahwah, NJ: Paulist Press, 2005), 21.

result of her connections with the Catholic Worker. Through her work as a liturgical artist, consultant, and designer, Bethune advocated for the integrity of the human person, the meaningfulness and necessity of liturgical participation, and the possibility of an integrated lifestyle in which labor was not divided from liturgy.

The second half of this chapter turns to a more radical realization of a liturgical lifestyle, in the American Grail Movement. The Grail was unique in its exclusive intent to educate young women in the lay apostolate. It did so by soundly ensconcing young women in the liturgical life and was generally recognized as a most affective school for realizing Catholic Action. The Grail, along with the Catholic Worker, realized the "back to the land" movement which, organized under the National Catholic Rural Life Conference (hereafter NCRLC), wholeheartedly embraced the holistic hope for living expressed by the liturgical movement. Though similar to the radical social movements founded by Dorothy Day and Catherine de Hueck Doherty, the Grail was able to mesh more frequently with mainstream American Catholic women, was particularly attractive to younger women, and anticipated the shifting interests of the liturgical movement toward liturgical life in the home.

WORK, PRAYER, ART, AND ADE BETHUNE

Early Life and Influences

Marie Adélaïde de Bethune was born in Brussels, Belgium, on January 12, 1914. The third of four children, her parents were Marthe Thérèse Terlinden and Gaston de Bethune. Her family were landowners and lived in the central area of Brussels where her father worked as a chemical engineer and inventor. Educated and financially comfortable, Bethune's family encouraged her imagination and her interests in history and art and were also surprisingly liturgically active. Bethune's great-grandmother went to daily Mass and was a frequent communicant, something quite unusual for a woman in the 1890s,[6]

---

[6] In an article titled "Revising our Conception of the Communion Rail," *Catholic Art Quarterly* 21, no. 2 (1958): 37–47, Bethune reflected on her grandmother, born in 1830, who attended daily communion: "Today we do not think this extraordinary, but in a nineteenth century still tainted with lingering Jansenism, it was so exceptional as to be noteworthy. Due to an intense but unbalanced sense of reverence for the Blessed Sacrament, good Catholics went to Communion but once or twice a year—at most, once a month. Even

and Bethune's mother, Marthe, attended a school where the religious sisters were very interested in liturgical study.[7] Ade Bethune herself recounted that she received Communion at the "age of reason" and began accompanying her grandfather to Mass. Using a simple child's devotional, which was popular at the time, however, left young Ade with too much room for imagination. Tiring of letting her mind wander along the window ledges and high at the tops of the columns, it occurred to her that time would be better spent in church if she simply brought her geography book along—to study.[8] When Ade Bethune's mother discovered this, she bought Ade a missal for Holy Week, into which Ade "sank her teeth" with joy and which also sparked her love of Scripture.[9] Years later, Bethune would reflect:

> The book Mother had given me proved to be most interesting and entertaining. It wasn't just a Holy Saturday book, nor even a Holy Week book. It was an "every day" book. I could pray with it every single day I went to *Mass*, because it was a *Mass* book (called a Missal I was told) with all the prayers of the *Mass* for every day of the year. At the end of the year I could start the book all over again and go through it day by day, year after year, as long as I lived.[10]

---

the most devout were judged 'unworthy to approach the Sacred Table' and the lengthy preparation considered necessary made frequent Communion practically impossible." Bethune, "Revising our Conception," 38.

[7] Judith Stoughton, *Proud Donkey of Schaerbeek: Adé Bethune: Catholic Worker Artist* (St. Cloud, MN: North Star Press of St. Cloud, 1988), 10.

[8] Adélaïde de Béthune, "Common Sense," *Liturgical Arts Quarterly* 5, no. 3 (1936): 79. The *Liturgical Arts Quarterly* preferred using the more formal version of Bethune's name. Bethune became "Ade Bethune" when, after signing her name as "A. de Bethune," it was accidentally set in type as "Ade Bethune," which she liked.

[9] Stoughton, 14. Bethune reflected: "I treasure that memory and the understanding of how the missal had come into our family through my mother's mother. . . . She did this in spite of the fact that there were no lay folks' missals in use; the only missals were the ones at the altar for the priests to use. . . . However, the publishing firm of Mame in Tours, France, had just started publishing a lay folks' missal. It may have been under the influence of Dom Guéranger, a great leader of the Liturgical Movement at the second half of the nineteenth century. Anyway, my grandmother wrote to Tours in France in order to procure a four-volume set of the missal in Latin and French, side by side. That was a novelty." Quoted in Stoughton, 15.

[10] Bethune, "Common Sense," 80.

Because of her father's career as an engineer and inventor, he and Marthe de Bethune decided to move the family to America in 1928, when Ade Bethune was fourteen. They hoped to encourage the de Bethune children to a life of work instead of growing up to be "idle, impoverished gentry in Europe."[11] Beginning life in New York, Ade Bethune attended high school during the week and Parson's School of Art on Saturdays; the following year, in 1929, she began going to high school for half days, in order to attend the National Academy of Design in the afternoons. The brightest and boldest forms of art interested Bethune, from iconography to the sharp cinematography of Communist propagandist movies. After finishing at the Academy, Bethune joined the Cooper Union Day Art School. Bethune was also very interested in stained glass and, in 1933, when Charles J. Connick of Boston, whom she knew from his lectures at the National Academy of Design, held a competition for the best design, Bethune submitted to it and won an opportunity to go to Boston to create her design in glass.[12]

Meeting the Early Catholic Worker

In the fall of 1933, Bethune first heard of the Catholic Worker at a gathering of friends from art school and went to investigate the Catholic Worker soup kitchen on East Fifteenth Street in New York, where she was impressed with the notion of hospitality in the midst of the depressed economy. Dorothy Weston (later, Coddington) gave Bethune some copies of the newspaper, *The Catholic Worker*, but Bethune was disappointed by the poor quality of the illustrations.[13] The Communist papers with which *The Catholic Worker* was competing were full of "big illustrations and biting cartoons." But, on closer examination, Bethune felt that "communist" drawings were "disappointing" and had "no substance" and that their ideas were "twisted." Bethune was filled with a desire to create "rigorous drawings about the truth, about the right ideas and the good things."[14] As she contemplated this problem, she turned to an old catechism to search for ideas. While she found it mostly full of "dry abstract material," nothing good for

[11] Stoughton, 21.

[12] Ade Bethune, "A Dream Come True," *Stained Glass* 28, no. 3 (Autumn 1933): 139–42.

[13] Ade Bethune, "The Work and Works of Mercy," *Orate Fratres* 15, no. 2 (1940): 53.

[14] Ibid.

pictures, she finally turned to the seven corporal works of mercy. With delight, she remembered Peter Maurin's "Easy Essay" in *The Catholic Worker* which spoke of hospitality, to which she connected the corporal work of mercy "harboring the harborless." Beginning with this, she depicted each work of mercy with a figure, or figures, in action.[15] These first pictures appeared in the March 1934 issue, and, in the same month, Bethune went to the Catholic Worker headquarters in New York and met Dorothy Day. After initially mistaking Bethune for a guest,[16] Day sat her down on a pile of newspapers, opened a missal, and pointed out which illustrations should be done for April, including Saints Don Bosco and Catherine of Siena.[17] Bethune found the

[15] Bethune sent several pictures to Dorothy Day and Dorothy Weston, with the accompanying note: "Dear Dorothies—There is but one thing I can make: that is pictures. So I send you a few already—I hope you can use them for *The Catholic Worker*. But this bothers me about them. Doesn't it cost you an awful lot of money to get the plates made? Can you find out if I couldn't possibly engrave or etch them directly upon wood or whatever the metal is they use? Please let me know in case you find out. I mean to do you more of the 'Corporal Works of Mercy' but I thought I'd start with 'Harboring the Harborless' as winter is yet far from finished. I also mean to do your Patron St. Joseph for his feast in March. And whenever you are in need of a picture please ask me. All right? With all my best for the Work. A de Bethune." Quoted in Stoughton, 37.

[16] When Bethune first came to the Worker, she brought bags of clothes, and Day thought she was looking for shelter. Bethune recalled, "A tall woman, with a face as though it had been carved by an axe, told me very kindly, 'I'm so sorry; we don't have any more room.' I was so shy that I stuttered, 'I'm the girl who made the pictures for you; and I brought these clothes for you.' 'Oh,' she said, 'You are? Fine.' [Day] took the two shopping bags and sat me on a pile of newspapers. Then she took out a missal and said, 'All right, we're going to use your Saint Joseph for March, but we'll need a picture for April. Saint Catherine of Siena's feast comes in April. She was the twenty-first child in her family and was cook for the big household, including the dye workers of her father's business. Catherine decided to make the kitchen her cloister, her place of prayer. Don Bosco's feast also comes in April; I'd like to have a picture of him too.'" Quoted in Stoughton, 37–38.

[17] Bethune, "The Work and Works of Mercy," 54. A discussion of Bethune's interest in the ordinary conveying a sacramental reality can be found in an article by the author, Katharine E. Harmon, "Drawing the Holy in the Ordinary: Ade Bethune, the Catholic Worker, and the Liturgical Movement," *American Catholic Studies* (Spring 2012): 1–23.

process of relying on the missal an excellent technique; the saints were busy, active, and working. Following the saints through the liturgical year provided a perfect avenue for drawing the Christ-life:

> The problem of making Elizabeth of Hungary nursing the sick, or Martin de Porres nursing the sick, was after all one and the same problem. It was reducible to the same terms: a nurse and a patient, the nurse tending the patient. The movements, the positions, the gestures were the same. It was the same problem of design. One had a black face, the other a white one. Above the one I painfully lettered the name Martin, under the other Elizabeth. But their work was the same. They were Christ, healing the sick. So I found out that an immense variety of pictures was possible of saints doing fourteen common works.[18]

Bethune thought it particularly appropriate that the saints who appeared in *The Catholic Worker* should themselves be workers. She did not draw the saints performing miracles but drew the saints doing ordinary work. As Bethune saw, the saints were remembered for their work, and their work was not extraordinary: "Works of mercy are not extraordinary actions which a few unusual people do. Everybody has to do them all the time anyway. Doing them with the love of Christ makes them works of love or mercy."[19] Therefore, any man's or woman's work could also be a work of mercy, especially when it was directed for the benefit of others. The saints who scrubbed floors and peeled potatoes might more easily reflect how ordinary work of ordinary men and women could be put to the service of the Mystical Body.[20]

Learning Liturgical Art with the John Stevens Shop
    Bethune's first encounter with the Catholic Worker began her long relationship with Dorothy Day and the Worker Movement and

---

[18] Bethune, "The Work and Works of Mercy," 55.
[19] Ibid.
[20] Bethune's image of Mary, "Our Lady of Homework" depicts Mary of Nazareth scrubbing floors; Bethune's image of St. Martha shows her peeling potatoes. See "Our Lady of Homework" (1937), Artwork by Ade Bethune from the Ade Bethune Collection, St. Catherine University Library, St. Paul, MN 55105, Image #3715; and "St. Martha" (1935), Artwork by Ade Bethune from the Ade Bethune Collection, St. Catherine University Library, St. Paul, MN 55105, Image #3537 [hereafter cited as "Ade Bethune Collection, St. Catherine University Library"].

provided a powerful venue for the realization of religious art which portrayed the message of the liturgical movement: an active faith which integrated prayer with life.[21] Day recognized the liturgical vitality latent in Bethune's work, and, in 1934, when Jesuit priest Daniel Lord offered Day several scholarships for Workers to attend the Summer School of Catholic Action in New York, Day turned to Bethune and told her to go. As Bethune recounted:

> I went to a two week course at St. Xavier's Academy on Sixteenth Street. You could take two classes. The first was called *The Mystical Body*. I was duly impressed. The other was *Liturgy*, a class on the Mass and the other Sacraments. The teacher, Father Gerald Ellard, SJ, was fantastic! Liturgy was really what I loved. I was elated because a lot of the things I had lived with and heard about vaguely I was now able to understand better and put in place in my mind. That class was a revelation, and how I got involved in the Liturgical Movement. I owe that to Dorothy.[22]

Bethune's interest in how the liturgical movement coincided with her desire to promote social welfare through art prompted her to join the Liturgical Arts Society in 1935. Here, she first met John Howard Benson (1901–56), artisan of the John Stevens Shop in Newport, Rhode

---

[21] In 1935, Bethune created a new masthead for the paper. She recounted: "*The Catholic Worker*'s first masthead was rather insignificant. When she began the paper, Dorothy Day had used two little illustrations of workers holding a mallet and pickaxe. These were in opposite corners at the top of the paper. After a few issues, she found an illustration of a black worker and a white worker. They still weren't on speaking terms, I guess, standing at opposite ends of the paper. I decided to follow the same idea, but bring them both together in the middle, with Christ's arms over their shoulders uniting them. That has been the masthead of *The Catholic Worker* for fifty years until 1985. I didn't know I was doing something so important, but there it was. It was pointed out that *The Catholic Worker* masthead had become 'sexist.' A new one was needed. I thought long and hard to offer Dorothy's spirit a new surprise, exactly half a century after the first. I thought of her love of little children, of the land, of feeding people. The result? Our new masthead: a woman, mother and agricultural worker, replaces the old male worker with the shovel. With this and minor changes, we present a new masthead, to quote Peter, 'with the philosophy of the old, a philosophy so old that it looks new.'" Quoted in Stoughton, 46–47.

[22] Quoted in Stoughton, 40.

Island, and Graham Carey (1892–1984), architect of Cambridge, Massachusetts. Meanwhile, as Bethune's work continued to appear in *The Catholic Worker*, liturgically minded persons began asking her to print her illustrations or to render her unique depictions of saints in three-dimensional media with which (little did her commissioners know) she was barely familiar.[23] These requests prompted Bethune to contact her friends Benson and Carey to begin the study of woodcarving and calligraphy at the John Stevens Shop in Newport, Rhode Island, where she might gain the skills to adequately render her commissioned projects. Bethune commuted between Newport and New York until she was offered a position teaching arts and crafts at Portsmouth Priory School, replacing Benson who left to teach at the Rhode Island School of Design. Teaching, plus her increasing involvement with the John Stevens Shop, prompted Bethune to move permanently to Newport.[24] Bethune would remain connected to the Priory School and Portsmouth Abbey for the rest of her life, becoming a Benedictine Oblate at the Abbey of Portsmouth in the summer of 1949, taking the name Leo.[25]

Ade Bethune's Philosophy of Labor, Art, and Lifestyle

Bethune's work was compelling to those interested in the liturgical movement for the philosophy of art, labor, and faith which it exuded. Bethune's philosophy of labor was strongly influenced by the

[23] Catherine de Hueck, for example, received upwards of a thousand cards from Bethune and wrote lavishing compliments regarding the inspiration drawn from Bethune's work by guests and workers at Madonna House in Toronto: "I love your work Ade, I really do, and I think it is your way to sanctification. Never for a moment stop drawing, for your drawings are inspirations. . . . [Your picture of] St. Adalbert graces our kitchen. He has not made a saint of our cook, but you never can tell. There is hope for even those impossible cases. No you must not stop drawing, for the Holy Spirit is with you. I know he guides your hands." Catherine de Hueck Doherty to Ade Bethune, January 17, 1936, Ade Bethune Collection 6 / Personal Correspondence, St. Catherine University Library.

[24] Bethune lived in the John Stevens Shop for two years but purchased a nearby colonial house where she moved her parents, happy to remove them from city life and return them to a home reminiscent of their life in Belgium.

[25] Letter from Ade Bethune to Godfrey Diekmann, December 10, 1949, Ade Bethune Collection 6 / Personal Correspondence, St. Catherine University Library.

philosophy of Eric Gill (1882–1940), and during her work at the John Stevens Shop, she developed her understanding of work more fully and in community. While perfecting her skills in woodcarving, metalwork, calligraphy, and design, Bethune eventually trained various apprentices, often young women.[26] The atmosphere was jovial and convivial, with delightful shared meals and imaginative nicknames for all the inhabitants of "John Stevens University" and the young Carey family. Throughout their long friendship, Ade Bethune and Graham Carey influenced and encouraged each other. While Bethune helped Carey simplify his artistic philosophy for his public lectures and writings, Carey served as a mentor for Bethune.

During her early years in the John Stevens Shop, Bethune compiled what Carey called "her thesis" for the "University," which neatly described her "philosophy of labor" in a booklet titled *Work*, published by the John Stevens Shop in 1939.[27] In this essay, Bethune described work as "man's great vocation" which "makes man human."[28] Not only this, but work was the way of expressing one's relationship with God: "For all human beings, created in the image and likeness of God, may be said to be God's material, which he, the Great Worker, shapes and makes into a perfect image of Himself."[29] Bethune believed that the first way to cooperate with the eternal creative work of God was by being good material—and employing good materials—ourselves. Thus, whenever "we work lovingly and well (regardless of the importance or smallness of the work) we have chosen to work well," and

[26] The first two apprentices were Mary Katherine Finegan and Mary Krenzer, young women who were affectionately called "Lion Cubs" of "Lion's College," in reference to Bethune and her nickname, "Leo," and the "university" of the John Stevens Shop.

[27] The *Liturgical Arts Quarterly* furnished the following review: "Readers of *Liturgical Arts* are familiar with the work of Miss de Béthune. . . . This booklet is written very much in the same vein and the chapter headings—'Work,' 'Raw Matter,' 'Ideas,' 'Skill,' 'Service,' 'the Dignity of Labor'—are an indication of the practical way in which the author views her subject. A reader of this booklet may not necessarily find any 'new' ideas for the simple reason that the author dwells on basic ideas which bear repetition, in and out of season." Review of *Work*, by Ade Bethune, *Liturgical Arts* 7, no. 2 (1939): 32.

[28] Ade Bethune, *Work* (Newport, RI: John Stevens Shop, 1939; repr. Breinigsville, PA: Catholic Authors Press, 2007), 1.

[29] Ibid., 8.

whenever we have chosen the good, we have directed our will toward the Good.[30]

Furthermore, Bethune outlined why she was convinced that art was not confined to the "fine arts," nor was the "artist" a special kind of man or woman. Instead, she believed that every human, by virtue of being human, had a creative faculty and the ability to be an "artist." The creativity of the human mind was applied in any situation—not simply in painting, music, and poetry.[31] To that end, becoming a good worker did mean acquiring skills and employing fine materials, but it also required forming one's ideas through study and contemplation and, finally, working out of love with an aim toward service.[32] That is, in work, the laborer found her gift to offer all humankind, a gift produced to meet real needs. As Bethune wrote, pouring oneself out to one's neighbor brought dignity to both the worker and the artist:

> All men who are dedicated to some human service are doing real work: builders, craftsmen, artisans, manufacturers, makers, producers, operators, actors, travelers, teachers, doctors, peasants, cultivators, laborers, mothers, workers of every kind. All men are called to this great vocation: their priestly office, to offer sacrifice. A sacrifice is a gift. What they offer is the gift of themselves—their power, their intelligence and their devotion—to their work.[33]

Art, then, widely conceived in many forms, was never an end in itself and was not for the glory of the artist. "Art" was work done well, for the other, and for the glory of God.

Working for the Liturgical Movement

Bethune's work attracted the attention of liturgical pioneers as she began writing for the *Liturgical Art Quarterly*. She advocated art that

---

[30] Ibid.

[31] Likewise, Eric Gill wrote, "We think creation only means creating special things, we don't realize that the creative faculty, the imagination, is necessary to the mere existence of humanity. The bank clerk and the shop assistant, the lorry-driver, the doctor and the lawyer must have the creative imagination as much as those other workmen, the artists." Eric Gill, "The Value of the Creative Faculty in Man," in *Work and Property & Church* (London: J.M. Dent & Sons, 1937), 90.

[32] Bethune, *Work*, 9.

[33] Ibid., 34.

would serve the faithful and would be truly liturgical, not caught by frills, the abstract, or controlled by an artistic principle. In short, liturgical art must serve a purpose: just as human hands were designed for acting in love, liturgical art should be designed to direct the human to contemplate, love, and experience the living God in liturgical worship. She extended this principle not only to two-dimensional art but to church architecture, a realm in which she would have increasing involvement throughout the liturgical movement. Bethune was adamant that the Sacrifice of the Mass was "the only reason for building the church," so, when making objects for use in the church, the starting point had to be the "meaning and value of the *Mass*":

> Our work may be anonymous. It may be communal. It may be subservient and quiet. It is not there to sing our own glory and talent as makers. It is there to sing the Glory of God in its beauty and perfection. So the most beautiful works of art on earth, from the point of view of their function, are sacred vessels, sacred vestments, sacred chant, and Scriptures, and especially the administration of all Sacraments. Our effort, then, whether in making objects, reciting office, or participating in the Sacraments, must be to make these works as perfectly as we can for their most beautiful function.[34]

Likewise, as objects crafted for worship should be beautiful and fitted to their service, so should the faithful be good servants by participating fully in the Mass. She recalled that Pius XI taught the faithful to participate in the Christ-life more abundantly by *participating* in the Holy Sacrifice:

> He asks it not just of the priests, but of us, the congregation, the laity. We are all priests, Saint Peter reminds us. We must all offer the *Mass* together (as one Body) with the ordained priest at the altar. We, the congregation, should all answer the prayers of the priest and sing together with the clergy and the choir. So we should show *outwardly* our *inner* Spirit of unity, harmony, and brotherhood in Christ: the Spirit of Christ.[35]

The whole Church, in one body, would work together through prayer, speech, and song; the outward sign of good work revealed the inner meaning of unity in God, or the Mystical Body of Christ.

---

[34] Bethune, "Common Sense," 84.
[35] Ibid., 82–83.

As Bethune's involvement with liturgical art societies continued and her artwork began to gain traction among those interested in liturgical renewal, she received a commission in 1937 from Gerald Ellard, who invited her to illustrate the 1940 edition of the liturgical textbook *Christian Life and Worship*. Originally published in 1933 by Bruce Publishing Company of Milwaukee, Ellard's book was the first collegiate textbook on the liturgy to appear. With twenty-seven chapters devoted to historical and theological aspects of the Eucharist and sacraments, Liturgy of the Hours, the Bible, basic Christian beliefs, and the central issues of the American liturgical movement, the book was widely used among colleges, reprinted in 1934, 1940, and 1950.[36] Also in 1937, Bethune was invited to illustrate the most popular missal in circulation, Msgr. Joseph Stedman's (1898–1946) *My Sunday Missal*, which began publication in 1932. Missal sales had climbed steadily since the late 1920s,[37] and Stedman's was the most popular, by far.[38]

[36] Keith Pecklers, *The Unread Vision: The Liturgical Movement in the United States of America: 1926–1955* (Collegeville, MN: Liturgical Press, 1998), 175. In the preface to the 1950 edition, Gerald Ellard referenced a national survey of college religion textbooks which ranked *Christian Life and Worship* as number three on a list of over one hundred textbooks on the college and university level. See Pecklers, 175–76.

[37] Pecklers, 49–50n77. Bethune was also invited to submit illustrations for a sequel to *The Christ Life Series*, published by Liturgical Press for use in primary grades and designed by Estelle Hackett, OP, Jane Marie Murray, OP, and Virgil Michel. This project, aimed for high school students, did not become a reality until after Michel's death. Including volumes on Christ's life, the Church's liturgy, and Christian social ethics, the series intended to ground religious education at the high school level on a solid liturgical basis. Though the works did not eventually include her illustrations, Godfrey Diekmann felt that Bethune's work would be extremely appropriate: "These four volumes, like the Christ-Life Series, are a series intended to bring the liturgical movement into the teaching of religion, in fact to make the full living of the Christ-Life the inspiration of the entire religion course. You would, therefore, be helping in a work of prime importance of the rechristianization of Christian life and worship in our young generation . . . since the subject matter is rather heavy (Christ's life, Church's liturgy the formative principle of our activity, Our Life in Christ [Virgil Michel's book], and Christian social ethics) and needs striking illustrations to drive home the lessons. Your work would be an important contribution to the liturgical apostolate." Godfrey Diekmann to Ade Bethune, 1940, The Godfrey Diekmann Papers 1013/9, Saint John's Abbey Archives.

[38] Pecklers, 50.

As Bethune's name became more common in liturgical circles, *Orate Fratres* began reporting on her work in the latter 1930s, frequently praising her prints and cards, produced at the John Stevens Shop and advertised in the newly christened *St. Leo Bulletin,* as being properly liturgical. In the "Liturgical Briefs" section in a 1940 issue, Godfrey Diekmann praised Bethune's introduction of Easter cards which were not bedecked with a Scottie dog or, gratefully, a "rakish yellow duck of patently low mentality."[39] At Christmastime, *Orate Fratres* reported with admiration Bethune's handmade crib sets with thirteen pieces, designed by Bethune and crafted by the men on the Catholic Worker Farm on Staten Island in New York. The set sold for $3.25 a piece; *Orate Fratres* concluded that not only:

> are we moving a step in the right direction by introducing a Christmas crib into the Catholic home, but by our support of these men we shall be offering a most acceptable Christmas gift to the Infant who was born in poverty that He might "bring glad tidings to the poor."[40]

Bethune's projects such as crèches, made by guests of a Catholic Worker, were powerful realizations of the liturgical movement's desire to unite life, liturgy, and social consciousness.

Writing and Speaking on the Liturgy

Aside from illustrating liturgical texts and textbooks and her production of liturgical cards and resources, Bethune began contributing articles to *Orate Fratres* as well as receiving invitations to speak at liturgically oriented conferences. At her first major speaking engagement, at the annual meeting of the Catholic Arts Association in St. Paul, Minnesota, in 1939, she gave a talk titled "The Industrial Counterrevolution" in which she discussed the dignity of labor in the arts. She continued to develop the relationship of life, work, and faith in a symposium talk given at the Sienna Heights Conference in 1940, where she

---

[39] "Liturgical Briefs," *Orate Fratres* 15, no. 1 (1940): 43: "The only Easter card this writer ever received was graced, not even with a friendly dog, but with a rakish yellow duck of patently low mentality even as ducks go. No wonder Christians haven't formed a habit of sending one another Easter cards if this example was typical of what the market offers! Heartening is the sign of the Easter greetings designed by Adé Bethune (29 Thames Street, Newport, R.I.), for whose Christian art we have more than once said a word of praise."

[40] Ibid.

described the integrated life. She urged her listeners to remember that it was through the humble tasks of work and living that they shared in the creative art of God:

> Our art, the very excellence of our workmanship, stands as a living testimony of the holy love and reverence which we have for one another and which integrates us one to the other whether inferior or superior, deserving or undeserving, proud or humble, clean or dirty, young or old, known or unknown, into one body, living one life.[41]

Thus, menial tasks, whether they were cleaning the cellar, ordering one's desk, or washing dishes, might seem to be actions of futility: for one might continually find "the cellar like a jungle, our desk a heap of a mess, and a stack of dishes waiting in the kitchen, so shortly after we thought we had it all nice and neat and put away."[42] This ordering, washing, and cleaning, however, Bethune viewed as a humble image of the resurrection and the renovation of the whole world. These tasks were not a drudgery but had a universal significance, imaging the work and care of Jesus, outpoured for humanity.[43]

Bethune connected the value of work with the liturgical life in one of her early articles in *Orate Fratres*, "The Work and Works of Mercy," which appeared in December 1940. In this piece, she related how she had begun drawing the saints in *The Catholic Worker* and her understanding of all work as having the potential to be works of mercy and works for Christ. For the readers of *Orate Fratres*, she compared all the varied human labor, which offered the skills and creativity of the self to all humankind, to the "work" of the Mass:

> [W]hen we offer the bread and the wine at Mass what is it that we offer but the works of our life? Thus there are not so many Masses, offered at seven, eight, nine thirty, ten fifteen and eleven forty-five. There is only *one* Mass. It was offered once, and we participate in it, each generation in turn. All day long, and all our life long, we fashion the offerings which we shall take to the altar whenever the priest officiates. They are the works of our life which are works of mercy when they are works of love.[44]

---

[41] Ade Bethune, "This 'Here' Life," p. 10, Ade Bethune Collection 11 / Writings, St. Catherine University Library.

[42] Ibid., 9.

[43] Ibid., 10.

[44] Bethune, "The Work and Works of Mercy," 56–57.

The ultimate work for the Christian was, then, the Mass; all work re-flected that one perfect offering of Christ:

> The mass feeds the hungry and instructs the ignorant. It visits the sick and the prisoner; and it admonishes and forgives the sinner. It gives alms to the poor; it consoles the sorrowful and it gives advice to those in doubt. It bears wrongs patiently. It buries the dead. It prays for all.[45]

She concluded that, for herself, who had drawn "so many pictures" of the saints, she had drawn only one picture in endless variation: the Mass. All human work, from the work of the saints to the work of our-selves, found its inspiration and its end in the one great work of Christ.

The Challenges of Liturgical Art, the Need for Active Participation
Bethune's more theological approach to folding all human efforts into the work of Christ was paired with her more practical desire to encourage all persons to take ownership over their art—including their liturgical art. At the point when Bethune entered liturgical arts circles in the mid-1930s, both she and her friends in the John Stevens Shop had been frustrated by the disintegration they had observed in the art world. While Bethune, along with Carey and Benson, believed that beauty existed in all forms of life, they felt that "artists" tended to take on a myopic view, defining beauty as adherence to method or principle and as that which should be executed by professionals. Bet-hune wrote in frustration to Graham Carey: "That's one reason why I *hate* artists. I can't bear them. They are so damned interested in their damned 'Art' that they don't know anything else exists."[46]

---

[45] Ibid., 57.

[46] Ade Bethune to Graham Carey, February 16, 1936, Ade Bethune Collection, 3 / Personal Correspondence, St. Catherine University Library. "And I have sometimes a violent suspicion that for a Christian artist it is far better to study Christ than to study Art, to pray than to draw. If he is interested first in the Kingdom of God. . . . 'Beauty will take care of herself.' It is so easy to become a 'Christian–*artist*' that I always want to exaggerate the direction of being a '*Christian*–artist.' Of course, we all agree, what is wanted is Balance. But whenever I see an exaggeration in one direction, I immediately leap to the other extreme—which however all by itself would be just as bad as the first. I guess it is a sort of instinct which I have developed from drawing lines. As soon as I see one running this way, it just hurts til I have put one running opposite to complete, hold, and satisfy it."

The members of the John Stevens Shop saw the problem of imbalance as even more dangerous for the Christian artist: one could not be consumed by an abstract ideal or artistic method when faith required an attentiveness and care for the concrete lives of men, women, and children. To this end, the promotion of "liturgical art" was beset by a twofold danger: first, the absorption of the "artist" in producing good "art" in abstract of its function or use in liturgical celebration, and, drawing from this, a tendency to place the liturgical arts in the hands of professionals to the exclusion of most people who would actually use or experience said "arts." Liturgical arts advocates had good reason for demanding the professionalization of the liturgical arts, as many saw the chief sin of Catholic art forms to be the cheap and sentimental commercially produced "religious" artifacts which flooded the world of Catholic art. Bethune herself was continually perturbed by what she saw as incredibly shoddy production of Christian religious art and artifacts. She wondered, for example, at renditions of cherubic but soundly realistic children surrounded by a fearsomely sentimental Virgin Mary:

> [W]hen it comes to the Blessed Virgin, oh dear, look what happens. Suppose I hadn't told you this is the Blessed Virgin, would you trust such a woman with your child, your cat, your dog or your canary? Not on your life. What do you suppose happened to that artist? Why is it that he can draw his children, his lamb, everything else quite decently, but when it comes to a sacred subject he falls down upon the worst sort of thing. There seems to be a split of the artistic person.[47]

In such examples, she felt that there was some disconnect between the rendering of art and the rendering of religious art; while "art" could be taken seriously, religious art was diffused into kitsch, similar to the disconnect between liturgical prayer and popular devotion.

This separation between the need for professionalism in the production of art and the conviction that art could be produced by anyone was a tension experienced between the two major Catholic liturgical arts associations, the Liturgical Arts Society (LAS) and the Catholic Art Association (CAA). While Bethune's writing and work was greatly appreciated by the *Liturgical Arts Quarterly*, the official journal of the

---

[47] Ade Bethune, "The Importance of Personal and Artistic Integrity," p. 1, Ade Bethune Collection 15 / Writing Book, St. Catherine University Library.

LAS, and her relationship with its secretary and editor, Maurice Lavanoux (1894–1974), quite positive, her philosophy tended to fall on the side of the CAA, which was more broad-minded in its evaluation of who could effectively produce quality liturgical arts. This was the mind-set with which Bethune approached the *Catholic Social Arts Quarterly*, the journal of the CAA, when she was asked to edit it in 1940, which she continued to do for three years. She was frustrated when arts—whether visual, kinesthetic, or aural—failed to engage formative action on the part of the people. Art, especially liturgical art, should direct the faithful to unity in Christ. In an editorial for the *Catholic Social Art Quarterly*, following a meeting of the CAA, during which a long exposition of Gregorian chant took place, Bethune remarked:

> Shall I repeat, shall I make plain, shall I shout loud and hard, shall I explain, I am *not* interested in trimmings?—but in the Liturgy. If we have to spend hours in the chapel to the strains of what most regal ceremonial our hosts can muster up, we shall all die with claustrophobia, asphyxiation, fainting spells, strained back, etc. . . . No one will be converted to Gregorian (e.g.) *by hearing it*—not even, or much less by hearing hours of it. But reasonable people will be converted by *singing* it. And if we are to sing it ourselves, we should begin in the smallest and humblest ways with a simple sung Mass, which hardly takes any time and has no trimmings.[48]

For Bethune, appreciating art—or liturgical arts—would only take place through action. People needed to be trained, in active participation, to the crafting or creation of a thing, including liturgical prayer. Without which, there was no formation, no transformation, and no hope of the liturgy being an effective venue for forming persons in the Mystical Body of Christ.

Bethune found forum to challenge the perception of the "artist" when she attended the first National Liturgical Week in 1940. At this first meeting, Bethune witnessed the recurring tension between those advocating for "professional artists" and the possibility of more ordinary people creating art for liturgical use. For two days, Bethune listened to speeches regarding the need for professional artists creat-

---

[48] Ade Bethune, "D.A. versus C.A.A. [Devil's Advocate versus Catholic Arts Association]," *Christian Social Art Quarterly* 3, no. 2 (1940): 24–25. This is Bethune's first job at editing and at writing editorials. See Ade Bethune Collection 3 / Writings, St. Catherine University Library.

ing liturgical art and peopling church building committees, including Maurice Lavanoux and Martin Hellriegel (1890–1981). During a discussion following Lavanoux's presentation, Bethune leapt in:

> We have been talking about fostering active participation of the laity in the Holy Sacrifice. I think we ought to talk also of fostering active participation of the laity in the building and furnishing of the church. I am sorry, Mr. Lavanoux, I don't agree with you in what you said about "well meaning amateurs." You are perfectly right in saying that good intentions can not replace skill. . . . It seems to me that they need leadership, and that they need the leadership of the ones who have the skill. Too often we have seen the ones who have the skill perform all kinds of fancy things which it is impossible for the small fry to carry out.[49]

Bethune compared the development of professional artists and the demeaning of amateurs to the development of chant: "once upon a time [congregations] all could sing those simple and easy tones, but when the experts came in and dolled it up with curlicues, nobody could sing it, save the experts."[50] While Bethune saw nothing wrong with the beautiful music of chant, she was adamant that emphasis should be placed not on beauty or aesthetics but on the purpose of the art, be it chant or otherwise. The liturgy demanded a display not of skill or beauty but of good work, of sacrifice and offering.[51] Liturgical art and architecture should not become showcases for artists' and artisans' but should invite the people of the liturgical community and space to contribute to their creation:

> There is a danger in letting the skilled people get away with their skill and show it off. . . . I think we would be horrified if we thought for one moment that the person who bakes the bread for the sacrifice would bake a pastry or a wedding cake. That won't do. Perhaps he can make a wedding cake. That is fine and good. But the LITURGY is not the place for him to display that. He has to bake just plain bread. Nor

[49] Ade Bethune, "Discussion," *1940 Liturgical Week Proceedings* (Newark, NJ: Benedictine Liturgical Conference, 1941): 207.
[50] Bethune cites Gerald Ellard's presentation regarding Gregorian chant. One might question how universal the singing of Gregorian chant was, but Bethune's point was that it had become increasingly complexified and the work of professional musicians, not congregation members. See Ade Bethune, "Discussion," *1940 Liturgical Week Proceedings*, 205.
[51] Ibid.

is the wine that is used for the sacrifice a smart cocktail mixture. The things that are needed of the Church do not need to display skill for their own sake. But we must remember that they must be made as well as they can possibly be made. Therefore it seems necessary to have competent leadership for the people to encourage their participation in every part of the Church: The building, the baking, the making of candlesticks and vestments, sweeping, and everything under the sun.[52]

The liturgy was a place not for smartness but for good work; nor was liturgy a place for frills. Instead, the Church, which had existed in many cultures and times, took up the ordinary things of the lives of ordinary people, adopting the attitudes and characters of the people, and making them Christian.[53] Ordinary things, crafted by ordinary people became extraordinary in liturgical use. For example, Bethune recalled that the Church had adopted many of the arts: the baker who makes bread, the weaver who makes linens and silks, the mason and the builder, the silversmith who makes chalices, and the winemaker who makes wine, the candlemaker who uses wax. These things all had clear uses which were reflected in ordinary life. The chalice was not so different from an ordinary cup, but it was made of precious metal because of its precious use. Ordinary elements of life, used liturgically, pointed to a greater reality, that is, a sacramental understanding of art. In the same way, images must accomplish this task, pointing beyond themselves to Christ.[54] Bethune believed "art" would be no use at all

[52] Ibid.

[53] Ade de Bethune, "Art and Christian Art," *Orate Fratres* 14, no. 8 (1940): 338. Bethune continued: "When the Church came to be, she came right into a pagan world. First she came from the Hebrews and so she took over many things from the Jewish race. Then she moved over into Greece and into the Roman Empire, which was a land of pagans, and she took over all the things the pagans held, and she Christianized them. Wherever the Church has gone she has done that. Now she is going into the Orient, China and Japan, and our Holy Father asks that there be not only native clergy but native Christian art. That is why we see those beautiful pictures that the Chinese make of the Blessed Mother looking like a Chinese woman. It is their idea of her. Through all the centuries, from the beginning, we see that in every country and in every time the Church just took the art of the people as it was and made it Christian."

[54] Bethune frequently pointed to the Churches of the East as an example, with iconography developed according to theological and scriptural traditions. She felt that Roman Catholics should look to the Eastern churches in order to

if the faithful simply looked at a set of pictures and exclaimed, "How pretty they are!" If so, then the art had failed in its purpose. Christian art should make one think, should remind the faithful of Christ, and should point toward love of neighbor.

At the same time, Bethune was aware of the "people's" poor taste in art and the love which so many harbored for devotions—or frightening statues of Mary. This was where the liturgical reformers could contribute, as teachers. In order for a reform of liturgical art to be successful, renewal had to be built up slowly. As she concluded during the discussion at the 1940 Liturgical Week:

> "[Reform] is coming but you can't rush it." If we are going to build up something superficial, we can build it right away, quickly and in a rush, but if we are going to build something radical that has roots and that can last for centuries, we have got to build the thing right. This does not mean we must do it slowly just because it is a good idea, in itself, to go slowly. We are doing it the best we can. It is just too bad that the liturgical restoration has to come slowly, but that is the way it is going to come. So, we must not be discouraged.[55]

Building slowly meant starting with the people's work and participation, not a change imposed by "professional" art authorities. Bethune took the task of educating and involving the people strongly in hand.

Liturgical Arts Education

Liturgical art served not only as an aid to devotion but as a field for enlightening understanding of the Christian mysteries, an exercise in ownership over one's place of worship, and identity of the self as a contributing, creative member of the Christian community. Bethune's promotion of the arts extended to all educational levels. In fact, her love for the simple and the childlike made her a special advocate for the ingenuity, freedom, and creativity of children. She took the work

---

learn from them and to interpret religious images in a more profound way: "That's one of the things I would really like to do, if I am given a few more years: namely, develop a theology of liturgical images that may help artists to fill our churches with the faces of those who have gone before us, faces that look at us, that tell us they are our brothers and sisters, faces that help us to see them all around us, and tell us that they are with us in celebrating the divine liturgy in heaven, as we celebrate it down here on earth." See Stoughton, 135.

[55] Ade Bethune, "Discussion," *1940 Liturgical Week Proceedings*, 208.

of children very seriously and cautioned adults against discouraging a child's crude artistic efforts. She reminded adults that children did not perceive their work as crude but instead looked for the beauty in their work. The child "forever strives to correct what minor mistakes he sees, aiming in everything to reach the perfection which he is slowly learning to appreciate better and better."[56] So too should the adult approach liturgical art, or the Christian liturgical life.

Her delight in children's curiosity and her enjoyment in helping them enter into the Catholic faith through hands-on creative means was evidenced through a number of involvements, including her work with Catholic elementary school programs.[57] She designed and produced a series of liturgical "wheel" calendars in the early 1950s that were published by Pio Decimo Press, decorated with explanations of various feast days and their ranks, and descriptions of the symbols chosen to ornament the calendars.[58] Similarly, her interest in encouraging children to interact with, learn, and experience the liturgical year prompted her to create an Advent calendar for use with children. The calendar included directions about how to help children count down the days before Christmas. Consisting of small windows which could be opened, one each day, during the Advent season, she suggested placing the calendar before a window or a lighted lamp, so that the pictures drawn on transparencies would shine more brightly,

[56] Ade Bethune, "Symposium: Should Children Draw Religious Subjects?" *Catholic Art Quarterly* 17, no. 4 (1954): 129.

[57] In one of her presentations, "The Work of our Hands Is Love Made Visible," included in an edited volume titled *Catholic Elementary School Program for Christian Family Living*, Bethune compared the love of Jesus to how humans might show their love: "By working—by working our fingers to the bone, as the saying goes—we make our love visible. Our Lord took our flesh, Himself love made visible. And what kind of man did He become, incidentally? He became a workman, an artist, a carpenter." Ade Bethune, "The Work of our Hands Is Love Made Visible," in *The Catholic Elementary School Program for Christian Family Living*, ed. Mary Ramon Langdon (Washington, DC: Catholic University of America Press, 1955), 125, Ade Bethune Collection 12, St. Catherine University Library.

[58] This Liturgical Calendar, published by Pio Decimo Press in 1953, included instructions from Bethune: "Tack your Map-Calendar on wall, bulletin board or kitchen door where all can refer to it easily. Use a map-tack to mark the day . . . and let children have the pleasure of moving it." "Liturgical Calendar," 1953, Ade Bethune Collection, St. Catherine University Library.

"till Christmas brings complete illumination. Christ is the light of the world."[59] With tools such as these, Bethune innovatively prepared tangible, interactive ways of involving children in the liturgical year:

> Parents are surprised all over again each year to observe how their children can experience a true sense of anticipation through the simple medium of little cardboard windows. It's not fair peeking, of course! But, even if one should peek and quietly close the shutter again no great harm is done, for part of the mystery is in fact the actual celebration of each day. And the parents are its ministers as they perform the rite of retelling the ever wonderful events of the Gospel.[60]

Such projects required training not only in the story of Advent but also in patience. Likewise, Bethune believed, not only interacting with but training in crafting one's own liturgical art would also form the child in a holistic life. The child would gain ownership over a craft and also engage dimensions of the Catholic faith. With this in mind, Bethune prepared instructions for children's art projects, including the interesting prospect of carving a crucifix, creating candleholders out of tin or plaster of Paris, stringing rosaries, and sawing and painting diptychs for the family altar. Children, of course, should be supervised in this work that involved knives, saws, and tin cutters, but such work also encouraged familial interaction and encouraged the responsible use of resources, using scrap materials to create beautiful and meaningful items. This work produced by hand had much more meaning than the crass commercialism and cheap manufacturing processes which plagued the production of devotional and religious materials.[61]

[59] "Mock-up on Cardboard," for "The Advent Calendar," Ade Bethune Collection, St. Catherine University Library.

[60] "Directions for 'The Advent Calendar,'" Ade Bethune Collection, St. Catherine University Library.

[61] Bethune, "The Work of Our Hands Is Love Made Visible," 133. Due to her relationship with the Catholic Arts Association, Bethune also recommended a number of resources for elementary school children regarding the use of religious art: Elementary Education Committee of the Catholic Art Association, *The Catholic Elementary Art Guide Vol. VII: Redeeming Used and Discarded Materials* (St. Paul, MN: 1954); Elementary Education Committee of the Catholic Art Association, *The Catholic Elementary Art Guide Vol. V: The Heart of the Home* (St. Paul, MN: 1952); Elementary Education Committee of the

Bethune also advocated for the importance of art for the high school student. Just as small children learned habits of patience and skill through the use of their hands, older students, through the work of their hands, helped others by practicing charity, prudence, and justice.[62] Her interest in young people also prompted Bethune to visit the Grail, which she had first discovered while in Holland during the summer of 1937. She had found the European group different from other youth organizations of Europe, observing that, while the Grail women were quite regimented, they had a serious orientation to Catholic liturgy and life. After the Grail moved to the United States, Bethune had many contacts with the group, including two of her apprentices, Peggy Maurer and Audrey Barton, who came from the Grail.[63] Like the Grail, Bethune worked internationally and, during her commission work at a four hundred-year-old mission church in Bacalar, Yucatan, she worked with three Grail-trained Chicana women from New Mexico, along with her other helpers.[64]

Work as a Liturgical Consultant

The realm of church architecture was one of the most concrete ways in which Ade Bethune was able to apply her skills as an artist and her hopes for advocating the laity's involvement and ownership of their faith. Her first commission came from Fr. Joseph L. Lonergan of St. Paulinus Church in Clairton, Pennsylvania. This particular parish, in

---

Catholic Art Association, *The Catholic Elementary Art Guide Vol. VI: Forming the Artistic Conscience* (St. Paul, MN: 1953).

[62] "A strong will—i.e., a will strengthened by habit—can be acquired only by action, and repeated action. The various works of the art class then, the art class in its broadest sense (i.e., all the arts, the dramatic arts, speech, music, painting, crafts, shop, etc.) are the living opportunities for action and repeated action which young people need to form their own will. This is why they are the most valuable character forming activities of the high school program (much more valuable than athletics) and that is why all students have a right to training in the arts." Ade Bethune, "The Value of Art to the High School Student," in *Art Today in Catholic Secondary Education (The Proceedings of the Workshop on Art in Catholic Secondary Schools Conducted at the Catholic University of America, June 12–23, 1953)*, ed. Augusta Zimmer (Washington, DC: Catholic University of America Press, 1954), 63, Ade Bethune Collection 11, St. Catherine University Library.

[63] Stoughton, 55.

[64] Ibid., 126.

the midst of the Depression, had been unable to acquire loans to build, nor could they afford an architect. So the parishioners, in 1936, decided to build a church themselves.[65] Lonergan had seen Bethune's pictures in *The Catholic Worker* and was so impressed that he contacted her, hoping that his parishioners might use her "Works of Mercy" designs for their stations and to see if Bethune herself might be willing to carve crucifixes for the altar and sacristy as well as a processional cross. Bethune (who had two lessons in woodcarving) accepted the commission, the first of a significant amount of artwork produced and directed at the parish, including stained glass for the baptistery and large panel paintings adorning the sanctuary walls. In line with her philosophy of art and labor for liturgy, the creation of liturgical art was not done by Bethune alone. She wanted the people, who had built the church building themselves, to also create its art so that the building might be fully theirs. She promised to teach them and set up an assembly line where young men and women applied the background to twenty-four heroic paintings of saints and apostles, and solicited volunteers to help paint the baptistery and the stations of the cross.[66]

[65] The ingenuity, care, and craftship embraced by the people of this parish echoed with Bethune's understanding of the production and purpose of art. In order to prepare their designs, St. Paulinus parishioners studied European churches, copying medieval buttresses and Byzantine designs. Work began in 1936, with stone acquired for free from the nearby New England Hollow, Spanish tile roofing purchased from a sheriff sale, and nine thousand square feet of Vermont slate found for eighteen cents a foot. Men and boys made the altar railing, candleholders, sanctuary and sacristy furniture, pews, stations, and narthex screen. Women embroidered altar frontals, sewed linens, surplices, and cassocks for the altar boys, and stained the finished pews. "Parish Directory, 50th anniversary, The Church of Saint Paulinus," pp. 10–11, Ade Bethune Collection, Series 1, Churches in the US 5, St. Catherine University Library.

[66] "Parish Directory, 50th anniversary, The Church of Saint Paulinus," pp. 13–14, Ade Bethune Collection, Series 1, Churches in the US 5, St. Catherine University Library. The Parish Directory related: "When Father Lonergan said, 'They don't know anything about art,' Adé replied, 'Oh, art is bunk. I can teach them.' And she did so." St. Paulinus continued as an autonomous parish until 1994, when declining congregations caused the bishop of the diocese to merge the parish with two other parishes in the area of Clairton. In 2007, with continuing financial difficulties, mounting costs of building repairs, accompanied by a shrinking congregation, the parishioners decided to close

In this project and throughout her career as a liturgical consultant, Bethune taught those with whom she worked. She emphasized the importance of paying attention to the best in artistic and religious traditions, including the churches of the East and their strong tradition of sacred images, the ancient use of natural light to illumine spaces (as opposed to artificial floodlights, for example), the people's ability to move through a space (not being stuck in a "forest of pews, or even a forest of chairs"), and the importance of attending to acoustics which allowed sound and congregational singing to reverberate through the space.[67] When asked about her work as a consultant in the late 1980s, Bethune would recall:

> So I became a liturgical consultant. And I started working on churches. I entered the field of architecture through the back door. I'm not a licensed architect. But I do know how to read blueprints and I can help the architect understand what the client wants from the liturgical point of view. The client's ideas are sometimes inchoate, you know, he doesn't always exactly know what he wants. At the same time I'm protecting the client from some of the vagaries the architect can produce, simply because they are novel or "interesting" or something like that, and it will not work. So I became a liturgical consultant.[68]

Bethune consistently rejected the use of commercially produced liturgical decoration and artifacts, bemoaning the "general tendency" for church builders to copy "washed out" nineteenth-century models of sanctuary space and stained glass, and warned pastors planning parishes not to fall into such traps of expectation.[69]

---

the parish permanently. See Mary Niederberger, "Tears accompany closing of St. Paulinus Church in Clairton," *Pittsburgh Post Gazette*, October 4, 2007.

[67] Stoughton, 135–36.

[68] Quoted in David Ramsey, *Ade Bethune*, The Archives of Modern Christian Art Series (Belmont, CA: College of Notre Dame, 1986), 15. Bethune continued: "In some cases I've designed the whole church, in the sense that I've done the schematic studies for the planning of the church. In fact, it's nicer if you can do that. But after Vatican II there was also no money. There was a depression—not a depression, but whatever you call it. . . . No money to build things. It was all mostly renovations."

[69] Ade Bethune to Valerion Lucier, May 14, 1956, Ade Bethune Collection, Series 1, Churches in the U.S. 6/3, St. Catherine University Library.

Bethune's liturgical consultant work, which extended to thirteen of the United States, was also international.[70] In 1951, Bethune was invited by a Maryknoll priest, Donald Hessler, who was working on a mission in the southern part of the Yucatan peninsula.[71] He asked Bethune to advise his congregation as to how to decorate their new mission church. Bethune arrived less than three months later, intending to create a plan for decorating the Church. But when she arrived and found a dozen village parishioners greeting her, eager to begin the project, she quickly decided to take a boat back to the nearest town in order to procure the necessary powder colors, glue, and three-quarter-inch brushes to begin the project immediately.[72] As Hessler would relate, many years after the event:

> Indeed Ade and her Mexican friends—trained on the spot—made our church walls preach the joyous news. I've visited Bacalar many times during these 35 years. Most of her murals are still intact, participating in the ever renewed parish life. A dynamic Mexican community has taken over from Maryknoll. We must joyously disappear in favor of the local church.[73]

Attentive to the cultural context of the congregation, Bethune picked themes and images which would attend to the Spanish language and Mayan heritage of the people. Over the sacristy door, she created a large scroll with psalm verses in Spanish and painted a large "three generation" mural on one of the interior church walls, depicting St. Anne as a Mayan grandmother.[74] Bethune's readiness in incorporating

[70] Bethune's liturgical consultant work is catalogued in the Ade Bethune Collection, held in the St. Catherine University Library. The Ade Bethune Collection has wonderful examples of Bethune's process of work, from letters and blueprints to three-dimensional models of projects on which she worked.

[71] See Adé de Béthune, "Font and Altar: Footnotes on Sacred Architecture," *Catholic Art Quarterly* 17, no. 3 (1954): 93–94.

[72] "Back in Bacalar, she found a broken floor tile to use as palette for grinding the colors. Two very young children collected sticks and shavings to keep the fire going under a double boiler of glue." Stoughton, 124–25.

[73] Donald Hessler to Judith Stoughton, March 6, 1986. See Stoughton, 127.

[74] Stoughton, 125. Bethune's use of St. Anne was an attempt to help balance the people's intense devotion to St. Joachim, who was seen as a powerful patron of the parish, with that of Mary and, more importantly, Jesus. Fr. Hessler, reflecting on the import of Bethune's work at this mission parish

every person in the creation of their worship space reflected her desire to promote active liturgical participation. Liturgical worship was not the property of experts. In fact, her interest in befriending and involving those around her even led to some of her neophyte artists reentering regular weekly liturgy attendance.[75]

Ade Bethune's Anticipation of the Liturgical Architecture of the Second Vatican Council

Bethune's work as liturgical consultant continued through the 1980s on projects from chapels to mission churches.[76] Bethune routinely emphasized the necessity of liturgical space which was functional, had the potential to aid the people's prayer, and was historically and theologically informed. For example, Bethune was hired to work as a liturgical consultant for St. Leo's Church in St. Paul, Minnesota. The pastor at the time, Fr. Bernard Murray, had spoken with her about the possibilities of a round church when they had met at Liturgical Weeks and CAA conventions. Bethune advised him on the difficulties of constructing a round church, something "fraught with every kind of pitfall, from Acoustics to Zoning." She also described some of the

---

some thirty years later: "Ade fit in perfectly with these young zealots and our Mexican sisters and brothers, who had gradually—during a hundred priestless years—divinized a wooden image of St. Joachim, our mighty 'Patron, Patriarca, Señor, San Joaquín.' I was eager that Ade find a way to 'put St. Joachim in his place' and end the idolatry. Ade corrected me at once, 'No, we're not going to put St. Joachim in his place, but rather give this Holy Man his own noble dignity. After all, he was the Father of the Holiest Woman on earth. He was the Grandfather of God.' So she began to paint a striking mural of the 'three generations', the Baby Jesus in the center on Mary's lap; with Joachim and Anne at their sides. Anne's presence brought all kinds of questions, and also cleared the way to humanize Joachim and promote holy marriages." Donald Hessler to Judith Stoughton, March 6, 1986. See Stoughton, 127.

[75] In a letter from Father Hessler to Ade Bethune, May 13, 1952, he wrote: "Warmest greetings from everyone in Bacalar, including Don José Cortes who says that the 'Señorita Artista' converted him, and he is going to go to church. . . . Who knows what you started?" See Stoughton, 126.

[76] Judith Stoughton details some of these projects in *The Proud Donkey of Schaerbeek*. Another of Bethune's projects which was highly reported in *Liturgical Arts Quarterly* was her work in the Philippines. See Adé de Béthune, "Philippines Adventure," *Liturgical Arts Quarterly* 19, no. 4 (1951): 10–13.

successfully rendered churches-in-the-round, including the Chapel of the Holy Sacrifice at the University of the Philippines, designed by Leandro Locsin of Manila in 1955, of which Bethune had also been the liturgical consultant, and included a four-page commentary on early Christian and contemporary churches-in-the-round.[77]

With regard to church interiors, Bethune stressed that form led to function and that function should attend to the need and culture of its users. She felt that liturgical spaces should be aware of the distinction between the "timeless, permanent teaching of the Church" and its "variable customs."[78] One such custom was the altar rail. At one point in the Church's history, until the turn to the twentieth century, a short kneeler or communion rail near the sanctuary was significant enough space for the small number of persons who might go to receive Communion. Following Pius X's advocacy for frequent Communion, however, the increasing number of frequent communicants had rendered an "almost general problem of crowding in an inadequate space" coupled with the inconvenient necessity of the priest rushing back and forth to people "in a manner that lacks the dignity fitting to the Sacrament."[79] Bethune indicated that a solution must be found to avoid unnecessary movement detracting from the "Sacred Action," as well as a more convenient and comfortable space for people.[80] She suggested two possibilities, both of which she had witnessed. The first example she offered was to receive Holy Communion standing, which, although "this custom may seem revolutionary," was also the custom in the early days of the Church, and perhaps as late as the thir-

[77] See Stoughton, 131. Stoughton describes the exchange as "typical of the responses which Ade gives her clients: unexpected 'short history courses,' plus astute and practical recommendations related to the present time and place."

[78] Adé de Béthune, "Revising Our Conception of the Communion Rail," *Catholic Art Quarterly* 21, no. 2 (1958): 37.

[79] Ibid., 38.

[80] Ibid., 39. "Some rubrical reforms are obviously needed to implement the twentieth century legislation. Chief among the reforms which have been suggested are a shortening of the formula 'Corpus Domini . . . ' (to perhaps the first two words only), and an extension of the diaconate to furnish the celebrant with sufficient assistance for distribution of Holy Communion. This latter need, as we know, has been particularly felt in mission territories where priests are few, and their congregations—brought up from the start on St. Pius X's reform—flock literally by thousands to receive Holy Communion at the hands of their overworked spiritual shepherd."

teenth century.[81] An alternative possibility, she suggested, would be a circular altar rail. While circular sanctuaries had their difficulties, she had seen two examples (one at the Chapel of the Holy Sacrifice at the University of the Philippines in Manila and the other at the Church of Christ the Sun of Justice in Benson, Vermont), which had used a circular plan: "It is not merely an idea that looks interesting on paper, but an awesome realization which penetrates into the soul by the help of an architectural setting so aptly suited to the action as to re-enforce its hidden meaning."[82] A circular altar rail emphasized Christ the Center, with communicants kneeling, facing Christ, and embodied the notion that all were made one in the social action of the Eucharist. And, from a practical viewpoint, the circular communion rail aided the efficient motion of the priest, who would no longer need to zigzag but could move in one, continuous motion.[83]

Bethune also offered instruction regarding the use of a baptistery. She admitted that, until she had her first godchild, the baptistery was merely a "blur" in her mind: "From the architectural point of view, my general impression of these baptismal experiences is a complex of drafty vestibules and narrow quarters in inconspicuous corners."[84] But during her experience working with Lonergan of Clairton, Pennsylvania, she applied her knowledge of baptism that she had garnered from study of ancient church architecture. The result at Clairton was a small, separate building, with "real dignity and beauty," in a round fieldstone room at the base of the bell tower.[85] Her practical approach to liturgical

[81] "No formal communion rail seems to have appeared in the West much before the eighteenth century—the sanctuary being closed off by chancels (i.e. latticed screens), often in the form of a marble enclosure or wrought iron grille. Standing has also remained unchanged in most of the Eastern Rites, where no communion rail is used to this day." Bethune, "Revising Our Conception of the Communion Rail," 39.

[82] Ibid., 40.

[83] Ibid.

[84] Adé de Béthune, "Font and Altar: Footnotes on Sacred Architecture," 88.

[85] She noted that she studied with Gerald Ellard and Dom Gregory Borgstedt while she was at Portsmouth Abbey, as well as being influenced by Father Régamy's *Cahiers de L'Art Sacré* (1946), in which a note described the possibility of a separate baptistry: "In its renewed life of today, the Spirit of the Liturgy demands that the rite of Baptism—by which the neophyte is united to the Christian community—should be followed by as many people as possible from that community. The baptismal ante-chamber and especially the baptistry

art and space, suggesting the possible removing of altar rails and the meaningfulness of a separate baptistery area, anticipated some of the most significant liturgical spatial changes which would occur after the Second Vatican Council.[86]

Trajectory of Ade Bethune

Ade Bethune's legacy in the liturgical movement is clear and comprehensive, though she is most frequently identified as "the Catholic Worker artist." Among Bethune's worldly accolades were honorary degrees from Saint Mary's College, Notre Dame, and the University of Notre Dame, among others, and the invitation to design the brass candlesticks for the papal altar in the Vatican at the closing session of the Second Vatican Council.[87] After many years with the John

---

proper should therefore open wide upon the church." Bethune, "Font and Altar: Footnotes on Sacred Architecture," 89.

Bethune wrote a number of articles on church design. See, for example, Ade Bethune, "Tabernacle and Altar," *Catholic Art Quarterly* 22, no. 4 (1959): 98–101; "Bell Towers in Sacred Architecture, Part I," *Catholic Art Quarterly* 21, no. 3 (1958): 80–88; and "Bell Towers in Sacred Architecture, Part II," *Catholic Art Quarterly* 21, no. 4 (1958): 118–23.

[86] While Bethune's visions for the future were, at times, surprisingly accurate, she could also be far off the mark. See, for example, "Small Churches," *Orate Fratres* 12, no. 11 (1937): 486–89, where Bethune described the importance of smaller, more intimate parishes: "Where will you get all the priests to take charge of this army of new small churches? Answer: The missionary days of America are over, at least in the East and the Middle West. Our huge parishes have to be manned by a pastor and at least three or four vicars. Make each one of these priests the pastor of a small parish, if necessary, under the supervision of an experienced confrere, and everything is taken care of. Seminaries throughout the country are full of future priests ready to go out to their work." Of course, Bethune wrote at the height of seminary numbers, so her suggestion may have been apt for the time, but precisely the opposite took place for the next generation of Catholics, with the joining rather than separating of parishes.

[87] "Parish Directory, 50th anniversary, The Church of Saint Paulinus," p. 13–14, Ade Bethune Collection, Series 1, Churches in the U.S. 5, St. Catherine University Library. Reflecting on the Second Vatican Council, Bethune noted: "I was happy when the documents of Vatican II came out and emphasized the presence of Christ, not only in the Eucharist, but also in the Scriptures, in the people, and in the priest. I am very sorry they left out the presence of Christ in his sacred image. Perhaps the reason they did this is that the images of

Stevens Shop, which continued to advertise religious art in its *St. Leo Bulletin* until 1981, Bethune joined the Terra Sancta Guild, to which she contributed designs for well-crafted liturgical art. She continued contributing to liturgical arts circles and creating liturgical art throughout her life, even as media for reproducing art drastically changed. Bethune adamantly became accustomed to using a computer[88] and, in 1986, oversaw the production of a collection of two hundred of her pictures into a clip-art book for use in "bulletins or programs, and for your school and church events."[89] Always present in Bethune's mind, however, was her advocacy for the welfare of the people of Newport, Rhode Island, and she worked on campaigns to reroute highways, as well as create a low-income housing program, Harbor House, for the elderly. Community members remember Bethune as incredibly active in promoting the safety of Newport citizens and that she personally drove the effort to renovate a convent near her home into low-income housing. Ade Bethune died in Newport in 2002, just months after the low-income housing project came to completion.[90]

Christ had become wishy-washy and feeble, too 'arty,' not liturgical enough. It belongs to our time to bring back a new life to the delineation of sacred images as a true part and expression of the liturgy." Stoughton, 135.

[88] Martha Marie Grogan, conversation with the author, May 22, 2012, Newport, RI. Grogan worked as Bethune's personal assistant during the last years of Bethune's life.

[89] Ade Bethune, "To the Reader," *Eye Contact with God through Pictures: A Clip Book of Pictures from the Ade Bethune Collection* (Kansas City, MO: Sheed & Ward, 1986). Produced after Bethune's works were assembled by the Saint Catherine University Library in St. Paul, Minnesota, Bethune included a short note to readers: "A few symbolic designs are included in these pages. But, by far, the greater number of pictures show people. Why? So that, rather than merely puzzle over symbols for abstract ideas, we may look directly at the goodness of Christ our Lord, and see—reflected in our brothers and sisters—the Icon, the very Image of the love of God himself."

[90] See James A. Johnson, "Artist on the Point helped shape the local landscape," *The Newport Daily News*, May 5, 2010. A visit by the author to this senior citizen facility in July 2010 gave opportunity for several conversations with current residents who remarked on the affordability and need for the housing project and the unfortunate event that Bethune died before she could make use of it herself. See also Anne Kumar, "Elderly have 'Cozy Nest,'" *The Newport Daily News*, February 4, 2002.

Other American Lay Women in the Liturgical Arts
Bethune was, of course, not alone as a lay female Catholic artist active in the liturgical movement. Two of the most active Catholic liturgical arts societies, the LAS and the CAA, bore witness to a significant number of women artists, beginning in the early years of the movement, one of the most prolific of whom was Miss E. Charlton Fortune (1885–1969) of California.[91] Active in liturgical arts on the West Coast, Euphemia Charlton (or "Effie") Fortune, director of the Monterey Guild, was familiar to liturgical circles and a trusted advocate for the liturgical art movement. Among her appointments was giving a series of eight lectures, delivered to the sisters of Kansas City, Missouri, under the direction of Bishop Edwin O'Hara (1881–1956) and the College of St. Teresa in February and March 1942. An audience member submitted a summary of some of Fortune's major points to *Orate Fratres*, noting how Fortune emphasized the relation of the liturgical art movement to the "great Catholic revival of liturgical prayer and living." As the attendee reported, liturgical art and architecture should not simply "not transgress the liturgical rules" but should adopt a "liturgical outlook," one which sought to "make the setting compatible in externals with the dignity of the liturgy."[92]

[91] Other examples include Elsa Schimd, whose work on a Stations of the Cross in mosaic for a church in New York City was reported by Hildreth Meière in "A Modern Way of the Cross in Mosaic," *Liturgical Arts Quarterly* 1, no. 1 (1931): 35–38. Meière was herself a director of the publication. See also Ann H. Grill, "What We Can Do about Catholic Art," *The Catholic Art Quarterly* 11, no. 1 (1947): 7–11; Ethel Thurston, "Medieval Dramas in New York," *The Catholic Art Quarterly* 21, no. 1 (1957): 25–26; Marykay Jones, "Impressions of an Idea," *Liturgical Arts Quarterly* 8, no. 3 (1940) : 54–55; Micaela Martinex, "Letter to the Editor," *Liturgical Arts Quarterly* 6, no. 1 (1937): 54; Beatrice L. Warde, "Printing Should Be Invisible," *The Catholic Art Quarterly* 21, no. 2 (1958): 33–36.
[92] "The Apostolate," *Orate Fratres* 16, no. 6 (1942): 284–85. For more on Fortune, see Rebecca Berru Davis, *Women Artists of the Early Twentieth Century Liturgical Movement in the United States: The Contributions of E. Charlton Fortune, Ade Bethune, and Sister Helene O'Connor, O.P.* (PhD diss., Graduate Theological Union, 2011).

The Liturgical Movement Goes Back to the Land

Bethune's interest in uniting labor, arts of all stripes, and lifestyle as developed by the liturgical movement also found a ready home in the various Catholic initiatives connected to Catholic agrarianism.[93] By the late 1920s, interest in promoting family life, religious life, and community life coincided with the "objectives" of Catholic Action, such as the promotion of Rural Life Sunday and Rogation Days, which were associated with blessing the fields in preparation for a fruitful harvest. Michael Woods describes the fluid beginnings of the correspondence between the liturgical movement pioneers and the rural life movement, which was organized by Edwin O'Hara into the National Catholic Rural Life Conference, an alternative organization to the Rural Life Bureau of the National Council of Catholic Bishops.[94] And, by the end of the 1930s, Catholics who were interested in rural reconstruction found an increasing base of literature available, with the benefits of rural living encouraged through diocesan papers[95] and journals such as *Land and Home*, the Catholic Rural Life Bulletin.[96] *Land and Home* frequently invited women to write about the healthful and moral benefits for children and young people who lived on the land, the process of preparing

[93] Michael Woods identifies the intersection of liturgy and rural life in his *Cultivating Soil and Soul*. See Woods, 10–25. See also Leo R. Ward, ed., "Ligutti and the Farmers," in *Catholic Life, U.S.A.: Contemporary Lay Movements* (St. Louis, MO: B. Herder Book, 1959), 202–20.

[94] There was significant tension over the founding of an "alternative" and competing organization, as it made the Rural Life Bureau of the National Conference of Catholic Bishops obsolete. See American Catholic History Research Center and University Archives, Catholic University of America, Washington, DC [hereafter cited as ACUA], 10, The Records of the Department of Social Action, Series 17, Records Relating to the Rural Life Bureau, 1929–1955.

[95] See, for example, the newspaper of the Diocese of Des Moines, Iowa, *Catholic Rural Life. Catholic Rural Life*, Archives of the Diocese of Des Moines, 601 Grand Avenue, Des Moines, Iowa.

[96] Wider reading was also advertised. For example, in 1940, Dr. Eva J. Ross conducted a study of Belgian rural cooperation, describing the program which "has aimed at integrating the whole life of the rural peoples and which, inspired and promoted by the Catholic clergy, has helped to remake a new rural Belgium since 1885. . . ." P.A.N., Review of *Belgian Rural Cooperation*, by Eva J. Ross, *Orate Fratres* 14, no. 11 (1940): 528.

food for a family, and working together to care for farms and animals. Such closeness to the land, peace, and familial cooperation, writers claimed, brought them closer to God.[97] At the same time, women who were involved in these agrarian movements resonated with the interests of the liturgical movement. For example, one of the initiatives lay women promoted and led were "vacation schools" for rural children, to help them learn a simple form of dialogue Mass participation.[98] Other women, such as Florence Berger and her husband, Alfred, found common ground between the NCRLC and the promotion of a familial liturgical lifestyle at the National Liturgical Weeks.

The intersection with the rural life movement and the liturgical movement was readily identifiable by liturgical pioneers. In fact, when the NCRLC meeting and the National Liturgical Week coincided in 1941, Martin Hellriegel of Holy Cross Parish in O'Fallon, Missouri, remarked to the assembled group:

> [W]hile speaking of rural life this pastor is going to raise a note of protest (please watch the smile) about the concurrence of the "National

[97] Ruth DeMars, "We Moved Out," *Land and Home* (March 1942): 5: "There is a closeness to God not felt in the city way of life. We all pitch in to do the work. Of course, the children are too young to do very much, but there is being developed in their little minds the right attitude toward country life and cooperation. That is what is needed to make this life successful." See also Luella Midgely, "Productive Farm Homes," *Land and Home* (February 1941): 21–22; Maude Taylor Sarvis, "Going to School in the Nineties," *Land and Home* (June 1942): 6–8; Roberta Hellrung, "Marriage," *Land and Home* (February 1941), 10; and Ruth Hartquist, ". . . And a Career," *Land and Home* (February 1941): 10–11.

[98] Miss Ellamay Horan of Silver Lake, Missouri, described her experience teaching catechesis along with several Sisters of Charity and Father Norbert Pohl, of St. Vincent's Catholic Parish and School, in nearby Perryville, Missouri. The two main objectives of the two weeks' vacation school were: (1) to get children of various ages to participate in Mass as a group, and (2) make them active participants as individuals, following the answer to Question 364 of the *Revised Baltimore Catechism*: "The best method of assisting at Mass is to unite with the priest in offering the holy Sacrifice, and to receive holy Communion." Thus, for three hours each day, for fourteen days, the Mass was the central figure in a catechetical program, the conclusion of which, she reports, was that the children "of this rural parish had learned a simple form of Dialog Mass participation." See "Teaching the Mass in a Rural Vacation School," *Orate Fratres* 17, no. 9 (1943): 424–27.

Liturgical Week" here at St. Paul and the "National Rural Life Conference" now convening in Jefferson City, Missouri. As a Missourian and as a lover of the Rural Life Conference I should this evening be in Jefferson City, and as a Catholic and a lover of the liturgical apostolate I am happy to spend these holy days here in St. Paul. But now I quit smiling as I say the following: In the future we should not permit such simultaneousness. These two movements are like two halves of a circle and the leaders of one should bring information and inspiration to the other. But that is impossible when the two are convening at the same time. The liturgical group is the "husband" and the rural group is the "wife" and what God has joined together, let no man put asunder. But right now they are "divorced."[99]

This connection was also embraced by one of the most readily identifiable groups of the liturgical movement, the American Grail Movement, which introduced thousands of young women to the intersection of liturgy, labor, and lifestyle.

The Grail Movement and Catholic Action in America

The Grail arrived on the American front in 1940, headed by Dr. Lydwine van Kersbergen (1905–98) who had joined the Dutch Grail in 1926, five years after its founding. Van Kersbergen had a PhD in Dutch literature from the University of Nijmegen and administrative experience in the Grail in London, England, and Sydney, Australia.[100] Her work with the European Grail had made her aware of the Catholic Intellectual Revival and Catholic Action, and, by the time she arrived in the States after necessary evacuation from Nazi-occupied Holland, she found a scene ripe for lay movements.[101] Inspired by Pius X's

---

[99] Martin B. Hellriegel, "A Pastor's Description of Liturgical Participation in His Parish," *1941 Liturgical Week Proceedings* (Newark, NJ: Benedictine Liturgical Conference, 1942): 82–83. Quoted in Woods, *Cultivating Soil and Soul*, 34.

[100] Brown, *The Grail Movement*, 25.

[101] "In the Grail, a veritable Trojan Horse, a portable arsenal of militant European Catholic ideas and trappings already specially formulated for a female constituency was smuggled into the American Catholic Church. During the postwar era, the American Grail volunteers adapted this thoroughly European movement to the exigencies of life in Catholic America. Sometimes van Kersbergen aided in this process and sometimes she strongly resisted Americanizing the Grail. She had one major strength, derived from her experiences with the Dutch, English and Australian Grail, that made her unique among the leaders of the American Catholic laity: she had thought

adage, "The primary and indispensable source of the true Christian spirit is the active participation of the faithful in the sacred mysteries and in the solemn prayer of the Church," she concluded that "the first principle in the training of lay apostles is the understanding that the experience of the sacred liturgy is the integrating center of life."[102] Thus, the Grail Movement, in concert with other grassroots groups led by women, the Catholic Worker and Friendship House, sought to create an alternative, small community in which its members might experience the radical social implications of the Mystical Body through group prayer and work.[103]

The Grail and Young Women

Unique to the Grail experience, however, was its explicit intention for the advocacy and education of young Christian women. While Virgil Michel had spoken of the role of Christian women, an emphasis on the specific role of women in establishing a reformed society had not been emphasized in many American liturgical movement venues. Yet, this would change with the advent of the American Grail Movement.[104] As Joan Overboss (1910–69), cofounder of the American Grail, would describe in an article for *Orate Fratres* in 1945:

> The Grail Schools are intensive periods of formation for positive Christian action. Their purpose is to prepare young women all over America as great-hearted *women*, radiant *Christians*, and generous *apostles* to enable them to meet the profound universal problems of our time and to

---

long and systematically about the niche that women could and should occupy within the lay apostolate." Debra Campbell, "Both Sides Now: Another Look at the Grail in the Postwar Era," *U.S. Catholic Historian* 11 (1993): 17.

[102] Lydwine van Kersbergen, *The Normal School of Sanctity for the Laity* (Loveland, OH: Grailville, 1959), 6.

[103] See Campbell, "Reformers and Activists," 175–76.

[104] At the 1943 Grailville summer session on the liturgy, titled "Cymbals of Joy," Godfrey Diekmann capped the week by "sketching a striking parallel between the nature and function of the Christian woman and that of the Church. . . ." Virginia Bogdan, "The Grail Training Course," *Orate Fratres* 17, no. 10 (1943): 465. See also Lydwine van Kersbergen, "Toward a Christian Concept of Woman," *Catholic World* 182, no. 1 (October 1955): 11; Debra Campbell, "The Heyday of Catholic Action and the Lay Apostolate, 1929–1959," in *Transforming Parish Ministry: The Changing Roles of Catholic Clergy, Laity, and Women Religious*, ed. Jay Dolan et al. (New York: Crossroad, 1989).

contribute in their specific capacity as women, in an organized postulate under the leadership of the hierarchy, towards a Christian future.[105]

The earliest members of the Grail Movement, then, emphasized the charisms available to young women, particularly their potential for the domestic vocation, and taught that women and men had complementary roles. As Grailville evolved over time, it continually grappled with the concept of the Christian "woman" and the role of woman in modern society.[106] Specifically inviting women to enter into the liturgical apostolate, the Grail Movement provided a unique way for women to enter into the aims of Catholic Action and, in the liturgical movement, to join in the goal of restoring society. Attending Grailville for a month, a summer, or one of its various short summer school programs afforded an opportunity for women to participate in an intense experience of communal living, prayer, and work.

The Grail and the Laity

At the 1949 Liturgical Week held in St. Louis, Missouri, van Kersbergen gave an address on the theological and cultural aspects of Sunday in Grailville, drawing on her publication, *The Normal School of Sanctity for the Laity* (1949). She described the modern world's capture by secularism in every sphere of life. It was the responsibility of the laity to Christianize all aspects of the lay vocation: the family, the business, the school, and all institutions. In this modern age, the Holy Spirit had raised up "a new organ in the mystical body," the apostolate of the laity, to accomplish this re-Christianization of society. How could lay people attain such sanctity? She referred to Pius X's locating the source for the true Christian spirit in the solemn prayer of the Church. The Christian, then, must seek this source of the liturgy:

[105] Joan Overboss, "Grail Offers Courses in 'Lived' Christianity," in "The Apostolate," *Orate Fratres* 19, no. 7 (1945): 325.

[106] Grail leaders Janet Kalven and Lydwine van Kersbergen each wrote a book describing the subject of women: Janet Kalven, *The Task of Woman in the Modern World* (Des Moines, IA: NCRLC, 1946), and Lydwine van Kersbergen, *Woman: Some Aspects of Her Role in the Modern World* (Loveland, OH: Grailville, 1956). After the Second Vatican Council, the character of the Grail would change, becoming more inclusive of other faiths and more attentive to bourgeoning women's movements and feminism.

[W]ith the Sacrifice of the Mass as the center of each day and the Divine Office as the consecration of the hours, with the Sunday to sanctify the week, the cycle of fasts and feasts to hallow the year, and the sacraments to elevate the span of life from birth to death, we find the fundamental plan for our growth in Christ.[107]

The Grail Movement sought to invite young women to take up this charge, training them in their Catholic faith through active participation and ownership in the liturgy, to re-Christianize the world.

Grail Summer Schools in Liturgy

The Grail courses sought to bring "young women all over America" into a deeper participation in the liturgical life *as young women*. Girls from high schools, colleges, parish cells, Catholic Action groups, and workplaces learned to sing Gregorian chant, participate in a *Missa Cantata*, practice meditation, attend lectures and discussions, and study important current trends in Christian theology.[108] Miss Virginia Bogdan of Rochester, New York, who attended a Grail training course in 1943, reported on her experience positively for the readers of *Orate Fratres*, enthusiastically relaying how the Grail women responded to Msgr. Hillenbrand, Benedict Ehmann, Max Jordan of the National Broadcasting Company, Mrs. Therese Mueller, Godfrey Diekmann, and Emerson Hynes.[109]

[107] Lydwine van Kersbergen, "The Restoration of Sunday: Goal of the Modern Lay Apostolate," *1949 Liturgical Week Proceedings* (Conception, MO: The Liturgical Conference, 1950): 35.

[108] A summer course offered by the Ladies of the Grail in Libertyville, Illinois, for the summer of 1943 offered two- to three-week courses on "The Role of Women in a Christian World Reconstruction," "Leadership Training and Work with Children," "The Liturgy and Plainchant of the Church," and "The Principles and Practices of Rural Living." As *Orate Fratres* reported in its "Liturgical Briefs" section, "Although only one of the courses is explicitly devoted to the liturgy, every day spent at the Grail brings a new awareness of the richness and practicality of the liturgical life. Two weeks will mean an unforgettable, formative experience in full Christian living, in learning initiative and in welcoming the responsibility of the lay apostolate. We recommend the courses enthusiastically and without reserve." "Liturgical Briefs," *Orate Fratres* 17, no. 7 (1943): 328.

[109] Virginia Bogdan, "The Grail Training Course," 464–66.

Not limited to liturgical worship and theoretical theology, girls who came to the Grail learned to take mundane chores and orient them to the Christ-life, integrating life, labor, and liturgy. City girls learned how to perform manual labor on the farm, clean the floors, and bake bread. Mary Alice Duddy, who attended a Grailville program in 1945, described the intensity of the experience of baking her own bread:

> The sunny kitchen at Grailville was full of the warm smell of baking. The bread makers had sifted and cleaned the wheat, ground it into flour, mixed and kneaded the dough. They had shaped the warm spongy mass into generous loaves and with a sharp knife had traced the sign of the cross atop each one. Now their task was almost finished. . . . In a few hours, the bread would be on the dinner table, the least noticed perhaps of all articles of food, the sturdy mainstay of life.[110]

Baking bread at Grailville did not end with creating healthy life-stuff. Through the process of bread making, Grail women were encouraged to contemplate how the work reflected Christ. The ordinary plants, grains, and flour became the new green blade that rose, the grain of wheat that fell, the matter transformed by fire. As Duddy explained:

> Bread is only bread, our common daily food. But to the bread bakers at Grailville who have followed the process from the planting of the wheat to the serving of the finished loaf, it will never again be commonplace. For them, young women, eager to share as lay apostles in the work of redemption, the parable of bread holds the secret of Christ's apostolate and their own.[111]

Similar to Ade Bethune, the Grail summer programs sought to unite life and labor with liturgy, calling for contemplation of the beauty of the ordinary and independence from commercialized materials.

The contemplation inspired by the process of labor proved fruitful for at least some women who experienced the slow intentionality of the Grail. The interest in focusing on actions which had meaning, which were both corporate in character and purpose and richly symbolic of the life and teachings of Christ, emphasized the use of ritual.

---

[110] Mary Alice Duddy, "The Parable of Bread," *Orate Fratres* 19, no. 7 (1945): 298.

[111] Ibid., 301.

Likewise, within liturgical worship, participation in the ritual, in reciting words, in partaking in Communion, and in symbols of corporate identity (such as the kiss/sign of peace) and being attentive to the story of the liturgical feasts and seasons asked for engagement with action.

Accounts of the Grailville summer programs of the 1940s through the 1950s present an outstanding roster of Catholic thinkers and writers, including leaders of the liturgical movement.[112] In turn, the women who participated in the Grail experienced the central liturgical events being promoted by liturgical pioneers in order to facilitate lay participation, long before similar reforms would be realized for the entirety of the Church. For example, during Holy Week of 1941, the Grail community, located in its first American home, Doddridge Farm in Libertyville, Illinois, held a retreat for about thirty young women who came from Catholic Action groups in Chicago, Milwaukee, Toledo, and New York. Under the direction of Fr. James Coffey (1908–2007), retreatants experienced the "full and solemn performance of the rites of Holy Week," not as witnesses, but as active participants.[113] The women took part in "exercises and ceremonies" which reflected the liturgy, including a paschal meal on Holy Thursday, stations on Good Friday, prayers inspired by the collects of the Mass of the Presanctified, and a renewal of baptismal vows individually on Holy Saturday. Janet Kalven, in reporting the group's retreat to *Orate Fratres*, described the event as being "so permeated with the spirit of the liturgy" that it was not only a time of individual sharing in the life of God but an experience of sharing in the Mystical Body.[114] Some of the participants were surprised that the communal experience of Holy Week would be so compelling. As one young participant reflected, "I wouldn't have

---

[112] Sometimes, liturgical leaders were somewhat overwhelmed by the Grail women's enthusiasm. Godfrey Diekmann, in a letter to Abbot Alcuin Deutsch, August 13, 1949, wrote: "The end of the first day at Grailville. They're nice people, surely; but they do expect a person to produce, *i.e.*, to shake 'inspiration' out of one's sleeve at a moment's notice, at least six times a day, besides the regularly scheduled conferences." Quoted in Kathleen Hughes, *The Monk's Tale: Biography of Godfrey Diekmann, O.S.B.* (Collegeville, MN: Liturgical Press, 1991), 137.

[113] Janet Kalven, "The Grail Spirit in Action," in "The Apostolate," *Orate Fratres* 15, no. 8 (1941): 383.

[114] Ibid.

believed that other people could be a help instead of a distraction during a retreat."[115]

Similar events were planned, with even more participants in attendance, for Christmas. In December 1941, fifty girls spent the days between Christmas and New Year's in an intensive Catholic Action course; girls came from diverse backgrounds, including college and university students, young teachers, working girls, and girls from various ethnic backgrounds, including an African American girl and a Puerto Rican girl. This group, under the direction of Gerald Ellard, attended talks directed by him, attended Vespers each afternoon, tried to "assist at Mass intelligently and actively as possible," and held a *Missa Recitata* each day, save for a *Missa Cantata* on the last. The event concluded with a mystery play, using familiar texts from the liturgy, dramatized "simply and prayerfully."[116]

In 1942, another liturgical leader, Fr. Reynold Hillenbrand (1904–79), lectured in the summer course titled "The Vineyard," during which participants experienced a dialogue Mass:

> Those to whom the Dialogue Mass was something new, found it a joyous event to chant the Offertory verse as we slowly filed up to place our own host in the Ciborium, and the idea of our offering ourselves with the priest and with Christ to God became very real.[117]

---

[115] Ibid.

[116] "We were not performing for an audience. But by recreating these scenes together, we made them more vivid and impressive for ourselves. And the familiar texts from the liturgy, cast in dramatic form, took on a new and deeper significance. . . ." Janet Kalven, "The Spirit of the Grail," 186. Likewise, during Christmastime, the Grail women planned a "living crèche: ". . . Doddridge Farm was transformed into Saintonville and we ourselves into the '*Saintons*.' '*Les Saintons*' is French for the little figures around the crèche. The name signified not only that we wanted to spend our days at the farm around the crib, but also that we wanted to fulfil [sic] our vocation as Christians—to be saints. All of the inhabitants were assigned tasks which had to be performed to keep Saintonville running smoothly; even a shepherd was appointed, to care for the livestock (one goat, one duck, three pigeons!). . . ." Janet Kalven, "The Spirit of the Grail," in "The Apostolate," *Orate Fratres* 16, no. 4 (1942): 186.

[117] Draft of press release for "The Vineyard," p. 2, Archives of the American Grail. Quoted in Alden Brown, *The American Grail Movement*, 36, 184n43. Brown notes that this is an unpaginated booklet, circulated privately, containing an introduction and the texts of the major addresses given during this course.

Women who attended lectures by liturgical scholars and studied their works also were exposed to daily communal prayer. For example, Anna Harmon of Cincinnati, Ohio, participated in a Grailville reading group which read liturgical scholars of the day, such as Louis Bouyer and Romano Guardini. Harmon paired her reading with attendance at theological lectures conducted at Grailville, which were framed by the communal singing of morning and evening prayer, a daily custom for the Grail women.[118] Such communal singing of liturgical prayer was central to the Grail vision, as Lydwine van Kersbergen stressed that the Grail participants should become fundamentally oriented to liturgical time, including the Mass at the heart of each day, Sunday as the summit of the week, and the liturgical year as the "unifying rhythm of the year."[119] Liturgy was also practiced in the most accessible ways for the diverse group of women. Kalven related how, in practicing the liturgy, the Grail favored liturgy in the vernacular, praying Vespers and Compline in English, using their own translations. When Saint John's Abbey published the *Short Breviary* (1944), the Grail made it a required text, along with the *St. Andrew Missal*, the *Liber Usualis*, and the Bible, in the Grailville Year's School for the Lay Apostolate.[120]

Thus, the developments of the liturgical movement, from the dialogue Mass to the use of congregational singing, were promoted at Grailville, exposing a significant swath of young women to the wider prayer of the Church. Francine Wickes, who first attended Grailville in July 1944, reflected on the effectiveness of Grail's radical liturgical life:

> My earliest recollection of that first summer is one of hot July afternoons and evenings, all of us standing outside in two facing lines, chanting Vespers and Compline. I was overwhelmed by it all, the graceful beauty of the chant, the poetry of the psalms, the rhythm of the antiphonal recitation, the sense that we were one voice in prayer. We sang the Mass daily in the parish church, sang the hours of the

[118] Personal correspondence with Kathleen Harmon, SNDdeN, August 6, 2012. Anna Harmon, born in 1918, also worked in the Grailville bookstore while in her seventies. Because of the Grail, Anna Harmon was familiar with the most current in liturgical thought and was excited about the developments of the Second Vatican Council. Her daughter is liturgical lecturer, writer, and musician, Kathleen Harmon, SNDdeN.

[119] Janet Kalven and Grail Members, "Living the Liturgy: Keystone of the Grail Vision," *U.S. Catholic Historian* 11, no. 4 (1993): 29.

[120] Ibid., 30.

office, sang short antiphons before and after meals and during work. I thought I'd gone to heaven.[121]

Nevertheless, not all innovations were universally received. And, interestingly, some of the tensions which would be experienced after the Second Vatican Council were also experienced in the community of Grailville. For example, as Kalven relates, the Grailville approach to liturgy called for congregational singing following the reception of Holy Communion as an expression of the Mystical Body. As Kalven noted, however, this practice was met with "significant resistance from those who had been formed in a more individualistic piety that regarded time after communion as a moment of private conversation with God."[122] Such an account echoed tensions which would be observed as liturgical reforms were promoted and practiced following the Council.

The Grail's Relation to Other Movements

The Grail is often grouped with other Catholic social movements led by lay women—the Catholic Worker and Friendship House. At the same time, the Grail and the Catholic Worker also shared characteristics with the NCRLC and the "back to the land movement." The groups, therefore, had significant overlap and, as Debra Campbell suggests, competed for the "attention and commitment of the same small but growing pool of volunteers: young, educated, primarily middle- or upper middle-class Catholic women seeking spiritual growth and

---

[121] Francine Wickes to Janet Kalven, April 4, 1993. Quoted in Kalven, "Living the Liturgy," 30.

[122] At Grailville, study was closely linked to meditation and private prayer. In addition, the Grail approach was experiential: "[W]e wanted participants to *experience* the Mass as the high point of their day and Sunday as the climax of their week. Whenever it was possible we recommended that the proper of the Mass be read in English while the celebrant read the Latin, the homily focus on the texts of the day or spirit of the season, and the congregation join in offertory and communion processions. We encouraged congregational singing as an expression of the unity of the Mystical Body, but found that it met with significant resistance from those who had been formed in a more individualistic piety that regarded time after communion as a moment of private conversation with God." Kalven, "Living the Liturgy," 30. Kalven noted that the Grail used "innovative offertory and communion processions" to highlight the importance of participation in the liturgy.

the opportunity to serve the church and humanity."[123] The competition was fairly friendly, and, as early as 1936, van Kersbergen first wrote to Dorothy Day to discuss the related natures of their movements. In 1942, Grail members Joan Overboss and Janet Kalven appeared on a panel with Day at the NCRLC annual convention in Peoria, Illinois. And, in the summer of 1943, the Grail summer program, titled "The Harvest," located at temporary quarters in Childerly, the Calvert Club retreat center in Wheeling, Illinois, included Day and her daughter, Tamar. During this Grail program, Day saw a clear integration of communal prayer and apostolic work: "We have learned to meditate *and* bake bread, pray *and* extract honey, sing *and* make butter, cheese, cider, wine, and sauerkraut."[124] Such activities would become staples of Catholic Worker Farms as well, with days structured by daily Mass, Compline, craftspersons, and conferences, realizing what Peter Maurin had described as "Cult, Culture, and Cultivation."[125]

Likewise, the Grail found considerable intersection with the NCRLC, particularly through women who had participated in the Grail and had since married. Several women, along with their husbands, crisscrossed

[123] Campbell, "Both Sides Now," 14–15.

[124] Ibid., 16.

[125] "On our farm at Easton there begins to be a synthesis. We have daily Mass (our chaplain is Fr. Pacifique Roy, the Josephite). Sometimes we have three Masses daily, when there are retreats going on and visiting priests. Mass is preceded by Prime. Also, we have daily sung Mass. . . . We now have a few woodcarvers, letterers, Gregorian enthusiasts, folk-dancers, writers, *etc.*, in our midst; we have husbandmen and gardeners, lecturers, talkers, but what we need is a few real farmers. . . . On our seventy acres we have three families with a total of five children and two more expecting. Half a dozen single people and constant visitors. We have retreats all summer every other week, lasting five days and everyone comes early and stays late. All the women have been taught to bake bread, and make butter. Some have learned how to milk cows and goats." Dorothy Day, "Cult, Culture and Cultivation," in "The Apostolate," *Orate Fratres* 19, no. 11 (1945): 574–75.

The return to the farm picked up one of Peter Maurin's solutions to the degenerate and destructive modern industrial society. While the Catholic Worker hospitality houses have continued to flourish throughout the US, the Farms proved to be a failure as a sustainable social experiment. See Jay Dolan, *The American Catholic Experience: A History from Colonial Times to the Present* (Garden City, NY: Doubleday, 1985), 411; see also, Mel Piehl, *Breaking Bread: The Catholic Worker and the Origin of Catholic Radicalism in America* (Philadelphia: Temple University Press, 1982), 131.

with National Liturgical Weeks, the NCRLC, and Grailville. For example, James Shea, a journalist and National Liturgical Week participant, wrote enthusiastically about the Grail: "I have discovered it is possible to make a beginning of living a Christian life, because we are *making* that beginning. For me it is quite a change. And for anyone who plans to live the life of the Church more fully, I would suggest as one possible means: marry a girl from Grailville!"[126] Another couple, Daniel Kane and Mary Cecilia McGarry Kane of Philadelphia, Pennsylvania, moved to a farm a short distance from Grailville; within the next two years, half a dozen other couples joined them (on separate parcels of purchased land) to form a cooperative.[127] Likewise, Alfred and Florence Berger of Cincinnati, Ohio, first came into contact with the liturgical movement through their attendance at Grailville events. The pattern of liturgy, combined with the rhythm of life and care at Grailville and the production of the arts, came to characterize the Grail from the 1940s onward.

The Grail's Move from Libertyville, Illinois, to Permanent Residence in Loveland, Ohio

After operating from Libertyville's Doddridge Farm for three years, tensions with their archbishop, Samuel Stritch of Chicago, over leadership and ownership of the space came to a breaking point when Auxiliary Bishop Sheil asked the Ladies of the Grail to yield their space to an incorrigible summer camp of the Catholic Youth Organization. The Ladies of the Grail admitted the inevitable need to relocate.[128] One of the charisms of the Grail being their fearless dramatizations of Scripture and liturgical feasts, Kalven related Lydwine van Kersbergen's response upon hearing that they would need to leave Doddridge Farm:

Our preparations for the summer were integrated into our Lenten program of prayer and penance. Mary Louise [Tully], back at Doddridge

---

[126] "Discussion," *1949 Liturgical Week Proceedings*, 65.

[127] See Brown, *The Grail Movement*, 56–57. See also Grace Elizabeth (Gallagher) Rogan, "A Red Brick Schoolhouse," in *Be Not Solicitous*, ed. Maisie Ward (New York, 1953), 148.

[128] "The bishop wanted to use the property as a recreation center for the armed forces and as a children's camp. Lydwine flatly refused and the bishop responded by urging the Grail to find its own property. . . ." Mary Gindhart et al., eds., *Histories of the Grail in Individual Countries* (Grailville: The Grail, 1984), 79, American Grail Archives.

for a Lenten retreat, had prepared a group meditation in dramatic form based on the Book of Job. We went in procession from place to place—the cross on the hill, the vegetable garden, the porch of one of the cottages—stopping at each site for a brief episode to be enacted to inspire our prayer. For a major scene in the drama, Mary Louise had chosen as a setting our new compost heap, built in the approved organic form of a truncated pyramid with sloping sides. Lydwine as Job, dressed in a burlap robe, sat on the compost pile and lamented her losses. We completed our meditation in peace; the next morning at breakfast, Lydwine told us that her laments were truly heartfelt, for the archbishop had ruled that we were to leave Doddridge Farm by the beginning of June.[129]

With the help of Msgr. Luigi Ligutti (1895–1983) of the NCRLC, van Kersbergen was introduced to Archbishop John T. McNicholas of Cincinnati, who invited Grailville to settle in his diocese, in Loveland, Ohio.[130] Beginning in the summer of 1944, sixteen women began the next stage of the Grail's existence at what became known as Grailville. The women of the Grail were grateful for the championship of McNicholas, who not only helped them acquire Grailville's land but encouraged pastors and teachers to send young Catholic women to the Grail's programs.[131]

Grailville Publications and Resources

As the Grail settled into their new home in Loveland, they continued their summer programs and increased the volume of resources in multiple forms of media, which they produced and sold. Kalven related that, as the Grail women discovered "ideas and activities which proved vivifying for the community at Grailville," they compiled them and shared them through programs and publications.[132] The Liturgical

---

[129] Janet Kalven, "Women in Search of Autonomy: The Move to Grailville, 1943–1944," in *Women Breaking Boundaries: A Grail Journey, 1940–1995* (New York: State University of New York Press, 1999): 59.

[130] Gindhart, *Histories of the Grail in Individual Countries*, p. 79, American Grail Archives.

[131] Brown, *The Grail Movement*, 6–9.

[132] Kalven, "Living the Liturgy," 32. Others include: *Epiphany* (Grailville, 1946); *Holy Advent Ember Days* (Grailville, 1949); *Spring, Lenten Sundays* (Grailville, 1949); *The Church Year in a City Parish* (Grailville, 1955); *The Twelve Days of Christmas* book and kit (Grailville, 1955); *Are you Ready? A Four-week*

Week of 1948 used the theme "Restore the Sunday" which inspired the Grail to create a resource of the same title *(Restore the Sunday*, 1949), an apostolic program with six meetings and a final celebration, as well as additional articles and practical suggestions for family use. As Alden Brown notes, many of the Grail's published materials were intended to draw Catholics—particularly Catholic families—into the liturgical life of the Church by emphasizing and describing how feasts and seasons of the liturgical year could be enacted.[133] *Restore the Sunday* was the most developed project that the Grail produced, followed by a companion volume, *Toward a Christian Sunday.* (1949). These texts referenced sources such as Florence Berger's *Cooking for Christ* (1949) as useful for putting the liturgy in the center of family life.[134]

The Grail women were also active in the liturgical arts. One of the Grailville projects involved the study and performance of music, which resulted in the recording of several long-playing records, such as "Grailville Sings" which contained folksongs, spirituals, polyphony, and Gregorian chant. The Grail also sustained an active art studio as well as a theater in which they staged liturgically based plays.[135] Like its European predecessor, the Grail certainly gained a reputation for its innovative paraliturgical rituals, many of which emphasized the connection of the unity in Christ and the Eucharist, spiritual gifts, and forgiveness,

---

Advent Program in Preparation for Christmas (1956); and *The Paschal Meal* (Grailville, 1956).

[133] Some pamphlets include: *This Is Marriage: A Simplified Version of the Encyclical 'Casti Connubii' (On Christian Marriage) by Pope Pius XI*, Introduction by Emerson Hynes (Grailville, 1946); *This Is Social Justice : A Simplified Version of the Encyclical 'Quadragesimo Anno' (On the Reconstruction of the Social Order) by Pope Pius XI*, Introduction by Carl F. Bauer (Grailville, 1946); *A Collection of Folk Melodies Drawn from Traditional Sources* (Grailville, 1947); *A Hymn to Work*, photographs by Abbé Albert Tessier, text by Josephine Drabek (Grailville, n.d.); *Families for Christ* (Grailville, 1949); *The Christian Observance of Candlemas* (Grailville, 1950); *Holy Spring* (Grailville, n.d.); and Anne M. Mulkeen, *New Life for New Year's Eve* (Grailville, 1951).

[134] See also Brown, *The Grail Movement*, 60–61; and *Restore the Sunday*, compiled and edited by Janet Kalven, Mariette Wickes, and Barbara Ellen Ward, with James M. Shea (Grailville: Grailville, 1949); *Toward a Christian Sunday, an Apostolic Program Based on the Volume*, Restore the Sunday (Grailville: Grailville, 1949).

[135] See Leo R. Ward, ed., "The Grail Movement," in *Catholic Life, U.S.A.: Contemporary Lay Movements* (St. Louis, MO: B. Herder Book, 1959), 116.

along with family and rural life. For example, the weeklong "Vineyard" workshop of 1942, focusing on the Mystical Body of Christ, included the celebration of the feast of St. Ephrem, accompanied with a silent breakfast of apples, cheese, milk, bread, and honey, eaten *in the wilderness* following Mass.[136] Aside from the performance of these rituals at Grailville, women also compiled these rituals into resources for outside use. Some of these included *Let Us Baptize Thanksgiving* (1949) and *New Life for New Year's Eve* (1950), which suggested ways in which the modern Catholic might borrow a leaf from the early Church and Christianize secular holidays. Other booklets, *Promised in Christ* (1955) and *The Church Blessed Motherhood* (1957), spoke of ways to "solemnize events" surrounding the female life cycle, including engagement, marriage, and motherhood.[137]

Grailville and the Vocation of Woman

In writing about lay Catholic movements, Leo Ward, CSC, praised the Grail for its training of young women in spiritual leadership, describing the "spirit" of Grailville as "perpetually uttered in a way of life":

> It is a joyous spirit, not bubbling or giggling, but a spirit expressing a deep and quiet joy. People sing, dance, and play, but the joy is attached as much to their work as to dance and play, a fact that some people may find difficult to understand. Visitors at once notice the joy, and soon begin to catch it. At Grailville there is joy in work and sometimes in hard work, and joy at prayer, too, even some times, as during Holy Week, at long and perhaps tiring prayer.[138]

Meanwhile, H. A. Reinhold described the Grail as "an answer to American needs," even though its name sounded as if it were "just

---

[136] Debra Campbell, "Both Sides Now," 20.

[137] Kalven, "Living the Liturgy," 32–33. In van Kersbergen's *Woman, Some Aspects of her Role in the Modern World* (1956), she described the need for women to understand their role: "Ultimately, she wants a relation not only to her husband and children, but to the universe. A complete concept of woman's nature must take into account all the levels of reality, not only the physical, but the riches of her intelligence, her intuition for mystery, her tendency to inwardness and contemplation, her capacity for selfless love, the hunger of her being for a total dedication." Lydwine van Kersbergen, *Woman, Some Aspects of Her Role in the Modern World* (Loveland, OH: Grailville, 1956). Quoted in Ward, "The Grail Movement," 112.

[138] Ward, "The Grail Movement," 110.

that kind of bourgeois escape [from] religion which became crystallized in the 'music drama' of Wagner."[139] Similarly, Joseph T. Nolan, writing in *America*, described Grailville as "a beginning, not a finishing school" where young women finally were affirmed in "the value of their traditional womanly role in contrast to the movie and magazine version of the Junior Miss and the successful woman."[140]

The Grail certainly walked a fine line between idealism and practicality. But even if the Grail was idyllic in its scope, liturgical pioneers, including Godfrey Diekmann, saw the Grail as an ideal which might help as a model:

> I used to suspect that the whole thing was pitched too high; that it was removed from the pressing problems of industrialized, urban life; that it was too "ivory tower." Well, maybe. But then, the Blessed Virgin herself is *turris eburnean*. And we badly need "places of escape" where the spirit can be refreshed and the vision enkindled. That has been a traditional apostolate of monasteries in regard to the laity. Perhaps in this more complicated age, the laity themselves must help, in a more definitely practical way.[141]

Of course, while on the one hand the Grail encouraged domestic homemakers, it also trained women for international mission fields. By the 1950s, the Grail had become a national group, with centers in a number of American cities, a School of Missiology in Grailville, established in 1950, and the Institute for Overseas Service, established in Brooklyn in 1956.[142] The Grail seemed to be answering some great need among

---

[139] H.A. Reinhold, "Grailville," *Orate Fratres* 23, no. 12 (November, 1949): 544.

[140] Joseph T. Nolan, "Grailville's Valiant Women," *America* 78 (October 1946): 9–11. Leo Ward commented that the "world mission idea" of Grailville was "breath-taking for a girl who was in part brought up on movies and television, on ads for beer and cigarettes, on the ideal of Hollywood, on the hope of getting a job and stitching fragmentized Christian and pagan parts together in a meaningful whole. It is a bold idea that this girl from Seattle or a Kansas farm is being formed for so great a vocation as mission work in Brazil or South Africa." Ward, "The Grail Movement," 112.

[141] Godfrey Diekmann, "The Apostolate," *Orate Fratres* 23, no. 11 (1949): 524.

[142] Campbell, "Reformers and Activists," 177. The Grail opened "city centers" in Brooklyn (1947); Cincinnati (1951); New York (1952); Philadelphia (1954); Lafayette, Louisiana (1957); Queens, New York (1958); and San Jose, California (1961). See Debra Campbell, "Both Sides Now," 13.

members of the lay apostolate, as evidenced by its packed summer sessions. Janet Kalven recalled the popularity of the Grail Movement:

> [E]very summer, carloads came from the cities to Grailville for week-long or summerlong courses, some staying on for the full year. Grail-ville burst at its seams, all the barns becoming sleeping places, the dining rooms spilling over to the porch and lawns. As strange as the lay apostolate, the liturgical movement, and social action were to most Catholics, the momentum was gaining on all fronts, a quiet revolution, for new life in the church.[143]

By 1962, when the Grail held its first national conference, an estimated fourteen thousand women had taken part in Grail programs.[144] After this point, the Grail entered its next phase, decidedly less "Catholic" in its approach, with increased involvement from women from various religious backgrounds and an increased interest in social and economic justice, including feminist concerns.[145] Writing in 1993, Mary Jo Weaver described the Grail as "no longer a youth movement, no longer engaged in missionary activity, no longer working in a national network of city centers."[146] Its goal was no longer conversion of the world, and its relationship with Catholicism had changed. Another major departure from its 1950s identity was the rejection of the "complementary status of women in the Church."[147] The Grail continues to exist today,

[143] Janet Kalven et al., "The Grail in America, 1940–82," (unpublished manuscript), p. 4. Quoted in Jay Dolan, *The American Catholic Experience*, 414.

[144] Dolan, *The American Catholic Experience*, 415.

[145] Campbell, "Reformers and Activists," 178. See also James O'Toole, *The Faithful: A History of Catholics in America*, 165; and Mary Henold, *Catholic and Feminist: The Surprising History of American Catholic Women* (Charlotte: University of North Carolina Press, 2008), 66–67, 142–43. Henold notes that both so called "new nuns" and communities such as Grailville were places where women were "committed to prayer and liturgy as instruments for communal worship and personal development. These women provided some of the first forces for feminist liturgical exploration."

[146] Mary Jo Weaver, "Still Feisty at Fifty," 6. See also Janet Kalven, "Grailville in the Seventies and Eighties: Structural Changes and Feminist Consciousness," *U.S. Catholic Historian* 11, no. 4 (1993): 45–57.

[147] Weaver, "Still Feisty at Fifty," 6–7. Weaver describes the Grail's shifting identity: "If Grail members in the 1950s were forceful in articulating women's role in the lay apostolate, they are equally forceful today in articulating women's roles in the church (broadly understood) and in the world. Grail

not as an exclusively Catholic organization, in Loveland, in southwestern Ohio.[148]

CONCLUSION

Trajectories into the Home

This chapter focused on the blossoming of efforts to integrate liturgy, life, and labor, as exemplified by the work of artist Ade Bethune and the American Grail Movement. Bethune sought to invite the faithful into liturgical participation, be it through identifying their own work with the work of Christ, building liturgical spaces which increased aural/oral and visual participation, or creating projects which trained young minds to the riches of the liturgical year. Likewise, the Grail Movement sought to educate young women in the liturgical life by introducing them to the best in liturgical prayer and a retrieval of an agrarian model of living in which labor tightly intertwined with home and family life. Yet, while some outcomes of these trends were highly practical, such as architectural plans or resources for family life, the most authentic experiences of this radical integration of living a liturgical life in community were attractive but simply impractical for

---

has indigenous teams in twenty countries involved in local attempts to train women for leadership in health care and community development. Grail members at an international level have worked to forge a new theology of women that is at once spiritually rich and politically responsive. They have steadily and consciously moved beyond the language of women's roles in a patriarchal world toward an understanding of themselves as active shapers of the world in which they live." She further elaborated that the Grail's explicitly feminist stance began in 1970 with a workshop with Mary Daly, followed by a week-long program titled "Women Exploring Theology" (1972), and continued through 1977 with an annual "Seminary Quarterly at Grailville," in which feminist critics, seminary students, and interested women discussed how the women's movement intersected with the post-Conciliar Catholic Church. Weaver, "Still Feisty at Fifty," 8–9.

[148] For more information on the Grail's Conciliar and post-Conciliar realization, see Janet Kalven, "Living the Liturgy," 33–35. See also Mary Jo Weaver, *New Catholic Women: A Contemporary Challenge to Traditional Religious Authority* (San Francisco: Harper and Row, 1985): 118–27; Janet Kalven, "Women Breaking Boundaries: The Grail and Feminism," in *Journal of Feminist Studies in Religion* 5 (1989): 119–42; and Eva Fleischner and Donna Myers Ambrogi, "Grailville in the Sixties: Catechetics and Ecumenism," *U.S. Catholic Historian* 11, no. 4 (1993): 37–44.

most. Grailville, for example, was designed for young, single, mobile women as a retreat experience, a learning experience, and an idealized version of the Christian life. Without Grailville, communal activities, from bread baking to prayer, were difficult to sustain on one's own. As Mary Perkins Ryan, during a roundtable discussion at the 1948 Liturgical Week, observed:

> Most of us are not so fortunate as to be able to live in such communities, but we can certainly learn from them what Christian family and community life may and can become, and we can learn from them ways in which liturgical living may be made concrete, may be incarnated in family and community customs.[149]

While many liturgical customs attesting to women's vocation in the liturgical apostolate were performed at the Grail, it remained for other venues to more concretely realize the possibilities for the liturgical movement's intersection with home life and the female vocation of wife and mother.

---

[149] Mary Perkins Ryan, "In the Home: Round Table Discussion," *1948 Liturgical Week Proceedings* (Conception, MO: The Liturgical Conference, 1949): 64.

Chapter 5

Cooking for Christ in the Liturgical Kitchen: Liturgy, the Home, and the Liturgical Apostolate (c. 1945–59)

INTRODUCTION

The Next Phase of the Liturgical Movement

For pioneers of the liturgical movement, the final frontier for living the liturgical life was not the public but the private realm. Liturgical reformers became more interested in the home as the location for the most basic and natural training for the liturgical life to occur. The family offered a whole new realm of liturgical instruction; rather than leaving liturgical instruction to the "experts," or to experimentation in radical lifestyles, families who knew each other well could work together to celebrate feast days, pray together, and conceptualize spiritual gifts through stories, activities, and art. Families could pray together saying the Office, the rosary, or table prayers. Families could go as a group to Mass to receive the Eucharist. The family—whether husband and wife, couples with children, or more extended units with grandparents, aunts and uncles, or other household members—offered a powerful symbol, serving as a microcosm of the Mystical Body of Christ, a dynamic community in which training the heart and mind to love of God and neighbor might occur. Liturgical reformers believed that the family could and should be the locus in which the integration of all aspects of life in Christ occurred most profoundly. Incorporating the family more specifically into the liturgical life, finding inroads from activities like family prayer and sacramental experiences to craft projects, extended the liturgical apostolate to a new sector of Catholics, those called to fully live out their liturgical apostolate as spouses and/or parents.[1]

---

[1] "We have discovered, although we are as yet far from acting consistently on our discovery, that the cooking and cleaning and mending and tidying, the earning of a living, the entertaining and recreation, which make up a large

There were many lay women involved during the latter stages of the liturgical movement—far too many, in fact, to aptly summarize. Many of the recurring trends of the liturgical movement continued to circulate: the use and construction of liturgical art and architecture; learning the Latin language, hymnody, and chant; social issues of poverty and race; increased participation in communal prayer such as the dialogue Mass; and the benefits of programs such as Grailville and liturgical study clubs. But the most distinctive new feature came with an increased attention on the liturgical life in the home. In this subject area, the majority of the women who wrote and lectured were married women and, usually, mothers. Though women writing about the liturgical life in the home appeared in the mainstream liturgical movement in the late 1930s, in the post–Second World War era, such writing increased dramatically.[2] Discussions frequently focused on the raising and teaching of children by Catholic parents, the charge to American

---

part of family life should be considered, not as interruptions to our life in Christ, but as essential parts of it; not as distractions from sharing in the 'Work of Christ' but as our special share in that 'Work' not as a means of purgation only, but of illumination and union with God. Otherwise marriage would not truly be our vocation, our way to holiness, the way in which Christ Our Lord has called us to share in his work of glorifying God, of saving and sanctifying men. Otherwise we should not be living our family life in Christ; we would be trying to be Christians on the one hand, and married people and parents and members of our community on the other hand, and our life would never become integrated, directed wholly with, as we now see, it is intended to be by God." Mary Perkins Ryan, "Liturgy and the Family Arts," *1946 Liturgical Week Proceedings* (Highland Park, IL: The Liturgical Conference, 1947): 106–7.

[2] Writings on the family and the liturgy had appeared earlier but were more often composed by priests and religious, not women. For example, Virgil Michel, "The Family and the Liturgy," *Orate Fratres* 11, no. 9 (1937): 393–96; Joseph Kreuter, "The Liturgy in the Christian Home," *Orate Fratres* 9, no. 3 (1935): 104–7; and Bede Scholz, "Sacramentals, II: Family Sacramentals," *Orate Fratres* 5, no. 3 (1931): 115–18. Donald Attwater, an English lay man, had submitted a piece in 1933: "The Liturgy and the Christian Family," *Orate Fratres* 7, no. 8 (1933): 349–56; and lay woman Therese Mueller's first article for *Orate Fratres* appeared in 1938: Therese Mueller, "Letters of a Godmother," *Orate Fratres* 12, no. 7 (1938): 289–93.

A good indicator of the rise in interest in the subject of home and the liturgy can be found in the National Liturgical Week's subject choice for 1946 (the first year with a title), which was "The Family Life in Christ." The Week featured sessions and panel discussions on restoring family life, marriage, the social

women to reject the thralls of commercialism, patent brands, and glossy magazine covers, and an encouragement of Catholics to arrange their homes and family pastimes according to the liturgical year. Finally, a notable amount of literature produced by and for women compelled those mothers and wives of Catholic families to embrace their apostolate as *lay women* as being fully capable of living a Christ-life to the fullest within the mundane work of the everyday—that is, to see their domestic lives of care and keeping children, husbands, and home not as an interruption to or departure from the sacramental realm but as *food* for the spiritual life and as liturgical arts.

Rather than a realm to which women were confined, an evaluation of "living the liturgical life" from the perspective of the mother/wife reveals careful theological reflection on this vocation in the lay apostolate as an authentic realization of the Christian life, revealing the degree of volition with which lay women sought to unite their role as wife and mother with that of the liturgical apostolate. As is clear from the language and descriptions of praxis of these women and their reflection on their roles as wife and mother, their understanding of their potential for leading a liturgical life was informed by the theological language foundational to the liturgical movement, particularly in the archetype of the Mystical Body.[3]

Thus, examining lay women who identified as having great potential to act as leaders and nurturers of the microcosm of the Mystical Body reveals how women embraced the vocation of wife and mother as fully integrated with the life of the liturgical apostolate to which all Christians were called. Women who chose to embrace this liturgical apostolate from within their vocations as wives and mothers had a strong desire to sacramentalize life and work within the home precisely because this sacramentalization or reclaiming of the most mundane tasks was identified as a resistance to the secularism and the breakdown of family life. The liturgical movement helped women take the liturgical life which they had learned through study, college, or parish life into the home, allowing the home to continue to feed the liturgical life, not interrupt it. Thus, the vocations of women—traditionally identified and self-identified as matrons of the home, nurturers of children, and

---

sanctification of liturgy, the Eucharist, family communion, the liturgical year, among numerous others.

[3] See, for example, Florence Berger, "In the Home," *Orate Fratres* 25, no. 2: 76.

helpmeets to husbands—served as the vital force in orienting families to Christ through the living of a liturgical life. As Florence Berger, author of the well-circulated cookbook *Cooking for Christ* owned, "This [housework, caring for family] I claim is woman's work—her share in the priesthood of Christ."[4] Such a mind-set suggested a powerful reclaiming of women's role and of the priesthood of Christ. Boundaries of public and private prayer, as well as gendered boundaries, became more permeable in this domestic liturgical life, where the kitchen table found resonance with that of the eucharistic table.

This chapter focuses on three of the most influential women in this period, Therese Mueller (1905–2002), Mary Perkins Ryan (1912–93), and Florence Berger (1905–83). These three were all participants in the National Liturgical Weeks, contributed to *Orate Fratres*, and were known as lecturers in many Catholic circuits, including Grailville, the Catholic Lay Women's Movement, and the National Catholic Rural Life Conference. Taking note of emerging trends in American Catholicism in the post–Second World War period, which primed the atmosphere with interest in family life and shifted the sails of the liturgical movement itself, provides context for the work of Mueller, Perkins Ryan, and Berger. Aside from these central characters, some other forums for discussion of women's contributions to the liturgical life, such as the National Liturgical Weeks, give a sense of the increasing breadth of the liturgical movement devotees. Looking at these venues reveals the number of women who were involved in the liturgical movement and experienced the first measures of reform in the restored Triduum and Holy Week with excitement. Yet, by examining women involved and concerned with the liturgical movement, one also gains a sense of the difficulties ahead for implementing and fully realizing liturgical renewal. Living the "liturgical life" would change rapidly after the Council's reforms, and women who were once in great demand as national speakers suddenly disappeared. As Therese Mueller described:

> And then came the Second Vatican Council—the Council, which fulfilled hopes beyond our wildest dreams, but which also brought changes that made many people uneasy and even perturbed. No one asked for any more talks.[5]

[4] Ibid.

[5] Therese Mueller, Review of *To Dance with God*, by Gertrud Mueller Nelson (1986), Therese Mueller Papers 1/1, St. Catherine University Library, St. Paul,

Thus, the late 1940s and 1950s represent a fascinating period of transition for the liturgical pioneers, taking the liturgy to the final frontier, the home, as the Church and modern world approached the changing social patterns and expectations of the 1960s.

SOCIAL CONTEXT
FOR AMERICAN CATHOLIC HOME LIFE

A Most Charming Connection between Liturgy and Cakes

Though the "heyday" of liturgical life and the home did not arrive until after the Second World War, the subject had been an ongoing discussion amid members of the liturgical movement. For example, in the first volume of *Orate Fratres*, Virgil Michel asked in his "Editor's Corner," "How many readers of *Orate Fratres* will grant offhand that there is or can be a most charming connection between liturgy and cakes?"[6] In his short article, he referred to days in which the preparation of a special bread or pudding was a "natural" cultural response in rhythm with the liturgical year. According to Michel, these days represented a time "when the liturgical spirit was of the life of the people, and flowed over, as it should, into their daily actions and their homes. . . . The joy of the Church's worship was carried to the family hearth, where it hallowed and enlivened everything it touched."[7] Michel implied that the liturgical movement's formulation in America identified a past way of life, a contrasting situation to that of the modern day. He also proposed the possibility of change and used the example of breads and puddings being prepared in the family home to mark the liturgical year as a way in which the modern family might invoke this lively past of the Church's worship. Michel's exclamation over the charming connection of "liturgy and cakes" seemed whimsical, at least, and served as a good analogy to stress the potential for readers of *Orate Fratres* to serve as a leaven in the world: those who would work like leaven would spread the spirit of the liturgy in a modern world beset by the plagues of secularism, selfish individualism, and commercialism.[8]

MN 55105 [hereafter cited as "Therese Mueller Papers, St. Catherine University Library"].

  [6] Virgil Michel, "Cakes and the Liturgy," *Orate Fratres* 1, no. 9 (1926): 282.
  [7] Ibid., 283.
  [8] Ibid.

Likewise, *Altar and Home*, published by the priests of Conception Abbey in Missouri, began circulating in February 1934. This short monthly sought to offer ways for Christian homes, which were at one time the setting for eucharistic worship, to become closely united to the worship of the faithful and to make the liturgical life which the monks at Conception Abbey were advocating more known among the "ordinary public" of Catholics through a simple but "good Catholic" paper.[9] In concert with the liturgical movement, *Altar and Home* hoped to foster healthy Catholic devotions in order to build up society. Articles gave a historical background to customs such as Candlemas, legitimizing the importance of practices which were "once carried on with great splendor" and the "deepest significance" but had been "somewhat lost sight of in this day."[10] Articles tended to speak about how true appreciation of the feasts of the Church and the meaning of the Mass would build up true Catholics.[11] Other articles played upon sensitive pictures of a struggling Depression-era family:

> Look into the Christian home. In these days of depression, what father does not fear the loss of position and money, if indeed, he still has either? He thinks of little hungry mouths and fear clutches his heart; only the sign of his King on the Cross lends him courage to carry on. There is mother. She too has her cross of life, caused, many times, by thoughtless children and careless fathers. Only the thought of another Mother and another Cross keeps up her failing strength. Even tiny John and Mary— why, surely, they have their little crosses, though they may be only the crosses of learning dates of history or rules of grammar. Let them but

[9] The first issue of the monthly described its aims: "The necessity of good Catholic reading cannot be emphasized too much in our day. As Catholics we all have the duty of praying for mankind; as clerical students we feel we have a special duty to do a bit of the active apostolate. We realize the fact that many books are written on various Catholic subjects; but we also feel that these books do not come into the hands of the ordinary public. Hence you will find some of the same truths in a shortened form appearing in our little paper. We feel that this work will be a great help to us in our future activities in explaining and preaching to the people the duties of our Catholic religion. We hope that the articles which appear in our paper will tend towards that end. One of the chief objects will be to keep our friends in touch with the liturgical life at Conception as it is also carried out in other places." "The Purpose of Our Paper," *Altar and Home* 1, no. 1 (February 1934): 4.

[10] "Candlemas," *Altar and Home* 1, no. 1 (February 1934): 1.

[11] For example, "The Mass," *Altar and Home* 1, no. 1 (February 1934): 3.

recall the faithfulness of that other John and Mary in the school of the Cross and their burden will become light.[12]

How successful such assurances would be might be questionable. But some practical ways to unite altar and home also were encouraged, in particular, the family uniting together at the communion rail.[13]

With instructions for how to inspire the family, *Altar and Home* encouraged women themselves to model Mary, as Mary was the ideal of motherhood:

> Without Mary, all motherhood loses its ideal. "Mother's Day," so appropriately assigned to the month of Mary, should show she is loved and appreciated by her children. Her deeds of kindness and sacrifice form a golden "rosary" that we love to "tell" without ceasing. Every mother's ideal is the red rose of Mary's motherhood.[14]

Consonant with this language in *Altar and Home*, another descriptive thread of the family's role as the Mystical Body of Christ in miniature appeared in describing the parents, the mother in particular, as Christ figures in the home. Virgil Michel asserted that "Everything the parents do as parents is an exercise of their participation in Christ's priestly powers. Whatever they do in exercise of their authority must be judged as an exercise of their priestly power."[15] Yet, as noted above, the spiritual expertise of the mother gave her a particular authority, or claim to leadership, as cultivator of her children's (and her husband's) spirits. Michel described:

> The mother is indeed a gardener of God doing a veritable priestly work in the Christian care of her children. It is she who has sent the child at the very beginning to the baptismal font of the supernatural re-

---

[12] "Calvary of Life," *Altar and Home* 2, no. 3 (April 1935): 3.

[13] "The family that models itself on the Holy Family partakes of graces innumerable and has a dignity of the highest order. What could be more noble than that which takes place at the Communion rail! Christ is received, body, soul and divinity. He becomes part of the individual, uniting with Himself just as truly as they are united by blood." "A Holy Family," *Altar and Home* 1, no. 12 (January 1935): 2.

[14] "The Loveliness of Mary," *Altar and Home* 2, no. 4 (May 1935): 2.

[15] Virgil Michel, "The Family and the Mystical Body," *Orate Fratres* 9, no. 7 (1934): 299.

birth. But the seeds of faith there sown into the child's soul by the hand of God will not sprout or germinate except in so far as the soil of the infant soul is tended and watered. This is the function of the mother. She is truly the priestess of the home; hers is the sacerdotal work of bringing the latent seeds of divine grace, the gifts of faith and of the Holy Ghost, to bud forth in the soul of the child, to sprout blossoms and to bear fruit in accordance with the developing age of the child.[16]

Michel was quick to affirm that women should "step actively into the affairs of the world, the world needs her," but that women's chief responsibility was in the home and that, in fact, social evils and ills were on the increase because of a breakdown in family life and the vanishing influence of the mother and wife.[17]

The provocative analogy of mother as priestess presiding over her family might be heartening or at least inspirational, but it might also be fearsome. The symbol of priestess in her own Mystical Body in miniature could seem frigidly daunting—an impossible ideal—debilitating to the woman not able to attain such an ideal. Though the methods and witness of these women were theologically and liturgically informed, and often enjoyed a good analogy, Mueller, Perkins Ryan, Berger, and others more firmly grounded themselves in practical experiences. One writer, Eileen Nutting, frequent contributor to *Orate Fratres*, aptly described this tension between analogy and reality of a family life:

> Analogies should be carried only as far as they do any good. There is nothing infallible about them. They are intended merely as helps, and the ones that fail to help should be skipped. Therefore I am not going to try to see the mother of the family as the symbol of the priest at the altar. At least in my home there is scant similarity. There in the kitchen stand I, the cook. It is the last ten minutes before the meal is ready. I call down to the boy painting his car in the basement to get ready to stop! I call the girl from the delights of her latest library book, to toss the salad! I tell the little fellow for the ninety-ninth time that he may not have a Milky Way just before dinner. The cake is lop-sided and the carrots a trifle—oh, just a mite—scorched. I am an overworked mother in a cluttered kitchen, and I do not feel like a priestess who is preparing a

[16] Virgil Michel, "The Christian Woman," *Orate Fratres* 13, no. 5 (1939): 250–51.

[17] Virgil Michel, "The Liturgy and Catholic Women," *Orate Fratres* 3, no. 9 (1929): 270.

sacrifice at the table of the Lord. But when the children finally get to the table and get some food into them and begin to relax; when the events of the day are brought up and admired or regretted, but at least placed in their proper niche; when the give and take of family life is indulged in and a little humor dares to raise its head, then a feeling of well-being comes over me and, though I still do not feel like a priestess, I do feel that this is a symbol of the table of the Lord—my home, my family meal, scorched carrots and all.[18]

The analogy of women's leadership in the home being like Christ the priest of clean and gold-leafed icons had its glorious aspects—but the more cluttered details of daily experience could also hold sacramental resonance.

Context of Postwar American Catholicism

How women moved beyond the rhetoric describing their role and took liturgical interests into the home was determined by the changing social context of post–Second World War Catholicism. Following the Second World War and the explosive population increase with the first wave of baby boomers, Catholic parishes of the 1950s experienced new strains of a shifting population, as urban parishes' constituencies began to move to the suburbs, and an unprecedented number of Catholic children entered the school systems. Leo Ward described the most serious problems of the Catholic parish of this era: diminishing contact between priest and parishioners, booming suburban parishes and languishing urban parishes, financial problems, poor worship services, and a pervading sense of "complacency" accompanying the sense of ascendency and success on the part of second-generation (nonimmigrant) Catholics.[19] In fact, the 1950s, despite the wide variety of Catholic Action groups and activities, were also characterized by a certain lethargy among the faithful. Historian Leslie Woodcock Tentler identifies the atmosphere following the Second World War as one pervaded by a sense of having "made it." One of the most influential elements was the G.I. Bill, which secured a college education for any man

[18] Eileen Nutting, "A Mother and Her Children," *Orate Fratres* 24, no. 7 (1950): 318.

[19] Leo R. Ward, *The Living Parish* (Notre Dame: Fides, 1959), vii–xii. See also Debra Campbell, "The Heyday of Catholic Action and the Lay Apostolate," in *Transforming Parish Ministry: The Changing Roles of Catholic Clergy, Laity, and Women Religious*, ed. Jay P. Dolan et al. (New York: Crossroad, 1990), 242–43.

returning from wartime service. The significant leap in college-educated Catholics, adding to a number which had been increasing since the early twentieth century, significantly improved the social standing of Catholics.[20] The same drive for social action was no longer present, as many American Catholics had escaped from the cycles of poverty, lack of educative opportunities, or work as union laborers, which had caused their parents to confront social injustice and social need. This coincides with, for example, the witness of Andrew Greeley, who described a similar phenomenon in *The Church and the Suburbs* (1959). While the laity was rising in educational and skill level, parish service and lay ministry remained in a more nineteenth-century model, with a lack of leadership by the lay people of the parish and an assumption that the priest, who had certainly been educated, would continue to serve with monolithic control over the parish's work.[21]

Lay People in Catholic Parishes

Despite some languishing conditions for Catholic lay involvement, at the same time, the unprecedented needs of Catholic parishes, fed by a more educated population and the institutional infrastructure which had been lacking in previous decades, afforded new opportunities for lay people. As Debra Campbell summarizes, increasing populations and growing parishes placed two strains on the Catholic Church: the need to provide services (such as parochial schools, athletic programs, scout troops, and the like) and demands for family oriented apostolates (including the Cana Movement and the Catholic Family Movement). Parish-based programs for children or families needed lay people to serve as leaders within the parish.[22] On the national level, the Cana Movement, originating in a series of retreats titled "Family Renewal Days" led by John Delaney, SJ, in 1942 in New York, became a lay-led movement in which couples met to discuss family issues. As a pamphlet describing the movement advertised, Cana couples sought to "become better husbands and wives, better parishioners with full

---

[20] Leslie Woodcock Tentler, *Catholics and Contraception: An American History* (Ithaca, NY: Cornell University Press, 2004), 9.

[21] Andrew M. Greeley, *The Church and the Suburbs* (1959; repr. New York: Paulist, 1963), 56–57, 84, 135. See also Debra Campbell, "The Heyday of Catholic Action," 244.

[22] Debra Campbell, "The Heyday of Catholic Action," 248.

and active participation in parish life, and better citizens."[23] Being a good Catholic had become connected to being a good citizen, as Catholics became increasingly inculturated into mainstream America. This coincided with the developing theology of the laity, begun in the 1930s, and the charge of Catholic Action, which invited Catholics to take responsibility in reforming the world through their vocations in the lay apostolate.

American Catholics and the Home

At the same time, the life of 1950s suburban America also challenged the traditional order of men in the home; while fathers drove long distances to work and were gone long days, mothers stayed home with children. In a city, surrounded by family ties, paternal family order could be more easily maintained by an extended network of male relatives, but in the suburbs, the family home was guarded only by the women and women of the neighborhood. This trend began to bifurcate the roles of men and women, placing men at the head of the workplace and women as head of the home.[24] Even with women's education increasing and "feminism" gaining traction in American society, many Catholics believed that adequate and appropriate schooling was needed to help young women prepare for motherhood and cultivate appropriate attitudes toward marriage, building a home, and establishing a family. General Catholic literature supported this emphasis and lauded the role of women in the home but stressed that the leading role in sustaining domestic religion should be the father's.

Of course, if evidence exists which stresses the father as the rightful head of domestic religion, one can safely assume that this was frequently not the case. And, as frequently appeared among witnesses to the liturgical movement, women were reported as being more receptive to the aims and practices of the liturgical movement than men.[25] For example, as early as 1934, *Orate Fratres* reported an article

[23] *Your Cana Club: A Basic Program* (Washington, DC: Archdiocese of Washington, 1959), 36. Quoted in Debra Campbell, "The Heyday of Catholic Action," 248.

[24] Debra Campbell, "Catholic Domesticity, 1860–1960," in *American Catholic Women*, ed. Karen Kennelly, The Bicentennial History of the Catholic Church in America, ser. ed. Christopher J. Kauffman (New York: Macmillan, 1989), 77.

[25] Historian Colleen McDannell notes that, unlike Protestants who had a long history of emphasizing the role of the father in family worship, substituting for a male minister, Catholics had no strong tradition of men

252

"of interest" to its readers with regard to the recent resolutions of the Catholic Women's Union which met in May of that year in Hermann, Missouri. The Catholic Women's Union adopted a resolution which supported the liturgical movement, asserting that it was *the* Catholic movement, following the inspiration of Pius X for restoring a more active participation in the Church. This move would result in lifting out that "half-Protestantism" into which so many had fallen in the past four hundred years.[26] The writer claimed that, according to experience across the world, "the steadily growing Liturgical Movement has received greater and more whole-hearted support from women than from men."[27] Perhaps this was due to men's being more prone to "individualism," thus slower to embrace "corporate piety," or because men had not the patience and quietude necessary for "the more tranquil forms and norms of the liturgy."[28] Meanwhile, women had great influence and were encouraged to do their share to live more intensely the life of the Church. They could do so by making use of the missal, reading the Mass text before Mass and attending study clubs, receiving holy communion at least monthly, and congregational singing. The same writer also suggested that liturgical celebrations in the evening would be particularly attractive to young women, such as those in the young women's Sodalities, who might, assumedly, want some wholesome activity for their evenings. Finally, this Catholic Women's Union article included a long list of ways to carry the liturgical spirit into the home, noting suggestions from the Christianizing of the parlor (with images of Christ, for example), to blessing children with holy water before bedtime, to discouraging birthday parties and returning to the observance of the saint's nameday, to obtaining a blessing before and after childbirth and preparing a home altar.[29]

leading family worship. McDannell suggests that it might have been difficult to encourage men for multiple reasons, compounded by Catholic writers' preference for rituals and family celebrations which involved craft projects. The intricacies of planning, organizing, and assembling small children and activities which focused around baking and cooking would be mother's tasks, not father's. See McDannell, "Catholic Domesticity," 77–78.

[26] "The Spirit Breatheth," in "The Apostolate," *Orate Fratres* 8, no. 12 (1934): 565.

[27] Ibid.

[28] Ibid.

[29] Ibid., 566–67.

The fundamental concept of liturgical renewal, "the doctrine of the Mystical Body," did not escape a discussion of the Catholic family. Some writers, such as Joseph Kreuter, OSB, of Saint John's Abbey, wrote on the subject of "The Family and the Eucharist," reflecting on the importance of attending family Communion as a "sure pledge of intimacy" among the various members of the household and a way to place Christ at the very center of the Christian home, training the children, especially, to the importance of the Eucharist.[30] Likewise, Virgil Michel wrote on the relation of the Christian family to the Mystical Body, speaking of the parents' role in exercising their priestly powers, first serving each other as Christ and extending this service to care and teaching of children.[31] Michel described his vision for the family's involvement in the liturgy more specifically in the article "The Family and the Liturgy," where he claimed that:

> The family life of the Christian should be in constant harmony with the liturgy of the Church and take its lead constantly from this same liturgy as it unfolds itself in the Church in the course of the ecclesiastical year. There is, in fact, no element of ordinary family life that can not take its inspiration directly out of the Church's liturgy.[32]

The miniature of the Mystical Body of Christ had its own mission of continuing the sanctifying mission of Christ through extending the seasons and feasts of the Church in the home. The liturgy should be the inspiration for a family's Christian home, with attendance at Mass and reception of Communion as a family instilling a family consciousness of unity in Christ.[33] Thus, the Mystical Body of Christ in miniature, supported by active participation in the services of the altar and in their liturgical life at home, would play an indispensable role in building up a truly Christian spirit in the world.[34]

---

[30] Joseph Kreuter, "The Family and the Eucharist," *Orate Fratres* 9, no. 8 (1935): 358. See also Joseph Kreuter, "The Christian Family and the Eucharistic Sacrifice," *Orate Fratres* 9, no. 11 (1935): 546–50.

[31] See Virgil Michel, "The Family and the Mystical Body," *Orate Fratres* 11, no. 7 (1937): 295–99; and Virgil Michel, "The Family and the Liturgy," *Orate Fratres* 11, no. 9 (1936): 393–96.

[32] Michel, "The Family and the Liturgy," 393.

[33] Ibid., 395.

[34] "Such a restoration of the liturgy to its proper place in the lives of the faithful should make a great difference not only in the active participation in

A DISCOVERY FOR *ORATE FRATRES*: THERESE MUELLER
AND THE FAMILY LIFE IN CHRIST

Sociology, Maria Laach, and the Nazi Socialist Regime

Despite trending interests in the family life and resources for the
religious instruction of children in the liturgical life, neither the priests
and monks of Saint John's nor the writers of popular devotionals
had yet struck a chord for liturgical movement followers which was
fully practical. The first developed guide to bringing the liturgical
movement fully into the life of the Catholic family came with German immigrant Dr. Therese Geuer Mueller. Therese Geuer was born
in 1905 in Cologne, Germany, daughter of physician Franz Geuer,
whose ancestors were agriculturists and landowners, and Maria Mül-
lers, who came from a family of industrial tradespeople, both from
the Rhineland. Therese Geuer was educated at a private grade school,
followed by six years at the city high school for girls. She began her
study of economics at the University of Cologne and then, due to her
father's death in 1925,[35] finished all her studies there. She completed
the *Diplom-Volkswirt Prüfung*, which she described as "something like a
Master's degree in economics," but was closely linked to sociology.[36]

---

the services of the altar, but also in their daily life and atmosphere at home.
A family that is thus truly imbued with the true Christian spirit through
intelligent participation in the liturgical life of the Church will have no
difficulty in producing and upholding a Christian atmosphere in the home
itself. Such a Christian atmosphere will be a natural result, and there will be
no effort needed for establishing the practice of Catholic reading and literature
in the home, for a common expression of the religious life by the members
of the family, and the like. All of this will be the natural outcome of their
consciousness of the family as a miniature mystical body that draws its true
Christ-life out of the indispensable source of this same life in the liturgy of the
Church." Michel, "The Family and the Liturgy," 396.

[35] Therese Mueller, "The Death of a Righteous," Therese Mueller Papers 1/1,
St. Catherine University Library. Mueller described the death of her father,
which was hastened by his negligence in caring for himself, though he was
a physician. Mueller related her struggle with his death and noted the sad
frustration of not having any prayers to say at his bedside except the same
Hail Marys or Our Fathers. She was able to recite some psalms by heart but
was deeply troubled by the experience.

[36] Therese Mueller, "Autobiography," Therese Mueller Papers 1/1, St.
Catherine University Library.

She did practical work in various social welfare agencies in Cologne and, in 1929, completed a doctorate with economics as a major and sociology as a minor. In 1930, she married Dr. Franz H. Mueller, who was an assistant at the Institute for Social Research at the University of Cologne. Influenced by both the Youth Movements in Germany and the monks of Maria Laach, both Therese and Franz became deeply interested in the work of this Benedictine Abbey during their early married life. Most compelling was Romano Guardini (1885–1968), whom they heard at gatherings held at Burg Rothenfels on the Main River. Guardini would influence many young German families who passed on the ideas of the liturgical movement to the next generation, just as the Muellers experienced.[37]

The Muellers' lives were interrupted, however, with Adolf Hitler's rise to power. Catholics could no longer hold university positions and the Muellers, both as educated persons and as Catholics, were likely in danger.[38] When Franz Mueller was invited to teach sociology in America in 1936 at St. Louis University in Missouri, he took the position. Therese Mueller followed with their three young daughters, Mechtild Elizabeth (1931), Hildegard Ursula (1933), and Gertrud Brigitta (1936), the following year. As Therese Mueller reflected, "We left home and friends and brought little more with us than our faith and our traditions. We began to build a new home, father, mother, and three little girls and put our trust in God's presence."[39]

Entering the Liturgical Movement in America

With the move to St. Louis, the Muellers continued their interest in the liturgy, establishing themselves with Fr. William Huelsmann's Holy Family Parish in St. Louis, a liturgical haven, and became quickly connected to the Catholic Workers of St. Louis, to Martin Hellriegel

---

[37] Some idea of the Muellers' familiarity with the liturgical movement in Europe can be seen in Franz Mueller's first (and only) submission to *Orate Fratres*: Franz Mueller, "Thoughts on Some Mass Texts," *Orate Fratres* 13, no. 1 (1938): 11–15.

[38] Gertrud Mueller Nelson, personal correspondence with the author, February 25, 2011. Though usually Jewish faculty were forced to resign under the Nazi regime, Gertrud Mueller Nelson recalls her parents' needing to leave Germany as being connected to their Catholic background.

[39] Therese Mueller, Review of *To Dance with God*, by Gertrud Mueller Nelson (1986), Therese Mueller Papers 1/1, St. Catherine University Library.

of O'Fallon, Missouri, and then to Dorothy Day and Ade Bethune.[40] Therese Mueller remembered that the Catholic Workers encouraged her and Franz to help them with a lecture series on the liturgy and the liturgical year. Though she was worried about speaking clearly, newly exercising her English skills with an American audience, with "all sorts of help and coaching" she wrote and delivered a lecture on bringing the "richness of the Church's liturgy into the home and family."[41] Following the lecture, a young man reached for her script and declared it was just the thing that the Benedictines at Saint John's would wish to publish in *Orate Fratres*. Contacting Saint John's began the Mueller's long association with Godfrey Diekmann and with the center of the liturgical movement in America. The Muellers only briefly met Virgil Michel, shortly after their first contact with Saint John's, when they saw him for just moments while he was concluding a visit with Huelsmann. Fr. Huelsmann asked the Muellers over so that they might be introduced and, Therese Mueller reflected, Michel told them that "One of our young monks [Godfrey] is strutting around as if he has made a discovery . . . for *Orate Fratres*."[42]

[40] Ade Bethune collaborated with Therese Mueller and Mignon McMenamy to manufacture a table prayer wall hanging which was produced as a kit by St. Leo's Shop in Newport. Kits for embroidery were another popular way that ritualized praying at family meals made its way into family homes and women's pastimes. Letter from Ade Bethune to Mary Naksone, curator at St. Catherine's, October 31, 1985, Ade Bethune Collection 9 / Personal Correspondence, St. Catherine University Library.

[41] Therese Mueller, Review of *To Dance with God*, Gertrud Mueller Nelson (1986), Therese Mueller Papers 1/1, St. Catherine University Library. See also, Therese Mueller, "Personal Reminiscences on Father Godfrey Diekmann, OSB," Therese Mueller Papers 1/1, St. Catherine University Library: "In 1938 some 'Catholic Workers' who befriended us, urged me to prepare a talk (within a program planned over several weeks) on Liturgy and the Family. They helped with the English and coached my enunciation. The reception was quite enthusiastic. One of the listeners reached for my notes: 'they must go to St. John's!' Where is St. John's? St. John's Abbey in Minnesota. Where is Minnesota? What did I know: I just had found out where Missouri is. Since the others agreed: it was a good idea, he got the copy."

[42] Therese Mueller, "Personal Reminiscences on Father Godfrey Diekmann, OSB," Therese Mueller Papers 1/1, St. Catherine University Library. Michel died only weeks after he met the Muellers, in November 1938.

A Practical Edge to the Theoretical Liturgical Movement

Diekmann's "discovery" was the practical edge which the liturgical movement needed to gain, particularly in light of developing Catholic interest in the family and family life. Mueller's knowledge as a sociologist specializing in the family, her experience in the German liturgical movement, and her motherhood/wifehood gave her work an authority and an authenticity which previous writers had lacked. Her work was particularly attractive because, as she herself described, it was "not in the academic line, but in a popular vein flowing from my experience as wife and mother."[43]

Interest in composing family rituals had increased by the end of the 1930s and more frequently became a topic of discussion amid reformers as a new venue which needed attention. For example, H. A. Reinhold wrote Godfrey Diekmann on March 14, 1940, noting the need for a book on family rituals which included table prayers and blessings to be said by father or mother, prayers for expectant mothers and mothers after childbirth, and prayers for sick children.[44] Instructions were also needed for helping parents educate their children in the liturgical spirit, make shrines in their homes or keep the Church seasons in the family, as well as crafts for children which would involve them in their faith.[45]

Mueller's interests perfectly met this growing need. The first article which Mueller submitted was titled "Letters of a Godmother," appearing in May 1938, and elaborated on the crafting of a baptismal robe with appropriate symbols which would denote the meaning of baptism.[46] The article, printed on the first page of *Orate Fratres*, was

[43] Therese Muller, "Autobiography," Therese Mueller Papers 1/1, St. Catherine University Library.

[44] Letter from H. A. Reinhold to Godfrey Diekmann, March 14, 1940, H. A. Reinhold Papers MS2003–60, John J. Burns Library, Boston College, Chestnut Hill, Massachusetts.

[45] Ibid.

[46] Letter from Virgil Michel to Mrs. Franz Mueller, September 14, 1938, Therese Mueller Papers 1/2, St. Catherine UniversityLibrary. "On the way back from St. Louis I spoke with several priests who are heart and soul in the Apostolate. They all read your article, liked it very well, and said that they did not see anything wrong in the article. I assure you most solemnly that the article was not only correct but very successful. There is a priest from Chicago visiting us here at the present. He incidentally remarked what he was going to do about Baptism and he stated exactly what you have in your article

received very well, and Diekmann convinced Mueller that she should enlarge her material into five or six articles to appear in *Orate Fratres*.[47] Both Virgil Michel and Diekmann assured Mueller not to worry about language barriers and encouraged her to write in German if she needed to, and they would help in the translating. Michel was interested in both her writings on baptism and her account of how things were done in Germany.[48] With such encouragement, every night after the children were in bed, Mueller sat to write. She eventually wrote four articles, a series which appeared in the fourteenth volume of *Orate Fratres*, which were assembled into a booklet in the Popular Liturgical Library, *Family Life in Christ*.[49] This pamphlet, which went through four editions (printed in 1941, 1946, 1952, and 1963), was received favorably by liturgical movement devotees and the wider Catholic Action circles.[50]

---

and mentioned that that is where he got the idea from. So there you are. If you have an idea for another article write it up in German and we will have someone translate. . . ."

[47] Letter from Godfrey Diekmann to Franz Mueller, October 13, 1939, The Godfrey Diekmann Papers 1020/5, Saint John's Abbey Archives, Collegeville, Minnesota [hereafter cited as SJAA]. "Mrs. Mueller's article has made the rounds; and every one that read it was heartily in favor of its acceptance and publication. It is just the sort of thing we have been looking for: to actualize the liturgy in the home. I think, too, that it will make a very good pamphlet later on, but that has not been decided as yet."

[48] Letter from Virgil Michel to Mrs. Mueller, September 21, 1938, Therese Mueller Papers 1/2, St. Catherine University Library. "I showed your recent letter to the editors of *O.F.* They would be glad to have you submit articles such as you mention in regard to the three topics. . . . Have you a number of pictures in regard to baptismal notices, death notices, *etc.* in the form of small cards in the liturgical spirit? If so, we should be glad to have an article sometime showing how these things are done in Germany. . . . P.S. I refuse to believe that your last article had any heresies in it in *O.F.*"

[49] Therese Mueller, "Family Life in Christ," *Orate Fratres* 14, no. 9 (1939): 391–96; Therese Mueller, "Family Life in Christ: Bringing Home the Sacraments," *Orate Fratres* 14, no. 10 (1939): 439–43; Therese Mueller, "Family Life in Christ, III: The Liturgical Year in the Home," *Orate Fratres* 14, no. 11 (1939): 487–91; and Therese Mueller "Family Life in Christ, IV: Daily Growth," *Orate Fratres* 14, no. 12 (1939): 533–38.

[50] Dr. A. H. Clemens favorably reviewed "Family Life in Christ," in the September 1943 issue of *The Holy Family*, pp.131–32: "The problem which vexed the great mind of Dr. Sorokin of Harvard, finds its simple solution

In 1940, Franz Mueller was offered a teaching position at the College of St. Thomas in St. Paul, Minnesota, soon after the birth of their fourth child, Reinhold Christopher. The family was both glad to already know people in Minnesota and found it more like their German home—and less strange. In St. Paul, Therese Mueller took care of her family and continued to write and lecture, becoming increasingly known as an authority on liturgical practices in the home. Recalling her family's time in St. Paul, the Mueller's daughter, Gertrud, recalled how Maria von Trapp, in "full-length dirndl regalia," came to gather information from Mueller for her own popular book, *Around the Year with the von Trapp Family* (1955).[51] In 1944, Therese Mueller took over a lecture course on economic principles in the extension program of the College of St. Catherine, to which she added a sociology course on the family, lecturing almost regularly during summer sessions or on weekends in various fields of sociology. The Mueller's fifth and last child, Francis Laurence, was born in 1948.

Parental Responsibility in Teaching the Liturgical Life

Therese Mueller was concerned with parents who assumed that they need not bother with religious instruction of children, as this was the job of priests and nuns attached to a well-oiled system of Catholic schools, a phenomenon particularly present in the United States.[52] She saw this as leading to indifference on the part of parents and compared this phenomenon to her experience in Europe:

> The experience of Christian parents in some European countries speaks
> in eloquent language on this matter. For decades they, too, relinquished
> to the Catholic school as many as possible of their parental rights and
> duties. They discontinued family morning prayer: for did not the chil-

---

in an unique pamphlet 'Family Life in Christ' by Mrs. Dr. Franz Mueller. Not only has the author of this remarkable booklet steeped herself in the traditions of the Church; she has also lived these traditions in the family circles of thoroughly Catholic provinces abroad. Her actual and long contact with families actually living their lives with Christ, has given her pamphlet a touch of the realistic and practicality not easily found elsewhere. "Review," Therese Mueller Papers 1/3, St. Catherine University Library.

[51] Gertrude Mueller Nelson, personal correspondence with author, February 25, 2011.

[52] Therese Mueller, *Family Life in Christ*, 3rd ed., Popular Liturgical Library Series IV, no. 6 (Collegeville, MN: Liturgical Press, 1946), 9.

dren pray in school? They no longer discussed or talked of religious problems at home: what was the need, since the priest or sisters were teaching in school whatever the children had to know? They did not attend Mass on Sunday as a family: there were school and sodality Masses with different members of the family in different pews and places.[53]

But after two or three generations of this attitude, suddenly there was a great abyss: due to political changes in the relationship of church and state, there was no longer any Catholic school education. As Mueller described, "An awakening followed, and with it a remarkable rebirth of Catholic family life, a renewal of 'the Church at home.' Can we not learn from this example instead of waiting for a similar experience?"[54] Mueller thus proposed strategies for parents to find significant and concrete ways to enhance their children's spiritual lives along with their own and, at the same time, develop a strong sense of family identity and tradition.

Mueller's suggestions required a transformation of the passivity which had come to characterize American Catholic families. Instead of indifference on the part of parents, she encouraged her audiences that all the family should pray together. Drawing upon the experience of her mother and father praying, she attested to how children were deeply impressed by a parent's example. When Mueller wrote in the 1940s her encouragement was needed, for a family praying together or coming as a group to Mass was exceptional. As she observed, "It is not the best practice of the children to be always in the school pews in church and for fathers and mothers to be in special benches. Family worship strengthens family ties, and frequent family days in our parishes would help to achieve this end."[55]

Likewise, Mueller stressed the use of the liturgical year as a way for the family, the Church in miniature, to follow the Church and live a liturgical life by following the changing seasons and customs associated with the various days. Activities which involved play and motion, such as processions, were frequently suggested as appealing to children.[56] While the liturgical year offered many ways of learning about

[53] Ibid., 10.
[54] Ibid.
[55] Ibid., 15.
[56] "If there should be no candle procession in church or if we are unable to attend, we may have one at home, going through the house with our blessed candles, singing the praises of God and His Blessed mother and repeating the

the liturgical life, sacraments, and seasons, Mueller suggested that the smallest liturgical cycle should be each day and its worship, that is, daily prayer:

> It should be the fruit and result of liturgical family life that we pray even the daily prayers with the Church, Lauds and Prime in the morning, Vespers and Compline in the evening, as well as the meal-prayers of the Church. Of course we shall rarely do so well as that. There are too many obstacles, external ones at least. But by ever keeping this ideal in mind as the ultimate goal, we can prepare for it.[57]

Home altars, where families could gather to recite prayers and texts suited to liturgical time and remember feasts and saints, could be decorated by children and thus be imbued with even more meaning. Agreeing with Ade Bethune's understanding of craftship and human development going hand in hand, Mueller wrote:

> We should realize that the simplest things carefully made by ourselves, with love and understanding, are far more worth-while than all the trinkets out of a dime store or even more expensive articles which can never, in all their sweetness and unreality, reflect the true liturgical spirit.[58]

Though living the liturgical life could be achieved by committing to a radical lifestyle, crafting a liturgical life at home, especially one in which children could be involved, was becoming a greater reality.

Feeling at Home in the Sacramental Life

Aside from her Popular Liturgical Library pamphlet *Family Life in Christ*, Mueller's other most popular publication was another short pamphlet titled *Our Children's Year of Grace* (1943). As Martin Hellriegel introduced, she had drawn from her own treasure trove: "her Catholic Faith, her Catholic education, and her Catholic home-life. What she suggests she practices and lives with her truly Catholic and inspiring family."[59] In it, Mueller described the practices of her family and gave

---

prayers of the candle-blessing. This way of celebrating religious feasts never bores the children; in fact, they can never get enough of it." Ibid., 19.

[57] Ibid., 24–25.

[58] Ibid., 25–26.

[59] Martin B. Hellriegel, foreword to *Our Children's Year of Grace: Considerations for Use in the Home-School by Parents Who Wish to Teach Their Children to Live*

histories for liturgical traditions which had become too rare a sight in the contemporary American world. The Christmas crib, for example, could be a project that was worked on year by year, as statues made by hand—even if in simple soap, flat board and painted, clay, or with wire and cotton and dressed in cloth—would be more dignified than deplorable mass-produced products. Year by year, the crib might increase, with the Holy Family one year, followed by shepherds the next, until the three kings and their "whole train" were made.[60] Interestingly, Mueller defended such practices as liturgical:

> This [making a Christmas crib] is not liturgy, you say? But it is. It is the representation of St. Luke's Christmas Gospel—from the worried arrival of Mary and Joseph after the vain search for an inn, the first adoration by the holy couple, the annunciation in the fields, and the coming of the shepherds, to the solemn procession of the three kings who were on their way all the time, to adore the King of Kings on Epiphany.[61]

She saw the nightly visit before the Christmas crib at bedtime as a "study" of the liturgy; liturgical study, therefore, was not and should not be confined to scholars and professionals but could be practiced by anyone, even children, who contemplated the story of the Gospel and sought to enact its meaning. Mueller's insisting that the "liturgy" could equally exist in the home and her interest in restoring rituals which intersected the boundaries of private and public, such as the churching of women, questioned the tight boundaries which had sequestered liturgy as "public and ecclesial" and devotions as "private and domestic." Mueller's suggestions sought to edge the liturgical movement out of "liturgics" and into the realm which would most affect the laity, the home, a trajectory recognized by many of the reformers as necessary to its success.[62]

Therese Mueller was interested in taking advantage of the visible and palpable things of the Church's ceremonies—like the water,

---

Throughout the Year with Christ and His Church, 2nd ed., by Therese Mueller (St. Louis, MO: Pio Decimo Press, 1943), 5.

[60] Therese Mueller, *Our Children's Year of Grace*, 2nd ed. (St. Louis, MO: Pio Decimo Press, 1943), 16.

[61] Ibid., 17.

[62] See also Teresa Berger, *Gender Differences and the Making of Liturgical History: Lifting a Veil on Liturgy's Past* (Farnham, UK: Ashgate, 2011), 10–11, where she discusses the shifting margins of "proper liturgy" and "popular piety."

candle, salt, oil, and baptismal robe of baptism—which would make an impression in the child's memory. Likewise, gifts for baptisms should emphasize baptism, taking the form of a Bible, a small holy water stoup for a room, a book about the child's patron saint, or a white baptismal garment. Receiving a baptismal garment instead of silver spoons, savings account books, or baby clothes would far better commemorate the day.[63] She also described the traditions of the "old country," noting how children celebrated the nameday, the feast of the patron saint to whom the child was committed at baptism, as being the anniversary of the baptismal day:

> Thus, besides serving as a reminder of his baptismal privileges and duties, the celebration impresses on the child the life and work, the struggle and the holiness of the saint whose name he bears, and teaches him to consider how he may follow the example of his patron in his own state and calling.[64]

Likewise, children should also be encouraged to identify with and participate in the other sacraments: "Even a small child should feel at home at the *eucharistic Sacrifice* and should be encouraged to imitate father and mother in going there daily or weekly."[65] Children should be shown that Mass was an impressive event, a sublime and memorable experience, as if it were a gift or reward. Mueller called Christian parents to the task of presenting the seriousness, awe, and wonder of worship to their children:

> Then Sunday after Sunday we prepare the child for holy Mass, reminding him of the mystery of the renewal of the death on the cross, the redemption of mankind. We shall always try to find new ways of explaining the parts of the Mass in words adapted to his understanding. . . . We must teach him to become consciously a part of

[63] Mueller, *Family Life in Christ*, 6. Mueller noted that, "In earlier times, however, the silver spoon (or silver mug) had a beautiful Christian significance. Used in the administration of baptism and a gift of the godparent, it was meant to be a lasting remembrance of baptism, and had the figure of the patron saint (or of some apostle, hence 'apostle spoon')—Mickey and Minnie Mouse had not yet entered the scene!—engraved on the handle." *Family Life in Christ*, 6n3.

[64] Ibid., 7.

[65] Ibid.

Christ and of His Sacrament, to be transformed with the bread and wine into Him who is going to offer us with Himself to the Father, and who gives us His flesh and blood, His love and grace in holy Communion.[66]

Mueller encouraged parents that they could take on this task and described her own family's practice as an example. Spending some time of quiet reflection together, reading the text of the next day's Mass, talking about it, and, if she and Franz Mueller had an article or a book in hand treating the Sunday's liturgy, they might read from it to explain it, giving the little ones opportunity to ask questions or say things in their own way.[67]

Another interest in Mueller's discussion of the liturgy and family life were the rituals which were specifically women's, and she believed strongly that ceremonies which sanctified unique moments in women's lives should be reappropriated, such as the churching of women. "What has become of this wonderful rite," she asked, which was marked by a joyful procession with family and friends, holiday clothes, and a blessing given by the Church and its priest in joy and thanksgiving for a successful pregnancy? Mueller contrasted the intent of the rite with the interpretation it had garnered in mid-twentieth-century America:

Little remains, unfortunately, of this observance of the mother's first visit to the church after childbirth. The respectful reception by the priest at the entrance of the church, an honor which is shown only to the bishop visiting the church officially, is now confused with the rites before baptism, when the unbaptized person is not allowed to enter the church before answering the questions and receiving the exorcisms. The lighted candles in the mother's hands symbolizes the new life that was enkindled in baptism from Christ's divine life, and thus the candle represents the child itself (nowadays, unfortunately the child, because of its weakness or because of danger of exposure, is not brought along to church). The blessing with holy water, too, what else is it but another mark of respect of the mother? But all this has been misinterpreted,

[66] Ibid., 8.

[67] Ibid., 9. Mary Sparks of South Bend, Indiana, originally of Boston, Massachusetts, recalled using such methods in preparing her children for Sunday Mass. Mary Sparks, interview with the author, September 2010, South Bend, Indiana.

and the rite has come to be considered a ceremony of purification which, needless to say, is entirely at variance with the Christian concept of matrimony.[68]

Mueller insisted that the rite, properly interpreted, was intended not to embarrass or disgrace but to convey joy and grace to this particularly important moment in a woman's life. Mueller's interest in focusing on the importance of ritual meaning, or the sacramental meaning of events, would later extend to her involvement with marriage preparation.

Working in the Midst of the Liturgical Movement

The Muellers had just entered the American liturgical movement when Virgil Michel's health rapidly declined, leading to his death in November 1938. The Muellers were deeply saddened by his passing, as he had been a great encouragement (and a fellow German-speaker) with whom they felt comfortable corresponding about their vocation in the liturgical movement.[69] Their German heritage was both advantage and disadvantage to the Muellers. In April 1942, Godfrey Diekmann had invited Therese Mueller to come and talk to a liturgical study club he was conducting in the seminary, with regard to family sacramentals. He told her that it would be a friendly crowd of theology and philosophy Benedictines-in-training, who would not mind her accent or her pronunciation one bit but simply wanted to hear her speak about the truly Catholic home, the customs and traditions that should take place in it, and her

[68] Mueller, *Family Life in Christ*, 29–30. See also, Therese Mueller, "Churching," *Orate Fratres* 15, no. 11 (1940): 519–22. Like sanctifying the birth of a child, other women wrote with regard to pregnancy itself. For example, Margaret Place, *Sanctifying Pregnancy: In the Light of the Joyful Mysteries of the Holy Rosary*, Popular Liturgical Library (Collegeville, MN: Liturgical Press, 1954), Family Life, Liturgy and Life Collection, Special Collections, Boston College, Chestnut Hill, Massachusetts.

[69] Letter from Franz Mueller to Godfrey Diekmann, December 6, 1938, The Godfrey Diekmann Papers 1020/5, SJAA: "I hope you understand that we as newcomers feel still somewhat lonely in this country, but it is true—in this special sense that we find so few with whom we could exchange ideas regarding liturgical movement, religious art, etc. We considered Father Michel one of the few who could and would help us to see the will of God expressed in our separation from our beloved home country and to learn to love our new situation and new tasks in *this* country."

experiences with her children.[70] As the United States entered the Second World War, however, the Muellers' travels, as resident "enemy aliens," became more restricted. In the summer of 1943, the Muellers canceled a trip to Saint John's, as they were unable to get the appropriate paperwork from the United States district attorney (five forms for each family member) in order to travel to Collegeville from St. Paul.[71]

Her invitations to lecture and travel also brought Mueller some frustration with regard to how she treated her own family; she felt the disconnect of being asked to travel around the country teaching about the family but choosing to leave her husband and children behind.[72] Yet her perspective as a lay woman and wife was one which was much needed for the liturgical movement as it entered 1940s American Catholicism. One of her frequent commitments was presenting at the National Liturgical Weeks, and, even by 1941, liturgical leaders referred to "Mrs. Dr. Mueller" as a familiar face to devotees of the liturgical movement.[73] Discussions following her presentations, such as that following her 1941 presentation on "The Christian Family and the Liturgy," inspired other young women to voice their opinions. For example, Miss Nancy Wagner, a student at the College of St. Catherine in St. Paul, attended Mueller's presentation on the family. Following Mueller's talk, Wagner predicted that the effectiveness of the liturgical movement would fall to the younger generations, to learn and apply Mueller's suggestions.[74] In light of this, some young people felt that uniting the

[70] Godfrey Diekmann to Therese Mueller, April 26, 1942, The Godfrey Diekmann Papers 1020/5, SJAA.

[71] Franz Mueller to Godfrey Diekmann, July 7, 1943, The Godfrey Diekmann Papers 1020/5, SJAA.

[72] Therese Mueller to Godfrey Diekmann, May 3, 1942, The Godfrey Diekmann Papers 1020/5, SJAA.

[73] The Chair for the 1941 meeting introduced Mrs. Mueller: "Many of us are familiar with the beautiful articles written by Mrs. Franz Mueller in *Orate Fratres*. We have her here tonight to read a paper to us. Mrs. Mueller has had considerable experience in Germany in the liturgical revival, especially in its relation to the parish and family." "The Christian Family and the Liturgy," *1941 Liturgical Week Proceedings* (Newark, NJ: Benedictine Liturgical Conference 1942): 162.

[74] "Finally, may I express my conviction in regard to the liturgical movement in general, that it is the part of the college student, especially, and of our younger generation today, to learn and apply these things, rather than the older generation. I don't mean this as a slam to the older people, nor to imply

Christian family should not only refer to corporate prayer in the home but, in a wider sense, be attentive to unity in the larger Christian family. Miss Nora Le Tourneau of Washington, DC, following this same presentation, felt that Mueller was right to affirm corporate prayer in the home but stressed it was also necessary to foster family prayer within the parish. She referenced, as an example, a "negro parish" she attended in Washington, where families went to Communion as families, then went home for family breakfast and family prayer, concluding that "more could be done along these lines in fostering corporate prayer itself in the church, and also in the home."[75]

Therese Mueller's work with the liturgical movement continued through the 1940s and 1950s, with numerous lecture tours and much writing. As noted above, *Family Life in Christ* was published by Liturgical Press, and, following this, friends of the Mueller's from Pio Decimo Press in St. Louis had asked for a "step-by-step" walk through the liturgical year as it was celebrated in the Mueller family: *Our Children's Year of Grace*, which went into seven editions.[76] Because of her being in demand as a lecturer, even though speaking was much harder for her than writing, Mueller joined the Speakers' Bureau of her local Confraternity of Christian Doctrine in St. Paul, which kept her quite busy, especially in Advent and Lent, until her fifth child was born in 1948.

As Mueller continued to write and lecture, preventing her audiences from thinking her stories about her liturgical work with her children as simply stories *about her children* was sometimes a challenge. As a sociologist, Mueller was very interested in the family and, when she wrote about the family, she did not always mean hers. *Our Children's Year of Grace*, for example, was meant to be about not Mueller's children but *any* children of any family who might wish to live liturgically.[77] Even if she drew on examples from her family's experiences, she intended her work to be suggestions, guides for how another family might plan its liturgical life. And women did find her work effective. For example,

---

that they are outdated or antiquated. They have done their best perhaps . . . if there is really a widespread decadence of moral standards, this could not happen in America if we had a majority of the kind of families Mrs. Mueller describes." "Discussion," *1941 Liturgical Week Proceedings*, 173.

[75] "Discussion," *1941 Liturgical Week Proceedings*, 174.

[76] Therese Mueller, Review of *To Dance with God*, by Gertrud Mueller Nelson (1986), Therese Mueller Papers 1/1, St. Catherine University Library.

[77] Gertrud Mueller Nelson, personal correspondence with the author, March 1, 2011.

Elizabeth Drevniok wrote in *Altar and Home* in 1959 that the beginning of her interest in the liturgical life in her home came when she first read Mueller's work in *Orate Fratres*: "It all started when we read Therese Mueller's *Family Life in Christ* and 'Letters of a Godmother.'"[78] In her article, Drevniok described living the liturgical life based on Therese Mueller's work and creating her own.

The Custom of the Advent Wreath

The most widely adopted practice which Mueller suggested to American Catholics was the Advent wreath, now a common sight in Catholic churches and homes during the Advent season. In Mueller's third book, *The Christian Home and Art* (1950), she more fully described the problem of the secularization of Christian holidays and offered activities, rituals, and crafts which would circumvent the erasure of the liturgical life from properly liturgical seasons. Among those methods was the "advent wreath," which Mueller "quietly introduced to family homes."[79] Mueller suggested this German custom, a wreath of greenery with red candles and ribbons, as a way to symbolize the joyous expectation of Christmas.[80] She admitted that the Advent wreath was as old as the Christmas tree and from the same source, the heathen sun cults. As a reminder that time was rolling on eternally, Germanic folks would take wheels from their carts and wagons, decorate them, and hang them up in their halls as an offering, signifying a day free from toil and labor (as their carts were out of service, lacking a wheel) for the glory of the sun godhead. German Christians took over this idea and changed its meaning to one which reflected the passage of time from the darkness of sin to the light of the promised redeemer: "The light is growing: each Sunday of Advent we light one more candle, until the pyramid of light, the countless lights on the 'tree of life,' the Christmas tree, represent the fulfillment of our hope and longing through the ages."[81]

[78] Elizabeth Drevniok, "A Letter Cake for Charlie," *Altar and Home: A Liturgical Review of the Laity* 26, no. 3 (February 1959): 2–5.

[79] Gertrud Mueller Nelson, personal correspondence with the author, February 25, 2011.

[80] Therese Mueller described the Germanic custom of the Advent Wreath at the Liturgical Week in 1941 in her talk, "The Christian Family and the Liturgy."

[81] Therese Mueller, "About the Advent Wreath," Therese Mueller Papers 1/1, St. Catherine University Library.

When Mueller suggested this custom to liturgical pioneers, Martin Hellriegel insisted that the German red be transformed to purple and pink to match the colors of penitence and hope seen in vestments and paraments. As the Advent wreath was being introduced, Mueller admitted that, not long ago, the Advent Wreath had been considered an outspokenly "Protestant" custom, especially in Germany. She suggested that it was one of the customs that had been somewhat "lost" to Catholics in the heat of the Reformation and had been "wintered over" by some small groups of Protestants. She saw no reason, however, why Catholics could not embrace the custom now, as a way to concretely bring home a deepened concept of the Advent of God.[82] The custom of lighting an Advent wreath has become a staple among Catholic parishes and homes.

Therese Mueller and the Sacrament of Marriage

As bringing liturgy into the home became more commonplace, Mueller began to focus on other sacramental realms in which she could more actively contribute. She began to feel that it was somewhat unbalanced to focus so much on the Christian family and its renewal when there was so little attention directed to the beginning of the family, particularly to the holy sacrament of marriage. As Mueller asked,

> [The sacrament of matrimony] *exists*, that it is present in our very homes, day in day out, year in year out, with every sign of love to the partner and to the children; with all its spiritual gifts and graces and powers from above, standing beside us, supporting us until we part in death. Why do we so soon forget this great treasure handed to us on our wedding day, meant to last for a lifetime?[83]

In her many talks to engaged couples and in other conference settings, Mueller stressed how many people simply did not understand the full liturgical meaning of their marriage, as the spiritual and sacramental aspects were so overpowered by the wedding ceremony. On the contrary, Mueller encouraged engaged couples to embrace their sacrament of marriage not as a day to be gotten through but as a call from God to

[82] Ibid.

[83] Therese Mueller, "Holy Matrimony—the saving signal for the Christian Family," Therese Mueller Papers 1/1, St. Catherine University Library.

a religious vocation which required cultivation in prayer and remembrance, at least yearly, of the holy sacrament which they lived.[84]

Mueller put much energy into serving the Archdiocese of St. Paul through her conversations with engaged couples, working to develop a better understanding of the "forgotten sacrament" of marriage. She also spent increasing amounts of time with part-time teaching at the College of St. Catherine and St. Thomas University and was active in her parish as a eucharistic minister and through involvement in its Christian home life commission.[85] As the Mueller children grew, the daughters attended Grailville in Loveland, Ohio, and each would eventually continue involvement with the liturgical life as lecturers, writers, and artisans. In particular, Therese Mueller's daughter Gertrud Mueller Nelson continued and transformed Mueller's work in a new resource for family life, titled *To Dance with God*, in 1986, and she is well known for her clip art produced by Liturgical Press for use in parishes, churches, and schools.[86] Mueller described her daughter's more modern book as "a full evolutionary turn to my simple beginnings forty years ago."[87]

With a full career and lengthy involvement with the liturgical movement as it evolved and changed, Therese and Franz Mueller were among the leading figures in advancing the liturgical movement into its last and necessary frontier—the Catholic home. As James A. Wilde,

[84] Therese Mueller, "Note Card Speech [untitled]," Therese Mueller Papers 1/1, St. Catherine University Library.

[85] Therese Mueller, Review of *To Dance with God*, by Gertrud Mueller Nelson (1986), Therese Mueller Papers 1/1, St. Catherine University Library. See also James A. Wilde, "Franz and Therese Mueller: The Domestic Church," in *How Firm a Foundation: Leaders of the Liturgical Movement*, ed. Robert Tuzik (Chicago: Liturgy Training Publications, 1990), 239–44.

[86] See also Gertrud Mueller Nelson, *Sisters Today* 68, no. 6 (1996): 403–9. Gertrud Mueller Nelson, *Clip Art for Feasts and Seasons* (Collegeville, MN: Liturgical Press, 2002), CD-ROM.

[87] Therese Mueller, Review of *To Dance with God*, by Gertrud Mueller Nelson (1986), Therese Mueller Papers 1/1, St. Catherine University Library.

Like Therese Mueller, Gertrud Mueller Nelson and her family celebrated and honored the feasts and seasons detailed in the book. Therese Mueller added, "Furthermore, they extended many of these celebrations to include their entire parish community. The book is filled with stories of these experiences and with practical suggestions as to how one can adapt these traditions and make them one's own."

in *How Firm a Foundation*, described, "Franz and Therese Mueller, by word and example, brought all they could to the movement and in doing so gave it an essential dimension."[88] After working closely with Therese Mueller in the liturgical movement and for nearly thirty years at St. Thomas University, Franz Mueller died in 1994. Therese Mueller died in St. Paul in 2002.[89]

CORRECT, CHEERFUL, AND CHARMING: MARY PERKINS RYAN

Editing, Writing, and Speaking of How to Pray

Mary Perkins was born in Boston on April 10, 1912, the youngest of four children, daughter to Charles Perkins and Elizabeth Ward Perkins and sister to Anna, Eleanor, and Francis Perkins. Her father was an architect, and her mother worked for many years with Charles Woodbury, printer and teacher, on improving art education in schools and

---

[88] James A. Wilde, "Franz and Therese Mueller: The Domestic Church," 23.

[89] Mueller left a significant amount of writing on the liturgy, sacraments, and family life in series produced for journals. Some of her work includes: "Teaching Children How to Pray," *The Catholic Family Monthly* (December 1944): 16–20; "Is the Church a Real Mother?" *Altar and Home* [hereafter *Altar and Home*] 22, no. 2 (1955): 10–14; "The Mystery of a Child," *Altar and Home* 23, no. 8 (1956): 7–11; "Liturgy and Living Room," *Altar and Home* 25, no. 1 (1957): 20–23; "Epiphany on Our Street," *Altar and Home* 25, no. 2 (1958): 7–11; "The Holy Candle," *Altar and Home* 25, no. 3 (1958): 3–5; "O Blessed Cross," *Altar and Home* 25. no. 5 (1958): 8–9; "Clothed in the Lord," *Altar and Home* 25, no. 6 (1958): 28–32; "A Mistake about Mother," *Altar and Home* 25, no. 7 (1958): 24–28; "Theirs Is the Kingdom," *Altar and Home* 25, no. 8 (1958): 2–6; "Liturgizing Our Family Prayers," *Altar and Home* 25, no. 9 (1958): 4–9; "Gate of Heaven," *Altar and Home* 25, no. 10 (1958): 7–11; "The Real Saint Nicholas," *Altar and Home* 27, no. 1 (1959) 5–9; "The Pope and Wedding Rings," *Altar and Home* 27, no. 4 (1960): 16–19; "Our Lady of Advent," *The Marianist* 48, no. 12 (1957): 5–7; "Sacramental Aspects of Christian Family Living," *Social Justice Review* (July/August 1987): 134–35; See Therese Mueller Papers 1/4, St. Catherine University Library.

colleges.[90] Mary Perkins' elementary and secondary education was completed in Boston and the Convent of the Sacred Heart in Connecticut, but she graduated after only two years at the age of fourteen, continuing her education in Europe. She went to college in New York City at Manhattanville College of the Sacred Heart in 1929. During her four years, she majored in English; edited her college magazine, the *Essay*; and was influenced by the message of the Sisters of the Sacred Heart to take an active role in Church and society.

Perkins graduated from Manhattanville in 1933 with a bachelor of arts and was hired as a secretary by Sheed & Ward, recently opened in New York.[91] She worked in a variety of secretarial positions there, none of them very well, but was deeply influenced by the Sheed and Ward's advocacy for lay Catholic's responsibility in Catholic Action. While she was at Sheed & Ward, she met Leonard Feeney, SJ, who, she later would say, gave her the idea for her first book, *At Your Ease in the Catholic Church*, published in 1938. This was among the first books of Catholic etiquette ever published, and Perkins was described as a "Spiritual Emily Post," instructing Catholics how to behave in Church.[92] Feeney was pleased with the result of Perkins' work, which

[90] See Maurice Brown and Diana Korzenik, *Art-Making and Education* (Urbana, IL: University of Illinois Press, 1993).

[91] At the recommendation of Msgr. John J. Hartigan, who taught religion at Manhattanville College, Sheed and Ward offered Mary Perkins a job: "[O]ne of my duties was to have some acquaintance with the Sheed and Ward list, which is an education in itself. But even more valuable was the contact with a mind as clear as Mr. Sheed's with such a passion for truth and straight thinking, and the atmosphere of Catholic action, or active Catholicism—the sense that lay men could and should use their abilities in the service of the Church—that there is a great and vital 'movement' afoot and that the most interesting thing one can do is to be a part of it." Mary Perkins Ryan to Matthew Hoehn, OSB, The Mary Perkins Ryan Papers, MS303-30 Series 1, 1/17, John J. Burns Library, Boston College.

[92] One reviewer favorably exclaimed: "It was a stroke of genius on the part of Mary Perkins to note that there was the need for a special kind of How to Behave book: and another stroke of genius to call it *At Your Ease in the Catholic Church*, since that it what we naturally want to be: there is an amazing total of minor misery in not knowing how to behave and a pleasing exhilaration in knowing so well that one can do it without having to give a thought to it. She thinks of everything. How to act if you meet a bishop, how to distinguish between a bishop and a monsignor . . . how to arrange a baptism; what the liturgical colors mean; whether you break your pre-communion fast

offered a theological background to explain postures and etiquette in the Catholic Church, and summarized, "So you see you have managed on the whole to be as correct as you have been cheerful and charming."[93]

Not only did Perkins' book receive favorable responses from reviewers, but she also began accepting requests for public discussions of her book, especially by women's clubs. Rose C. Downey (Mrs. Edward J.), secretary of St. Ann's Women's Club in Wollaston, Massachusetts, wrote to Perkins on March 1, 1939, to say that her club members were looking forward to Perkins' visit: "We feel sure your review of your own book, 'At Ease in the Catholic Church' will be as interesting as your many admirers have found this literary gem to be."[94] Perkins' authorship of this book also prompted her inclusion in the *Book of Catholic Authors* published by Walter Romig in 1942, a book designed for high school students, describing Catholic authors and their works.[95] Likewise, Perkins' work was well received by women's colleges, including Saint Mary's at Notre Dame. Perkins' next work, *Speaking How to Pray* (1944), a book about the use of Latin in the Church, was complimented

---

by smoking or by biting your nails . . . the difference between an ordinary wedding and a Nuptial Mass; the rules about attending Protestant services; preparation of a sick-room where Communion is to be administered, and hundreds of like manners." "A Spiritual Emily Post" in *The Publishing Business* (March 1939): 6–7, The Mary Perkins Ryan Papers, MS303-30 Series 2, 2/3, John J. Burns Library, Boston College.

[93] Leonard Feeney to Mary Perkins, 1938, The Mary Perkins Ryan Papers, MS303-30 Series 1, 1/6, John J. Burns Library, Boston College.

[94] Rose Doyle to Mary Perkins Ryan, December 18, 1939, The Mary Perkins Ryan Papers, MS303-30 Series 1, 1/4, John J. Burns Library, Boston College. Perkins Ryan continued to receive invitations to speak regarding etiquette into the 1940s. For example, Constance Armstrong, of the Catholic Young Women's Club in New York City, wrote to Miss Mary Perkins on March 13, 1949, to thank her for speaking at an Annual Communion Breakfast: "The note of true simplicity rang in all your words. And I know that many more girls will enjoy your book than would have had they not seen you. And in reading your book they will be brought closer to Our Lord—the purpose for which you wrote it." Constance Armstrong to Mary Perkins Ryan, March 13, 1949, The Mary Perkins Ryan Papers, MS303-30 Series 1, 1/1, John J. Burns Library, Boston College.

[95] Walter Romig (of publishers and booksellers Walter Romig & Company) to Mary Perkins, March 20, 1942, The Mary Perkins Ryan Papers, MS303-30 Series 1, 1/13, John J. Burns Library, Boston College.

by Mother Madeleva of Saint Mary's: "Our students are making their annual retreat this week. Your books are part of their spiritual reading. 'Speaking of How to Pray' comes at a most opportune moment. They, too, can share its wisdom and its understanding."[96]

Promoting Latin Resources

Though Perkins' entry into the realm of Catholic writing was through "Catholic etiquette," her debut with the liturgical movement was the result of her skills as a Latin translator. And, interestingly enough, Perkins had long been exposed to liturgical reform, as she was the niece, by marriage, of Justine B. Ward.[97] Like Justine Ward's focus on restoring chant to congregational use so as to facilitate sung prayer, Perkins was interested in restoring Latin to the Catholic faithful so as to provide them with the tools for active participation. And, as witnessed through the examples of Ellen Gates Starr and Justine Ward, among others, those involved with the liturgical movement had long sought to increase active lay participation through comprehension of the media of worship, missals, breviaries, and chant.

Members of the liturgical movement were divided about the use of the vernacular, but the subject of learning Latin so as to gain access to liturgical texts had frequented the pages of *Orate Fratres* since Starr had advocated the use of the breviary in the late 1920s. By 1940, Godfrey Diekmann believed that discussion of the vernacular would necessarily remain in the theoretical sphere, for he felt that "there is very small hope of any major change of the policy on the part of Rome in this respect."[98] In the meantime, he felt that *Orate Fratres's* responsibility to its readers was to promote the use of the Latin language and to point readers to resources which would, at least, give children a fundamental acquaintance with the language so as to help them become active assistants.

To this end, one of the first Latinists Diekmann contacted was Ella Francis Lynch (1882–1945), whom he had first read in the *Wanderer*

---

[96] Madeleva Wolff, CSC, to Mary Perkins Ryan, October 25, 1944, The Mary Perkins Ryan Papers, MS303-30 Series 1, 1/7, John J. Burns Library, Boston College.

[97] George Cabot Ward, who married Justine Bayard Cutting in 1901, was Elizabeth Ward Perkins' (Mary Perkins' mother) brother.

[98] Godfrey Diekmann to Ella Francis Lynch, December 18, 1940, The Godfrey Diekmann Papers 1165/12, SJAA.

and whom he felt would provide a valuable resource in contributing to *Orate Fratres*.[99] Lynch, founder of the National League of Teacher-Mothers, had been writing articles and producing pamphlets regarding the teaching of kindergarten- and primary school–aged children since the late 1910s.[100] Lynch broached the possibility of incorporating Latin into already crowded school curricula, a perennial obstacle for those interested in teaching Latin to Catholic children.[101] Of course, Lynch felt that any time devoted to Latin would be an improvement and would provide the foundations for a revival in learning, even if it were only for five minutes a day. A complete change of mind-set was

[99] "I am writing to request an article by you for our periodical on the subject of teaching small children the first rudiments of ecclesiastical Latin. I have been an interested reader of your contributions to the *Wanderer*, and I'm certain that your experience in the field of child education guarantees an article that will prove most useful for the large minority of laity-subscribers to *Orate Fratres*." Godfrey Diekmann to Ella Francis Lynch, December 18, 1940, The Godfrey Diekmann Papers 1165/12, SJAA.

[100] For example, Ella Frances Lynch, "Preparedness in Teaching Children: Inculcation of the Habit of Daily Work among Them May Have as Great Military Value as Army Drills," *The New York Times*, August 19, 1917.

As Perkins Ryan would evaluate at the 1942 Liturgical Week, "Miss Ella Frances Lynch, founder of the National League of Teacher-Mothers, has been hammering away at the subject of more Latin, and early Latin, for many heroic years in pamphlets and articles and letters. Any parent or kindergarten or primary school teacher who wants to find out how best to go about giving the children the Latin best suited to them, could not do better than to write to Miss Lynch, Minerva, New York, for her *Orbis Vivus*." Mary Perkins Ryan, "Our Language of Praise," *1942 Liturgical Week Proceedings* (Newark, NJ: Benedictine Liturgical Conference, 1943): 129.

[101] "The principal difficulty in conducting the experiment has been the crowded condition of our elementary curriculum, which allows very little opportunity for a serious effort to attempt a good job with Latin. Probably not more than forty percent of our schools have made a serious effort to carry on the experiment. The Latin Course was never made compulsory in all the schools. Where the materials have been used, the reports have generally been that the children were able to grasp the material, and made satisfactory progress. It is my opinion that the texts in this Series would be found very serviceable if they could be given an adequate trial." Letter from Rev. N. M. Shumaker (Superintendant of Catholic Schools of Toledo, Ohio) to Mary Perkins Ryan, September 30, 1942, The Mary Perkins Ryan Papers, MS303-30 Series 1, 1/15, John J. Burns Library, Boston College.

needed for American Catholics, who seemed to view the Latin of Mass as something that should simply be "gotten through" as quickly as possible. With such separation of ritual and meaning, it was impossible to legitimize its curricular incorporation.

The Use of Your Catholic Language

As the liturgical movement entered the 1940s, many liturgical pioneers believed that learning Latin would be essential in advancing lay participation in worship. Mary Perkins entered this fray and applied her skills in Latin to preparing a textbook which was accessible to teachers, catechists, and families, titled *Your Catholic Language: Language from the Missal* (1940).[102] While she had been preparing *At Your Ease*, Perkins began to think that Catholics would be infinitely "more at ease" if they understood their language. Reflecting on her own experience, she realized that she considered all the years she spent on Latin in school and college to be completely ineffectual in understanding Church Latin. This led her to begin to plan a book about Latin, one which would allow the reader to become familiar with the Mass through familiarity with its language.[103] The Latin lessons in her book were built on examples which used the Propers of the Mass, hymns, and lectionary readings. She also assured readers that there were many shortcuts and tactics to learning the language: "As you will see . . . most of the Latin words in the Liturgy have English derivatives, so that you can at least make a good guess as to their meaning."[104] Perkins emphasized that Latin should not be the language of the elite, especially when so many Catholics had the tools to educate themselves.[105] She intended *Your Catholic Language* to be used by anyone learning the language, from new seminarians to catechists.[106] Moreover, she saw

[102] Perkins Ryan described Latin as "one of the most essential human tools for taking an active part in the official life and worship of the Church." Mary Perkins Ryan, "Our Language of Praise," *1942 Liturgical Week Proceedings*, 126.

[103] Mary Perkins Ryan, "Some People Seem to Know What God Wants," und. typescript, The Mary Perkins Ryan Papers, MS303-30 Series 2, 1/35, John J. Burns Library, Boston College.

[104] Mary Perkins, *Your Catholic Language* (New York: Sheed & Ward, 1940), 7.

[105] Ibid., 2.

[106] At the National Liturgical Week which met in 1944, a list of useful liturgical texts was distributed. The list had been compiled with the assistance of many members of the Liturgical Conference, by means of a questionnaire sent to them after the Chicago meeting the previous October (1943). Among

providing Catholics with the tools they needed to develop theologically and spiritually as directly useful for the liturgical movement.[107]

A New Member of the Liturgical Conference

In the same year that she prepared *Your Catholic Language*, Perkins also attended her first (and *the* first) National Liturgical Week held by the Benedictine Liturgical Conference. She described her involvement in the Liturgical Week as "a matter of chance—or of providence" and explained that it had a most singular effect on her life.[108] During the summer of 1940, she had been promoting Sheed & Ward books in the New York area, which included contacting librarians of major Catholic institutions. During her visit to Saint Mary's Abbey in Newark, New Jersey, she was introduced to Fr. Michael Ducey, who was organizing the first Liturgical Week in America. Perkins recalled:

> I remember asking, "What is a liturgical Week?" I don't remember Fr. Ducey's answer. What I do remember is that he asked me whether by any chance I used some part of the Divine Office for my daily prayer. When I admitted to doing so (I was always embarrassed when caught by a cleric engaging in what was then such a typically clerical activity.) he said, "Splendid. We need another layperson in that session." And so I was invited to attend the Week and act as a discussion leader.[109]

Though Perkins had been interested in liturgical matters, or, at least used the breviary, she was quite cloudy as to what a "liturgical week"

---

the texts recommended was *Your Catholic Language*, by Mary Perkins Ryan, published by Sheed & Ward and available for $2.00. The book was described as: "Very practical aid in surmounting the Latin language difficulty is furnished by Mary Perkins in her readable volume." "Reading List," *1944 Liturgical Week Proceedings* (Chicago: The Liturgical Conference, 1945): 165.

[107] "We hope that the book will be useful to lay-people who are taking part in the Liturgical Movement, to young men about to enter a seminary, whose Latin needs improvement, to novices who need Latin for taking part in the Office. We also hope that it will be useful to teachers of Doctrine and Religion in Catholic Schools, to show how the Latin of the Church might be easily taught as a language, without further over-crowding the curriculum." Mary Perkins Ryan to Matthew Hoehn, 1938, The Mary Perkins Ryan Papers, MS303-30 Series 1, 1/17, John J. Burns Library, Boston College.

[108] Mary Perkins Ryan, "The First National Liturgical Week," The Mary Perkins Ryan Papers, Series 1, 1/22, John J. Burns Library, Boston College.

[109] Ibid.

would be and envisioned a program concerned with Gregorian chant, Gothic church architecture, and the Office. Upon entering the hall, which was filling up with clergy "of all shapes and sizes, with a sprinkling of women religious and laity," however, she related that "I realized the program would certainly have a wider focus."[110] The titles of the programs, "The Parish," "The Mass," "The Divine Office," "Devotions," "Parish Worship: Its Artistic Expressions," and "The Living Parish," did not adequately describe the scope of the liturgical week. As Perkins recounted:

> As the Week progressed, I began to realize that this meeting was concerned with nothing less than changing both the focus and the atmosphere of catholic living. A vision of "The living parish" was emerging, quite different from the individualistic, legalistic, sentimental piety that too often characterized our parishes. In the new vision, as Vatican II would put it twenty years later, the liturgy is the summit toward which all the activity of the Church is directed and at the same time it is the fountain from which all her power flows. Christ is present in many ways in the Church's liturgical celebrations so that we may worship the Father by, with and in Him, as members of his body, sharing his Spirit. At the same time, we can learn from Him and grow up in all things in Him, our Head. Thereby taking part in the building up of God's kingdom. The inspiration of this vision was the statement of Pius X: "The primary and indispensable source of the true Christian spirit is active participation in the sacred mysteries and the public and solemn prayer of the Church." The purpose of the Week, then, was to clarify the meaning of "active participation" and "the true Christian spirit," and then to explore the implications of Pius X's statement for pastoral life and personal spirituality.[111]

Perkins would later reflect that she remembered most vividly "the sense of happiness" amid a thousand-plus dedicated people. The Liturgical Week participants were filled with a sense of joy, simply by realizing there were other "liturgical nuts" with whom to work. Perkins felt that this newfound awareness of being in concert with others who shared a liturgically centered vision helped her gain a profound sense of community:

[110] Ibid.
[111] Ibid.

And I remember my own joyful realization that I really belonged to the Body, the community of the Church, that I had a right to take an active part in both the internal and external worship and work of the Church, and further, that I felt somehow called to direct my efforts in whatever ways opening out to me, to promote this liturgical vision of Christ living and active in the Church.[112]

Within this Body, her perspective as a lay woman was appreciated. On some occasions, such as the National Liturgical Week which met at St. Meinrad, Indiana, in 1942, Perkins was one of two lay people listed in the entire program.[113] Perkins herself felt that lay people were needed to present Catholicism to other lay people, as lay persons could consider practicalities of lay, non-religious life and speak on a level which was more accessible to other lay persons.[114]

How to Use Your Latin, the Living Language of the Church

By 1942, debate over the use of Latin was increasing amid members of the liturgical movement, and Perkins was invited to speak on the subject of "Our Language of Praise" at the 1942 Liturgical Week meeting. During her presentation, she noted that members of the liturgical movement must envy the angels, who did not have to concern themselves as to whether they said, *Sanctus, Sanctus, Sanctus* or *Holy, Holy, Holy*. While angels had no need of a special language to praise God, only humans could use "actual physical sound to express spiritual ideas to other human beings, and to God" through voice, song, and

[112] Ibid.

[113] Elmer A. Steffen of Indianapolis gave a talk titled "The Organist and Choir Director." "Program for the Liturgical Week of St. Meinrad, Indiana," The Mary Perkins Ryan Papers, MS303-30 Series 2, 2/9, John J. Burns Library, Boston College.

[114] "I think such writing is needed today, because the expert is usually too busy at his own work to undertake it, and being an expert, he cannot know what a layman wants or needs to learn, as well as another layman. I should like to improve my writing—and myself—so as to be capable of being a sort of literary errand-boy for the Faith, doing what lies in my power to persuade people that the Catholic Religion is most interesting, as well as most true, and that the life of the Liturgy is for every Catholic to lead." Mary Perkins Ryan to Matthew Hoehn, 1938, The Mary Perkins Ryan Papers, MS303-30, Series 1, 1/17, John J. Burns Library, Boston College.

language.[115] Speaking together animated the faithful, allowing them to act as fully human and Christian beings and as active members of the Mystical Body of Christ. Because the Holy Spirit ruled the Church, one should not think that historical circumstances alone had determined the liturgical use of language. Latin, with its discipline, its "conciseness combined with beauty," its singability, and its ability to hold together the concrete and the abstract, had powerful force to affect the "whole" human person: intellect, senses, and imagination.[116] Perkins claimed that, since Latin was "the living language of the living Church," it remained vital to the Church's identity and prayer. But Latin was also an unchanging language. Why, she asked, should we pick and choose what should be easily comprehended, bowing to the insatiable human tendency to pick the easiest route?[117] Rather:

> [W]e explain the Church's symbols in [the people's] own terms and so bring [them] to an appreciation and understanding of the symbols themselves. And so with Latin—instead of changing the language of the liturgy to suit a changing people, why not teach the people to understand the language?[118]

She acknowledged the objections to teaching Latin to Catholics, particularly surrounding the necessity of training and practice: "But people are too stupid!" "Nobody would do it." "Nobody has time." "You don't mean to say that people can't save their souls without Latin!" Perkins reminded the audience that those objections were familiar "for they are exactly the objections which are brought up against the whole liturgical movement."[119]

Her point was astute, as the difficulty, training required, concern over pastoral questions (if our parish does not have a dialogue Mass, does that mean our Mass is not as good?), and occasional laziness on the part of clergy and laity alike did coincide neatly with the difficulties of the liturgical movement. Likewise, the use of a Catholic language for Catholic liturgy coincided with the formation of Catholic identity. For liturgical movement advocates, the liturgy was the source

[115] Mary Perkins Ryan, "Our Language of Praise," 1942 *National Liturgical Week Proceedings*, 121–22.
[116] Ibid., 122–23.
[117] Ibid., 123.
[118] Ibid., 124.
[119] Ibid., 121–22.

of and inspiration for all of Catholic life, thus the liturgy was a chief marker of identity. Reformers such as Mary Perkins regarded retaining the use of a holy language, one which was truly universal, as a powerful conduit for preserving Catholic religious, social, and cultural values.[120] For the first time, as Catholics became more assimilated to mainstream American culture, rose in social status, and increased in numbers, Catholics had the means and facilities to preserve their culture through means of Catholic schools, organizations, newspapers, Catholic Action groups, sodalities, and the like. As Perkins described, "more and more of the laity are growing to feel that they want to acquire for themselves whatever is necessary for a full Catholic life, even if it means a great deal of work."[121] Thus, with the proper machinery in place for Catholics to fully live a Catholic life, through networks and social supports, Catholics had an ideal situation for learning Catholic values, including their language.[122]

[120] At the same time, these values were of a decidedly Western-European stamp, again reflecting a somewhat myopic view of "culture" shared by members of the liturgical movement.

[121] Ibid., 127. In concluding remarks following Perkins Ryan's paper presentation, Thomas J. Carroll summarized: "Under the heading of literature, we might include Mary Perkins' (Mrs. Ryan's) very excellent paper on the Latin language. The mention of the vernacular in one session struck a familiar key for many, but we all know that the use of the vernacular is something to dream of in the future, that if it comes at all it will be in the Holy Spirit's own good time. Meanwhile Mrs. Ryan has showed us not only good reasons to love the language we have, but methods of making it more widely known and loved. We may well say that a wider teaching of Latin is important for the functional purpose of allowing people to enter more fully into the prayer of the Whole Christ, and through Christ giving praise to God." "Summary and Conclusion," *1942 Liturgical Week Proceedings* (Newark, NJ: Benedictine Liturgical Conference, 1943): 198.

[122] In the discussion following Dietrich von Hildebrand's talk titled "Liturgy and the Cultural Problem" at the liturgical week in 1941, Perkins Ryan advocated for Catholics to take advantage of their new-found resources: "We all have to go to school. We all have to learn to read. Why then don't we take advantage of this, and show people how to use their education in God's service? If people can read the comic strips and newspapers, they can be shown how to read the Missal." "Discussion," *1941 Liturgical Week Proceedings* (Newark, NJ: Benedictine Liturgical Conference, 1942): 198.

Beginning Married Life, Adding the Family to the Liturgical Movement

In March 1942, Godfrey Diekmann contacted Mary Perkins about writing a booklet for Liturgical Press's Popular Liturgical Library, a companion booklet for Pius Parsch's *Study the Mass*, translated by William Busch. Diekmann thought that Perkins would be able to successfully tackle the subject with an approach that would be "sufficiently popular and sprightly (is that the right word?) for popular appeal." For, as Diekmann wryly observed, the liturgical movement had suffered from "stodginess," and Liturgical Press had not a "single really 'popular' pamphlet in our 'Popular Liturgical Library.'"[123] Unfortunately, though Perkins drafted a general scheme, this work was not completed in time for Diekmann's proposed publication date of fall 1942, perhaps because of her marriage to John Julian Ryan (1898–1983), followed by a move to Cambridge, Massachusetts. John Ryan, a 1921 Harvard graduate and teacher at Holy Cross College in Worcester, Massachusetts, had met Mary Perkins through mutual friends. John shared Mary's interest in liturgy and joined her in attending the National Liturgical Weeks, occasionally jointly presenting as a couple.

---

[123] Letter from Godfrey Diekmann to Mary Perkins Ryan, March 2, 1942, The Mary Perkins Ryan Papers, MS303-30 Series 1, 1/4, John J. Burns Library, Boston College. "You see, I have great confidence in you. The booklet should perhaps be written by a priest; but I know of none who can combine substance and style in the manner I believe desirable for this text. And perhaps too, the laity (who will be principal users of booklet), may be encouraged to overcome their initial prejudices against such an 'ecclesiastical' subject as liturgy by recognizing a lay author.—Please think favorably of the request."

Diekmann explained that the pamphlet was to reflect on the spiritual quality of the Mass in the context of the growing liturgical movement: "The general scheme for it as you briefly outlined it in your letter is about what we would want. An introductory chapter on how we got where we are, another on the liturgical movement in recent decades, particularly in the U.S., and then the works, showing also its ramifications in social fields and, in general, its vital import for the whole of life. Just keep in mind that it will be used principally for study groups, for people who have heard the term liturgy and liturgical movement, and were perhaps vaguely interested to know what the fuss was about. Above all, the essentially spiritual, ascetical character of the liturgical movement has to stand out clearly: perhaps we can finally convince the laity that the liturgical movement is like the flame of the Holy Ghost: it burns once you pick it up; you can't just dawdle with it." Godfrey Diekmann to Mary Perkins Ryan, June 21, 1942, The Mary Perkins Ryan Papers, MS303-30 Series 1, 1/4, John J. Burns Library, Boston College.

During the early part of their marriage, while John Ryan taught at Holy Cross College from 1937 to 1946, Mary Perkins Ryan continued her writing career while also beginning her career as a mother. In 1944, Perkins Ryan offered another collection of simple ways for Catholics to understand how "dogmas of faith" related to the sacraments and sacramentals, the Mass, the liturgical year, and the public prayers of the Church through her book *Speaking How to Pray*. As a reviewer described, Perkins Ryan aimed "to show the lay person how to live the more abundant life of the spirit by integrating into his own life the whole doctrine of faith, the means of grace, the beauty of the liturgy."[124] As with her previous projects, Perkins Ryan received a number of favorable reviews regarding her intersection with the liturgical movement, including a letter from William Busch:

> I am deeply impressed at what your book supplies as compared with older books which confine themselves to the individual aspects and neglect the thought of the Mystical Body and the Liturgy. You have done a truly remarkable piece of work and I trust that the book may be a best seller to the great profit of those who will read and study it and who will follow its guidance. You have given us a Liturgical Week all by yourself and I trust that it will also be a National one.[125]

Likewise, she received an evaluation from Abbot Alcuin Deutsch of Saint John's Abbey expressing his impressions of her work. Addressing her as "My dear Oblate," as both Perkins Ryan and John Ryan were Benedictine oblates, Deutsch wrote:

> I think you will have gotten some idea of the impression it [the book] created in me from the last issue of THE OBLATE, which I trust you

[124] P. P. Parente, Review of *Speaking How to Pray*, by Mary Perkins Ryan, March 1944, The Mary Perkins Ryan Papers, MS303-30 Series 2, 2/1, John J. Burns Library, Boston College. Other reviews include: "Catholic Women's Interest, Review," *Our Sunday Visitor* (November 5, 1944): 10; Richard M. Green, "Book Review," *America* (December 9, 1944): 196–97; "Book Review," *The Grail* (January 1945): 31; Werner Hannan, OFM, "Book Review," *The Catholic Educational Review* (April 1945); and "Book Review," *Catholic Book Club Newsletter* 23, no. 1 (November 1944).

[125] William Busch to Mary Perkins Ryan, October 21, 1944, The Mary Perkins Ryan Papers, MS303-30 Series 1, 1/2, John J. Burns Library, Boston College. Fr. Busch also congratulated her on her new baby.

have received. I think I promised to write to you again to tell you what impression I got from reading your book. I am not going to go into detail, nor indulge in any criticism of your style. I do not think I am sufficiently qualified to venture on such a thing. I do, however, wish to say that I marveled at your theology and wondered how you got it, never having attended a school of theology. Evidently you have done a great deal of reading and thinking, and God must have blessed you with a wonderful memory. You have written with great fluency and enthusiasm—proceeding, no doubt, from your love of Christ, of His Church, and her liturgy. I can only hope and pray that the book finds many readers who will derive from it the same love and enthusiasm that fills your soul.[126]

Indeed, as had Therese Mueller's vocation been viewed as a valuable lens for the liturgical movement, so was Perkins Ryan's expertise as a lay female writer seen as a real contribution. Another commentator, Martin Carrabine, SJ, the moderator of Chicago Inter-Student Catholic Action group who was working in the office of Bishop Sheil, wrote to Perkins Ryan on October 24, 1944, to explain how important her work as a lay person and as a young mother was. He believed that the "excessively celibate slant of so much of our spiritual reading" was a hindrance to many Catholic readers seeking a spiritual entrance into Catholicism.[127] Similarly, Abbot Albert Hammenstede, OSB, of St. Meinrad Abbey in Meinrad, Indiana, echoed the concern regarding the need for the liturgical movement to become less theoretical and more accessible to lay persons. In a letter to Perkins Ryan praising her latest book, *Speaking How to Pray*, in 1944, he assured her that she had chosen wisely in leaving out copious footnotes which might put off the average Catholic reader, yet she had still made sound connections

---

[126] Perkins Ryan also received a motherly note alongside accolades for her professional accomplishment, as Abbot Deutsch continued, "You indicated in your letter to me that you were expecting to have a joy shortly, that of the birth of a child. I surmise that by this time, if I judged rightly from the wording of your letter—your expectation has been realized. If so, my congratulations to you and your husband and my prayer that the child may draw the mother's spirit with the mother's milk and be a source of abiding joy to you and its father and a blessing to the world." Alcuin Deutsch, OSB, to Mary Perkins Ryan, November 20, 1944, The Mary Perkins Ryan Papers, MS303-30 Series 1, 1/4, John J. Burns Library, Boston College.

[127] Martin Carrabine to Mary Perkins Ryan, October 24, 1944, Mary Perkins Ryan Papers, MS303-30 Series 1, 1/3, John J. Burns Library, Boston College.

between liturgical renewal and Catholic teaching: "You have done what I suggested 25 years ago when I told Abbot Herwegen that I thought it absolutely necessary to introduce the friends of liturgy in a deeper understanding of the Dogma."[128]

Living the Liturgical Life, a Christian Life Conscientiously Lived

In 1946, John Ryan was offered a position as an assistant professor at Boston College, and the Ryans remained in Boston from 1947 to 1950, during which time they attended the National Liturgical Weeks as a couple. While participating in a roundtable discussion with other married couples, Perkins Ryan described what was meant by the term "liturgical life": "When you first hear the phrase, *a liturgical life*, it certainly sounds strange and terrifying, but of course it is only a short way of saying, *a life of active Christian worship*, a life whose vital force and pattern is the Holy Sacrifice of the Mass."[129] Perkins Ryan oriented an understanding of the liturgical life around the eucharistic liturgy, drawing on the structure of the Mass by noting that the pattern of the Mass suggested a pattern for life, one which was characterized by giving and receiving, that is, giving to God and receiving God's grace-filled presence in return. Perkins Ryan suggested that a certain awareness of the meaning of the sacraments the faithful experienced, fueled by an active participation in them, allowed the sacraments to have not only a meaning within the church walls or the ordered life of the cloister but also a wider meaning, one which all the apostolate could cultivate. One did not need a large and sacred amount of time for prayer and study; nor did one need solitude and sequestering in order to lead a liturgical life:

> [O]ne simply has to have the supernatural life given one by baptism, for the ability to take part in the worship of God through Christ in the Church is one of the great powers given us by baptism . . . a power that enables us to take part in the Mass itself and make our whole lives part of the offering of the Mass.[130]

[128] Albert Hammenstede, OSB, to Mary Perkins Ryan, November 29, 1944, The Mary Perkins Ryan Papers, MS303-30 Box 1, 1/7, John J. Burns Library, Boston College.

[129] Mary Perkins Ryan, "In the Home: Round Table Discussion," *1948 Liturgical Week Proceedings* (Conception, MO: The Liturgical Conference, 1949): 62.

[130] Ibid.

Attending Mass was the "best way," Perkins Ryan claimed, but not being able to attend Mass daily (which was the situation of many mothers, she noted) should not divide one from living a liturgical life. One could consciously live the Mass each day in the world because of the grace God had imbued in creation. And a Christian participating in the Church's own "training program" to grow in all ways in the grace of Christ might lead a fully Christian life anywhere—in a factory, in a school, in the workplace, on the open road, or on any sort of job.[131] As Therese Mueller, Ade Bethune, and others had approached in their own ways, Perkins Ryan affirmed that the liturgy might permeate all of life.

For Perkins Ryan, the Christian home was a unique place for living the liturgical life—in fact, she proposed that perhaps it was *easier* to lead a liturgical life at home than anywhere else and that it was easier to live a liturgical life as a member of a family, a member of a community, than as an individual.[132] Drawing on an increasingly familiar image, Perkins Ryan described the home, the domestic community, as a symbol of the Mystical Body. The Christian home was first sanctified by matrimony, a sacrament foundational for the family and the practice of homemaking. With marriage came the hope for children who, like their parents, were temples for the Holy Spirit and little members of Christ. Parents who tried to live liturgical lives, she observed, had to help the children to see the world imbued with God's grace, the beauty of creation, and remind the children that they themselves were full of dignity and glory. As Perkins Ryan proposed:

> [I]f we tell our children about it when we are washing the dishes or the clothes (or the children themselves, for that matter) they will begin to think about water the right way, and they will begin daily to think about their baptism and its wonders.[133]

Thus, any moment of the family's life, from mundane breakfast cereals to singular baptism days of younger siblings, had the potential for

---

[131] Ibid.

[132] "It is possible to try to lead a liturgical life as an individual; it is far easier and more fruitful to be trying to lead such a life as a member of a whole family leading the life of the Church, the Christ-life, together, not only in each one's own soul, but as a family." Mary Perkins Ryan, "In the Home: Round Table Discussion," *1948 Liturgical Week Proceedings*, 64.

[133] Ibid.

sacramental remembrance. All things might point the faithful's minds to Christ, the reality made present in the eucharistic experience, and all things might be oriented to a life of praise of God:

> Whenever we are doing anything about feeding our family and guests, we can let the fact of food, our work with food, bring us to the thought of the Holy Eucharist; whenever we are dealing with the house itself, we can let its walls and floors and fixtures remind us of the house which God is building for His own habitation for all eternity, the temple to God in the Spirit of which we are the chosen building-blocks. Whatever the thought or the phrase from the day's Mass that we are trying to remember and make our own through the day may be, we can easily find something in the course of the day's occupations to remind us of it, to bring it home to us, to make it vital and relevant and grace-bringing.[134]

As Perkins Ryan assured her listeners, the liturgical life was not hard, but it required practice; it was "nothing odd, it is merely a Christian life conscientiously lived."[135]

Identity and Vocation

Mary Perkins Ryan's understanding of liturgical life and a Christian conscientiousness underlined the key of *integration* of liturgy and life, a fundamental aspect of the liturgical movement. Perkins Ryan identified that every aspect of the family's living might reveal Christ and stressed that one need not pine for the sanctuary of cloisters to rest deeply in a liturgical life. What she proposed instead was a *changed mind-set*, a *shift in worldview*:

> [T]hat the cooking and cleaning and mending and tidying, the earning of a living, the entertaining and recreation, which make up a large part of family life should be considered, not as interruptions to our life in Christ, but as essential parts of it; not as distractions from sharing in the "Work of Christ" but as our special share in that "Work" not as a means of purgation only, but of illumination and union with God.[136]

---

[134] Ibid.

[135] Ibid., 62.

[136] Mary Perkins Ryan, "Liturgy and the Family Arts," *1946 Liturgical Week Proceedings* (Highland Park, IL: The Liturgical Conference, 1947): 106–7.

The "Work" or the "Art" of the home should not be circumscribed by popular help ads and how-to books. The practice of homemaking was not only an art but a liturgical art, an art by which Perkins Ryan and her husband, John Julian, could worship God together as members of the Mystical Body of Christ. Adopting a worldview which allowed the liturgical experience to permeate life came from an acceptance of one's vocation, particularly when one was called to the lay apostolate, to marriage, and to parenthood. It was necessary to unite the work of the home with the work of the Church because the alternative was to live two separate vocations—for women, the life of the housewife and mother on the one hand and the life of the Christian on the other. To divide the work proper to those called to marriage and family life from Christian life would be to deny the vocation to which Christ had called them to share in his work of glorifying God.[137]

The Liturgical Life for Women Responds to the Modern Woman

The impulse for embracing the vocation of the lay apostolate, as women, was driven by a desire to act in contrast to the many pressures and expectations of modernity—pressure to cut corners, get it done "in as short a time and as inexpensively as possible, chiefly by using well-advertised products; to include all the necessary vitamins and calories; to impress guests with the look of your dishes."[138] That is, the liturgical movement encouraged its adherents to orient the self differently, to reorient life around that which was the Source of Life and well-being, to reject popular pressure to feed on food which would not sustain. Women interested in liturgical renewal were well aware of the "popular" projection of the harassed American housewife, with annoying children and a husband who was "slipping away from her," and, rather than "face the real cause of their dissatisfaction, they leap eagerly at a laxative or soap powder which promises to fill the household with joy and love."[139] The modern woman, "our woman of the ads," as she was often characterized, was driven by foolishness and selfishness—and lack of faith. If women were to take seriously the baptism which poured forth the grace of Christ, the Holy Spirit which anointed hearts in confirmation, then they might see that the cure for ignorance

[137] Ibid., 107.
[138] Ibid., 114.
[139] Mrs. Cort, "What Is So New?: A Panel Discussion," *1948 Liturgical Week Proceedings* (Conception, MO: The Liturgical Conference, 1949): 14–15.

or stupor or a bad temper was not "Carter's little liver pills, but more frequent Communion."[140]

The woman who drew on the rich food of the liturgy to lead her family to Christ had chosen to sacramentalize her life, to believe in her vocation and in the unique position afforded to her as the mother of children and wife of a husband, to help form her small community in the way of the Mystical Body. Mary Perkins Ryan, during the 1946 Liturgical Week, described homemaking as a "sacramental, liturgical art."[141] She advocated that the same full and active participation in the Church's work of worship could "be continued and carried out by active charity throughout our daily lives."[142] The liturgy, in fact, was:

> teaching us that we should plan our whole family life and each of its various aspects as a work of sacramental, liturgical art, reflecting the life of the Church, ordered to the loving worship of God and the loving service of our neighbor, our parish, our community and country, the whole Mystical Body of Christ.[143]

But, how would one know that Christian family lives were continuations of the sacramental life of the Church and of the Mystical Body of Christ? Just as the symbols of the sacraments were of created and material things and our very bodies were created and material, we, in turn, used creation:

> We receive the very life and powers of Christ Our Lord, through the ministry of our priests, by means of created and material things, in the Sacraments, the sacramentals, the prayer, the full life of the Church. We in turn now can use created things—ourselves, our talents, our time, our actions, the materials we work with—in the worship of God, for the salvation and sanctification of men, because we share in the priesthood of Christ through the Sacraments of Baptism and Confirmation. We are continually taught and trained in this sacramental use of created things by the whole sacramental life of the Church.[144]

---

[140] Ibid., 15.

[141] Mary Perkins Ryan, "Liturgy and the Family Arts," *1946 Liturgical Week Proceedings*, 108.

[142] Ibid., 109.

[143] Ibid.

[144] Ibid., 107.

Perkins Ryan's view of the sacramental echoes the work of previous women pioneers but develops the notion of a liturgical home life as a point of theological reflection. Nevertheless, any of these musings was in danger of becoming idealism if one could not bridge between the theoretical and the practical. Perkins Ryan reminded, "The ways of sacramentalizing this art [of homemaking] are not difficult. The only difficulty comes in consistently practicing them!"[145] She continued:

> I do not pray that we theorize on theology but that together we find a thousand little ways of bridging the gap between principle and practice. I do not pray that we speculate on the nature of Christ and his mystical life today but that together we create a thousand situations in the family which make His life real to us and in us. I do not even pray that we contemplate the fresh and vital beauty of the liturgy with its roots in the past, its flower in the present, and its tendrils reaching out to the future. But I do pray that together we can carry this beauty into a thousand homes where it will inspire young lives, give point to middle-age and yield a reward for long years of service.[146]

She hoped that, in challenging young Catholic families to "make real" Christ in their lives, the faithful would pick up the task, seeking concrete ways to enact the liturgical life, and form their families in lasting ways.

Choosing a Christian Lifestyle: Community, Consumption, and Time

One of the recurring tactics in women's language about the liturgical life was an emphasis on the joy of or superiority of life in the country or, at least, the problems presented to Catholics who lived in giant, somewhat impersonal suburban parishes. Echoing the views of the National Catholic Rural Life Movement, there was a substantial amount of opinion that life in the country was "better for the majority of families" than crowding in cities and towns. Mary Perkins Ryan observed:

> [I]f it is God's will, there will be more and smaller parishes in cities and towns, there will be more small villages each with a church, with farms spread around them. There will be less inhuman overcrowding in cities and less inhuman isolation in the country, and more and more Christian

[145] Ibid., 116
[146] Ibid.

families will be able to be situated sufficiently near a church to participate as fully as possible in its full sacramental, liturgical life. Then also
Christian families will be more easily able to be true neighbours to each
other, and to the stranger and the destitute, and to supplement and fulfill their family life by a fully Christian community life.[147]

While this vision was more like a medieval parish than modern mid-
century American life, it is interesting to see the stress on *community*
established by the country parish family, as well as the Christian work
ethic produced by manual labor and production of one's own household work, whether in canning, repairing, baking, tailoring, or teaching children.[148]

As Perkins Ryan and others were aware, not every family had opportunity to change its life-space, but choices within the home might
be made which synchronized with a Christian lifestyle: employers
might pay fair wages, housewives might become suspicious of bar-
gains which actually gouged other persons, and care could be taken
with regard to what time-saving devices were bought. For example,
while washing machines or cars might improve lifestyles palpably and
save time for more productive tasks, canned dishes and "easy dinners" should be "shunned like the plague."[149] It was not Christian to
be "puritanical," but good work, especially work which tended to the
care and flourishing of the family, should be taken seriously and with
care, not sped through with Crisco and instant oatmeal. Perkins Ryan
suggested that this responsibility was particularly in the hands of the
mother, the one most often trusted with charge of the kitchen:

> For the family will not be as well, and certainly not as lovingly fed by
> the mother who uses nothing but such foods, as by the mother who
> tries to use the best materials available, to produce the most nourishing
> and welcome dishes for her own particular family. Nor will the mother
> have so perfect an offering to make in the Holy Sacrifice of the Mass if

---

[147] Ibid., 110.

[148] Ibid., 110–11. Many more examples of the benefits of rural life are
witnessed in resources such as the journal *Catholic Rural Life Bulletin/Land
and Home*. See Michael J. Woods, *Cultivating Soil and Soul: Twentieth-Century
Catholic Agrarians Embrace the Liturgical Movement* (Collegeville, MN: Liturgical
Press, 2009).

[149] Mary Perkins Ryan, "Liturgy and the Family Arts," *1946 Liturgical Week
Proceedings*, 113

she brings mostly "time saved" from one of her most important works [of caring for her family].[150]

Such censure regarding how a woman chose to allocate her time and resources was strong, indeed. Yet, on the other hand, liturgical pioneers sought to stress that the liturgical life should be taken just as seriously in the home as it should be anywhere else. One could not be a worshiping member of the Mystical Body without caring properly for the Mystical Body in one's own home. The home too should be a place of social regeneration.[151]

Mary Perkins Ryan's The Sacramental Way *and Other Projects*

Perkins Ryan's work was not limited to discussion of the family and home life, and her skills as an editor and translator were continually drawn upon by liturgical leaders, writers, and publishers. For example, one of her projects was a joint effort with Fr. Shawn G. Sheehan to produce an edited volume of the Liturgical Conference, titled *The Sacramental Way* (1948). Drawing on papers given during the first six Liturgical Weeks, Perkins Ryan and Sheehan sought to present an introduction to the general themes of the liturgical movement and crafted accompanying study questions so as to produce a "readable and saleable book" to attract the general reader, priest, sister, or non-religious lay person, or to be used as a college religion text or by study clubs.[152] Perkins Ryan's introduction to the volume stressed the importance of integrating matters of doctrine with Christian action in the world, an integration which would be fed through active participation.[153] In order to avoid "datedness" of the text, references to the

---

[150] Ibid.

[151] Interestingly, the desire to promote fair wages, just labor practices, and conscious-driven consumption, which Perkins Ryan described, anticipated the growing interest among twenty-first century Catholics with regard to economic justice and environmental sensibilities. See, for example, Kyle T. Kramer, *A Time to Plant: Life Lessons in Work, Prayer, and Dirt* (Notre Dame, IN: Ave Maria Press, 2011).

[152] Reynold Hillenbrand to Mary Perkins Ryan, Octave of the Epiphany, 1947, The Reynold Hillenbrand Papers 28/27, UNDA.

[153] "It is characteristic of the Liturgical Movement in this country that it has always stressed the interdependence of the three factors of doctrine, holiness of life and Christian action in the work of re-establishing all things in Christ. In seeking above all to restore to the laity that active participation in the sacred

actual week or current events were omitted—including references to the Second World War.[154]

Perkins Ryan's projects during the 1950s followed a series of relocations with her family; in 1950, the Ryans left Boston because they wanted John Ryan to take a position where he could specialize in writing and to give the children the opportunity to live in the country and near a monastery. They chose Conception Seminary, Conception Missouri, but found it was too far in the country, poorly located with poor transportation and not enough leisure. John was offered a job at Saint Mary's College at Notre Dame but had deep disagreements with Mother Madeleva over teaching methods and stayed for only one academic year. In 1953, he was hired by Fr. Michael Mathis, CSC, director of the University of Notre Dame Liturgy Program, as a consultant to the Notre Dame University Press on their liturgical services and as a member of the Notre Dame liturgical committee. Mary Perkins Ryan joined in this work and actually took it over in 1956. While in South Bend, Indiana, in the spring of 1955, Perkins Ryan had begun translating Louis Bouyer's *Bible et l'Evangile*, which would be published by the Notre Dame Press in 1958 as *The Meaning of Sacred Scripture*. At this time, she was also commissioned to prepare the translation of Pius XII's *Novum Psalterium* (1945), which was published by Fides in 1955.[155]

---

mysteries which Pius X declared to be the primary and indispensable source of the true Christian Spirit, it has constantly sought to set forth the doctrinal foundations and implications of this statement and to point out the far-reaching results which such active participation should bring into the personal and social life of Catholics, as well as to discover the practical means by which this active participation may be achieved under modern conditions." Mary Perkins Ryan, introduction to *The Sacramental Way* (New York: Sheed & Ward, 1948), 1.

[154] Reynold Hillenbrand to Mary Perkins Ryan, Octave of Epiphany, 1947, The Reynold Hillenbrand Papers 28/27, UNDA.

[155] This translation eventually was used in the English edition of the *Book of Hours* (1955) and *The Office of Our Lady* (1962), and also by William Storey, in his breviary, *Morning Praise and Evening Song* (1963). Bill Storey relates the delight with which he and Mary Perkins Ryan convinced their bishop to approve her translation. They had the volume sent to him, with no indication of whom the translator was; the bishop was so impressed he approved it, which, Storey surmises, may have turned out differently had he known that Mary Perkins Ryan, lay woman, was the translator. William Storey, conversation with the author, October 11, 2010, South Bend, Indiana.

With Perkins Ryan's increased involvement at Notre Dame, John Ryan took a position as an editorial assistant for *Catholic Boy*, also published by Notre Dame Press. Unfortunately, his tenure was brief, and he was retained only for a year before *Catholic Boy*, which was "in the red," could not afford to retain a "lay editor." Mary Perkins Ryan's work with Mathis at the Notre Dame Liturgy Program was not enough to sustain their family with five small boys, John Jr., Peter, Tom, Michael, and David, so the family was forced to move again, this time to St. Anselm's College in Goffstown, New Hampshire.[156] Here, John was a much-beloved professor of English and also had opportunity to write.

Liturgical Pioneer, Catechetical Pioneer

Aside from Mary Perkins Ryan's involvement at National Liturgical Weeks, including serving as a member of its board of directors along with John Julian Ryan from 1953 until 1963, her other earlier writings included *Mind the Baby* (1949) and *Beginning at Home* (1955). In these works, she sought to guide parents in finding ways to give their children meaningful opportunities to teach a basic pattern of Christian living, encouraging them to view others as members of the Mystical Body. Even children who went to Catholic school with regular instruction in religion still needed help *incorporating* morality and faith into daily life. As Perkins Ryan wrote:

> If we are trying to sacramentalize our daily lives, to live the life of the Church inwardly and as outwardly also as circumstances permit, then the course of each day and week and year should offer its own opportunities to teach the children as much as they are capable of learning

---

[156] Perkins Ryan wrote to Godfrey Diekmann: "At the moment I have no very rosy vision of the future anywhere—it seems more and more as if we simply didn't have what it takes to bring up a family. We can only cling to the hope that God will see them through somehow in spite of our age, impracticality and growing inability to cope with things. I seem more and more to be two different people—a reasonably competent writer and editor, and a hopelessly incompetent wife, mother and housekeeper. If we could afford it, it would be better to give up everything but a minimum of writing, *etc.*, but that doesn't seem advisable either under all the circumstances. So please keep us in your prayer—solvitur ambulando. . . ." Mary Perkins Ryan to Godfrey Diekmann, May 14, 1957, The Godfrey Diekmann Papers 1021/5, SJAA.

about God, about the truths of the faith. The guide in general to what the children are capable of understanding and absorbing is, here again, mainly the children's own interest and span of attention.[157]

Yet, though Perkins Ryan was able to articulate the potential for the Catholic family to live the liturgical life, she also struggled with identifying herself and her family as effectively living this out. This tension became particularly poignant when the Ryans were invited to attend the program as two "experts" discussing family life and liturgy. When Godfrey Diekmann invited the Ryans to attend in 1957, Perkins Ryan wrote back:

> There was some talk last fall about putting us on the program as two of the "experts" for discussing family life and liturgy—but God knows we are no experts on the family and anything, and since we are unsure of our plans, there is every reason for not including us. Thank you again for all your trouble on our behalf and for many other things as well . . . and excuse this gloomy letter. John is in a particularly gloomy state about selling this house, finances, how the children act, etc. and I have got right in it with him![158]

Just as Therese Mueller had grappled with the irony of being thought an "expert" while feeling quite inept, Mary Perkins Ryan was keenly aware of the difficulties of living the liturgical life.

As the trajectory of her career developed, Perkins Ryan's adamancy that children needed continual, incarnational (practical/sensory), and holistic education bridged her involvement in the liturgical movement with the catechetical movement, in which she became increasingly involved in the post-Conciliar era. Perkins Ryan continued her work in producing catechetical materials, such as her *Key to the Psalms* (1957) as well as frequent writing for journals such as *Orate Fratres/Worship* and *Commonweal*.

Perkins Ryan's continual interest in connecting liturgical catechesis and parochial education resulted in her writing the controversial *Are Parochial Schools the Answer?* (1964), which questioned the value of the

---

[157] Mary Perkins Ryan, *Beginning at Home* (Collegeville, MN: Liturgical Press, 1955), 126.

[158] Mary Perkins Ryan to Godfrey Diekmann, May 14, 1957, The Godfrey Diekmann Papers 1021/5, SJAA.

Catholic educational system's role in teaching religion. According to a review by Gerard A. Pottebaum of Pflaum Publishing Company, this book focused on Catholic education within the broader mission of the "new climate" in the Church:

> The new climate . . . calls for a new diffusion of responsibility. When the bishops of the Church assembled in solemn council, they found that they had not been called together to rubber-stamp a set of conclusions already arrived at but to act as successors of the Apostles: as a body responsible, under the leadership but not the domination of the Holy Father, for the well-being of the Church. . . . The same principle of subsidiarity may then be expected to be extended throughout the Church. . . . The spirit of renewal calls every Catholic to share, according to his place and function in the Church, in responsibility for its growth and welfare and for the communications of the life and charity of Christ to all men.[159]

"Responsibility," according to Ryan, might involve attentiveness to shifting patterns in Catholic life and subsequent adjustments in strategy. As parochial enrollment figures began to shrink and the cost of employing qualified teachers and administrators increased as numbers of clerical and religious men and women declined, parochial schools became a deficit mark against their respective parishes. Perkins Ryan increasingly questioned the equanimity of requiring parish families—including those who did not have children attending the parish school—to support this burdensome effort. Instead, she proposed, a wiser investment would be made if monies were put toward educational efforts which would benefit the entire parish community:

> [T]he resources now spent in providing protective or segregating services for Catholics [should] be used instead, on the other hand, to foster a mature and responsible Christian vitality which is our best

---

[159] Mary Perkins Ryan, *Are Parochial Schools the Answer?* (New York: Holt, Rinehart and Winston, 1964). Quoted in Gerard A. Pottebaum, "In Gratitude for the Life of Mary Perkins Ryan," *CIC Update: The Christian Initiation of Children Newsletter* 4, no. 4 (1993): 2. Due to Perkins Ryan's expertise, Pottebaum made arrangements for her to serve as a consultant to Geo. A. Pflaum Press while Pottebaum was starting a new religious education division at the Publishing House. Gerard A. Pottebaum, personal correspondence with the author, March 12, 2011.

safeguard, and on the other, to serve the needs of the community in the sharing of Christ.[160]

Rather than investing in a parallel system of schools and other services for Catholics, Perkins Ryan felt that more energy should be placed on education of men, women, and children within the parish itself.

After the Second Vatican Council, Perkins Ryan focused her involvement more completely on developing religious catechesis, contributing to this effort by serving as founding editor for *The Living Light* (1964–72) and also serving as editor for *Professional Approaches for Christian Education* (*PACE*; 1973–88), from which she retired at the age of seventy-six. As Ann Morrow Heekin notes in a dissertation detailing Mary Perkins Ryan's involvement in the field of religious catechesis, Perkins Ryan's editorial leadership at both *The Living Light* and *PACE* allowed her to broaden her vision of liturgical catechesis to a more comprehensive vision of religious education. Perkins Ryan saw the primary importance of *adult education*, as it was the cornerstone for communal or familial religious education, and the need to incorporate modern theories of learning and development within catechesis.

With regard to liturgy, Perkins Ryan's liturgical writings were featured in a number of journals and magazines between the 1930s and the 1960s,[161] and her liturgical work continued to be used after the

---

[160] Ann Morrow Heekin, "The Life and Work of Mary Perkins Ryan: The Interplay of Liturgy and Catechesis in Whole Community Education," *Religious Education for Peace and Justice Proceedings* (November 4–6, 2005): 12; http://old.religiouseducation.net/proceedings/2005_papers.htm. See also Ann Morrow Heekin, "Reclaiming a Lost Leader: Mary Perkins Ryan, Visionary in Modern Catholic Education," *Religious Education* 103, no. 2 (2008): 196–217; Roy Deferrari's rebuttal, *A Complete System of Catholic Education Is Necessary* (Boston: St. Paul Editions, 1964); and Mary Perkins Ryan *We're All in This Together: Issues and Options in the Education of Catholics* (New York: Holt, Rinehard and Winston, 1972) in which she took up the issues of after-school programs and adult catechesis. See also Ann Morrow Heekin, "Mary Perkins Ryan: Twentieth Century Religious Educator, Education to a New Vision of Church," (PhD diss., Fordham University, 2006).

[161] Some include: Mary Perkins, "Distributism and the Guilds," *Free America* 1, no. 6 (June 1937): 12–13; Mary Perkins Ryan, "Strangers No Longer," *St. Joseph Magazine* (October 1945): 13; "My Sacrifice and Yours," *St. Joseph Magazine* (November 1945): 10, 28; "Come!" *St. Joseph Magazine* (December 1945): 14–15; "This Is the Victory," *St. Joseph Magazine* (May 1946): 2–4, 18;

Second Vatican Council, such as the 1966 revised edition of *The Spirit of Holy Week*, originally published in 1958.[162] As Gerard Pottebaum, close friend and colleague of the Ryans reflected, she saw the liturgical movement as a process, not an end in itself.[163] The goals of the liturgical movement, from participation to ethical responsibility, should continue to flourish and evolve. Indeed, Perkins Ryan's own projection of the future of the liturgical movement, summed up at the conclusion of her speech, titled "Family Life in Christ," given at the National Liturgical Week in 1946, belied her hopes for the continuing evolvement of the movement:

> Further generations, trained in the full liturgical life and outlook of the Church from childhood, will, please God, be able to smile at such an elementary effort to show how the work and play of family life can be integrated into true family life in Christ. The idea will be a truism, self-evident, not needing to be said at all, let alone explained at such length. But to all those who have begun, or who might begin family life as we did, with as little notion for the glorious possibilities of its most ordinary aspects, as well as to you, fathers and sisters, who must train and help and encourage us, my husband and I humbly offer this paper, hoping that it may be of some service in achieving our common aim of family life in Christ.[164]

With this spirit, Perkins Ryan was also ready to adjust her views on liturgy and liturgical catechesis as needs of Catholics changed. For

---

"Fire of Thy Love," *St. Joseph Magazine* (June 1946): 12–14, 31; "Growth in All Things," *St. Joseph Magazine* (August 1946): 11–12, 31; "Seek First," *St. Joseph Magazine* (September 1946): 10–11, 26; "To the Last," *St. Joseph Magazine* (October 1946): 10–11, 32; "He Is Coming," *St. Joseph Magazine* (November 1946): 9, 26; and "Meditations on a Baby," *St. Joseph Magazine* (December 1948): 3–4, 15. The Mary Perkins Ryan Papers, MS303-30, Series 2, 1/19-1/41, John J. Burns Library, Boston College.

[162] Mary Perkins Ryan, *The Spirit of Holy Week*, rev. ed. (Notre Dame, IN: Ave Maria Press, 1966), Liturgy and Life Collection, Special Collections, Boston College.

[163] Gerard A. Pottebaum, personal correspondence with the author, March 2011.

[164] Mary Perkins Ryan, "Family Life in Christ," *1946 Liturgical Week Proceedings*, 118.

example, while she had so strongly supported the teaching of Latin to Catholics so all could actively participate in liturgical prayer, she adjusted this view when it became clear that the vernacular would become the norm for Roman Catholics in the United States.[165]

Mary Perkins Ryan continued to work as a freelance writer through the 1970s and 1980s. Throughout her life, she authored, edited, and translated over twenty-five works on topics of theology, philosophy, and, primarily, liturgy. As with so many of the eclectic and active liturgical pioneers, and as is particularly characteristic of its women, Perkins Ryan can be identified in two separate spheres. She is included among leaders of both the liturgical movement and the catechetical movement, especially as religious catechesis shifted from the responsibility of religious sisters to lay teachers with the shifting populations of parochial school systems. Mary Perkins Ryan died on October 13, 1993, after a struggle with Parkinson's disease, in New Hampshire.[166] John Ryan died in 1983.

COOKING FOR CHRIST IN THE LITURGICAL KITCHEN: FLORENCE BERGER

Beginning with the Grail Movement

Florence Sudhoff Berger was born on June 22, 1909, in Cincinnati, Ohio, daughter of A. Bernard Sudhoff, born in Germany (in Barmen Elberfeld), and Mary Emma Ruthman, also of German heritage (Oldenberg). Florence Sudhoff was the youngest of five children (others being Etheol, Edward, Arthur, and Mary). In Ohio, Florence went to St. Ursula Academy,[167] St. Ursula High School, and the University of

---

[165] Mary Perkins Ryan, "I'm Going to Like More Vernacular," *Amen* 9 (1 July 1954): 5–7, 12.

[166] See M. C. Bryce, "Mary Perkins Ryan," *The Living Light* 12 (1975): 276–81; P. O'Hare, "Mary Perkins Ryan (1912–1993): Mulier Furtis," *The Living Light* 30 (1994): 3–8. Mary Charles Bryce, "Pioneer Women in Catechetics," *The Living Light* 23 (1986): 313–24. Another biography of Mary Perkins Ryan can be found at http://www2.talbot.edu/ce20/educators/view.cfm?n=mary_ryan#bio.

[167] In 1949, following the publication of *Cooking for Christ*, Berger was invited to be the "guest speaker" for the annual alumnae reunion of St. Ursula Academy. "Local Author to Speak at Alumnae Reunion," January 23, 1950, newspaper clipping, Florence Berger File, The Ohioana Library Association, Ohioana Library, 274 East First Avenue, Columbus, Ohio [hereafter Ohioana Library Association].

Cincinnati, where she graduated Phi Beta Kappa in 1930, returning for a master of arts in 1931 and a bachelor of education in 1932, specializing in early childhood education.[168] She worked in the public school system of Cincinnati for several years. In 1933, she married Alfred (Al) Berger, born in 1904, also of Cincinnati. Alfred Berger had also gone to college, attending Xavier College, where he majored in chemistry. He graduated, however, in the midst of the Great Depression, and so, unable to find a job, he chose graduate school, completing a PhD in inorganic chemistry from the University of Cincinnati.[169] He worked for thirty years at the Institum Divi Thomae and started the Massasoit Chemical Company which made dishwashing compound. In 1940, the Bergers and their first two children, Mary Florence (1936) and Ann Marie (1938), moved from their small apartment home in Cincinnati to a thirty-five-acre farm in Delhi, Ohio.[170] When they first came to the farm, they had few Catholic friends and their feelings about their country parish, St. Aloysius, were tepid, as their daughter, Ann Berger

[168] She exercised her leadership skills during college, acting as president of Theta Phi Alpha, the Catholic Women's fraternity, and as a founding member of the Newman Club. "About the Author," book jacket, Florence Berger File, Ohioana Library Association.

[169] A family website provides a history of the Berger family: http://bergerhill.info/BG_Alfred.html.

[170] In a fascinating history of Al and Florence Berger, written and compiled by their six children (Mary, Ann, Fred, Christina, Kathy, and Kia [Rose]), the Berger's lives are collectively detailed. The move to the Farm is described as arriving at "an old farmhouse, partially propped up by rain barrels," at the end of a dirt road. Alfred Berger, who delighted in fixing, building, and tinkering, slowly worked on the house, building additions, installing plumbing, and improving the bathrooms and kitchen. Ann Berger Frutkin, *Florence and Al Berger: A Collaborative Memory of a Cincinnati Family* (Hilton Head Island, SC: Studiobooks, 2009), 8–12.

Regarding the family's move out of the city and into the country in 1940, Ann Berger Frutkin reflects that it may have been a move to spare the German family from anti-German sentiment during wartime: "One of the reasons that I now believe that my parents were interested in the farm life was that they wanted to keep their children from the pre-war haranguing that had begun in the city. Alfred had experienced anti-German sentiment in Clifton during WWI and had been appalled. Neither of them wanted to have newspapers in the house and they closely monitored our radio listening. Florence would mutter even during the Vietnam War, 'The first casualty of war is truth.'" Ann Berger Frutkin, 12.

Frutkin, would recall.[171] By the end of the war, the Berger's third child, Alfred (Fred) Joseph (1942), and fourth, Katherine (Kathy) Marcia (1945), had been born. The birth of the Berger's fifth child, Christine Angela (1947), however, was something of a turning point, especially for Florence Berger's life. Overextended, Florence Berger caught pneumonia while pregnant with Christine; her life was saved by the new miracle drug penicillin, and she delivered Christine while in an oxygen tent. As her daughter, Ann Berger Frutkin, would recall, "Both she and Dad thought that she would die. All of this turmoil must have strengthened their understanding of their vulnerability, the fleetingness of time, and a belief in God."[172]

Following Christine's birth, Florence Berger became more active in church life. She took a turn at being president of the Catholic Women's Club, of which she had been a member, and explored the new group for women which had developed near their home, in Loveland, Ohio, the Grail. She and Alfred Berger had been involved with the National Catholic Rural Life Conference (hereafter NCRLC), having themselves been "lured to the country by its wholesome lifestyle and now thought that the simplicity was also a way to be more active religiously."[173] Luigi Ligutti, whom the Bergers knew from the NCRLC, had acquainted them with the Grail, which was teaching young women to live more simply and make their home life "more meaningful in a religious way."[174] The women at the Grail were also trained to work in homes to help families, and a young Grailville woman, Mary Hayes, who had come from an orphanage, was the first who came to live with the Bergers, the first of several caretakers.[175] This connection to Grailville was the Bergers' introduction to the broader liturgical movement.

Equipped with space, house, and garden that she did not have before, Florence Berger became more interested in combining the life of her family with her Catholic faith. One of these experiments was creating a resource for women to use for recipes which would be suited to the liturgical calendar. She claimed to first get the idea from a statement of the bishops on secularism as the "greatest evil of today" and from Pius XI "who is reported to have said that festival days did more

[171] Ibid., 16.
[172] Ibid., 17.
[173] Ibid.
[174] Ibid.
[175] Ibid., 17–18.

to further religion than any official pronouncements of the church."[176] She experimented with many of the Church's feast days with her five children—Mary, Ann, Fred, Christina, and Kathy (she and Alfred later had a sixth child, Rose)—trying to emphasize "the why of religious feast days by preparing special food for the children, and explaining its significance as they ate."[177] Meanwhile, the Bergers had maintained their involvement with the NCRLC and their contact with their friend, Ligutti, its executive secretary. When Berger explained what she was doing with her family, Ligutti suggested that she make a book of her recipes to be published by the NCRLC.[178] Berger, "in the midst of babies and a growing family," spent "the nights on the typewriter and the days in the kitchen trying out recipes."[179] Mary Berger, a twelve-year-old at the time, worked on illustrations (which were not, in the end, used). After two years of work, and assisted by her husband, Florence Berger produced one of the most interesting artifacts of the liturgical movement, the book *Cooking for Christ*.

Cooking for Christ

A study of Berger's cookbook reflects some of the key impulses noted by women, particularly uniting women's work/vocation with that of the liturgical life and by training her family to stewardship, good work, and creativity. As Berger wrote, the kitchen was a place uniquely the woman's and thus offered unique opportunity for women to bring Christ into the home and live out their own apostolates:

[176] "Writes Religious Cookbook," Florence Berger File, Ohioana Library Association.

[177] "Religion: Christ in the Kitchen," *Time* 54, no. 12 (September 19, 1949): 81.

[178] Shortly before *Cooking for Christ*'s publication in 1946, Mary Perkins Ryan had suggested that someone should produce just such a resource which could guide one's creation of liturgical dishes throughout the year: "In this connection, somebody should get together a book of recipes for the traditional Christian dishes of all countries throughout the liturgical year. Then we each could choose and adapt those which best fit in with our way of life, which are best suited to our family's traditional foods on feasts and fasts." Mary Perkins Ryan, "Liturgy and the Family Arts," *1946 Liturgical Week Proceedings* (Highland Park, IL: The Liturgical Conference, 1947): 115.

[179] Berger Frutkin, 18.

If I am to carry Christ home with me from the altar, I am afraid He will have to come to the kitchen because much of my time is spent there. I shall welcome Him on Easter and He shall eat new lamb with us. I shall give homage to Him on Epiphany and shall cook a royal feast for him and my family. I shall mourn with Him on Holy Thursday and we shall taste the herbs of the Passover and break unleavened bread. Then the cooking which we do will add special significance to the Church Year and Christ will sanctify our daily bread. That is what is meant by the liturgical year in the kitchen.[180]

In this creative resource, which would become a recommended textbook for Catholic schoolgirls,[181] "liturgically appropriate" meals were interspersed with brief lessons on the meaning of feasts, the histories of saints, and the social implications of liturgical practice. For example, following Easter, during the octave, Berger gave an example of how to use a family's leftover lamb in creating an "Easter Soup." Christians "garnered and saved their Easter blessings" by wasting nothing and neither should we:

Too many children still hunger for bread in this world of mal-distribution. . . . Christ, Himself, gave us the example of gathering up remnants—and no meat lends itself to stews and casseroles so well as lamb does.[182]

Berger saw wastefulness as a sin not only against one's fellow human community but also against God. Resonating with interests of the National Catholic Rural Life Movement for responsible use of resources,

---

[180] Florence Berger, introduction to *Cooking for Christ: The Liturgical Year in the Kitchen* (Des Moines, IA: National Catholic Rural Life Conference, 1949).

[181] For example, an article in the *Catholic Digest* (1964) reported: "Sister Francesca, O.S.U., is teaching girls [at Brescia College in Owensboro, Kentucky] to be women: Christian, feminine women. . . . Those students must read Gertrude Von le Fort's *Eternal Woman* and Solange Hertz' *Searcher of Majesty*. Other books include *Woman in Wonderland, Destiny of Modern Woman, A Tour of the Summa, The Year and Our Children* [by Mary Reed Newland], *Around the Year with the Trapp Family* [Maria von Trapp], *Woman-Words and Wisdom, Cooking for Christ*, and *How to Dress Well on $1 a Day*. The list blends the sublime with the practical!" Ethel Marbach, "The Eternal Woman," *Catholic Digest* 28 (October 1964): 79–81.

[182] Berger, *Cooking for Christ*, 76–77.

Berger believed that not only farmers but city dwellers as well were called to good stewardship of their gifts and resources.

Culling up liturgically sensitive meals also required delving into multiple cultural backgrounds, though limited to those which were European. For example, a "Pease Porridge," or split-pea soup, was suggested as an appropriate Palm Sunday dish, for in Scotland Passion Sunday was called "Car-Sunday." Peas were called "carlings," and Pease Porridge was a Sunday dish in Lent. Berger explained how to make the rather old dish with a bit of modern convenience:

> If you have a pressure cooker you can finish the soup in 15 minutes at 15 pounds pressure, and the peas will need no soaking. Add a ham bone or two slices of diced, fried bacon if it is not a fast day. May you enjoy your carling, but especially your Sunday. Even in Lent our Sunday is a day of joy, an anniversary of the Resurrection, and "it would be unlawful to be sad today."[183]

Other recipes suggested Polish carp at Christmastime, Italian sausage and peppers for St. Valentine's Day, an Armenian vegetable dish for Lent, and Finnish pancakes for St. John's Day.

A liturgical year in the kitchen had immense potential to orient a family around a meaningful center. In the face of the lethargy which had "crept upon the Christian spirit," Berger proposed that "perhaps mothers and daughters can lead their families back to Christ-centered living and cooking," thus echoing the charge of her contemporary liturgists and Scripture scholars calling for more active lay participation and understanding.[184] Just as liturgical participation and comprehension of Scripture had opened the Christian spirit to the reality of God, so might the work of the kitchen perform this task; the woman as caregiver and cook might rest in the sacramental sense of her vocation to feed the little members of the Mystical Body a more substantial meal. Eating together as a family would add to and complement other venues of "churching" the domestic church, including family Mass and family prayer. But despite the immense value of setting aside time and making it sacred through Mass and prayer, Berger found that making things of everyday life fostered a more holistically liturgical lifestyle:

---

[183] Ibid., 59.
[184] Ibid., "Introduction."

[Mass and family prayer] are the big things, but so many little things have been won as well. The celebration of feast days has made the liturgy active. It permeated our cooking, our table decorations, our songs, our pictures, our games and even our flower arrangement. It has intensified the unity of our family group. There is so much work to be done to prepare a feast that just everyone has to work together. It has won friends for us, for the Church, and for Christ.[185]

As Berger suggested, though the kitchen was usually associated with women's work, it could also serve as the center for family activity, creativity, and spiritual development. Accordingly, many of her recipes suggested how children could be involved. For example, during the O Antiphon days, each family member took a turn at providing a dessert to surprise the others:

We begin with the smallest child. Her treat may be only a graham cracker for dessert. Freddie cracked and picked some black walnuts for us. All the pounding didn't give it away because little boys are so often pounding. Ann made some Advent wreath cookies and used up all the cinnamon drops for decoration—on the cookies, her face and her fingers. Mary made a big casserole of baked beans and we couldn't quite decide if she was treating herself or the family. Finally, it was mother's turn, and then, at last, father's turn to produce something really outstanding. At dessert time father rose from the table without a word, put on his hat and coat without a smile, and left us sitting at the table with our mouths open in amazement. After five minutes which seemed like hours, he stamped back into the house—with a big bowl of snow ice cream. The squeals of delight would have pleased an abbot.[186]

Such cooperation in private family meals and liturgical awareness complemented parallel moves toward families participating together in domestic prayer and, on the parish level, family communion.

Cooking for Christ offered a valuable resource for developing a liturgical life which specifically targeted the lives of women. As Berger asked in her introduction to the volume, if she had been given the vocation of mother—of cook—then why should not her work proclaim the glory of God:

---

[185] Florence Berger, "Liturgy in the Family," *Orate Fratres* 24, no. 3 (1950): 127.
[186] Berger, *Cooking for Christ*, 12.

If I am to create, and I believe God made me to do just that, why can't I create feast day specials from eggs and milk and butter? These are materials which I know. I once tried to paint a picture, but the colors ran and the perspective was poor. I tried to write music, but even the dog howled to hear it. I tried to weave a piece of cloth, but the warp broke and the woof tangled. So I have resolved to stick to my cooking and beat my way into heaven.[187]

A woman's work of creatively planning and preparing meals followed in the footsteps of ancient traditions. For example, the Jewish Passover was but one example of eating particular foods appropriate to the season, and the custom of associating certain foods with certain days continued with the spread of Christian feasts. With the "Protestant revolt," however, the feasts scattered and, in the present day with its secularist attitude, the faithful had only a remnant: a "drummed up," so-called Mother's Day and "silly little Easter bonnets to cover our silly little heads."[188] Berger's idea, then, was a restoration of Christian tradition with modern conveniences, making the liturgical year alive and accessible to a wider sector of the faithful.

Cooking for Christ, which went through numerous editions, was introduced at the NCRLC meeting November 7–9, 1949, at the Neil House in Columbus, Ohio. The exhibit was titled "The Liturgical Year in the Kitchen" and was arranged as a series of "sets," with twelve of the family's feast day tables replete with decorative settings and traditional foods for viewing.[189] The tables were themed for Advent,

[187] Berger, introduction to *Cooking for Christ*. Berger actually became an accomplished weaver, so her dismissal of her skill is probably rhetorical.

[188] Berger, introduction to *Cooking for Christ*. The language "against" Protestants is also, unfortunately, quite common amongst those active in the Roman Catholic liturgical movement and reveals either an obliviousness or disinterest in the initiative of numerous Protestant churches in liturgical renewal which were contemporary to them. See Jeremy O'Sullivan-Barra, "Protestantism and Economic Life," *Integrity* 1, no. 5 (1947): 11–25; and Peter Michaels, "Contemporary American Protestantism," *Integrity* 1, no. 5 (1947): 26–39. More accurate evaluations of the protestant churches' liturgical revival include, for example, Michael J. Taylor, *The Protestant Liturgical Renewal* (Westminster, MD: Newman Press, 1963); and John R. K. Fenwick and Brian D. Spinks, *Worship in Transition: Highlights of the Liturgical Movement* (Edinburgh: T. and T. Clark, 1995).

[189] Florence Berger to Mrs. D. Head, Executive Director of the Ohioana Library, October 14, 1949, Florence Berger File, Ohioana Library Association.

Christmas, Epiphany, and so on through the year, as Berger explained to a newspaper reporter:

> There will be an advent table deep in the preparation of plum pudding and Christmas cakes and cookies. An advent wreath, symbol of the four centuries of waiting for the Messiah, will burn overhead to mark the four long weeks of waiting before Christmas.
>
> The Christmas table itself will be a more formal one, for this is the birthday feast of our King. All of the best recipes now come out of the kitchen to give joy to our families and glory to God. The Christ candle at the table's center tells us that the Son of God is born and lives with us and in us on this day.[190]

As Berger described, "So we have taken the material things of field and flower and food to each liturgy. In a way they are little sacraments because they are signs of spiritual things, and, although they give no grace of themselves, yet they are arteries of the Christ-life for us."[191] She described the focus of the family life and the Church:

> Our dining room table with its daily bread is but a sign of the altar at church on which lies Christ's body, the food of our souls. When we bring our finest linens, silver and flowers to try to make that home table attractive, we too, are sacristans preparing holy things in our "Little Church."[192]

Such a production was prime material for inclusion in *Orate Fratres* and, at the same time as the NCRLC meeting, *Orate Fratres* included an article by Florence Berger in which she described the goal of the book and her presentation at the NCRLC, replete with sets. For *Orate Fratres* readers, she described her work as "a strange hybrid" that aimed to bring the liturgy closer to home as a "most informal study of liturgy."[193]

---

[190] "Writes Religious Cookbook," Florence Berger File, Ohioana Library Association.

[191] Ibid.

[192] Ibid.

[193] Florence Berger, "The Liturgical Year in the Kitchen," 550. *Orate Fratres* reviewed *Cooking for Christ* in January 1950: "The reviewer's competence in the field of creative cooking is strictly a minus quality. But he spent several hours on the evening of the book's arrival, devouring recipe after recipe (*in voto*), and absolutely fascinated by the running commentary of the text. The book is a feast for soul as well as stomach. (Lucky Mr. Berger and children!) Even most

Doing so, Berger noted, made theories about liturgical living practical and available to a wider audience.[194]

In her article for *Orate Fratres* in 1949, Berger summarized her involvement with the liturgical movement through the production of this cookbook as follows:

> Great leaders are men of vision who can point out a path of action with the surety of a prophet. Faithful followers may often be women who appreciate the revelation and set their feet upon the new way in trust and love. It sometimes takes years for the following in practice to catch up with the leadership, but women are notorious for bringing the stars down to earth and centering all ideas in themselves.[195]

Interestingly, Berger chose to divide "men of vision" from, it seems, "women of action." Though she seems to be belittling herself and other "followers," she also reflects a tension between theory and practice which continually plagued the liturgical movement. Liturgical pioneers had spoken, in theories, about how the liturgical life should permeate the home, but more practical measures were created by women.

Other liturgical pioneers resonated with Berger's emphasis on the importance of food and the liturgical life, including Mary Perkins Ryan. As Perkins Ryan had claimed, an indifference to food was the result of secularism. Christians should cultivate the same care toward food which compelled Jesus "in the glory of his risen life to prepare bread and cook fish for the hungry disciples after their night of fishing."[196] Cooking, like other aspects of work, should be embraced as an opportunity to mirror, in the family's little corner of God's creation, the Lord's skill and wisdom in making himself the Bread of Life.[197]

---

of the fast-day recipes sound attractive; if less so, there is always the good sauce of an interesting and edifying story. Without a doubt, this is, in a field all its own, a book of the year." "Cooking for Christ, Review," *Orate Fratres* 24, no. 2 (1950): 91.

[194] Berger, "The Liturgical Year in the Kitchen," 550.

[195] Ibid., 549.

[196] Ibid.

[197] "We are attending to the physical nourishment of members of the Mystical Body of Christ, children of God and heirs of heaven, who need to be able to find, in the food we set before them not only bodily food but an analogy, a reflection of that heavenly food which has in itself the 'sweetness of

Reception of Cooking for Christ

Cooking for Christ received much coverage, from Florence Berger's alumnae club to *Orate Fratres* to *Time* magazine, who reported on the success of the "blonde, fortyish" housewife of Cincinnati.[198] The address she had given at the annual NCRLC meeting appeared in *Orate Fratres'* "Apostolate" section in February 1950, where more readers could note her methods for living the liturgical life in the family. According to Berger, there were three chief methods which her family had found successful. The first was the importance of participating during Mass as a family group, not as a divided entity. Like many others, she found the divisions of fathers from mothers, children from parents, and children from each other as antithetical to living out the Mystical Body or trying to take on the identity of a "little church" as a family:

> We are annoyed by all diversions which divide us as a family group on Sunday at mass. If we want to sing the Mass, my husband has to climb to the choir on the first Sunday of the month. The girls and I can sing on the second Sunday; men and women on the third Sunday, while the children squirm downstairs. Often it isn't customary for families to even sit together at Mass. Children are arranged by age in closed classes and none of us learn to participate in the Mass together. I see no reason why we couldn't all sing the Mass together in the body of the church as families—except the insignificant cost of simple chant booklets for everyone, plus a few strenuous rehearsals. We could do it if we wanted to, and I for one think there are many lay people who do want it.[199]

---

every taste.' It was by no accident that Our Lord chose food and drink as the materials of the greatest of the Sacraments. We should, therefore, try to cure ourselves of that curious inhuman indifference to real food which is such a strange characteristic of many Americans, which is not the result of asceticism, but of secularism, of that separation of man's physical from his spiritual life which is now resulting in contempt for the physical, equally with a neglect of the spiritual. We should cultivate, rather, that loving attention to the needs and desires of our family, which caused Our Lord himself, in the glory of his risen life to prepare bread and cook fish for the hungry disciples after their night of fishing; should see our cooking as an opportunity to mirror, in this lower order, his skill and wisdom and love in making himself the Bread of life." Mary Perkins Ryan, "Liturgy and the Family Arts," *1946 Liturgical Week Proceedings*, 114–15.

[198] "Religion: Christ in the Kitchen," *Time* 54, no. 12 (September 19, 1949): 81.

[199] Florence Berger, "Liturgy in the Family," 124.

Berger saw all this division as organizing the family "to death" and felt it subsequently fueled the passivity with which many parents approached religious education.[200] Second, Berger described the benefits of family prayer—which her family drew from sources such as the *Short Breviary*. She noted that she and Alfred Berger had been amazed by the speed with which their two eldest girls memorized the psalms while she and her husband still had to keep their eyes on the page.[201] Finally, she spoke of the importance of the liturgical year, which helped her family to keep the liturgy active, in celebrating feasts at home. She noted to her audience that the record of their feasts was found in *Cooking for Christ*:

> As an introduction to the liturgy you may find it helpful. As a cookbook you will find it quite different. Some of the recipes you may not like—we did not like them all—but it was written for Christians and not for nationalists. Your neighbor may often desire what you decry. It is our hope that this true story will help "to bring all things to a head in Christ, both the things in the heavens and the things on the earth."[202]

Her note with regard to "nationalists" reflects the strong ethnic borrowings which characterized these resources. Yet, although recipes recalled Dutch, Greek, Finnish, French, and Italian heritages, among others, ethnicities beyond western and southern Europe were wholly neglected.

Though *Cooking for Christ* was very popular in the years immediately following its release, it is also a very early example from Florence Berger's thought regarding the liturgical life and, according to her daughter, Mary (Berger) Kelly, the work did not reflect her later

---

[200] Florence Berger echoed both Therese Mueller and Mary Perkins Ryan, noting, "Outside agencies have taken over the education, the recreation and now even the spiritual instruction of children so that mothers and fathers feel they are not needed. As a result, they have done less and less in these matters. When a mother is not needed, she no longer loves. When a father is not needed, he no longer cares. If you, as priests or sisters or mothers or fathers, have any influence in the arrangement of your Sunday Masses, I beg you to let us be together as families. Let us pray and participate in the Lord's sacrifice together." Florence Berger, "Liturgy in the Family," 125.

[201] Ibid., 126.

[202] Ibid., 127.

thought.[203] While *Cooking for Christ* was her only published volume, Berger submitted a number of pieces to *Orate Fratres* which appeared in its "Apostolate" section, reviewed books,[204] and composed a series of articles titled "In the Home" which appeared in the twenty-fifth volume of *Orate Fratres* (1950–51).

Florence Berger and the Experience of Liturgical Reforms

In their home parish and through the Diocese of Cincinnati, the Bergers were very active in promoting the liturgical movement in a variety of venues, especially after the liturgical reforms of the 1950s, such as the restored Holy Week, which were being implemented in parishes. In a letter to Godfrey Diekmann in December 1956, Florence Berger described some of these methods of the liturgical commission, of which she and her husband were members, utilized to keep both priests and laity "up-to-date" on liturgical reforms. One such source was the use of bulletins, which were sent directly from the archbishop and were given to the laity through means of the diocesan paper, covering issues such as the appreciation of the sacrament of baptism. A second method of instruction was a sermon series, in which priests and pastors could further the understanding of Holy Week and its relation to baptism. Suggestions were also made to lay Catholic Action groups, especially ones that attended to religious activities or family life. She related that these groups were especially helpful in promoting the feasts and seasons of the liturgical year. A third means the Bergers' liturgical commission used was the speakers bureaus of the Archdiocesan Council of Catholic Men and the Archdiocesan Council of Catholic Women; series of talks were prepared by these bureaus in order to encourage discussions at the parish level on topics such as liturgy, active participation, the dialogue Mass, and baptism.[205]

The Bergers' experience with their liturgical commission was somewhat extraordinary, as Diekmann informed them, and he encouraged

---

[203] Mary Kelly, personal correspondence with the author, March 7, 2011.

[204] Alfred and Florence Berger, Review of *The Family Book: A Book for Parents* by Rosemary Haughton, *Worship* 36, no. 4 (1962): 295–97; Review of *Your Life of Our Lord*, by Aidan Pickering, *Worship* 36, no. 4 (1962): 295–97; Review of *The Seven Sacraments: In Mime and Choral Speech*, by L. P. B. Stiven, *Worship* 36, no. 4 (1962): 295–97.

[205] Florence Berger to Godfrey Diekmann, December 9, 1956, The Godfrey Diekmann Papers 1013/6, SJAA.

the Bergers that advertising the example of Cincinnati in *Orate Fratres/ Worship*[206] would be helpful in goading other dioceses to establish active liturgical commissions:

> There are all too few liturgical commissions actually functioning in the States. The Archbishop [of Cincinnati] is a man of considerable stature to whom fellow bishops look up. Any report therefore, however brief, would prove of real value. Even if the report is no more than a good paragraph, I will be very grateful to you for it.[207]

In 1957, the Bergers' responsibilities increased even more, as Alfred was asked to be the National Chairman of Family Life of the National Council of Catholic Men.[208] Diekmann pointed out the importance of liturgical movement members being appointed to these posts, as they would thus be able to help influence these Catholic organizations to take the liturgy into account in defining the family: "Avenues are opening up which would have been unthinkable even a few years ago. May the Lord help us with His grace not to fail the family apostolate."[209] In the late 1950s, both Bergers were involved with the National Liturgical Weeks, and Florence served on the board of directors along with several other lay women.[210] As had Therese Mueller, the Bergers made efforts to connect the "liturgical life" to an interpretation of the psychological, sociological, and physical aspects of

[206] The twenty-fifth volume of *Orate Fratres* became *Worship*, reflecting shifting attitudes toward use of the vernacular. See Keith Pecklers, *The Unread Vision: The Liturgical Movement in the United States of America: 1926–1955* (Collegeville, MN: Liturgical Press, 1998), 163–64.

[207] Godfrey Diekmann to Florence Berger and Alfred Berger and Family, November 28, 1956, The Godfrey Diekmann Papers 1015/11, SJAA.

[208] "It will be a big job and one that will take every bit of spare time he can muster. We ask your prayers of the success of the work, because that success will be a spiritual one." Florence Berger to Godfrey Diekmann, September 12, 1957, The Godfrey Diekmann Papers 1013/6, SJAA.

[209] Godfrey Diekmann to Florence Berger, October 24, 1957, The Godfrey Diekmann Papers 1013/6, SJAA.

[210] Rev. John P. O'Connell to H. A. Reinhold, May 22, 1958, H. A. Reinhold Papers, MS2003-60 Series 1, 6/4, John J. Burns Library, Boston College. The Liturgical Week of 1958 included on its board of directors Miss Sarah Marquardt of Urbana, Illinois; Mrs. John Julian (Mary Perkins) Ryan of Goffstown, New Hampshire; Miss Mariette Wickes of Detroit, Michigan; and Mrs. Alfred (Florence) Berger of Cincinnati, Ohio.

Christian marriage. To this end, the Bergers planned the workshop for Family Life at the Liturgical Week in 1958.[211]

The Bergers' Introduction of Technology to the Liturgical Movement

The Bergers also forged the way for the liturgical movement in the field of technology, coordinating and providing the materials for a short-lived but booming "Tape-of-the-Month Club." In 1956, Alfred Berger, who had attended many Liturgical Week sessions and who had a history of tinkering with machinery, thought it would be valuable to record the speakers. Beginning with messy wire recorders which "spun around into messes that often made Christmas tree tangles look like child's play," he was grateful for the development of reel-to-reel tapes which could be spliced and patched "carefully with scotch tape."[212] The tapes were assembled in the Bergers' kitchen, with one master copy and ten copies produced of each talk. The "Tape-of-the-Month Club" was first advertised among members of the Liturgical Conference, 120 of whom wanted to use the tapes for two discussion groups a month which meant, Florence Berger calculated, that "240 more discussions on the liturgy [would be taking place] than there were before we began six weeks ago."[213] The work of assembling, cutting, and mailing the tapes was somewhat overwhelming for the family who had tape reels "for breakfast." Still, Florence Berger admitted to Diekmann, "But, Father, isn't it worth it? When I think of the colleges and seminaries and sister novitiates hearing these wonderful things and then discussing them, I wonder why in heaven's name we didn't get use out of them before. The lay people have answered too, and they are all so grateful."[214]

---

[211] Alfred Berger to Godfrey Diekmann, June 12, 1958, The Godfrey Diekmann Papers 1013/6, SJAA.

[212] Berger Frutkin, 18.

[213] Florence Berger to Godfrey Diekmann, March 11, 1959, The Godfrey Diekmann Papers 1013/6, SJAA.

[214] Ibid. When the Bergers were "swamped" with requests for the tapes after Godfrey Diekmann included the Berger "Tape of the Month" project in the Liturgical Briefs, Diekmann offered a tongue-in-cheek apology: "I apologize if this action was precipitous and swamps you with requests so numerous that you cannot fill them. Perhaps you will have to expand your staff? Or simply resign as mother of your family." Godfrey Diekmann to Florence Berger, March 18, 1959, The Godfrey Diekmann Papers 1013/6, SJAA.

An interesting array of people from across the United States made use of the tapes done by the Bergers. The monks of Blue Cloud Abbey of Marvin, South Dakota, used the tapes for discussion and found "greater appreciation of 'the Work of God' because of them." Sr. Mary Teresa, SSND, of Roxbury, Massachusetts, was a teacher and guidance director who moderated a Young Catholic Students Group which used the tapes and later made the tapes available to faculty members. Sisters and high school girls of St. Margaret's Academy, in Minneapolis, Minnesota, used the tapes to prepare for discussion; and Sister Clarissima, OSF, served as the distributor of the "Tape-of-the-Month Club" in the states of Arkansas and Missouri. A musician and choir director in her community, she used the tapes to teach the aspirants.[215]

In addition to thirty years of work in the NCRLC, national Catholic women's and men's associations, and the liturgical movement, the Bergers also traveled widely, both domestically and internationally, and continued to renovate their nineteenth-century farmhouse and experiment with various forms of farming. As the Bergers approached their seventies, Florence wanted to move to a warmer climate, and the Bergers chose Hilton Head, South Carolina, making summer trips to Cincinnati. Today, the family website simply says, with regard to the liturgical movement, "Alfred and Florence had a great passion for Church and international students."[216] Florence Berger died in Hilton Head, South Carolina, on April 13, 1983, and Alfred, who continued to split his time between Ohio and South Carolina, died in Cincinnati in 1994.

PROMOTING THE LITURGICAL FAMILY LIFE

A Truly Popular Liturgical Movement

Mueller, Perkins Ryan, and Berger are three representatives of a larger constellation of women who were working on family life and its intersection with the liturgy in the late 1940s into the 1950s. Their work characterizes a growing concern among liturgical pioneers to make the liturgical movement more accessible and practical, less abstract, and truly popular, that is, a movement of the people. For example, Diekmann's inviting Therese Mueller and Mary Perkins Ryan (though Perkins Ryan's was never actually rendered) to produce truly "popular"

---

[215] "Posterboard," Alfred Berger Collection 1, John J. Burns Library, Boston College.

[216] Fred Berger, "Alfred Joseph Berger," http://bergerhill.info/BG_Alfred .html.

books for the Popular Liturgical Library encouraged the collection to move in a new direction, and a series of pamphlets produced by other women in the 1950s discussed family customs for the liturgical year. One of these was Helen McLoughlin, who compiled *Family Advent Customs* (1953), in which she acknowledged Florence Berger and the NCRLC for using recipes from *Cooking for Christ*. McLoughlin believed that simple blessings in which the family could participate were important media for introducing union between altar and home.[217] She suggested that it was best to begin with one or two customs, gradually adding as years passed, and stressed the importance of families developing their own customs to suit their personal circumstances. One project which she described was the Advent wreath:

> When our children were small we bought a large, permanently-preserved pine wreath and used it year after year. Now that they are going to school they help to make a new one each Advent. Inexpensive and easy to assemble is the wreath we make from a bunch or two of laurel leaves bound to a circle of wire from coat hangers. The evergreens are secured by fine wire to the circle. Candles and ribbons are added as the wreath is put together. Laurel is practical because it does not shed when suspended over the dining room table. Moreover, laurel is a symbol of victory, and thus reminds us that Christ's coming means victory over sin and death. Loveliest of wreaths and fragrant, too, is one of fresh princess pine. When we use that type, we hang it in the living room and add a single silver star to it each evening in Advent when the candles are lighted for prayers. Stars are cut from metallic paper. City dwellers may make an attractive wreath of fireproof green paper, while country folks will find a metal barrel hoop ideal as a frame for whatever evergreens are at hand. In our children's classrooms in Corpus Christi School, New York City, Advent greens are sometimes kept fresh in inexpensive plastic rings.[218]

Other instructions detailed "Gifts for Jesus," an "Advent House" calendar, and an Advent home liturgy to accompany the blessing of the aforementioned Advent wreath. In concert with the move to conserve resources, McLoughlin included instructions as to how to transform

---

[217] Helen McLoughlin, *Family Advent Customs*, Popular Liturgical Library (Collegeville: Liturgical Press, 1953), 4, Liturgy and Life Collection, Special Collections, Boston College.
   [218] Ibid., 5.

the Advent wreath for use at Christmastide; the wreath, unless it began to shed, should be kept until Epiphany.[219] Another resource by McLoughlin, *My Nameday*, sought to establish the child's saint namesake as the primary feast (as opposed to the birthday). The book had hymns, music, special prayers, feast day gifts, and, helpfully, names and addresses of places where one could order cake molds, shaped cookie cutters, gummed decorations, and the like to perfect such a feast day.[220]

The resources produced by Grailville were also touted as excellent resources for living a Christian family apostolate. As Vincent S. Waters, bishop of Raleigh, North Carolina, and president of the National Liturgical Conference, wrote in the foreword to Grailville's *The Paschal Meal: An Arrangement of the Last Supper as an Historical Drama*:

> As the liturgical movement in America matures, there is a growing interest among the laity in living more closely with the Church and carrying over the spirit of her feasts and seasons from the sanctuary into the home, the school, and other spheres of daily life. Recent years have seen an encouraging increase in popular books and pamphlets on Christian family customs, ceremonies, practices and celebrations, which while not part of the official prayer of the Church, nevertheless reflect the spirit of her liturgy and serve to strengthen the bonds between altar and home.[221]

As evidenced both in young women witnesses to *Orate Fratres* recalling the importance of their Grailville experiences, as well as leaders such as Florence Berger, who were strongly influenced by the work of Grailville, the Grail's role in advancing the liturgical movement in the home was far-reaching.

---

[219] Ibid., 7. Other sources include Zella Boutell, *The Christmas Cook Book* (NY: The Viking Press, 1953), and Virginia Pasley, *The Christmas Cookie Book* (Boston, MA: Little, Brown, 1949).

[220] Other pamphlets written by Helen McLoughlin and published by the Liturgical Press's Popular Liturgical Library Series were: *Easter to Pentecost Family Customs* (Collegeville, MN: Liturgical Press, 1956); *My Nameday—Come for Dessert* (Collegeville, MN: Liturgical Press, 1962); and *Christmas to Candlemas in a Catholic Home*, 2nd rev. ed. (Collegeville, MN: Liturgical Press, 1979).

[221] Vincent S. Waters, foreword to *The Paschal Meal: An Arrangement of the Last Supper as an Historical Drama*, by Grailville Community College, Loveland, Ohio (St. Paul, MN: North Central, 1956), 5.

The Broader Constellation of Pioneers: Mary Reed Newland

Aside from the Popular Liturgical Library and other such resources, another figure who should be included in a review of important lay-women pioneers is Mary Reed Newland (1917–89) of Monson, Massachusetts. Mary Reed Newland also wrote popular works for use, one of the most comprehensive being *The Year and Our Children*.[222] More detailed than Berger's *Cooking for Christ*, the book elaborated more in its descriptions of feast days, along with suggestions for activities and anecdotes of how Newland's family chose to commemorate the days. For example, Newland, in writing about the "Summer Saints," described how feast day dinners in her family began with singing "Happy Feast Day to You" to the tune of the birthday song. She admitted, "While not liturgical, it is a custom of long standing and comes from the heart."[223] One of these summer feasts was devoted to remembering the apostles, a number of whom had summer feast days. How did one celebrate the apostles? With gingerbread men:

> Any good gingerbread biscuit dough will do, and any good ginger-bread-boy biscuit cutter will make a gingerbread Apostle (or you may cut them freehand with a knife). The twist is the decoration. We decorated each one with his own symbols, tied a ribbon through a hole pierced (before baking) in the top of each biscuit, served them on a tray, covered, with only the ribbons showing; you got your dessert by choosing a ribbon, finding the biscuit, and identifying it. This is an excellent way to learn all the Apostles. The combination of head and stomach is hard to beat.[224]

---

[222] Mary Reed Newland's other writings include: *We and Our Children: Molding the Child in Christian Living* (New York: P. J. Kenedy, 1954); *The Family and the Bible* (New York: Random House, 1963); *Our Children Grow Up* (New York: P. J. Kenedy, 1965); *Religion in the Home: A Parent's Guide to the Our Life with God Series*, Grade 1 (New York: W. H. Sadler, 1967); *Youth: What Happened?* (Notre Dame, IN: Ave Maria Press, 1970); *The Resource Guide for Adult Religious Education*, (Kansas City, MO: National Catholic Reporter, 1974); and *The Saint Book: For Parents, Teachers, Homilists, Storytellers, and Children* (New York: Seabury Press, 1979), Liturgy and Life Collection, Special Collections, Boston College.

[223] Mary Reed Newland, "Summer Saints and Some Are Not," in *The Year and Our Children, Planning the Family Activities for Christian Feasts and Seasons* (New York: Longmans, Green, 1956), 228–29.

[224] Ibid.

Newland admitted that training in the liturgical life could be limited to feasts of the liturgical year, which generally lent themselves to imaginative creations with which mothers could plan to occupy and subtly teach their children. But reflection on wider family practices could also be oriented to refining a life in Christ. For example, in her section on Lent in *The Year and Our Children*, Newland spoke of the discipline of silence, reflecting on Jesus' silence when he was condemned to death, tormented by soldiers, or fell under the weight of the cross. She related silence to a "commonplace of childhood": bickering. She wrote that bickering was:

> [A] verbal form of cannibalism. The one who holds out longer with his pecking at another is victor, having reduced the victim to tears, goaded him to losing his temper, striking, or some other form of retaliation. . . . There is no real remedy for this but silence on the part of victims. Abstinence from it on the part of attackers is the perfect solution, of course, but if someone does start, silence will stop him. This however, is awfully hard on the one who is silent.[225]

Newland maintained that if Christian parents taught children that whatever one does to a brother or sister was done to Christ, thus to provoke a brother or sister was to provoke Christ, children might see (and so might adults) that to be silent under provocation was to be silent with Christ. Newland concluded that this practice was not quite impossible but might take a lifetime to achieve. She also encouraged that, if parents were spectators to such a moral victory, they must be sure to congratulate the hero:

> Darling, I heard ——— today when he called you a pig and tried to make you angry. It was wonderful, the way you didn't answer back and only walked away. You used silence the way Our Lord used it, the way He wants you to use it. When you are silent in union with Him you are growing in the likeness of Christ.[226]

Other holidays, Newland mentioned, had been abused and mixed with all sorts of vandalism, even if they were connected to the liturgy. For example, she gave a quick summary of the history of All Hallow's

[225] Mary Reed Newland, "Ash Wednesday and Lent," in *The Year and Our Children*, 151.
[226] Ibid.

Eve and spoke of traditions involving food, prayers, and hopes for loved ones who had passed in contrast to the confusion of pagan ideas, where Halloween was beset with goblins, witches, and the like.[227] Throughout this resource, Newland offered helpful historical explanations of feast days and prayers and details about the saints which were likely to catch the attention of children.[228]

Men, Family Life, and the Liturgical Movement

Of course, it is also important to realize that women were not the only ones interested in the liturgical life in the home, and liturgical pioneers who were men also contributed to this realm. H. A. Reinhold and Martin B. Hellriegel, for example, both wrote rather substantial amounts of literature or composed "home liturgies" for use by families,[229] and Virgil Michel frequented the subject of women and liturgy numerous times in his prolific output of theological and

---

[227] In Reed Newland's Halloween section, she noted how children, who showed up on the Newlands' lawn on Halloween night, were beset by a witch who cackled and demanded that the children pray for the dead so that their souls would be released from torment. "I am forced to tell ye this, miserable dearies, whether I would or no; so mark it well. If ye pray for the dead, they are released sooner from their torment of waiting in Purgatory and speed on the wings of light to their eternal reward. So go and knock and the woman will open to your knock, and sing as loud as ye can. . . ." The children apparently responded, praying for grandfathers, grandmothers, aunts, and uncles, etc., and Catholic and non-Catholics alike said the one prayer they shared in common: the Our Father.

[228] In teaching about St. John the Baptist, Reed Newland reported how she talked with children about "Isaias," who, "in addition to discovering how and what he prophesied, we looked for some autobiographical facts about him. He came to a violent end, we discovered, sawed in half by his son-in-law, Manasses. 'Sawed in half,' said one. 'Heavens! Which way?' This is a minor detail alongside his prophecies, I agree, but the children consider it one of the more interesting facts they have picked up about saints and martyrs." Mary Reed Newland, "Summer Saints and Some are Not," in *The Year and Our Children: Planning the Family Activities for the Church Year*, 2nd ed. (Garden City, NY: Image Books, 1964), 228–29.

[229] For example, see Martin B. Hellriegel, "Family Life, the Liturgical Year, and the Sacramentals," *1946 Liturgical Week Proceedings* (Highland Park, IL: The Liturgical Conference): 103–5; and Martin B. Hellriegel, "Seasonal Suggestions," *Worship* 30, no. 6 (1955): 374–90.

philosophical texts.[230] Perhaps more significantly, however, were lay men who were fathers and husbands. Men were frequently very much involved in promoting the liturgical life in the family, along with their wives. Buoyed by experience in the Catholic Family Movement, a number of "husband-wife" teams were invited to describe their experience of living the lay apostolate—examples of these can be found in *Orate Fratres/Worship*, in the National Liturgical Week *Proceedings*, and in other journals such as *Integrity*.[231] Additionally, all three of the "main characters" discussed in this chapter married men who were active, interested, and involved in the liturgical movement: Franz Mueller, John Ryan, and Alfred Berger, coexisted with numerous other lay men, such as James Shea (of Loveland, Ohio, who attended and presented at Liturgical Week conferences), Patrick Crowley (cofounder of the Christian Family Movement with Patricia Crowley), and Willis Nutting (professor of history at the University of Notre Dame, participant in Liturgical Weeks, and writer for *Orate Fratres*).

Other Lay Women Supporting the Liturgical Movement

Perhaps primarily, lay women supported the liturgical movement by picking up resources designed for their use and implementing them in their home. Women (and men) who sincerely sought to teach their children about full participation in the liturgy and the liturgical life made use of a plethora of liturgically minded methods, picking and choosing customs which suited them best. For example, Mary E. Lydon McGann

---

[230] See Pecklers, 131. See, for example, Virgil Michel, "The Liturgy and Catholic Women," 270.

[231] For example, see Emerson and Arleen Hynes, "Holy Week in the Home," *Orate Fratres* 30, no. 4 (1955): 257–66; Ernst and Johanna Winter, "Lent in the Home," *Orate Fratres* 31, no. 3 (56): 178–87; and John and Katherine Mella, "Holiness and Hospitality," *Integrity* 6, no. 9 (1951): 40–43; Discussion amongst four panelists, husband and wife Mr. and Mrs. John Julian and Mary Perkins Ryan of Cambridge, Massachusetts, and Mr. and Mrs. Emerson and Arleen Hynes of Collegeville, Minnesota, "Liturgy and Life," *1946 Liturgical Week Proceedings* (Highland Park, IL: The Liturgical Conference): 122–27; and round-table discussion with Mr. and Mrs. John Julian and Mary Perkins Ryan of Cambridge, Massachusetts, and Mr. and Mrs. James Shea of Loveland, Ohio, "In the Home," *1948 Liturgical Week Proceedings* (Conception, MO: The Liturgical Conference, 1949): 61–66. Ed Willock, founder of *Integrity* magazine and father of eight children, also reflected on the man's view of homemaking. See Ed Willock, "The Father in the Home," *Integrity* 6, no. 9 (1951): 9–15.

(1913–2004) drew upon liturgical cookbooks to develop family rituals and feasts for the year. For the First Sunday in Advent, she made "stir-up pudding," to echo the Advent introit, "Stir up your power and come"; for St. Nicholas's day, she made a "bishop's punch" (according to Florence Berger's recipe), while her husband, Harold, dressed up as St. Nick; during Holy Week, the Easter Vigil began with a festive breakfast, with braided "stollen" bread. Drawing more deeply on her talents, Mary McGann often paired such feasting with special songs which she, herself a graduate of the Pius X School of Music, accompanied on the family piano. Expanding the liturgical life to commemoration of the sacraments, McGann also designed baptismal robes for each new child in her family, which she subsequently embroidered with symbols for each sacrament the child received (as Therese Mueller had suggested). The McGann family, which included eleven children, also prayed together, praying Compline on Sunday evenings, using the English version in the *Pius X Hymnal*.[232] Such interaction inspired both leadership, especially on the part of older children who helped to organize family activities, and a deep appreciation among the family members of how ritual and symbol served to bring Christ near.[233]

Certainly, examples such as McGann reflect the broadening realization of how the family might together partake in liturgical activities and, more particularly, who should take charge of children's religious instruction. On the one hand, many religious sisters had an immense interest in promoting the liturgical movement in their classrooms, evidenced by the high number of sisters who attended Liturgical Weeks and prepared catechetical materials.[234] But reformers such as Therese

---

[232] The *Pius X Hymnal* (Boston: McLaughlin & Reilly) was compiled by the faculty of the St. Pius X School of Liturgical Music; an edition for unison or mixed voices was produced in 1953 and a congregational version in 1956.

[233] Interview with Mary E. McGann, RSCJ, January 9, 2010; and personal correspondence with Mary E. McGann, August 2012. Mary E. McGann's mother, Mary E. Lydon McGann, was deeply impressed with the liturgical movement in multiple venues (including music, the Cana Movement, Grailville, the Catholic Family Movement, and the NCRLC) and its resources, with a "liturgical library" full of literature from the liturgical movement. The family moved several times but was living in Syracuse, New York, from 1955 onward, when the fullest extent of the family celebrations were realized in the home.

[234] For example, a series of articles by Sr. Esther, SP, described taking the liturgy home throughout the liturgical year, providing pictures, illustrations,

Mueller had warned of the dangers of sequestering children's education to the school alone. At the same time, the field of Catholic education itself was changing. By mid-century, American lay women had increasingly entered the field of education. Yet those who hoped to serve in Catholic schools and potentially teach children to love the liturgy, found it frustrating to enter a system which was overwhelmingly run by religious who did not need the same pay that a lay teacher would, with no need for housing, transportation, clothing, and food. As Frances McMahon, a student at Loretto Heights College in Denver, Colorado, pointed out during the session on "The Family and Religious Families" during the Liturgical Week of 1946, she appreciated the atmosphere of Catholic schools and wanted to teach in them with a Catholic point of view, but she found it unsustainable:

> Is there any way this situation could possibly be cleared up so that the lay teachers could be paid a decent salary, and more girls from the Catholic colleges could teach in Catholic schools? I would be more than happy to teach in the Catholic Schools.[235]

---

and anecdotes intended to be useful to parents of school children; the series appeared in five parts in volume twenty-two of *Orate Fratres*, over 1946–1947, all under the title, "Bringing Liturgy to Life in Home and School." Other examples include Sr. Marie Imelda, OP, "The Kindergarten Child and the Liturgy," *The Catholic Educator* 13, no. 9 (1942–43): 351–56; Andrea Rodgers, "Making the Liturgy Live," *The Catholic Educator* 16, no. 9 (1945–46): 822–27; and A Sister of St. Joseph, "The Priesthood of Christ as Embodied in the Liturgy," *Catholic Educational Review* 46 (1948): 595–600.

[235] In a discussion following Rev. Charles Schmitt, "The Family and Religious Families," Frances McMahon, student at Loretto Heights College, recounted: "I would like to speak from the standpoint of a future lay teacher. I am doing my practice teaching this year in a public high school, and I do not like it. I also attended a Catholic school, and I like the atmosphere. If I am to teach I would want to teach in a Catholic school. For example, in teaching Geoffrey Chaucer, you can see the problems that would present themselves when you come to the little footnotes in the book that slam the monks of that time, and you are unable to defend it from a Catholic's point of view. Lay teachers do have to make a living, and as you know, the Catholic schools do not pay enough. Since the public schools pay more, we naturally go to the public schools to do our teaching." Frances McMahon, "Discussion," *1946 Liturgical Week Proceedings* (Highland Park, IL: The Liturgical Conference, 1947): 148–49.

Yet again, a lay woman raised a practical problem to question the ideal hopes of the liturgical movement.

Finally, not only did women advance the conversation regarding liturgy and religious instruction, but lay women also simply supported the liturgical movement through prayer and monetary contributions. One such contributor was Suzanne Jobert of New York City, who asked Diekmann to use her donations to fund gift subscriptions of both nationally and internationally in mission territories.[236] Diekmann later reported that Jobert's gift helped supply free subscriptions to bishops, which was one of the strategies liturgical movement advocates used to change the bishops' minds to a more favorable view:

> Even if they do not find the time to read the magazine, merely looking at the table of contents with its list of rather outstanding authors and its substantial themes, often suffices to convince them that the liturgy is not merely a matter of ceremonial externals. And unless the bishops are favorable, any liturgical apostolate on lower levels cannot really succeed.[237]

Directly and indirectly, then, American lay women advanced the boundaries of the liturgical movement.

CONCLUSION

The Close of the Movement

Reviewing the work of women liturgical pioneers during the Second World War and post–Second World War period reveals the unfolding breadth and depth of the liturgical movement as it became increasingly networked with interests of Catholic Action movements, the National Catholic Rural Life Movement, attention to the Christian family,

---

[236] Suzanne Jobert to Godfrey Diekmann, January 2, 1956, The Godfrey Diekmann Papers 1016/14, SJAA. She enclosed a check for two hundred dollars, a rather hefty sum for 1956.

[237] Godfrey Diekmann to Suzanne Jobert, January 19, 1956, The Godfrey Diekmann Papers 1016/13, SJAA. Jobert continued to send monetary gifts, writing checks regularly to Godfrey Diekmann. In 1960, he wrote: "Quite a number of others in 1959 wrote to express their thanks. In every case I tell them that the gift is possible because of the generosity of a kind laywoman, and that they should keep her in their prayers. So you are gradually acquiring a spiritual family!" Godfrey Diekmann to Suzanne Jobert, February 15, 1960, The Godfrey Diekmann Papers 1016/13, SJAA.

and catechesis, among others. Evaluating the work of women in the context of these more diverse movements adds a new dimension to the study of liturgical reform. On the one hand, the most universally recognizable liturgical changes in the late 1950s came with the reform of the Easter Vigil and Holy Week at the instruction of Pius XII. Yet the liturgical movement's denouement was never meant to be the crafting of rites, in which lay women would have had little input. The liturgical movement sought the transformation of life, to realize the call of all the faithful to strive to better be the Mystical Body. Many of those lay Roman Catholics interested in liturgical reform did take personal ownership over their family's involvement in liturgical worship, liturgical prayer, and marking the liturgical year within their homes. With this alternative vision in mind, the following concluding chapter considers some of the issues concerning the effectiveness of women's involvement and the difficulties which women encountered who were involved with and interested in the liturgical movement, and it offers some trajectories for the future of the wider work of discovering American lay women in the liturgical-historical landscape.

Lay Women and the Future
of the Liturgical Apostolate

DID GENDER PLAY A ROLE?

Viewing the sources and resources for the liturgical movement with an attentiveness to women's presence puts into startling relief the breadth of their involvement, their creativity, and their shaping of the central concerns of the liturgical movement. Lay women were present in all the contours of the liturgical movement, from promoting and practicing strategies for increased participation and intellectual engagement in the liturgy, to crafting improved aesthetics for mediating liturgical experiences and devotions, to realizing the social implications of the liturgy in both the public and private spheres. Thus far, an evaluation of these sources leads one to conclude that gender, or these women's "womanhood," played an inconsistent role in their approach to liturgical reform. In some cases, the increasingly socially acceptable occupations of women, such as social work, enabled women to apply their knowledge from one field to another, such as Ellen Gates Starr's application of her knowledge as a social worker to her understanding of the Christian churches' role in social reform. Some women, like Maisie Ward, found it difficult to pursue the same academic training as their male peers but were able to assume leadership roles in venues more acceptable to women, such as the Catholic Evidence Guild, which prepared her for involvement in the liturgical movement. On the other hand, some women, such as artist Ade Bethune, betrayed little of how their role as women affected their involvement in the liturgical movement. On the other extreme, the national Catholic women's organizations (for example, the National Council of Catholic Women [NCCW]), the American Grail Movement, and the increased attention on Catholic women's role in sustaining family life in the 1940s and 1950s very explicitly made reference to women's unique contributions in advocating for liturgical renewal.

To some extent, concluding that gender plays little or an insignificant role supports one of the goals of this history, which is to present a story of the liturgical movement which reveals how women were fully active, present, and contributing to the liturgical movement along with their male peers. Women should not be an additional note or appendix to the history of the American liturgical movement but should be fully incorporated into a telling of its history. Developing the landscape of the liturgical movement with witnesses from lay women renders a more robust and accurate picture of the liturgical movement, its goals, and its challenges.

In some cases, however, paying particular attention to the role of gender uncovers important tensions in the history of the American liturgical movement. One valuable resource for evaluating the role of gender in liturgical renewal comes in the *Proceedings* of the National Liturgical Weeks. At times semi-informal and spontaneous, presenters also occasionally posed specific challenges to the women who were in attendance. During the National Liturgical Week of 1946, the active chairman leading the discussion following a paper titled "Marriage as a Sacrament" attempted to rally the organizational and communal charisms of modern Catholic women:

> You belong to bridge organizations; you belong to study clubs, book clubs, library organizations. You could take an interest in some of the discussions by your communities under the auspices of the women's clubs or the Red Cross and various other organizations, particularly talks on married life and the bringing up of children. There is a big field today for the Catholic woman in watching what is going on in the community, challenging very clever speakers who are eating at the vitals of married life and who are teaching birth control. It is an obligation incumbent upon the conscientious Catholic woman to take part in those things and challenge these speakers; and she can only do it when she has the proper information. That is the information we are trying to impart tonight in this session and through the work of the Liturgical Conference in the proceedings of the various Weeks that have been held throughout the nation.[1]

Because of their particular status as Catholic women, lay women who were active in the world were clearly expected to have some significant amount of influence in affecting liturgical change. This coincided with the self-perception that women in national Catholic women's organizations usually carried, such as the women in the NCCW, that women were

---

[1] "Discussion," *1946 Liturgical Week Proceedings* (Elsberry, MO: The Liturgical Conference): 59.

charged in a special way to promote Catholic life. While this example affirms women's volition, other comments in the very same session in 1946, however, somewhat goaded the women who were present with sarcasm: "Come on, girls, step up now. Here is your chance." While the ladies paused, not a woman but one of the men stood up in the crowd. The discussion leader exclaimed, "Here is a man [who will say something in discussion]. Thank God we have a man in the crowd."[2]

Surely, comments such as this reflect the collegiality of the discussions following the presentations during Liturgical Weeks. But they also belie some underlying strains within discussions of liturgical renewal. First, a recurring concern for venues such as the National Liturgical Weeks was their accessibility for lay people or "amateurs." While lay women were, at times, appealed to to engage in discussions, even those who were well-read in liturgical matters found it difficult to respond on command.[3] Other women, even one as well-known as Florence Berger, found it difficult to be taken seriously by male peers. As Florence Berger's daughter, Ann, recalled:

> With *Cooking for Christ*'s publication, Florence became an oddity—an educated, creative laywoman with a voice in church activities. I remember her saying in frustration, that if she wanted to say anything that those priests would listen to, she had to tell Alfred to say it for her. He always would as best he could.[4]

Likewise, while lay women in Liturgical Week audiences listened to the ideas and ideals of liturgical renewal, their questions often focused

---

[2] Ibid., 58.

[3] Fr. William J. Leonard, SJ, wrote to fellow member of the Liturgical Conference Committee, the Most Rev. William T. Mulloy, in September 1953, regarding the lack of subscribers to *Worship* (just over five thousand) and the approximate membership of two hundred attendees for the Liturgical Conference. Leonard wrote, "We go into a diocese like Grand Rapids, where there has been good advance preparation, and where five to seven hundred people—priests, sisters, and laity—turn out for our program. Then we proceed to perplex and bore them by reading at them lengthy, learned papers, which they are totally unprepared to assimilate." William J. Leonard to William Mulloy, September 1953, The Reynold Hillenbrand Papers 28/25, University of Notre Dame Archives [hereafter cited as UNDA].

[4] Ann Berger Frutkin, *Florence and Al Berger: A Collaborative Memory of a Cincinnati Family* (Hilton Head Island, SC: Studiobooks, 2009), 18.

on the practical application of such ideals. For example, following H. A. Reinhold's "The Family and the Eucharist," Miss Jean Crew asked, "I would like to ask why family communion has never been preached, or why isn't a day set aside for it every month?"[5] It seemed obvious to Crew that, in order to encourage family Communion, Catholics should hear about it in the context of their weekly worship. For similar reasons, when Ellen Gates Starr wrote about the breviary, she explicitly wrote "from the perspective of a lay woman," thus suggesting that her approach to the breviary would be *different* as a lay person and would address questions about its use and meaning which lay people would have.

Just as women were impressed with the possibilities afforded by knowledge of the liturgical movement, women also witnessed to the difficulties presented by attempting to enact its ideals. For example, following Martin Hellriegel's "Family Life, the Liturgical Year, and the Sacramentals," Mrs. Newberg of Colorado gave the following testimony:

> I grew up in the same surroundings as you did, Monsignor. When I came over to this country with my children, we started naturally the same training that I had received in the house of my parents; but, I must say, it isn't so easy to keep true.
>
> For instance, we celebrated the saints' days and the family given names of the children. But now already, after eight years, we started to drop that, and to celebrate birthdays because of the surroundings. Because the customs around us are so different and they have so impressed the children, they don't like our ways any more. They want to celebrate the same way as the surrounding children.
>
> So I fight for this old way I have been trained in, and the children had the same foundation, but it is very hard to swim against the stream.[6]

Newberg spoke to a real tension for mid-century American Catholics, especially those who had memories of the "old country": young American Catholics sought to blend in as Americans, not be readily identified as tied to old, backward, or embarrassing customs, even if such customs were attempts at living a more authentically Christian life.

---

[5] "Discussion," *1946 Liturgical Week Proceedings* (Elsberry, MO: The Liturgical Conference, 1947): 70.

[6] "Discussion," *1946 Liturgical Week Proceedings* (Elsberry, MO: The Liturgical Conference, 1947): 105.

Indeed, idealistic scenarios in which a radical liturgical life might be lived were appealing, but laywomen liturgical advocates afforded other liturgical pioneers glimpses of its difficulties. For example, Mrs. Charles Perkins of Boston, Massachusetts, related a story during the National Liturgical Week in 1946, during the "Marriage as a Sacrament" speech by Austin Staley, OSB, in which enacting the Christian way of life did not work as well as one might have hoped:

> When I came back from the last meeting in New Orleans to the City of Boston, I thought it would be a good idea to manifest the idea I was a Christian by reverting to the old form of "Goodbye" which is "God be with you." When I was leaving a friend, I said, "God be with you," instead of "Good-bye." Seeing astonishment on her face, I said, "What is the effect on you when I say that? It is the old form of something you say every day." And the person, who was a good average type, said, "Well, the impression on me is that you are very affected."[7]

Lay women such as Mrs. Perkins had on-the-ground experiences which other liturgical pioneers did not.

In other cases, lay women asked questions regarding family life and the liturgy and did not receive satisfactory answers. For example, in the discussion following the presentation of Rev. Fred Mann, CSSR, at the Liturgical Week in 1947, Miss Jean Gray asked:

> I would like to know how you connect the liturgy with the question of mixed marriages. Everybody here knows that mixed marriages are frowned upon by the Church, but they do exist and create a problem. In a lot of vicinities in the United States non-Catholic fellows far outnumber the Catholic fellows.[8]

Mann responded by relating that, in his experience, children who were taught about the Catholic faith did not end up in mixed marriages, citing a statistic of children he had known between 1932 and 1942, with only two of 103 in mixed marriages. Gray responded:

> That is very good, but that doesn't always happen, does it? We are not all in schools where that is taught. It is a pity, but it is true. Therefore,

[7] "Discussion," *1946 Liturgical Week Proceedings* (Elsberry, MO: The Liturgical Conference, 1947): 58.

[8] "Discussion," *1946 Liturgical Week Proceedings* (Elsberry, MO: The Liturgical Conference, 1947): 169.

how do you suggest we handle that when there are only non-Catholic fellows. It is pretty natural to date them, and marriage follows pretty soon. I know there must be some answer somewhere.[9]

In response, Mann assured her:

[T]he mind is made for truth, and if it is presented tactfully—and the girls can usually do that—and carefully and if along with it there is prayer and sacrifice, the Catholic party may exercise a tremendous influence with the non-Catholic that could be God's providential way of bringing the non-Catholic into the complete truth.[10]

Miss Gray simply responded, "That is very fine, Father. Thank you."[11] The conversation had ended.

In Gray's exchange with Fr. Mann, there was no actual discussion of reality—which was the number of mixed marriages—and how mixed marriages could attend to any liturgical life or perhaps some ecumenical common ground in which liturgical understanding could be engaged. Rather, the theoretical was stressed, noting the "mind" which was made for truth and the "tremendous influence" women might impress upon their husbands. Hope of persuasion did not satisfy Miss Gray when she hoped for practical answers.

Interestingly, another woman, Barbara Dells of Sunnyside, Washington, who was actually married to a non-Catholic and happened to be a parishioner of H. A. Reinhold's, was able to identify a way in which the liturgical movement intersected with the social issue of mixed marriages. She wrote to Reinhold that, as a woman in a "mixed marriage," she found the efforts of liturgical renewal to be a powerful force in affecting her family life. She was dismayed when she learned Reinhold would be leaving her parish in Sunnyside:

This is the only parish in which I've ever participated in a dialog Mass—and the Mass has come to mean so much more to me in these past two months—and it seems that I have come to understand the Mass *so* much better and to feel so much more a part of the Mass. My husband is not a Catholic and naturally I have hopes that someday, not this year, or next, or maybe even several years, but someday I hope that he will join the Church. And I have felt and still feel that with a

---

[9] Ibid.
[10] Ibid.
[11] Ibid.

dialog Mass it will be easier for him to understand what's going on. So you see, I feel that if we were not to continue to have a dialog Mass it will be a personal blow to my hopes.[12]

While a lecturer on Christian marriage was unable to describe how the efforts of liturgical renewal might be connected to the issue of "mixed marriages," a lay woman simply noted how she felt the accessibility and comprehensibility of practices such as the dialogue Mass might be helpful in exposing her "non-Catholic" husband to the Catholic faith.

LEARNING TO LOVE THE LITURGY

Though fully evaluating the role of gender in the liturgical movement certainly warrants further study, one can conclude that examining the activity and participation of lay, non-religious women in the liturgical movement serves as a valuable resource in identifying the challenges of the liturgical movement and its potential for transforming the lives of American Catholics. Lay women could often readily identify potential pitfalls that the liturgical movement would have to overcome in order to be successful, including the social challenges confronting twentieth-century American Catholics, who had inherited a Church where devotionalism, ethnic allegiances, and minimal liturgical activity were the norm.[13] Writing in 1941, Paula Sinclair described the juxtaposition of increased education for American Catholics in the secular realm with the dearth of liturgical education for the lay faithful. She noted that, in previous generations and in her own, many Catholics had not gone to Catholic school and many had not gone to any school past the eighth grade. While an increasing number of men and women had gone on to high school and college, only a few people were aware of the "philosophical and sociological implications of our faith" or had known "exquisite joy in participation in the spiritual fullness of Catholicism."[14] What was needed was education, an extension of the knowledge gained by the preparatory experience of the clergy, in teaching the full liturgical significance of the Mass. Congregants

---

[12] Barbara Dells, parishioner to Hans Anscar Reinhold, March 26, 1956, H. A. Reinhold Papers, MS2003-60 Series 1, 9/13, John J. Burns Library, Boston College, Chestnut Hill, Massachusetts.

[13] See Jay Dolan, *The American Catholic Experience: A History from Colonial Times to the Present* (Garden City, NY: Doubleday, 1985), 417.

[14] Paula Sinclair, "From Pew to Pulpit," *Orate Fratres* 15, no. 7 (1941): 296.

should learn how to *assist* at Mass rather than "be polite (or impolite!) spectators."[15] The education of lay Catholics in liturgical matters, as women such as Justine Ward, Maisie Ward, Sara B. O'Neill, and Nina Polcyn Moore attempted to promote, was one of the chief factors in achieving any expansion of the liturgical movement among Catholics.

Other women activists, such as Mary Fabyan Windeatt (1910–79), a Canadian who moved to New York City and then southern Indiana (near St. Meinrad), expressed similar concerns over the disconnect between hopes of the reformers and the form and quality of the liturgical catechesis to which the faithful were exposed. Windeatt was known in liturgical circles as a frequent contributor to the Catholic press, an author of Catholic children's books, a Dominican tertiary, and an advocate for interracial justice.[16] In an article appearing in *Orate Fratres* in March 1942, she described with resignation her parish bulletin, noting its quarterly finance reports and recommendations for hearing sermons on dogmatics and the "sad story that Sunday Vespers was not well attended." Windeatt concluded that "it is going to take more than a page in the Parish Bulletin, more than a preacher at Sunday Vespers, more than a group of competent musicians, to put a love of the liturgy in many of our people."[17] Parishioners in her experience were "nearly all individualists," with little way of knowing what the communal scope of the Church of Christ meant:

[15] Ibid., 297.

[16] See Mary Fabyan Windeatt, "Good-Will Tour," *Orate Fratres* 16, no. 9 (1942): 393–98. Her children's books, for which she sometimes traveled internationally in order to secure quality material and background information, were published throughout the 1940s, and included *Lad of Lima: The Story of Blessed Martin de Porres* (New York: Sheed & Ward, 1942); *David and His Songs: A Story of the Psalms* (St. Meinrad, IN: Grail, 1948); *Little Sister: The Story of Blessed Imelda, Patroness of First Communicants* (St. Meinrad, IN: Grail, 1944); *Song in the South: The Story of Saint Francis Solano, Apostle of Argentina and Peru* (New York: Sheed & Ward, 1946); and *The Children of Fatima* (St. Meinrad, IN: Grail, 1945). Her books, such as *The Children of Fatima*, were recommended in the "Catholic Elementary Art Guide" prepared by the Catholic Arts Association as appropriate for helping children bring a sense of devotion and history to their art projects and assignments. "Catholic Elementary Art Guide," October 1948, Catholic Arts Association 2/19, UNDA.

[17] Mary Fabyan Windeatt, "Whom Shall We Love," *Orate Fratres* 16, no. 5 (1942): 208.

They assist at Mass each in his own fashion, some with beads, others with books of novena prayers, some with neither of these, having no notion that everyone assisting at a Mass is meant to be spiritually united to all others doing the same.[18]

While the people may have known what a missal was, they still did not see the value in reading long prayers from a book—that was the work of the priest. Windeatt suggested that the "modern apathy" surrounding common prayer had its roots in economics and politics. While Christians might theoretically admit that they were all one in Christ's Mystical Body, in practical social realization, American Christians were a loose collection of independent individualists:

> Each child born in our land has a chance to be president, a millionaire, a self-made person through his own initiative. Our fathers came to this New World to be free, religiously and politically. We, their descendants, are reaping the harvest of this ideal. We accumulate our own little capital; we work to get the things we consider necessary and desirable. We consider minding our own business a virtue highly to be esteemed. We choose the type of clothes we wear, the car we drive, the toothpaste that appeals to us. And we pray along the same lines—*in a manner that appeals to us.*[19]

Worship had been formed by the manner of life which Americans had been encouraged to embrace—one which promoted a "hands-off" approach, freedom to be an individual, and taking pride in the distinction of having "the best" money could buy; in short, a tradition of ascendency. As an example, Windeatt related her parish's experience of church music, admitting that she herself was a music lover. The organ was "one of the finest in the country," and the choir, composed of "fifty men and boys," was presided over by "an unquestionable authority on church music." Her parish had, in fact, gained an "enviable reputation" in the field of choral art, even performing in New York City's Town Hall. Yet, while Windeatt could not deny the skill of the choir, she did not believe that such expertise was actually "adding anything to the Catholic family spirit in our parish" but rather was enforcing the passive quality of the congregation during the Mass; the choir sang the responses for the congregation who was encouraged to

[18] Ibid., 209.
[19] Ibid.

334

"sit back and listen to their efforts."[20] Windeatt emphasized that it was in *"assisting, uniting as a family at the holy Sacrifice,* that Catholics really achieve unity."[21] The congregation would not learn to love the liturgy by being encouraged to listen. Again, Windeatt's concerns illustrate the fundamental disconnect between *action* and *being,* as described by Catholic Action and as expressed by Ade Bethune with her philosophy of liturgical art and production. While congregants might not execute Latin or chant with virtuosity, the value in giving the faithful voices in communal prayer far outweighed a lack of excellence.[22] How else would congregants become nearer to one another, less of strangers, and less anonymous in the liturgy?

Windeatt presents an interesting disconnect between the vivid social life of American Catholic churchgoers and the liturgical life of these same congregants. Catholic clubs, evening activities, and sports teams were at a height during the mid-twentieth century, following years of increasing advocacy for Catholic identity, a growing Catholic population, and a growing awareness, if not acceptance, of Catholics in the American mainstream. While Catholics presumably had significant contact with each other through a number of social or political venues, despite the widespread participation and familiarity with devotional practices, they had little contact with each other *during* worship and, particularly, during the Mass. Even less so did Catholics readily extend the social implications of the liturgy beyond their own congregations, as Dorothy Day or Catherine de Hueck Doherty would model in their liturgical apostolates. While many Catholics had viewed the Mass as a venue for personal devotion and as a duty to fulfill as faithful Catholics, an emphasis on the purpose of the Mass was focused on dogmatic principles and not, in the experiences of most Catholics, on the communal nature of prayer and its implications for a life in Christ.

One of the most significant drawbacks of the liturgical movement, noted above, was its tendency toward elitism. Paula Sinclair, writing

[20] Ibid., 211.

[21] Ibid., 212.

[22] "Those of us who appreciate an artistic rendering of motets and sacred songs would undoubtedly writhe at having to listen to congregational singing where Mrs. O'Flaherty bungles the *Kyrie* and deaf old men mispronounce their Latin. But these things are all externals. . . . Always underneath there is the eternal truth—the sense of kinship through Christ which our modern manner of living does so much to thwart." Windeatt, "Whom Shall We Love," 212.

in *Orate Fratres* in 1943, noted that she had attended Liturgical Weeks and had been impressed by their efforts, evaluating their attendance as "visible, numerical proof of the progress the movement has made since its beginning."[23] Yet the Liturgical Weeks, she warned, "have not made converts," drawing only the clergy and religious who were *already liturgically inclined*. While some parishes boasted a congregation which "to a man, follows the Mass, missal in hand, with intelligent, reverent concentration," such instances were scarce in number.[24] By far, more lay people experienced the Mass pruned and plucked to "the bare bone of the essential act of worship," where services were reduced "to a sort of perpetual *Requiem*" and where choir and preacher alike were "compromising to the clock at the sacristy door."[25] In Sinclair's view, the liturgical movement had failed to reach into the locations in which it was most sorely needed, with an oblivious elite-ness existing among those of the liturgical intelligentsia who met together. Compounding this, in her vision, was the fact that education of the laity was somewhat trapped in a catch-22. Many clergy were reluctant to institute change because they believed that the "quick-Mass, no ceremony, cut-the-sermon school" was the laity's preference.[26]

The recurring problem of elitism in the liturgical movement can be illustrated through the example of the breviary. Even liturgical leader Ade Bethune had difficulty using the Office, an experience which she related to Godfrey Diekmann. While she wished to pray the Office, she found it difficult on several accounts and, in fact, gave away a breviary given to her by the Abbot at Saint John's.[27] Her experience of com-

---

[23] Paula Sinclair, "Give Us Our Heritage," *Orate Fratres* 17, no. 3 (1943): 117.

[24] "I know of one, on the far western extremity of our city, where a vested choir chants the proper Sunday after Sunday, where the Church's rules of divine service are observed to the letter. . . . The sermon there each week is carefully composed, well delivered on a subject that is an integrated part of a program directed toward renewing and sustaining the spiritual and intellectual vigor of parochial life." Paula Sinclair, "Give Us Our Heritage," 117–18.

[25] Ibid.

[26] Ibid., 117.

[27] "Nothing is wrong with the office except that it involves reading. I am a punk reader I'll admit. But usually by the time I get around to reading, I am so tired I can't see straight, and after two or three pages (especially at night) my eyes go on the blink and I go to sleep. Of course I have never wanted the breviary as badly as for the past week that it's been gone and it was a

munal prayer on Catholic Worker farms also indicated that the regular monastic office was too complicated for regular lay use. For example, in August 1940, at a Catholic Worker farm, the group abandoned Compline because "nobody came," except for a few "intellectuals," while everyone would come to say the rosary. Bethune hoped for a version of the Office which would be more suited for "uneducated people" who remained unreached by the "unfortunately too intellectual literature of the Liturgical Movement."[28]

Other women writers commented on the need for "practical things" to appear in *Orate Fratres*, not only in terms of the less abstract, but "more articles on the spiritual life and prayer," so that one who could not afford to buy many books or to make retreats could access liturgical resources.[29] And, a growing interest in practical resources for living the liturgical life became the major concern of liturgical reformers in the latter 1940s and 1950s, particularly in the work of Therese Mueller, Mary Perkins Ryan, and Florence Berger. On the other hand, others found it disconcerting that popular devotions, which were so often the center of the "uneducated" Catholic's prayer life, were identified as mere distractions. One writer asked *Orate Fratres* if it could stress the harmony between popular Catholic devotions and the liturgical life:

> Why look upon other devotions in the Church, such as that to the Sacred Heart or to the Sorrowful Mother, or to the Little Flower, as rivals in the field? Why not show rather how all these enrich, embellish, and beautify our liturgical life? It seems to me, Father, that a kindlier regard for what appeals to the *Ecclesia Discens* and a utilizing of this for the enhancing of the liturgical life would be a better approach

---

real heartbreak to see it go away. But in honesty I could not keep it when another was more in need of it than I am. I still have the monastic Day Hours and I guess I'm doing pretty well if I get that much done. I chewed off a bigger chunk than I could stomach when I presumed to try matins anyway. I wish laymen would learn to stay in their place." Ade Bethune to Godfrey Diekmann, November 9, 1940, The Godfrey Diekmann Papers 1013/9, Saint John's Abbey Archives, Collegeville, Minnesota.

[28] Ibid.

[29] Margaretta Van Winkle, "Suggestions," in "The Apostolate," *Orate Fratres* 12, no. 11 (1938): 526. Van Winkle identified herself as a tertiary Oblate of Saint Benedict from Northampton, Massachusetts.

than that wherein we attack popular devotions, and the faithful are antagonized.[30]

The writer does not identify as a man or woman but, as we have seen, it is no longer safe to assume that this writer was not a liturgically minded lay woman. In any case, witnesses such as these illustrate how those involved in the liturgical movement were frequently able to identify how the liturgical movement might better meet its goal of social transformation. The difficulties that lay women pointed out, such as the accessibility of the breviary for lay use, attendance at Sunday Vespers, and the potential for liturgical participation to form communal identity, would continue to be issues following the liturgical reforms of the Second Vatican Council.

CONCLUSION: UNFINISHED AND UNBEGUN

From the inaugural issue of *Orate Fratres* in 1926 to the eve of the Second Vatican Council, Roman Catholic lay women reflected on and realized the impulse to lead the liturgical life during the liturgical movement in the United States. Analysis of major women contributors, sociocultural shifts in American Catholicism, and the witness of scores of Catholic lay women who utilized and reflected on liturgical resources recovers how lay women identified and were identified as having a vocation to serve as cultivators of the liturgical apostolate and how lay women practiced living the liturgical life through spiritual, intellectual, artistic, and social venues. Though these women's gender is, at times, at play, the more significant result achieved by reexamining the sources is to reveal how important the involvement of the liturgical apostolate of lay persons was for making the liturgical movement in any way successful. The liturgical movement was not a priest-led movement. Finally, the impulse for Catholic living in the mid-twentieth century was very much a part of the encouragement to produce and maintain, or salvage and restore, a truly Christian way of life in the face of the evils of industrialism, modernism, secularism, and individualism. Attention to multidimensional factors of the American liturgical movement provides crucial context for how American Roman Catholic women participated in the liturgical way of life. Such historical work, simply revealing that "there were also many

---

[30] M. H. of Massachusetts, "Letter to the Editor," *Orate Fratres* 14, no. 5 (1940): 234.

women there," prepares the ground for further exploration of the land-scape of the liturgical movement and catalogues valuable historical precedence for the development and practical realization of liturgical reforms among American Catholic laity.

At the end of the day, as liturgical scholar Aidan Kavanagh, OSB, would summarize more than ten years following the Second Vatican Council, the work of the liturgical movement was at once "unfinished and unbegun."[31] So too is an appreciation of its advocates. Nathan D. Mitchell, liturgical scholar, writer, and teacher, identified the andro-centric vision of the liturgical movement in 1994. As Mitchell noted, save Teresa Berger's *Women's Ways of Worship* (which he indicated was a much-needed history), "To date, the history of the modern liturgical movement has been written primarily as *history for, by and about men*."[32] Yet, Mitchell assured, women's absence from the narrative "does not mean, of course, that women have failed, factually, to make any contribution to worship studies and pastoral praxis in the twentieth century—only that their contributions have been neglected or, more commonly, sought for in the wrong places."[33]

Indeed, one finds a liturgical foremother in places one would not expect: in Hull-House, in a publishing house, or in her own house. But these women's liturgical contributions are not "un-liturgical," "lack-ing seriousness," or "on the fringes." Lay women's work was integral to the development of the liturgical movement and to its success or failure. The practical experiences of laywomen liturgical pioneers tes-tify to the liturgical movement as a work in progress—a work which evolved and a work which increasingly needed lay Catholics to under-stand and embrace it. Certainly, there were also many women there during the liturgical movement in America—women who knew that the work of the liturgical life had only just begun.

[31] Aidan Kavanaugh, "Liturgical Business Unfinished and Unbegun," *Worship* 50, no. 4 (1976): 354–64.

[32] Nathan D. Mitchell, "The Amen Corner: A Mansion for the Rat," *Worship* 68, no. 1 (1994): 66.

[33] Ibid., 68.

Bibliography

The bibliography is divided into four sections. The first section, "Manuscript Collections," contains archival resources and unpublished materials. The second section, "Published Sources," contains works composed by American liturgical pioneers during the liturgical movement, 1926–59. The third section, "Related Works," contains works which provide context for the various eras and issues of the women in the United States liturgical movement, including Catholic Action, feminism, the European liturgical movement and its leaders, and American Catholic history. Some liturgical movement contributors who appear in the "Published Sources" section also appear in the "Related Works" section, when their writing does not directly address the liturgical movement, as do writers in the European context. The fourth section, "Supplementary Materials," contains secondary source materials relating directly to the liturgical movement.

MANUSCRIPT COLLECTIONS

The Ade Bethune Collection. University of St. Catherine Library, St. Paul, MN.

The Alfred Berger Collection. John J. Burns Library. Boston College, Chestnut Hill, MA.

Catholic Arts Association. University of Notre Dame Archives, Notre Dame, IN.

Catholic Daughters of America. Papers. The American Catholic History Research Center and University Archives. Catholic University of America, Washington, DC.

The Daughters of Isabella. Records. The American Catholic History Research Center and University Archives. Catholic University of America, Washington, DC.

Ellen Gates Starr Papers. Sophia Smith Collection. Smith College, Northampton, MA.

Florence Berger File. Ohioana Library Association, Columbus, Ohio.

General Collection Printed Materials. University of Notre Dame Archives, Notre Dame, IN.

Gerald Ellard Papers. John J. Burns Library. Boston College, Chestnut Hill, MA.

The Godfrey Diekmann Papers. The Archives of Saint John's Abbey, Collegeville, MN.

H. A. Reinhold Papers. John J. Burns Library. Boston College, Chestnut Hill, MA.

Judith Stoughton Papers. Archive Department of the Sisters of St. Joseph of Carondelet, St. Paul Province, St. Paul, MN.

Liturgical Arts Society Records. University of Notre Dame Archives, Notre Dame, IN.

The Liturgy and Life Collection. John J. Burns Library. Boston College, Chestnut Hill, MA.

The Mary Perkins Ryan Papers. John J. Burns Library. Boston College, Chestnut Hill, MA.

National Catholic Welfare Conference. Records. The American Catholic History Research Center and University Archives. Catholic University of America, Washington, DC.

Nina Polcyn Moore Collection. University of Notre Dame Archives, Notre Dame, IN.

The Reynold Hillenbrand Papers. University of Notre Dame Archives, Notre Dame, IN.

Sheed & Ward Family Papers. University of Notre Dame Archives, Notre Dame, IN.

Therese Mueller Papers. University of St. Catherine Library, St. Paul, MN.

The Virgil Michel Papers. The Archives of Saint John's Abbey, Collegeville, MN.

PUBLISHED SOURCES

Antcliffe, Herbert. "A Dutch Catholic Pageant." *The Ave Maria* 36, no. 2 (1932): 49–52.

"The Apostolate." *Orate Fratres* 1, no. 6 (1927): 188–90.

"The Apostolate." *Orate Fratres* 3, no. 8 (1929): 253.

"The Apostolate." *Orate Fratres* 4, no. 2 (1929): 89.

"The Apostolate." *Orate Fratres* 8, no. 4 (1934): 182.

"The Apostolate." *Orate Fratres* 8, no. 7 (1934): 330.

"The Apostolate." *Orate Fratres* 11, no. 2 (1936): 87.

"The Apostolate." *Orate Fratres* 15, no. 1 (1940): 43.

"The Apostolate." *Orate Fratres* 16, no. 6 (1942): 284–85.

Berger, Florence S. *Cooking for Christ: The Liturgical Year in the Kitchen*. Des Moines, IA: National Catholic Rural Life Conference, 1949.

Berger, Florence. "In the Home." *Orate Fratres* 25, no. 2 (1951): 76–78.

———. "In the Home." *Orate Fratres* 25, no. 5 (1951): 229–31.

———. "Liturgy in the Family." *Orate Fratres* 24, no. 3 (1950): 124–28.

———. "The Liturgical Year in the Kitchen." *Orate Fratres* 23, no. 12 (1949): 549–52.

Bethune, Ade. "D.A. versus C.A.A. [Devil's Advocate versus Catholic Arts Association]." *Christian Social Art Quarterly* 3, no. 2 (1940): 24–30.

———. "A Dream Come True." *Stained Glass* 28, no. 3 (Autumn 1933): 139–42.

———. "Revising our Conception of the Communion Rail." *Catholic Art Quarterly* 21, no. 2 (1958): 37–47.

———. "Small Churches." *Orate Fratres* 12, no. 11 (1937): 486–89.

———. "Symposium: Should Children Draw Religious Subjects?" *Catholic Art Quarterly* 17, no. 4 (1954): 125–34.

———. "Tabernacle and Altar." *Catholic Art Quarterly* 22, no. 4 (1959): 98–101.

———. "To the Reader." In *Eye Contact with God Through Pictures: A Clip Book of Pictures from the Ade Bethune Collection*. Kansas City, MO: Sheed & Ward, 1986.

———. *Work*. Newport, RI: John Stevens Shop, 1939. Reprint, Breinigsville, PA: Catholic Authors Press, 2007.

———. "The Work and Works of Mercy," *Orate Fratres* 15, no. 2 (1940): 53–57.

———. "The Work of Our Hands Is Love Made Visible." In *The Catholic Elementary School Program for Christian Family Living*. Edited by Mary Ramon Langdon. Washington, DC: Catholic University of America Press, 1955.

Bogdan, Virginia. "The Grail Training Course." *Orate Fratres* 17, no. 10 (1943): 464–66.

Boland, E. "The Grail Movement." *Catholic Mind* 31 (1933): 289–98.

Breen, Florence. "League of the Divine Office." In "The Apostolate." *Orate Fratres* 12, no. 2 (1937): 88–89.

Burns, Kathleen. "Liturgy and the College English Class." *Orate Fratres* 2, no. 11 (1928): 214–19.

Burton, Katherine, and Helmut Ripperger. *Feast Day Cookbook*. New York: David McKay, 1951.

Busch, William. "Liturgy and Farm Relief." *Catholic Rural Life* 8 (April 1930): 2–3.

Byrne, Mrs. R. A. "Liturgy and the Laity." In "The Apostolate." *Orate Fratres* 10, no. 6 (1936): 280.

Caldwell, Helen. "Dear Enemy." *Orate Fratres* 25, no. 10 (1951): 457–61.

Calpin, Helen M. "An Education in the Faith." In "The Apostolate." *Orate Fratres* 7, no. 4 (1933): 187.

"Calvary of Life." *Altar and Home* 2, no. 3 (April 1935): 3.

"Candlemas." *Altar and Home* 1, no. 1 (February 1934): 1.

Carroll, Thomas J. "Summary and Conclusion." *1942 Liturgical Week Proceedings* (Newark, NJ: Benedictine Liturgical Conference, 1943): 193–200.

Casey, Genevieve M. "The Liturgy as the Solution of the Negro Problem." *Orate Fratres* 11, no. 8 (1937): 369–71.

Catholic Church. *Leaflet Missal*. Chicago: Lawrence N. Daleiden, 1931.

"Catholic Women Are Studying the Liturgy." In "The Apostolate." *Orate Fratres* 7, no. 1 (1932): 30–31.

Clendenin, Mrs. John W. "Study-Club Accomplishments." In "The Apostolate." *Orate Fratres* 7, no. 11 (1933): 523.

Coddington, Dorothy. "Let Those Who Can, Do." *Orate Fratres* 19, no. 10 (1947): 433–39.

———. "Teaching Psalms to Children." *Orate Fratres* 23, no. 9 (1947): 403–8.

Day, Dorothy. "Cult, Culture and Cultivation," in "The Apostolate." *Orate Fratres* 19, no. 11 (1945): 574–75.

———. "Fellow Worker in Christ." *Orate Fratres* 13, no. 3 (1938): 139–41.

Day, Gertrude. "A Business Woman's Interest." In "The Apostolate." *Orate Fratres* 7, no. 11 (1933): 523–24.

de Bethune, Ade. "Art and Christian Art." *Orate Fratres* 14, no. 8 (1940): 337–41.

———. "Bell Towers in Sacred Architecture, Part I." *Catholic Art Quarterly* 21, no. 3 (1958): 80–88.

———. "Bell Towers in Sacred Architecture, Part II," *Catholic Art Quarterly* 21, no. 4 (1958): 118–23.

———. "Font and Altar: Footnotes on Sacred Architecture." *Catholic Art Quarterly* 17, no. 3 (1954): 82–102.

de Béthune, Adé. "Philippines Adventure." *Liturgical Arts Quarterly* 19, no. 4 (1951): 10–3.

de Béthune, Adélaïde. "Common Sense." *Liturgical Arts Quarterly* 5, no. 3 (1936): 79–84.

de Hueck Doherty, Catherine. "I Saw Christ Today." *Orate Fratres* 12, no. 7 (1938): 305–10.

DeMars, Ruth. "We Moved Out." *Land and Home* 5, no. 1 (March 1942): 5.

Diekmann, Godfrey. "Editor's Note." In "The Apostolate." *Orate Fratres* 27, no. 6 (1953): 330.

———. "Liturgical Briefs." *Orate Fratres* 23, no. 11 (October 1949): 523–25.

———. Review of *The Year of Our Lord*, by Aemiliana Löhr. *Orate Fratres* 11, no. 7 (1937): 335–36.

"Discussion." *1940 Liturgical Week Proceedings*. Newark, NJ: Benedictine Liturgical Conference, 1941, 157–62.

"Discussion." *1940 Liturgical Week Proceedings*. Newark, NJ: Benedictine Liturgical Conference, 1941, 207–12.

"Discussion." *1941 Liturgical Week Proceedings*. Newark, NJ: Benedictine Liturgical Conference, 1942, 171–75.

"Discussion." *1941 National Liturgical Week Proceedings*. Newark, NJ: Benedictine Liturgical Conference, 1942, 212–17.

"Discussion." *1942 Liturgical Week Proceedings*. Newark, NJ: Benedictine Liturgical Conference, 1943, 62–65.

"Discussion." *1942 Liturgical Week Proceedings*. Newark, NJ: Benedictine Liturgical Conference, 1943, 73–76.

"Discussion." *1943 Liturgical Week Proceedings*. Ferdinand, IN: The Liturgical Conference, 1944, 116–21.

"Discussion." *1946 Liturgical Week Proceedings*. Elsberry, MO: The Liturgical Conference, 1947, 57–61.

"Discussion." *1946 Liturgical Week Proceedings*. Elsberry, MO: The Liturgical Conference, 1947, 70.

"Discussion." *1946 Liturgical Week Proceedings*. Elsberry, MO: The Liturgical Conference, 1947, 104–5.

"Discussion." *1946 Liturgical Week Proceedings*. Elsberry, MO: The Liturgical Conference, 1947, 166–71.

"Discussion." *1946 Liturgical Week Proceedings*. Highland Park, IL: The Liturgical Conference, 1947, 148–49.

Drevniok, Elizabeth. "A Letter Cake for Charlie." *Altar and Home* 26, no. 3 (1959): 2–5.

Duddy, Mary Alice. "The Parable of Bread." *Orate Fratres* 19, no. 7 (1945): 298–301.

Dunne, Lambert. "Towards Christian Order in Labor Relations." In *The Sacramental Way*. Edited by Mary Perkins. New York: Sheed & Ward, 1948, 337–46.

The Editor. "Calvary of Life." *Altar and Home* 2, no. 3 (April 1935): 3.

———. "The Loveliness of Mary." *Altar and Home* 2, no. 4 (May 1935): 2.

———. "The Purpose of Our Paper." *Altar and Home* 1, no. 1 (February 1934): 4.

The Editors. "From *The Catholic Worker*." In "The Apostolate." *Orate Fratres* 8, no. 6 (1934): 284.

Ellard, Gerald. "The American Scene, 1926–51." *Orate Fratres* 25, no. 11/12 (1951): 500–508.

———. "The Liturgical Movement: In and For America." *The Catholic Mind* 31 (1933): 61–76.

———. *Men at Work at Worship: America Joins the Liturgical Movement*. New York: Longmans, Green, 1940.

A Former Parishioner. "Candlemas Day in a Negro Parish." *Orate Fratres* 21, no. 6 (1947): 130–35.

"Grail Offers Courses in 'Lived' Christianity." In "The Apostolate." *Orate Fratres* 19, no. 7 (1945): 325–26.

Harrigan, Ann. "Whites and Negros on a Wisconsin Farm." *Orate Fratres* 21, no. 7 (1947): 318–22.

Haus, Rose E. "A Friend Writes." In "The Apostolate." *Orate Fratres* 8, no. 6 (1934): 284.

Heidt, William George. *A Short Breviary: for Religious and Laity*. Collegeville, MN: Liturgical Press, 1941.

Hellriegel, Martin B. "Family Life, the Liturgical Year, and the Sacramentals." *1946 Liturgical Week Proceedings*. Highland Park, IL: The Liturgical Conference, 1947, 103–5.

———. Forward to *Our Children's Year of Grace: Considerations for Use in the Home-School by Parents who Wish to Teach Their Children to Live Throughout the Year with Christ and His Church*, by Therese Mueller. 2nd ed. St. Louis, MO: Pio Decimo Press, 1943.

———. "A Pastor's Description of Liturgical Participation in His Parish." *1941 Liturgical Week Proceedings*. Newark: Benedictine Liturgical Conference, 1942, 82–90.

———. "Seasonal Suggestions." *Worship* 30, no. 6 (1955): 374–90.

———. *The True Basis of Christian Solidarity: The Liturgy an Aid to the Solution of the Social Question*. Central Bureau Publications "Follow Me!" Brochure Series. St. Louis, MO: Central Bureau of the Central Verein, 1928.

Heywood, Robert B. "At Chicago University." In "The Apostolate." *Orate Fratres* 15, no. 5 (1941): 234.

———. "The Spirit of the Grail." *Orate Fratres* 15, no. 8 (1941): 360–67.

Hoonaert, Rodolphe, and William Busch. *The Breviary and the Laity*. Popular Liturgical Library Series I, no. 7. Collegeville, MN: Liturgical Press, 1936.

Horan, Ellamay. "Teaching the Mass in a Rural Vacation School." *Orate Fratres* 17, no. 9 (1943): 424–27.

Hynes, Emerson, and Arleen Hynes. "Liturgy and Life." *1946 Liturgical Week Proceedings*. Highland Park, IL: The Liturgical Conference, 1947, 122–27.

Hynes, Emerson, and Arleen Hynes. "Holy Week in the Home." *Worship* 30, no. 4 (1956): 257–66.

Kalven, Janet. "The Grail Spirit in Action." In "The Apostolate." *Orate Fratres* 15, no. 8 (1941): 382–83.

———. "The Spirit of the Grail." In "The Apostolate." *Orate Fratres* 16, no. 4 (1942): 185–86.

———. *The Task of Woman in the Modern World*. Des Moines, IA: NCRLC, 1946.

Kalven, Janet, Mariette Wickes, and Barbara Ellen Ward, with James M. Shea, eds. *Toward a Christian Sunday: An Apostolic Program Based on the Volume, Restore the Sunday*. Grailville: Grail, 1949.

Kalven, Janet and others, eds. *Restore the Sunday*. Grailville: Grail, 1949.

Krueter, Joseph. "The Christian Family and the Eucharistic Sacrifice." *Orate Fratres* 9, no. 11 (1935): 546–50.

———. "The Family and the Eucharist." *Orate Fratres* 9, no. 8 (1935): 354–59.

"League of the Divine Office." In "The Apostolate." *Orate Fratres* 12, no. 2 (1937): 88–89.

"Liturgical Briefs." *Orate Fratres* 1, no. 3 (1927): 95–96.

"Liturgical Briefs." *Orate Fratres* 4, no. 3 (1930): 137.

"Liturgical Briefs." *Orate Fratres* 4, no. 11 (1930): 475. "Liturgical Briefs." *Orate Fratres* 5, no. 5 (1931): 245–46.

"Liturgical Briefs." *Orate Fratres* 7, no. 2 (1932): 88.

"Liturgical Briefs." *Orate Fratres* 7, no. 3 (1933): 134.

"Liturgical Briefs." *Orate Fratres* 7, no. 5 (1933): 233.

"Liturgical Briefs." *Orate Fratres* 7, no. 6 (1933): 282.

"Liturgical Briefs." *Orate Fratres* 7, no. 8 (1933): 373–74.

"Liturgical Briefs." *Orate Fratres* 7, no. 9 (1933): 420.

"Liturgical Briefs." *Orate Fratres* 8, no. 2 (1933): 86.

"Liturgical Briefs." *Orate Fratres* 8, no. 3 (1934): 136.

"Liturgical Briefs." *Orate Fratres* 9, no. 9 (1935): 422.

"Liturgical Briefs." *Orate Fratres* 9, no. 10 (1935): 472.

"Liturgical Briefs." *Orate Fratres* 11, no. 2 (1936): 87.

"Liturgical Briefs." *Orate Fratres* 13, no. 11 (1939): 519–20.

"Liturgical Briefs." *Orate Fratres* 15, no. 1 (1940): 43.

"Liturgical Briefs." *Orate Fratres* 16, no. 6 (1942): 284–85.

"Liturgical Briefs." *Orate Fratres* 17, no. 7 (1943): 328.

"Liturgical Briefs." *Orate Fratres* 20, no. 7 (1946): 428.

"Liturgical Briefs." *Orate Fratres* 25, no. 10 (1951): 469.

Liturgical Conference, Inc., *What Is the Liturgical Movement?* Boston: The Liturgical Conference, 1948.

"The Loveliness of Mary." *Altar and Home* 2, no. 4 (May 1935): 2.

M. H. "Letter to the Editor." *Orate Fratres* 14, no. 5 (1940): 234–35.

Madigan, Dona. "Problems of a Convert Catechist." In "The Apostolate." *Orate Fratres* 7, no. 9 (1933): 424–25.

Marceron, Agnes M. "Study Club on the Mass." In "The Apostolate." *Orate Fratres* 7, no. 12 (1933): 570.

McAllister, Joseph B. "The Ball and the Cross." *Catholic World* 146 (February 1938): 602–5.

McKenna, Norman. "The Liturgy and Reconstruction." *Orate Fratres* 12, no. 8 (1938): 337–38.

McLoughlin, Helen. *Family Advent Custom*. Popular Liturgical Library Series. Collegeville, MN: Liturgical Press, 1953.

Meière, Hildreth. "A Modern Way of the Cross in Mosaic." *Liturgical Arts Quarterly* 1, no. 1 (1931): 35–38.

Mella, John, and Katherine Mella. "Holiness and Hospitality." *Integrity* 6, no. 9 (1951): 40–43.

Mellinger, Mary Roberta. "The Liturgy in the Primary Grades." *Journal of Religious Instruction: The Catholic Educator* 17, no. 1 (1946): 186–91.

Michel, Virgil. "The Apostolate." *Orate Fratres* 4, nos. 9–10 (1930): 426.

———. "The Apostolate." *Orate Fratres* 8, no. 6 (1934): 277.

———. "Cakes and the Liturgy." *Orate Fratres* 1, no. 9 (1926): 282–83.

———. "Christian Culture." *Orate Fratres* 13, no. 7 (1939): 296–304.

———. "Christian Reconstruction Cells." In "The Apostolate." *Orate Fratres* 9, no. 4 (1937): 179–82.

———. "The Christian Woman." *Orate Fratres* 13, no. 5 (1939): 248–56.

———. "The Cooperative Movement and the Liturgical Movement." *Orate Fratres* 14, no. 4 (1940): 152–60.

———. "The Family and the Liturgy." *Orate Fratres* 11, no. 9 (1936): 393–96.

———. "The Family and the Mystical Body." *Orate Fratres* 11, no. 7 (1937): 295–99.

———. *The Liturgical Movement and the Catholic Woman*. Popular Liturgical Library Series. Collegeville, MN: Liturgical Press, 1959.

———. "The Liturgy and Catholic Women." *Orate Fratres* 3, no. 9 (1929): 270–76.

———. "The Liturgy the Basis of Social Regeneration." *Orate Fratres* 9, no. 12 (1935): 536–45.

———. "Only a Layman." *Orate Fratres* 1, no. 11 (1927): 346–47.

———. "The Parish, Cell of Christian Life." *Orate Fratres* 11, no. 10 (1937): 433–40.

———. Review of *Jahr des Herrn*, by Aemiliana Löhr. *Orate Fratres* 9, no. 3 (1935): 140–41.

———. Review of *The Saints and Social Work*, by Mary Elizabeth Walsh. *Orate Fratres* 11, no. 8 (1937): 335.

Miss B. M. "A Neglected Parish Church." In "The Apostolate." *Orate Fratres* 7, no. 12 (1933): 571.

Miss M. C. "Laity and the Liturgy." In "The Apostolate." *Orate Fratres* 12, no. 2 (1937): 43.

Miss M. E. J. "In Answer to a Circular." In "The Apostolate." *Orate Fratres* 11, no. 2 (1936): 91.

Miss T. "A Lay Reader's Comment." In "Communications." *Orate Fratres* 6, no. 1 (1931): 47.

Miss. G. "From an Old Friend." In "The Apostolate." *Orate Fratres* 12, no. 1 (1937): 42.

Montessori, Maria. Preface to *The Mass Explained to Children*. London: Sheed & Ward, 1932.

Moynihan, Katherine E. "Enthusiastic Friend of the Liturgy." In "The Apostolate." *Orate Fratres* 7, no. 11 (1933): 524.

Mrs. Cort. "What Is So New?: A Panel Discussion.'" *1948 Liturgical Week Proceedings*. Conception, MO: The Liturgical Conference, 1949, 14–22.

Mrs. J. S. M. "Liturgy of the Layfolk." In "The Apostolate." *Orate Fratres* 9, no. 7 (1935): 334.

Mueller, Franz. "Thoughts on Some Mass Texts." *Orate Fratres* 13, no. 1 (1938): 11–15.

Mueller, Mrs. Franz [Therese]. "The Christian Family and the Liturgy." *1941 Liturgical Week Proceedings*. Newark, NJ: Benedictine Liturgical Conference, 1942, 162–71.

Mueller, Therese. "Churching." *Orate Fratres* 15, no. 11 (1940): 519–22.

———. "Family Life in Christ." *Orate Fratres* 14, no. 9 (1939): 391–96.

———. *Family Life in Christ*. 3rd ed. Popular Liturgical Library Series IV, no. 6. Collegeville, MN: Liturgical Press, 1946.

———. "Family Life in Christ, II: Bringing Home the Sacraments." *Orate Fratres* 14, no. 10 (1939): 439–43.

———. "Family Life in Christ, III: The Liturgical Year in the Home." *Orate Fratres* 14, no. 11 (1939): 487–91.

———. "Family Life in Christ, IV: Daily Growth." *Orate Fratres* 14, no. 12 (1939): 533–38.

———. "Letters of a Godmother." *Orate Fratres* 12, no. 7 (1938): 289–93.

———. *Our Children's Year of Grace: Considerations for Use in the Home-School By Parents Who Wish to Teach Their Children to Live Throughout the Year with Christ and His Church*. St. Louis, MO: Pio Decimo Press, 1943.

N. N. "The Story of a Negro Parish." *Orate Fratres* 20, no. 7 (1946): 370–75.

Nash, Elizabeth. "'Et Cum Fratribus nostris absentibus.'" In "The Apostolate." *Orate Fratres* 12, no. 1 (1937): 38–39.

Newland, Mary Reed. "Television and Children." *The Torch* (April 1951): 7–9.

———. *The Year and Our Children: Planning the Family Activities for Christian Feasts and Seasons*. New York: Longmans, Green, 1956.

Nolan, Joseph T. "Grailville's Valiant Women." *America* 78 (October 1946): 9–11.

Nutting, Eileen. "A Mother and Her Children." *Orate Frates* 24, no. 7 (1950): 317–21.

Nutting, Willis D. "Religious Education at Home." *Orate Fratres* 22, no. 4 (1948): 167–68.

Overboss, Joan. "Grail Offers Courses in 'Lived' Christianity." In "The Apostolate." *Orate Fratres* 19, no. 7 (1945): 325.

P. A. N. Review of *Belgian Rural Cooperation*, by Eva J. Ross. *Orate Fratres* 14, no. 11 (1940): 528.

Perkins, Mary. *Your Catholic Language*. New York: Sheed & Ward, 1940.

Pius X. *Tra Le Sollecitudini*. Vatican City: ASS, 1903.

Pius XII. *Mediator Dei*. Vatican City: AAS, 1947.

———. *Mystici Corporis*. Vatican City: AAS, 1943.

"Reading List." *1944 Liturgical Week Proceedings*. Chicago: The Liturgical Conference, 1945, 157–66.

Reinhold, H. A. *The Dynamics of Liturgy*. New York: Macmillan, 1961.

———. "Grailville." *Orate Fratres* 23, no. 12 (1949): 544–48.

———. "House of God and House of Hospitality." *Orate Fratres* 14, no. 1 (1939): 77–78.

———. "More or Less Liturgical." *Orate Fratres* 13, no. 4 (1939): 152–55.

"Religion: Christ in the Kitchen." *Time* 54, no. 12 (September 19, 1949): 81–82.

Review of *Cooking for Christ*, by Florence Berger. *Orate Fratres* 24, no. 2 (1950): 91.

Rowe, John G. "The Grail: the Modern Movement for Catholic Girls." *The Ave Maria* 39 (1934): 424–27.

Ryan, Mary Perkins. *Beginning at Home*. Popular Liturgical Library Series. Collegeville, MN: Liturgical Press, 1955.

———. "I'm Going to Like More Vernacular." *Amen* 9 (July 1, 1954): 5–7, 12.

———. "In the Home: Round Table Discussion." *1948 Liturgical Week Proceedings*. Conception, MO: The Liturgical Conference, 1949, 61–68.

———, ed. Introduction to *The Sacramental Way*. New York: Sheed & Ward, 1948, vii–xii.

———. "Liturgy and the Family Arts." *1946 Liturgical Week Proceedings*. Highland Park, IL: The Liturgical Conference, 1947, 106–18.

———. *Mind the Baby!* New York: Sheed & Ward, 1949.

———. "Our Language of Praise." *1942 Liturgical Week Proceedings*. Newark, NJ: Benedictine Liturgical Conference, 1943, 121–32.

———. *The Spirit of Holy Week*. Rev. ed. Notre Dame, IN: Ave Maria Press, 1966.

S. C. "Letter to the Editor." *Orate Fratres* 14, no. 5 (1940): 234.

Sartori, Kate E. "Not a Newcomer." In "The Apostolate." *Orate Fratres* 7, no. 7 (1933): 329.

Scanlon, Marie. "Letter to the Editor." *The Catholic Choirmaster* 12, no. 4 (1926): 128–29.

Schumacher, Heinrich. *Social Message of the New Testament*. Milwaukee: Bruce, 1937.

Schutte, Grace. "The Divine Office and the Liturgy." *Orate Fratres* 7, no. 11 (1933): 492–95.

Shannon, Mabel. "League of the Divine Office." In "The Apostolate." *Orate Fratres* 12, no. 2 (1937): 88–89.

Sinclair, Paula. "From Pew to Pulpit." *Orate Fratres* 15, no. 7 (1941): 295–97.

———. "Give Us Our Heritage." *Orate Fratres* 17, no. 3 (1943): 117–18.

"The Spirit Breatheth." In "The Apostolate." *Orate Fratres* 8, no. 12 (1934): 564–68.

Starr, Ellen Gates. "A Bypath into the Great Roadway." In *On Art, Labor, and Religion.* Edited by Mary Jo Deegan and Ana-Maria Wahl. New Brunswick, NJ: Transaction Publishers, 2003.

———. "The Delights of the Breviary." *Orate Fratres* 1, no. 8 (1927): 263–68.

———. "A Few Trials of a Happy Convert." *The Abbey Chronicle* 3, no. 2 (March 1929): 33–34.

———. "The Liturgy of Palm Sunday and Holy Saturday." *Sponsa Regis* 8, no. 7 (March 15, 1937): 151–57.

———. "On the Feast of the Assumption: Reflections on Some Breviary Texts." *Orate Fratres* 1, no. 10 (1927): 295–300.

———. "Praying the Mass Aside from Mass." *The Sentinel of the Blessed Sacrament* 37, no. 2 (February 1934): 63–70.

Struble, Agnes L. "Liturgical Study Club Activity." "The Apostolate." *Orate Fratres* 7, no. 10 (1933): 474–75.

Tobin, Elizabeth. "The Liturgy: A Remedy for Industrial Evils." *Orate Fratres* 3, no. 12 (1929): 389–91.

Tracy, Eleanor. "Perfection in New Mexico." In "The Apostolate." *Orate Fratres* 9, no. 2 (1934): 91.

van Kersbergen, Lydwine. *The Normal School of Sanctity for the Laity.* Loveland, OH: Grailville, 1959.

———. *Woman, Some Aspects of Her Role in the Modern World.* Loveland, OH: Grailville, 1956.

Van Winkle, Margaretta. "Suggestions." In "The Apostolate." *Orate Fratres* 12, no. 11 (1938): 526.

von Trapp, Maria Augusta. *Around the Year with the Trapp Family.* New York: Pantheon, 1955.

Walsh, Mrs. D. M. "Study Club Activity." In "The Apostolate." *Orate Fratres* 7, no. 6 (1933): 275–76.

Ward, Justine B. "Dom André Mocquereau of Solesmes." *Orate Fratres* 4, no. 5 (1930): 199–207.

———. "Liturgical Music: How to Bring About Its Reform." *Liturgical Arts Quarterly* 10, no. 1 (1941): 7–14.

———. "A Response to the Call of Pius X." Edited by Blanche M. Kelly. New York: Pius X Institute of Liturgical Music, 1922.

———. "Winged Words." *Orate Fratres* 1, no. 4 (1927): 109–12.

Ward, Maisie, ed. *Be Not Solicitous.* New York: Sheed & Ward, 1953.

———. "Changes in the Liturgy: Cri de Coeur." *Life of the Spirit* 16, no. 183 (October 1961): 127–36.

———. "Maisie Ward." In *Born Catholics.* Edited by Frank J. Sheed. New York: Sheed & Ward, 1954.

———. "Problems of the Apostolate." *Orate Fratres* 24, no. 1 (1949): 28–29.

Waters, Vincent S. Forward to *The Paschal Meal: An Arrangement of the Last Supper as an Historical Drama*, by Grailville Community College, Loveland, Ohio. St. Paul, MN: North Central, 1956.

Wesseling, Theodore. *Liturgy and Life*. New York: Longmans, Green, 1938.

Wilcox, Charlotte. "Sodalists' Liturgical Activities." In "The Apostolate." *Orate Fratres* 10, no. 5 (1936): 235.

Willock, Ed. "The Father in the Home." *Integrity* 6, no. 9 (1951): 9–15.

Windeatt, Mary Fabyan. "Good-Will Tour." *Orate Fratres* 16, no. 9 (1942): 393–98.

———. "Whom Shall We Love." *Orate Fratres* 16, no. 5 (1942): 208–12.

Winter, Ernst, and Johanna Winter. "Lent in the Home." *Orate Fratres* 31, no. 3 (1957): 178–87.

Woods, Will. "Mass-Hands." *Orate Fratres* 16, no. 7 (1942): 321–22.

Young, Cecilia. "Liturgical Drama Movement." *Orate Fratres* 7, no. 5 (1933): 226–27.

RELATED WORKS:

Abell, Aaron. "Preparing for Social Action: 1880–1920." In *The American Apostolate: American Catholics in the Twentieth Century*, 11–28. Edited by Leo R. Ward. Westminster, MD: Newman Press, 1952.

Beauduin, Lambert. *Liturgy the Life of the Church*. Popular Liturgical Library Series. Collegeville, MN: Liturgical Press, 1926.

Bednarowski, Mary Farrell. "Outside the Mainstream: Women's Religion and Women Religious Leaders in Nineteenth-Century America." *Journal of the American Academy of Religion* 48, no. 2 (1980): 207–31.

Brown, Victoria Bissell. *The Education of Jane Addams*. Philadelphia: University of Pennsylvania Press, 2004.

Bryce, M. C. "Mary Perkins Ryan." *The Living Light* 12 (1975): 276–81.

Campbell, Debra. "Both Sides Now: Another Look at the Grail in the Postwar Era." *U.S. Catholic Historian* 11, no. 4 (1993): 13–27.

———. "Gleanings of a Laywoman's Ministry: Maisie Ward as Preacher, Publisher and Social Activist." M.A. Thesis, Colby College, 1985.

———. "The Heyday of Catholic Action and the Lay Apostolate, 1929–1959." In *Transforming Parish Ministry: The Changing Roles of Catholic Clergy, Laity, and Women Religious*, 222–52. Edited by Jay P. Dolan and others. New York: Crossroad, 1990.

———. "'I Can't Imagine Our Lady on an Outdoor Platform': Women in the Catholic Street Propaganda Movement." *U.S. Catholic Historian* 26, no. 1 (2008): 103–14.

———. "Reformers and Activists." In *American Catholic Women: A Historical Exploration*, 152–81. Edited by Karen Kennelly. The Bicentennial History of the Catholic Church in America. Edited by Christopher J. Kauffman. New York: Macmillan, 1989.

Carr, Anne E. "The New Vision of Feminist Theology." In *Freeing Theology: The Essentials of Theology in Feminist Perspective*, 5–29. Edited by Catherine Mowry LaCugna. San Francisco: HarperSanFrancisco, 1993.

Carroll, Catherine A. *A History of the Pius X School of Liturgical Music, 1916–1969*. St. Louis, MO: Society of the Sacred Heart, 1989.

Cather, Willa. Prefatory note to *Not Under Forty*. New York: Alfred Knopf, 1936.

Chenu, R. P. "Catholic Action and the Mystical Body." In *Restoring All Things: A Guide to Catholic Action*, 1–15. Edited by John Fitzsimons and Paul McGuire. New York: Sheed & Ward, 1938.

Cott, Nancy. "The Birth of Feminism." In *The Grounding of Modern Feminism*. New Haven: Yale University Press, 1987.

Cummings, Kathleen Sprows. *New Women of the Old Faith: Gender and American Catholicism in the Progressive Era*. Chapel Hill: University of North Carolina Press, 2009.

Day, Dorothy. *From Union Square to Rome*. Silver Spring, MD: Preservation of the Faith Press, 1938.

———. *The Long Loneliness*. 1952. Reprint, San Francisco: Harper & Row Publishers, 1997.

———. *On Pilgrimage*. New York: Curtis Books, 1972.

Diliberto, Gioia. *A Useful Woman*. New York: Charles Scribner's Sons, 1999.

Dolan, Jay P. *The American Catholic Experience: A History from Colonial Times to the Present*. Garden City, NY: Doubleday, 1985.

Dolan, Jay P. and others. *Transforming Parish Ministry: The Changing Roles of Catholic Clergy, Laity, and Women Religious*. New York: Crossroad, 1989.

Donders, Rachel. *History of the International Grail 1921–1979: A Short Description*. Loveland, OH: Grailville, 1983.

Fiorenza, Elisabeth Schüssler. *In Memory of Her: A Feminist Theological Reconstruction of Christian Origins*. 2nd ed. New York: Crossroad, 1994.

Fisher, James T. *Communion of Immigrants: A History of Catholics in America*. New York: Oxford University Press, 2000.

Fleischner, Eva, and Donna Myers Ambrogi. "Grailville in the Sixties: Catechetics and Ecumenism." *U.S. Catholic Historian* 11, no. 4 (1993): 37–44.

Foucault, Michel. "Technologies of the Self." In *Technologies of the Self: A Seminar with Michel Foucault*. Amherst: University of Massachusetts, 1988.

Franchot, Jenny. *Roads to Rome: The Antebellum Protestant Encounter with Catholicism*. Berkeley: University of California Press, 1994.

Frisbie, Margery. *An Alley in Chicago: The Life and Legacy of Monsignor John Egan*. Evanston, IL: Sheed & Ward, 2002.

Gill, Eric. *Work and Property & Church*. London: J.M. Dent & Sons, 1937.

Gindhart, Mary and others, eds. *Histories of the Grail in Individual Countries*. Grailville: The Grail, 1984.

Greeley, Andrew M. *The Church and the Suburbs*. 1959. Reprint, New York: Paulist Press, 1963.

Guéranger, Prosper. *Institutions liturgiques*. Vol. 4. Paris: Société Génerale de Librairie Catholique, 1885.

Hall, Douglas John. "'The Great War' and the Theologians." In *The Twentieth Century: A Theological Overview*. Edited by Gregory Baum. Maryknoll, NY: Orbis Books, 1999.

Haquin, André. "The Liturgical Movement and Catholic Ritual Revision." In *The Oxford History of Christian Worship*, 696–720. Edited by Geoffrey Wainwright and Karen Westerfield Tucker. Oxford: Oxford University Press, 2006.

Hartmann-Ting, L. E. "The National Catholic School of Social Service: Redefining Catholic Womanhood through the Professionalization of Social Work during the Interwar Years." *U.S. Catholic Historian* 16, no. 1 (2008): 101–119.

Henold, Mary. *Catholic and Feminist: The Surprising History of American Catholic Women*. Charlotte: University of North Carolina Press, 2008.

Hieronimi, "Wie lehre ich mein Kind mit der Kirche beten?" *Bibel und Liturgie* 2 (July 1928): 346–47.

Irwin, Kevin W. *Models of the Eucharist*. Mahwah, NJ: Paulist Press, 2005.

James, Janet Wilson. "Women in American Religious History: An Overview." In *Women in American Religion*, 1–25. Edited by Janet Wilson James and others. Philadelphia: University of Pennsylvania Press, 1980.

Johnson, James A. "Artist on the Point helped shape the local landscape." *The Newport Daily News*, May 5, 2010.

Johnson, Kathleen Carlton. "Radical Social Activism, Lay Catholic Women and American Feminism 1920–1960." PhD diss., University of South Africa, 2006.

Kalven, Janet. "Grailville in the Seventies and Eighties: Structural Changes and Feminist Consciousness." *U.S. Catholic Historian* 11, no. 4 (1993): 45–57.

———. "Women Breaking Boundaries: The Grail and Feminism." *Journal of Feminist Studies in Religion* 5 (1989): 119–42.

———. *Women Breaking Boundaries: A Grail Journey, 1940–1965*. Albany, NY: State University of New York Press, 1999.

Kaplan, Wendy. *The Arts & Crafts Movement in Europe and America: Design for the Modern World, 1880-1920*. New York: Thames & Hudson in association with the Los Angeles County Museum of Art, 2004.

Kaplan, Wendy, and Elizabeth Cumming. *The Arts and Crafts Movement*. New York: Thames and Hudson, 1991.

Kelly, J. "La Réforme grégorienne aux Etats-Unis." *Revue Grégorienne* (1920): 69.

Kenneally, James J. "A Question of Equality." In *American Catholic Women: A Historical Exploration*, 125–51. Edited by Karen Kennelly. The Bicentennial History of the Catholic Church in America Series. Edited by Christopher J. Kauffman. New York: Macmillan, 1989.

Knight, Louise W. *Jane Addams: Spirit in Action*. New York: W. W. Norton, 2010.

Leo XIII. *Rerum Novarum*. Vatican City: ASS, 1891.

Löhr, Aemiliana. Review of *Priestertum der Frau*, by Oda Schneider. *Jahrbuch fur Liturgiewissenschaft* 14 (1934): 278.

———. *The Year of Our Lord: The Mystery of Christ in the Liturgical Year*. Translated by A Monk of St. Benedict. New York: P. J. Kenedy & Sons, 1937.

MacCarthy, Esther. "Catholic Women and War: The National Council of Catholic Women, 1919–1946." *Peace and Change* 5 (1978): 23–32.

Manzetti, L. P. "Echoes of the Gregorian Congress." *Cathedral Choir* (1920): 114.

Marbach, Ethel. "The Eternal Woman." *Catholic Digest* 28 (October 1964): 79–81.

McDannell, Colleen. "Catholic Domesticity, 1860–1920." In *American Catholic Women: A Historical Exploration*, 48-80. Edited by Karen Kennelly. The Bicentennial History of the Catholic Church in America. Edited by Christopher J. Kauffman. New York: Macmillan, 1989.

McGuinness, Margaret Mary. "Response to Reform: An Historical Interpretation of the Catholic Settlement Movement, 1897–1915." PhD diss., Union Theological Seminary, 1985.

Merriman, Brigid O'Shea. *Searching for Christ: The Spirituality of Dorothy Day*. Notre Dame, IN: University of Notre Dame Press, 1994.

Michel, Virgil. *The Social Question: Essays on Capitalism and Christianity*. Edited by Robert L. Spaeth. Collegeville, MN: St John's University Office of Academic Affairs, 1987.

Morton, Keith, and John Saltmarsh. "A Cultural Context for Understanding Dorothy Day's Social and Political Thought." In *Dorothy Day and the Catholic Worker Movement: Centenary Essays*. Edited by William J. Thorn, Phillip M. Runkel, and Susan Mountin. Marquette Studies in Theology, no. 32. Milwaukee, WI: Marquette University Press, 2001.

O'Brien, David J. *American Catholics and Social Reform: The New Deal Years*. New York: Oxford University Press, 1968.

O'Reilly, Bernard. *The Mirror of True Womanhood; A Book of Instruction for Women in the World*. New York: Peter F. Collier, 1878.

O'Toole, James M. *The Faithful: A History of Catholics in America*. Cambridge, MA: Belknap Press of Harvard University Press, 2008.

Orsi, Robert. *The Madonna of 115th Street*. New Haven, CT: Yale University Press, 1985.

Parrish, Marilyn McKinley. "Seeking Authenticity: Women and Learning in the Catholic Worker Movement." EdD thesis, College of Education, Pennsylvania State University, 2004.

Parsch, Pius. "Die Mitarbeit der Frau in der liturgischen Bewegung." *Bibel und Liturgie* 8 (1933/1934): 436–44.

Perkins Ryan, Mary. *Are Parochial Schools the Answer?* New York: Holt, Rinehart and Winston, 1964.

Piehl, Mel. *Breaking Bread: The Catholic Worker and the Origin of Catholic Radicalism in America*. Philadelphia: Temple University Press, 1982.

Piott, Steven L. "Jane Addams and the Settlement House Idea." In *American Reformers 1870–1920: Progressives in Word and Deed*. Lanham, MD: Rowman & Littlefield, 2006.

Pius XI. *Quadragesimo Anno*. Vatican City: AAS, 1931.

———. *Ubi Arcano*. Vatican City: AAS, 1922.

Power, David. "Sacramental Theology: A Review of Literature; Feminist Theology." *Theological Studies* 55, no. 4 (1994): 693–702.

Quigley, Jr., Martin, and Edward M. Connors, eds., *Catholic Action in Practice: Family Life, Education, International Life*. New York: Random House, 1963.

Rauschenbusch, Walter. *Christianizing the Social Order*. New York: Macmillan, 1912.

Reher, Margaret Mary. "The Path to Pluralism, 1920–1985." In *Catholic Intellectual Life in America: A Historical Study of Persons and Movements*, 91–141. Makers of the Catholic Community Series. Edited by Christopher J. Kauffman. New York: Macmillan, 1989.

Ross, Susan A. "The Bride of Christ and the Body Politic: Body and Gender in Pre-Vatican II Marriage Theology." *The Journal of Religion* 71, no. 3 (1991): 345–61.

Ruether, Rosemary Radford. "Women-Church: A Feminist Exodus Community." In *Women-Church: Theology and Practice of Feminist Liturgical Communities*. San Francisco: Harper & Row, 1988.

Senser, Bob. "Library in the Marketplace." *The Catholic Digest: The Golden Thread of Catholic Thought* 11, no. 2 (1947): 31–33.

Sheed, Frank J. *The Church and I*. Garden City, NY: Doubleday, 1974.

Sicherman, Barbara. *Alice Hamilton: A Life in Letters*. Cambridge, MA: Harvard University Press, 1983.

Skok, Deborah A. "The Historiography of Catholic Laywomen and Progressive Era Reform." *U.S. Catholic Historian* 26, no. 1 (2008): 1–21.

Starr, Ellen Gates. "Hull-House Bookbindery." *Commons* 47 (June 30, 1900): 5–6.

———. "Settlements and the Church's Duty." *Publications of the Church of Social Action*, no. 28. Boston: n.p., 1896.

Tarry, Ellen. *The Third Door: The Autobiography of an American Negro Woman*. Tuscaloosa: University of Alabama Press, 1992.

Tentler, Leslie Woodcock. *Catholics and Contraception: An American History*. Ithaca, NY: Cornell University Press, 2004.

Tuchman, Barbara. *The Guns of August*. New York: Dell Publishing Co., 1962.

Twose, George M. R. "The Coffee-Room at Hull House." *House Beautiful* 7 (January 1900): 107–9.

Vance, John G. *The Ladies of the Grail*. London: Catholic Truth Society, 1935.

Vatican II. *Sacrosanctum Concilium*. Vatican City: AAS, 1963.

Walsh, Mary Elizabeth. *The Saints and Social Work*. Silver Spring, MD: Preservation of the Faith, 1936.

Ward, Justine B., and Elizabeth Ward Perkins. *Music First Year*. Washington, DC: Catholic Education Press, 1914.

Ward, Leo R., ed. *Catholic Life, U.S.A.: Contemporary Lay Movements*. St. Louis, MO: B. Herder Book, 1959.

———. *The Living Parish*. Notre Dame, IN: Fides, 1959.

Ward, Maisie. *Unfinished Business*. New York: Sheed & Ward, 1964.

Weaver, Mary Jo. *New Catholic Women: A Contemporary Challenge to Traditional Religious Authority*. Bloomington: Indiana University Press, 1995.

———. "Still Feisty at Fifty: The Grailville Lay Apostolate for Women." *U.S. Catholic Historian* 2, no. 4 (Fall 1993): 3–12.

Weber, Joanna. "The Sacred in Art: Introducing Father Marie-Alain Couturier's Aesthetic." *Worship* 69, no. 3 (1995): 243–62.

Your Cana Club: A Basic Program. Washington, DC: Archdiocese of Washington, 1959.

SUPPLEMENTARY MATERIALS

Berger, Fred. "Alfred Joseph Berger." http://bergerhill.info/BG_Alfred.html.

Berger, Teresa. "The Classical Liturgical Movement in Germany and Austria: Moved by Women?" *Worship* 66, no. 3 (1992): 231–50.

———. *Fragments of Real Presence: Liturgical Traditions in the Hands of Women.* New York: Crossroad, 2005.

———. *Gender Differences and the Making of Liturgical History: Lifting a Veil on Liturgy's Past.* Farnham, UK: Ashgate, 2011.

———. *"Liturgie und Frauenseele": Die liturgische Bewegung aus der Sicht der Frauenforschung.* Stuttgart: Verlag W. Kohlhammer, 1993.

———. *Women's Ways of Worship: Gender Analysis and Liturgical History.* Collegeville, MN: Liturgical Press, 1994.

Berger, Teresa, and Albert Gerhards. *Liturgie und Frauenfrage: ein Beitrag zur Frauenforschung aus liturgiewissenschaftlicher Sicht.* St. Ottlien: EOS Verlag Erzabtei, 1990.

Bosch, Jennifer Lynne. "The Life of Ellen Gates Starr, 1859–1940." PhD diss., Miami University, 1990.

Botte, Bernard. *From Silence to Participation: An Insider's View of Liturgical Renewal.* Translated by John Sullivan. Washington, DC: Pastoral Press, 1988.

Brancaleone, Francis. "Justine Ward and the Fostering of an American Solesmes Chant Tradition." *Sacred Music* 136, no. 3 (2009): 6–26.

Brien, Dolores Elis. "The Catholic Revival Revisited." *Commonweal* (December 21, 1979): 714–16.

Brown, Alden V. "The Grail Movement to 1962: Laywomen and a New Christendom." *U.S. Catholic Historian* 3, no. 3 (1983): 149–66.

———. *The Grail Movement and American Catholicism, 1940–1975.* Notre Dame Studies in American Catholicism Series. Notre Dame, IN: University of Notre Dame Press, 1989.

Chandlee, H. Ellsworth. "The Liturgical Movement." In *The New Westminster Dictionary of Liturgy and Worship.* Edited by J. G. Davies. Louisville, KY: Westminster/John Knox Press, 1986.

Combe, Pierre. *Justine Ward and Solesmes.* Washington, DC: Catholic University of America Press, 1987.

Cunningham, Jim. "Specialized Catholic Action." In *The American Apostolate: American Catholics in the Twentieth Century*, 47–65. Edited by Leo Richard Ward. Westminster, MD: Newman Press, 1952.

Davis, Rebecca Berru. "Women Artists of the Early Twentieth Century Liturgical Movement in the United States: The Contributions of E. Charlton Fortune, Ade Bethune, and Sister Helene O'Connor, O.P." PhD diss., Graduate Theological Union, 2011.

Diekmann, Godfrey. "Is There a Distinct American Contribution to the Liturgical Renewal?" *Worship* 45, no. 10 (1971): 578–87.

Dougherty, Joseph. *From Altar-Throne to Table: The Campaign for Frequent Holy Communion in the Catholic Church*. ATLA Monograph Series, no. 50. Lanham, MD: Scarecrow Press, 2010.

Dower, Catherine. "Patrons of the Arts, The Wards: Justine and George, Symbolic Illusions." In *Cum Angelis Canere*. St. Paul, MN: Catholic Church Music Associates, 1990.

Duquin, Lorene Hanley. *They Called Her the Baroness: The Life of Catherine de Hueck Doherty*. New York: Alba House, 1995.

Fenwick R. K., and Brian D. Spinks. *Worship in Transition: Highlights of the Liturgical Movement*. Edinburgh: T. and T. Clark, 1995.

Franklin, R. William. "The People's Work: Anti-Jansenist Prejudice in the Benedictine Movement for Popular Participation in the Nineteenth Century." *Studia Liturgica* 19, no. 1 (1989): 60–77.

Frutkin, Ann Berger. *Florence and Al Berger: A Collaborative Memory of a Cincinnati Family*. Hilton Head Island, SC: Studiobooks, 2009.

G. H. Review of *Music: First Year*, by Justine B. Ward. *Orate Fratres* 8, no. 2 (1933): 94.

Greene, Dana. *The Living of Maisie Ward*. Notre Dame, IN: University of Notre Dame Press, 1997.

———. "Maisie Ward as 'Theologian.'" In *Women and Theology*. Edited by Mary Ann Hinsdale and Phyllis H. Kaminski. The Annual Publication of the College Theology Society Series. Vol. 40. Maryknoll, NY: Orbis Books, 1994.

Heekin, Ann Morrow. "The Life and Work of Mary Perkins Ryan: The Interplay of Liturgy and Catechesis in Whole Community Education." *Religious Education for Peace and Justice Proceedings*. November 4–6, 2005. http://old.religious education.net/proceedings/2005_papers.htm.

Herr, Dan. "The Gentle Firebrand." *U.S. Catholic* (1964): 10–13.

Hinsdale, Mary Ann. *Women Shaping Theology*. 2004 Madeleva Lecture in Spirituality Series. New York: Paulist Press, 2006.

Hughes, Kathleen, ed. *How Firm a Foundation: Voices of the Early Liturgical Movement*. Chicago: Liturgy Training Publications, 1990.

———. *The Monk's Tale: Biography of Godfrey Diekmann, O.S.B.* Collegeville, MN: Liturgical Press, 1991.

Kalven, Janet, and Grail Members. "Living the Liturgy: Keystone of the Grail Vision." *U.S. Catholic Historian* 11, no. 4 (1993): 29–38.

Kavanagh, Aidan. "Liturgical Business Unfinished and Unbegun." *Worship* 50, no. 4 (1976): 354–64.

Koenker, Ernst B. *The Liturgical Renaissance in the Roman Catholic Church*. Chicago: University of Chicago Press, 1954.

MacEoin, Gary. "Lay Movements in the United States before Vatican II." *America* 165 (August 1991): 61–65.

Mandell, Gail Porter. *Madeleva: A Biography*. Albany: State University of New York Press, 1997.

Marx, Paul. *Virgil Michel and the Liturgical Movement*. Collegeville, MN: Liturgical Press, 1957.

McConnell, Helen H. "Aemiliana Löhr's Theology of Liturgical Worship." PhD diss., Catholic University of America, 2001.

McGuire, Anne C. "The Reform of Holy Week, 1951–1969: Process, Problems, and Possibilities." PhD diss., University of Notre Dame, 2001.

McKeown, Elizabeth. "The National Bishop's Conference: An Analysis of Its Origins." *Catholic Historical Review* 66 (October 1980): 565–83.

McMahon, Leo M. "Towards a Theology of the Liturgy: Dom Odo Casel and the 'Mysterientheologie.'" *Studia Liturgica* 3, no. 3 (1964): 129–54.

Mitchell, Nathan D. "The Amen Corner: A Mansion for the Rat." *Worship* 68, no. 1 (1994): 64–72.

Nelson, Gertrud Mueller. *Sisters Today* 68, no. 6 (1996): 403–9.

Pecklers, Keith F. "The Liturgical Movement." In *The New SCM Dictionary of Liturgy and Worship*. Edited by Paul F. Bradshaw. 2nd ed. London: SCM Press, 2002.

———. *The Unread Vision: The Liturgical Movement in the United States of America: 1926–1955*. Collegeville, MN: Liturgical Press, 1998.

Pottebaum, Gerard A. "In Gratitude for the Life of Mary Perkins Ryan." *CIC Update: The Christian Initiation of Children Newsletter* 4, no. 4 (1993): 1–2.

Ramsey, David. *Ade Bethune*. The Archives of Modern Christian Art Series. Belmont, CA: College of Notre Dame, 1986.

Rousseau, Oliver. *The Progress of the Liturgy: An Historical Sketch from the Beginning of the Nineteenth Century to the Pontificate of Pius X*. Translated by the Benedictines of Westminster Priory. Westminster, MD: Newman Press, 1951.

Ruff, Anthony. *Sacred Music and Liturgical Reform: Treasures and Transformations*. Chicago: Hillenbrand Books, 2007.

Shepherd, Massey Hamilton. "History of the Liturgical Renewal." In *The Liturgical Renewal of the Church: Addresses of the Liturgical Conference in 1958*. Edited by Massey Hamilton Shepherd. New York: Oxford University Press, 1960.

———. *The Reform of Liturgical Worship: Perspectives and Prospects*. New York: Oxford University Press, 1961.

Starr, Ellen Gates. *On Art, Labor, and Religion*. Edited by Mary Jo Deegan and Ana-Maria Wahl. New Brunswick, NJ: Transaction Publishers, 2003.

Stoughton, Judith. *Proud Donkey of Schaerbeek: Adé Bethune: Catholic Worker Artist*. St. Cloud, MN: North Star Press of St. Cloud, 1988.

Taylor, Michael J. *The Protestant Liturgical Renewal*. Westminster, MD: Newman Press, 1963.

White, Susan. *Art, Architecture, and Liturgical Reform: the Liturgical Arts Society (1928–1972)*. New York: Pueblo Publishing, 1990.

Wilde, James A. "Franz and Therese Mueller: The Domestic Church." In *How Firm a Foundation: Leaders of the Liturgical Movement*. Compiled and edited by Robert Tuzik. Chicago: Liturgy Training Publications, 1990.

Woods, Michael J. *Cultivating Soil and Soul: Twentieth-Century Catholic Agrarians Embrace the Liturgical Movement*. Collegeville, MN: Liturgical Press, 2009.

Zwick, Mark, and Louise Zwick. "Dom Virgil Michel, OSB, the Liturgical Movement, and the Catholic Worker." In *The Catholic Worker Movement: Intellectual and Spiritual Origins*, 58–74. Mahwah, NJ: Paulist Press, 2005.

Index of Names

Mitchell, Nathan D., 339
Mocquereau, André, 63–65, 69, 74
Moore, Nina Polcyn, 152, 156n90, 157–61, 170, 180, 181
Morrison, Joseph P., 185
Mueller, Franz, 256, 257, 260, 265, 266n69
Mueller, Therese, 227, 243n2, 245, 255–72, 272n89, 285, 287, 296, 315, 322, 323
Mullen, Mrs. Mary, 137–38
Murray, Jane Marie, xviiin8, 96n150, 201n37

Nelson, Gertrud Mueller, 256n38, 269n79, 271
Newberg, Mrs., 329–30
Newland, Mary Reed, 304n181, 318–20
Nolan, Joseph T., 238
Nutting, Eileen, 249–50
Nutting, Willis, 321

O'Hara, Edwin V., 221, 222
O'Neill, Sara Benedicta, 93, 147–56, 157, 158–59, 160
O'Reilly, Bernard, 35n11
Osborne, Catherine, 160n102
Overboss, Joan, 48, 49n134, 225, 233

Parrish, Marilyn McKinley, 172
Parsch, Pius, 19–20, 32, 283
Pecklers, Keith F., xv, 12, 151, 153n81, 158n96, 177–78n158
Perkins, Mary. See Ryan, Mary Perkins
Perkins, Mrs. Charles, 330
Piehl, Mel, 161, 172
Pinsk, Johannes, 15
Pius Christ, 3, 7, 8, 17, 25, 26, 45n123, 53, 61, 62n26, 63, 69, 86, 142, 217, 224, 226, 253, 279, 293–94n153
Pius XI, 66, 129, 152n170, 188, 200, 302–3
Pius XII, 177–78n158, 294, 325

Polcyn, Nina. See Moore, Nina Polcyn
Pottebaum, Gerard A., 297, 299
Prosper of Aquitaine, Saint, 189

Redwood, Vernon, 134
Reinhold, H. A., xvin4, xvii, 74, 153n80, 154, 156n90, 175–76, 237–38, 258, 260, 320, 329, 331–32
Ryan, John Julian, 283, 284, 286, 294, 296, 300, 321
Ryan, Mary Perkins, xvin4, xix, 241, 242–43n1, 249, 272–300, 303n178, 309, 309–10n197, 210, 315, 321n231, 337

Senser, Bob, 153, 154n82, 154–55n85
Shannon, Miss Mabel, 108
Shea, James, 234, 321
Sheed, Frank, 134, 135, 146, 147, 151, 273
Sheil, Bernard J., 152, 152n76, 158n95, 181, 181n168, 234, 285
Shepherd, Massey, 8, 11, 12, 13, 17n42
Shuster, George H., 150, 164
Sparks, Mary, 137n26, 140, 265n67
Staley, Austin, 330
Starr, Eliza Allen, 76, 77n76, 82n92
Starr, Ellen Gates, 75–97, 98, 103, 105, 123, 124–26, 148, 149n67, 159, 170, 275, 326, 329
Stedman, Joseph, 201
Stevens, Mother Georgia, 62, 74, 74n66
Storey, William, 294n155
Stritch, Samuel, 234
Struble, Agnes L., 125, 125–26n241
Sullivan, Elizabeth, 159

Tarry, Ellen, 186, 186n180
Tentler, Leslie Woodcock, 250
Terranova, Noel, 179n164
Tobin, Elizabeth, 97, 98, 100
Tracy, Eleanor, 101–2
Tuchman, Barbara, 1

van Kersbergen, Lydwine, 42, 42n115, 43, 48, 224, 224–25n101, 226, 226n106, 231, 233, 234–35, 237n137
Vishnewski, Stanley, 167
von Trapp, Maria, 260, 304n181

Wahl, Ana-Maria, 78
Walsh, Mrs. D. M., 120
Ward, George Cabot, 61
Ward, Justine Bayard, 60–75, 97, 100, 124, 126
Ward, Leo R., 129, 131, 237, 238n140, 250
Ward, Maisie, 132–47, 151, 153n80, 154, 155, 158n97, 177, 178, 273, 326, 333
Weaver, Mary Jo, 57n16, 239, 239–40n147

Weltzer, Isabelle, 161
Weston, Dorothy. *See* Coddington, Dorothy Weston.
White, Susan, 72n59
Wickes, Francine, 231–32
Windeatt, Mary Fabyan, 333–35
Wintersig, Athanasius, 15–16
Wolff, Mother Mary Madeleva, 138, 275, 316
Woods, Michael, 190, 222, 224n99, 292n148
Woods, Will, 176

Young, Cecilia, 99–100
Young, John, 62

Zwick, Mark, and Louise Zwick, 164, 164n159, 165n121, 166, 167

Subject Index

Abbey of the Holy Cross, Herstelle, 5, 13, 32

adolescents. *See* liturgical education

adult education. *See* liturgical education

Advent wreath, 269–70

African Americans, 179, 181, 186, 230

altar. *See* liturgical architecture

Altar and Home, 111, 247, 248, 269, 272n89

America, 238

American Catholic, 127–28, 129–32, 136, 171–72, 245, 250–54, 334
 education, 112, 121, 132, 136
 social history, xv–xvi, 4–6, 327, 338–39

Americanization, 56, 224n181, 282, 329–30

Anglicans, 10n21, 51n136, 60, 77, 94, 126, 162, 183

architecture. *See* liturgical architecture

Archiv für Liturgiewissenschäft, 31

art, 76, 77–79, 97, 174
 and Christian art, 76, 204n46, 205, 209
 and liturgical participation, 199–200, 206–9, 221
 and the liturgical movement, 3, 65–66, 81–83, 185–99
 as aid to worship, 65, 69
 as modern art, 190
 of the home, 203, 210–11, 228, 243–45, 289–91

artists, 76, 98, 102n170, 103, 199, 204, 206–9, 221

Arts and Crafts Movement, 78–81, 190–91

Ave Maria, 35

Bacalar, Mexico, 212, 215

baptism, 26, 218, 229, 258–59, 263–64, 265, 273n92, 286, 287, 289–90, 312, 322
 and priesthood of the baptized, 122, 245, 290

Benedict, Saint, 9, 149, 167

Benedictine, 5, 8, 10n22, 12–13, 26–27, 30, 64, 82, 149, 166–67
 oblates, 65, 75, 168, 197, 284

Benedictine Liturgical Conference, 278

bookstores, 147–51, 231n118, 159–60
 St. Benet Bookshop, 149–61

Breviary, 50, 59, 81–91, 103–6, 148, 231, 275, 278, 311, 336

Caecilia, 74, 113

Calvert Club, 93, 96, 148, 149

Campion Propaganda Movement, 172–73

Cana Conference, 141, 251, 322n233

capitalism, 5, 38, 40, 54, 163

catechesis, 30, 31, 94, 103, 107, 223n98, 296–98, 333

catechism, 94, 193

Catholic Action, 23, 24n61, 26, 35, 45–46, 53, 108, 114–15, 121, 129–31, 138, 153, 173, 252
 and social responsibility, 23–24, 114–15, 129, 188, 191, 273
 and the liturgical movement, 129–31, 222, 259, 312, 335
 and women's duty, 45–46, 114–15, 119–20n222, 121, 224–25
 summer schools, 196, 226, 230

Catholic agrarianism, 191, 222–23, 248, 292

dialogue Mass, 137, 143, 144, 145–46n56, 233, 230, 231, 243, 281, 312, 332
Divine Office. *See* Liturgy of the Hours
Doddridge Farm, Libertyville, Illinois, 229, 230n116, 234–35
drama, 35, 47, 99–100, 230, 234–35

Easter Vigil, 142, 322, 325
Eastern Catholics, 168
education
    and Catholic schools, 261, 296–98, 311, 323
    and the family, 211, 243–45, 260–61, 265, 295–96
    and the goals of the liturgical movement, xix, 54, 94, 97, 101, 333, 336
English in the liturgy, 83n97, 144, 156, 231, 232n122, 275, 282n121, 300
Eucharist
    and family, 242, 254
    and food, 244–45
    and reception during Mass, 70, 217–18, 223n98

family, 141, 173, 241, 242–45, 249, 251, 252–53, 260, 287–88
    activities, 190, 211, 236, 246, 262–63, 302–3, 316–17
    and children's participation, 258, 261–62, 306
    and Eucharist, 140, 248, 264, 329
    and men, 320–21
    and prayer, 131, 268, 305
    and women's responsibility, 20, 55, 111, 119–20n222, 245, 288–89, 292–93
    as little church, 308, 310
    as Mystical Body of Christ, 242, 244, 248, 254, 290
Family Life in Christ, 259, 259–60n50, 262, 264n63, 269

femininity, 6, 18–20, 138, 139–40, 190, 304n181
feminism, xviin7, 38–39, 41n112, 50, 57, 226n106, 239, 239–40n147
feminization of liturgy, 18–20
Friendship House, 98, 132, 180–81, 184, 185–86, 225

gender, xviin7, 6, 109, 110, 111, 140, 245, 326–32
Grail Movement, the, 33–49, 130, , 178–79, 212, 224–41
    American Grail Movement, 224–41, 302
    and courses for study, 227–32, 277
    and feminism, 38–40, 41n112, 190, 226n106, 239, 239–40n147
    and liturgical prayer, 229–30, 231–32
    and liturgical resources, 159, 235–37, 317
    and liturgical scholars, 227, 229, 237–38
    and participation in the liturgy, 44–49, 226, 228–30
    Dutch Grail Movement, 33–49
Grailville. *See* Grail Movement, the
Gregorian chant. *See* liturgical music

high schools. *See* liturgical education
Holy Spirit, 16, 33–34, 226, 281, 287, 289
Holy Week, 31, 120n222, 142, 192, 229–30, 237, 245, 312
home
    and Catholic life, 40–41, 56, 137, 243–45, 247, 252
    and women's role, 20, 21n53, 38, 55, 57, 111, 244–45, 249, 250, 266, 289–90, 302, 303–4
    liturgical activities, 112, 119n222, 125, 202, 240–41, 253–54, 258–59, 262–65, 287–89, 308–9, 311, 316–17, 318–20

Hull-House, 75, 80–81, 94, 95, 170

immigrants, 52, 53, 56, 80–81, 126, 180–81
individualism, 5, 10, 49, 98, 109–10, 189
industrialization , 53, 97–98, 109–10, 189
Integrity, 146, 321
International Congress of Gregorian Chant, 63
interracial justice, 138, 178–79, 180–81, 185–86, 333

Jahrbuch für Liturgiewissenschaft, 6, 7, 13, 14
Jansenism, 10, 138n27, 191n6
Jesuits, 115n207, 157, 182
Jocists, 45
John Stevens Shop, 196–97, 198, 202
Junipero Serra Bookshop, San Francisco, California, 159–60

kitchen, 194n16, 203, 228, 245, 249–50, 292–93, 302–10
Knights of Columbus, 56, 140

labor, 25, 54–55, 56, 77–80, 98, 167–68, 251, 292
    and liturgical renewal, 170, 190–91, 195, 197–200, 202–3, 213, 228
    strikes, 77, 81, 126
Land and Home, 222, 223n97
Latin, 9, 83, 156
    and liturgical music, 35, 60, 63–64, 69, 206, 236, 279
    and liturgical reform, 9–10, 50, 71, 105, 280–81, 335
    learning Latin, 274–78, 300
lay apostolate, 16, 18, 22, 24, 26, 45, 46, 48, 84, 129–31, 146, 151, 186, 191, 231, 239, 244, 252, 289, 321
lay participation, 3, 13, 17, 21–22, 29–30, 58, 89, 97, 121, 131, 137, 141, 142–44, 168, 188, 206–9, 216, 223,

227, 229–31, 254, 275, 286, 293, 299, 312, 321–22, 332, 338
League of the Divine Office, 105
Lex Orandi, Lex Credendi, Lex Agendi, 189
liturgical architecture
    altar, xvi, 113n203, 144
    altar rail, 213n65, 217, 218, 219
    and participation, 144, 214
    baptistery, 213, 218, 219
    bell tower, 218
    church buildings, 52, 207, 212–13, 218, 240
    consulting, 212–19
    mission churches, 215–17
liturgical art, 100–103, 158–59, 236–37
    and education, 88, 209–12, 214
    as opposed to "kitsch," 159, 205
    production, 160, 202, 212–15
    promoting, 161, 175n151
liturgical artists. *See* artists
Liturgical Arts Quarterly, 73, 102, 103, 123, 205–6
Liturgical Arts Schola, 72
Liturgical Arts Society, 72–73, 102, 196, 205
Liturgical Briefs, 64, 70, 82, 112, 202
liturgical changes, 143–44, 219, 245
liturgical education
    academic programs in liturgy, 5, 138, 147–48
    and adolescents, 36, 43, 44, 45–46, 120n223, 160n104, 201n37
    and adults, 196
    and catechesis, 31, 332
    and children, 107–8, 141
    and culture, 282n122, 261
    and goals of the liturgical movement, xix, 3, 101, 333, 336
    and preaching, 329
    and study clubs, 56, 109, 112–13, 116–23, 125, 136, 147, 178–79, 182–83, 186, 188, 200, 243, 253, 254, 266, 293, 327

in colleges and universities, 97–99,
201
in high schools, 101n166, 120n223,
135, 165n121, 210n37, 212, 227,
315, 323n235
tools and media, 59, 101, 113, 190,
275, 277–78
liturgical minimalism, 227, 289, 332, 336
liturgical movement
and Catholic Action, 129–31, 222,
259, 312, 335
and Catholic Agrarianism, 191,
222–23, 248, 292
and religious sisters, xviiin8, 108,
172, 192, 300, 322
and social regeneration, 54, 58,
131–32, 158–59, 171–72
and support of bishops, 130, 324
and women. *See* women
in Austria, 48, 110
in Belgium, 16–18, 143
in France, 8–12, 63–65
in Germany, 12–16
in the United States, xv–xvi, 4–6,
12n26, 26–27, 48–51, 52–60, 63,
118, 188–89, 317
liturgical music
and chant, 61–62, 64–72
and children, 60, 62–63, 70, 72, 101
and choirs, 71, 72, 100n165, 101,
101n166, 310, 334, 336
and congregational singing, 64n30,
75, 142–43, 214, 231–32, 253, 275,
335n22
and education, 62–64, 67, 69,
70–72, 100
and Gregorian chant, 60, 63–64, 69,
206, 227, 236, 279
and Ward Method, 62, 64n30, 66,
70–71
at Solesmes, 9, 60, 64–65, 74
liturgical participation
and mystical body, 3–4, 103–4,
168–69

as "assisting" at Mass, 22, 82n92,
86, 117, 119n221, 129, 223n98,
230, 333–34, 334
with missal, 59, 67n42, 86, 97–98,
103
liturgical prayer, 3, 60, 63, 70, 81–82,
87, 97, 104, 130–31, 137, 166–67,
189, 205–6, 221, 231, 240
and use of the psalter, 81–82, 83,
115, 155n88, 156–57n91, 294
Liturgical Press, 106, 112, 118, 120,
125, 148, 166, 240, 266, 268, 271,
283
liturgical seasons, 9, 47, 116, 210, 261–
62, 269–70, 304–6, 312, 316, 322
Liturgical Weeks. *See* National
Liturgical Weeks
liturgical year, 9, 26, 27–32, 47, 65,
82n92, 112, 116, 125–26n24, 210–11,
231, 236, 240, 244, 246, 257, 261–62,
268, 284, 303n178, 304–6, 311, 319,
322–23n234, 329
liturgy
and accessibility, 328n3
and amateurs, 207, 328
and arts, 3, 65–66, 81–83, 114–15,
119–20n222, 121, 195–202,
224–25
and Catholic Action, 129–31, 222,
259, 312, 335
and cooking, 242–43, 245, 249–50,
288–89, 303–9, 317, 318, 322
and crafts, 210–11, 242
and culture, 102, 168–69, 190,
217–18, 282n120
and education. *See* education
and indifference, 107n184, 260–61,
329, 334
and interracial justice, 138, 180–81,
185–86, 333
and Sacred Scripture, 155–56, 201,
231, 264
and social regeneration, 131, 153,
170, 176, 188, 293

and the family. *See* family
and the home. *See* home
as solution to individualism, 49,
    98, 189, 279, 333–34
feminine nature of, 18–20
participation in. *See* liturgical
    participation
pastoral nature of, 9, 16, 17, 31,
    143–44, 145, 177–78n158, 281–82
simplification of, 71, 105, 107–8,
    190
social aspect, 54, 58, 131–32,
    158–59, 171–78
study of. *See* liturgical education
syllogism, 129
teaching. *See* liturgical education
versus devotion, 171, 205, 245,
    332–33
Liturgy of the Hours, 67n42, 84n101,
    87–88, 103–4, 106, 124n236, 138,
    155, 156, 168, 227, 278, 279

Madonna House, 181n166, 186,
    197n23
Manhattan College, New York, New
    York, 273
Manhattanville Academy. *See*
    Manhattanville College
Maredsous Abbey, 12
Maria Laach Abbey, 12, 30, 143, 154
Marquette University, Milwaukee,
    Wisconsin, 157
marriage, 40, 141, 216n74, 234,
    236n133, 237, 242–43n1, 243, 243–
    44n2, 252, 266, 270–71, 286, 287,
    289, 313–14, 321, 327, 330–32
Marygrove College, Detroit,
    Michigan, 98
masculinity and masculinization, 5,
    19, 20n51, 39, 40
Mass
    and participation, 22–23, 30, 32, 71,
        85, 86–87, 101, 124, 137, 141, 144,
        206, 223, 230, 242, 310

and social quality, 47, 48, 97–98,
    129, 160, 179, 204, 287
as sacrifice, 103, 118, 200, 203, 227,
    286, 292
study of, 107–8, 112, 116, 265, 277
Mediator Dei, 177–78n158
men
    and liturgy, 13, 101, 110, 111, 121,
        252, 321n231, 234, 328
    involvement in family, 252, 258,
        261, 264, 306, 310, 311
Minneapolis School of Music,
    Minneapolis, Minnesota, 100
Missa Cantata, 227, 230
Missa Recitata. *See* dialogue Mass
Missal
    and family, 124n236
    and prayer, 81, 86, 103, 143, 192
    intelligent use of, 83, 91, 96,
        130–31n5, 133n9, 336
    study of, 59, 93, 99, 112, 116–17,
        119, 121, 122, 125, 253, 277–78,
        282n122
Modernism, 1–3, 5, 45, 131, 125–
    26n65, 338
Mont Cèsar, Belgium, 12, 16
music. *See* liturgical music
My Sunday Missal, 201
mystagogy, 29–31
Mysterientheologie, 13, 22, 31
Mystical Body of Christ
    and American popularity, 4, 13, 132
    and communion, 140, 168–69, 182,
        232
    and participation, 103–4, 137,
        168–69, 188, 200, 254
    and social justice, xix, 3–4, 18,
        22n57, 24–26, 127n242, 170, 186,
        189, 225
    theology of, 3–4, 13, 22–23, 48, 177

National Catholic Rural Life
    Conference, 169, 191, 222, 223–34,
    245, 291, 302–4, 308, 315–16

Sheil School of Social Studies, 152, 181

Social Gospel Movement, 154, 172

social justice, 56, 98, 132, 138, 164, 166, 170, 190

socialism, 76n70, 81

sodalities, 56, 115, 120n223, 123n233, 127, 172, 253, 261, 282

Solesmes, 5, 7, 8, 9–10, 12, 60, 61, 63–65, 74

Sponsa Regis, 95, 96, 126

St. Aloysius Parish, Delhi, Ohio, 301

St. Andrew Missal, 125, 231

St. Ann Parish, Wollaston, Massachusetts, 274

St. Anselm College, Goffstown, New Hampshire, 295

St. Benet Bookshop, Chicago, Illinois, 149–56

St. Benet Library. *See* St. Benet Bookshop

St. James Parish, Aitkin, Minnesota, 100

St. Joseph Parish, South Bend, Indiana, 140

St. Leo Bulletin, 202, 220

St. Leo Parish, St. Paul, Minnesota, 216

St. Louis University, St. Louis, Missouri, 256

St. Margaret Academy, Minneapolis, Minnesota, 315

St. Matthew Parish, Milwaukee, Wisconsin, 157

St. Meinrad Archabbey, St. Meinrad, Indiana, 280, 285

St. Paulinus Parish, Clairton, Pennsylvania, 212–13

St. Pius X School of Chant, 66, 72n58

St. Procopius Abbey, Lisle, Illinois, 168

St. Thomas University, St. Paul, Minnesota, 260, 271

St. Ursula Academy, Cincinnati, Ohio, 300

St. Xavier Academy, New York, New York, 196

study club, 56, 109, 112–13, 116–23, 125, 127, 136, 147, 178–79, 182–83, 186, 243, 253, 266, 293
and women, 109–23, 126, 327

Tape of the Month Club, 314–15

technology, 2, 19, 40, 190, 220, 314–15

Thomistic Revival, 131–32

Tra le Sollecitudini, motu proprio, 3n6, 7, 17, 53, 61

Ubi Arcano, 129

universities. *See* liturgical education

University of Chicago, Chicago, Illinois, 45, 82, 149

University of Notre Dame, Notre Dame, Indiana, 219, 294, 321

vernacular, 156, 275, 282n121, 300, 313n206

Vespers, 29, 71, 106n162, 108, 230, 231, 262, 333

Ward Method. *See* liturgical music

Women of Nazareth. *See* Grail Movement, the

women
and education, 5, 15, 39, 42, 54, 78, 121, 127, 159
and idealism in the liturgical movement, 249–50
and housework, 228, 245, 287–89, 303–7
and marriage, 270–71, 330
and motherhood, 111, 243–45, 265, 278
and perspective (point of view), 229, 249–50, 258–59, 267, 280, 315–16, 323–24, 331–32
and pregnancy, 258, 265
as needed in the liturgical movement, 258–59, 278, 285, 315–16